¶ ALKIBIADES' LOVE

Alkibiades' Love

Essays in Philosophy

Jan Zwicky

MCGILL-QUEEN'S UNIVERSITY PRESS
Montreal & Kingston · London · Ithaca

© McGill-Queen's University Press 2015

ISBN 978-0-7735-4463-5 (cloth)
ISBN 978-0-7735-4464-2 (paper)
ISBN 978-0-7735-9699-3 (ePDF)
ISBN 978-0-7735-9700-6 (ePUB)

Legal deposit first quarter 2015
Bibliothèque nationale du Québec

Printed in Canada on acid-free paper that is 100% ancient forest free
(100% post-consumer recycled), processed chlorine free

McGill-Queen's University Press acknowledges the support of the Canada
Council for the Arts for our publishing program. We also acknowledge the
financial support of the Government of Canada through the Canada Book
Fund for our publishing activities.

LIBRARY AND ARCHIVES CANADA CATALOGUING IN PUBLICATION

Zwicky, Jan, 1955–, author
Alkibiades' love : essays in philosophy / Jan Zwicky.

Includes bibliographical references and index.
Issued in print and electronic formats.
ISBN 978-0-7735-4463-5 (bound). — ISBN 978-0-7735-4464-2 (pbk.). —
ISBN 978-0-7735-9699-3 (ePDF). — ISBN 978-0-7735-9700-6 (ePUB)

1. Philosophy. I. Title.

B21.Z85 2014   100   C2014-907108-6
                                       C2014-907109-4

The text faces used in this book are Aldus Nova, Heraklit Greek, Palatino
Sans, and Euler Greek, all designed by Hermann Zapf. The titling face is
Diotima, designed by Gudrun Zapf von Hesse.

Contents

A Note on the Text

¶ In the essays that follow, readers of Greek will notice two systems for the spelling of Greek names. Where I felt I could, I have used transliterations, because I believe this practice to be more respectful of the indigenous culture. Transliterations bring ancient Greek out from under the shadow of Roman conquest. For related reasons, many of us now use Pinyin romanizations of Chinese names, because that system, developed by the Chinese themselves, better represents Chinese in English than Wade-Giles. But, of course, the cases are not entirely parallel. Among other things, there are no ancient Greeks around to put pressure on us, making a general overhaul less likely. And so, in cases where a quick Internet search of the transliterated name does not lead immediately to the Roman name familiar to general readers, I have used the Roman spelling: Plato, Meno, Phaedo, Crito, Euthyphro, Porphyry, Aetius, Plutarch. I have also retained familiar English versions of some of the titles of Plato's dialogues: *Apology, Republic, Statesman, Sophist.* And, although 'Aristoteles' does indeed lead directly to Aristotle, I have retained 'Aristotle' to keep 'Plato' company. Except in strict phonemic transcriptions, I have followed the ancient practice of using *y* for upsilon.

¶ Notes are keyed either to section numbers or to page numbers and phrases in the text. Although the text does not contain superscripts, full bibliographic information for all quotations is provided. An asterisk (∗) in the margin indicates the presence of a note that contains bibliographic information for material I have paraphrased or mentioned rather than quoted. A dagger (†) indicates a note that includes commentary on the main text.

¶ ALKIBIADES' LOVE

What Is Lyric Philosophy?

PREAMBLE

Lyric meaning resists summary and paraphrase as much as it resists analysis. Paul Klee, speaking about lyric visual art, said:

> It is not easy to arrive at a conception of a whole which is con-structed from parts belonging to different dimensions ... It is difficult enough, oneself, to survey this whole, whether nature or art, but still more difficult to help another to such a comprehensive view. This is due to the consecutive nature of the only methods available to us ... [W]e lack the means of discussing ... an image which pos-sesses simultaneously a number of dimensions ... However, with each [dimension], irrespective of the amount of study which it may itself require, we must not lose sight of the fact that it is only a part of the whole ... And, if, as the number of dimensions grows, we find increasing difficulty in [comprehending] all the different parts of the structure at the same time, we must exercise great patience.

What follows may tax readers' patience in a different way, for it is a summary from which a number of dimensions have been omitted. It is an attempt to provide a brief overview of two much longer and interrelated works, *Lyric Philosophy* and *Wisdom &' Metaphor*, whose structure can only be described here, and not replicated. Yet one of their most central theses is that meaning is a function of form — that there is no 'content' detachable from form. Since the present discussion lacks their form, it cannot hope adequately to convey their meaning. It should, thus, be regarded as something like the signposted boardwalk tour of a wetland: it provides a few stops at examples of especially colourful species and allows one to gather an initial impression. ("Hm: green; and wet; and full of insects.") But such a tour can say nothing of the countless other species about which an observer might also wonder, nor can it offer more than the most cursory sense of how the wetland, as a complex ecology, goes about the business of being what it is.

Each numbered entry in what follows should be regarded as something like a musical phrase. Cumulatively, they constitute a melodic line of sorts. In *Lyric Philosophy* and *Wisdom & Metaphor*, the line constituted by my remarks is only one of many: there is a second, parallel, text composed of excerpts from other authors, excerpts from musical compositions, photographs, mathematical proofs, etc. The text constituted by my own remarks itself consists of two voices, one that lays out and develops thematic material, and an interlocutor, skeptical of and hostile to the claims of the first voice. The second text, in combination with my own, attempts to enact a multi-dimensional polyphonic structure. Even given the resources of a book-length document, however, it is impossible to fill in all the phrases in even one other voice; and so, in *Lyric Philosophy* and *Wisdom & Metaphor*, the second text becomes, also, a series of invitations to further reading (or looking, or listening). All it can aim to show are the most salient contrapuntal gestures.

In a brief introduction, though, not even this much is possible. In the larger books, the skeptical interlocutor tends to attack points of detail from a position of cultural authority; a number of exchanges are usually required to bring the assumptions that underlie the attacks to some degree of explicitness. Here, I have introduced the interlocutor's voice only once. And in one section, but only one section, I have opened the text up into multiple voices to try to give readers a sense of the bare bones of a polyphonic structure. For the rest, I have confined myself to the slimmest of hints.

LYRIC PHILOSOPHY: A GUIDED TOUR

1. The characteristic formal properties of lyric thought are resonance and integrity.

2. For lyric thought, the foundations of meaning lie in the world, and in human experience of the world, unconditioned by language.

3. Lyric meaning can underlie and inform linguistic meaning but it is, at the same time, broader in scope. Its root is gestural.

4. To read analytic thought sympathetically is to be favourably disposed towards the presupposition that meaning is essentially a linguistic phenomenon although, in any given case, the exact words may not matter.

   The reading of lyric compositions presupposes that, in significant ways, meaning exists prior to and independently of language — but that if language is to bear its trace, the choice of words must be exact.

5. No two of lyric thought, philosophy, and poetry are identical with one another; but neither is any one fully disjoint from the other two.

6. Philosophy's eros is clarity. The eros of lyric is coherence.

7. 'Lyric' in this sense quite deliberately sets aside historical associations with Romantic poetry in order to focus on what it is we could be meaning when we use it to characterize Vermeer's interiors, Wittgenstein's *Tractatus*, Schubert's use of diatonic tonality, and the poetry of Ezra Pound.

8. My use of 'philosophy,' too, sets to one side a characterization that identifies the discipline with systematic logico-linguistic analysis. That use is too narrow to capture our pre-systematic intuitions about what philosophy is. A good definition will include the thought of Herakleitos, as well as that of the best Anglo-American analysts.

9. Resonance is a form of clarity.

ERNEST KLEIN: **clear**, adj. — fr. I.-E. base *klā-*, var. of *kal-*, 'to shout, resound.'

10. Philosophy is thinking in love with clarity.

·

11. Philosophy, then, may assume lyric form when thought whose eros is clarity is driven also by profound intuitions of coherence. When it is also an attempt to arrive at an integrated perception or understanding of how something might affect us as beings with bodies and emotions as well as the ability to think logically.

  When philosophy attempts to give voice to an ecology of experience.

  Under such circumstances, it is not useful to distinguish between art and philosophy.

12. Lyric resonance is a function of attunement.

  It requires an open structure with distinguishable aspects or distinguishable axes of experience that stand in a non-linear relation to one another.

  Being drawn apart, it is brought together with itself.

13. The coherence that lyric awareness intuits, and that lyric thought attempts to render, is ecological in form.

  Ecological structure is a form of resonance.

·

14. Form and content are inextricably bound up with one another — how you say is what you mean.

15. In lyric, nothing is accidental: if a detail fits into a composition, the possibility of this fitting must be written into the detail itself.

  In lyric form, each detail is informed by the whole, is revealing of it to a greater or lesser degree. (Lyric part and lyric whole are indisseverable with respect to meaning. Yet they

are distinct.) The more intensely lyric the gesture, the greater
the degree of this information.

> MAX WERTHEIMER: It has long seemed obvious — and is,
> in fact, the characteristic tone of European science — that
> 'science' means breaking up complexes into their compon-
> ent elements. Isolate the elements, discover their laws, then
> reassemble them, and the problem is solved. All wholes are
> reduced to pieces and piecewise relations between pieces.
>   The fundamental 'formula' of Gestalt theory might be ex-
> pressed in this way: There are wholes, the behaviour of which
> is not determined by that of their individual elements, but
> where the part-processes are themselves determined by the
> intrinsic nature of the whole.

16. We can imagine any given detail — any identifiable part of
    a lyric composition — as a set of possibilities of resonance,
    some of which are actuated by situating the detail in the
    context of the composition.

    The set of actuated possibilities of resonance is the res-
    onant structure of the composition, its gestural architecture.

    What is expressed by the purposive arrangement of possi-
    bilities of resonance is a lyric thought.

17. Romanticism, as a cultural attitude, is characterized funda-
    mentally by the claim that there is an absolute distinction
    between an activity called 'Art' and another called 'Science,'
    and that this distinction carries normative weight. (Whether
    it's 'Art' that is merely subjective and 'Science' that is true,
    or 'Science' that is pernicious and 'Art' that is sublime, is
    irrelevant.)

18. A Romantic attitude toward the arts is further characterized
    by the thought that all meaning is properly (or essentially,
    or necessarily, or originally) a linguistic phenomenon — spe-
    cifically, that poetry is pre-eminent among the arts; by the

idea that the artist's ego ('genius') is an appropriate object of worship; and by the idea that 'true art' must wear sectarian liberationist politics on its sleeve.

19. Lyric thought is characterized by none of these commitments; indeed, it eschews them.

20. At the moment, in the West, lyric thought is marginalized by a late-Romantic culture that also marginalizes 'Art.' This occasionally leads to confusion.

21. Lyric desires wordlessness, a condition that it intuits as phenomenologically selfless, and as an extra-linguistic plenitude of meaning. What it achieves, if its medium is words, is speech that integrates various human modes of understanding — emotional, logical, physical, among others.

22. The power of the technocratic world view is not fundamentally illustrated by the extent of its achievements, but rather — as Heidegger thought — by the extent of its ability to disguise from itself that it is a perspective, a way of viewing the world.

23. What characterizes the philosophical subculture of technocracy is a cluster of related features: the assumption that any meaning worthy of the name is linguistic in form; a methodology that, for the most part, appears to be analytic — that is, appears to proceed on the assumption that understanding is a function of breaking a whole into its component parts, and that such parts are metaphysically independent of and prior to the wholes into which they are combined; a conviction that the breaking of a whole into its parts is thus not attended by any loss of meaning; a willingness to pursue unintuitive taxonomies, apparently because they facilitate an analytic approach; a distrust, evinced as much in the style of thinking as in what is said, of intense emotion; and an insistence on

the generic superiority of the rational intellect to emotions, desires, and sensations.

24. Most middle-class North American children know (or used to know) that there are things you can model better with Plasticine than with the biggest Lego set money can buy. And stuff you can do with a few bits of paper that you can't do with either. And stuff that no matter what you use, you can't get right.

Language is a limited instrument — vast, supple, complex, but limited.

> HERAKLEITOS: One thing, the only truly wise, does — and does not — consent to be called by the name of Zeus.

25. Some things can be known that cannot be expressed in technocratically acceptable prose. And there is another danger here, which is to try to express in technocratically acceptable prose *why* this is so.

To feel we are required to explain a gesture in terms the technocracy finds acceptable is, of course, to grant that the technocracy constitutes the final court of appeal. This is a view that lyric philosophy attempts to challenge.

26. There are indeed circumstances in which we may wish to insist on 'legitimating' explanations of the sort the technocracy prefers. (They were historically effective in pre-revolutionary France, for example, against certain forms of bigotry, despotism, and intolerance.) But this does not mean that explanations of this sort are the only ones that could possibly count — either conceptually or in practice — as genuine.

27. It is doubly mistaken then to assume that a certain way of using language (key terms that are frequently coinages unintelligible to non-specialists, a preference for certain kinds of convolute grammatical constructions, restricted use of metaphor, the elimination of emotional tone unless it is ag-

gressive, a tin ear) captures all that is true, or significant, or meaningful in human experience.

28. Analysis is not only different from lyric, it is at best structurally indifferent to its claims.

➤

29. By 'metaphor' I mean the linguistic expression of the results of focussed analogical thinking.

Strictly speaking, '*x* is *y*' is not a metaphorical claim unless '*x* is not *y*' is true. In the general case, an expression is not metaphorical unless it implies — or insinuates — a claim of the form '*x* is *y*' where '*x* is not *y*' is true. That *x* is not *y* is nearly always implicit.

TOMAS TRANSTRÖMER:
Construction cranes on the horizon want to take the big leap ...

30. Metaphor is a species of understanding, a form of what Wittgenstein called 'seeing as.'

It has, we might say, flex: we see, simultaneously, similarities and dissimilarities: we experience things as both metaphysically distinct and ontologically connected.

CHARLES SIMIC: My poems (in the beginning) are like a table on which one places interesting things one has found on one's walks: a pebble, a rusty nail, a strangely shaped root, the corner of a torn photograph, etc. ... where after months of looking at them and thinking about them daily, certain surprising relationships, which hint at meanings, begin to appear.

LUDWIG WITTGENSTEIN: The work of the philosopher consists in assembling reminders for a particular purpose.

31. Lyric thought is a kind of ontological seismic exploration, and metaphors are charges set by the seismic crew. A good metaphor lets us see more deeply than a weak one.

> LUDWIG WITTGENSTEIN: *Astonishment* is essential to a change of aspect. And astonishment is thinking.

32. The experience of understanding something is always the experience of a gestalt shift: the dawning of an aspect that is simultaneously a perception or reperception of a whole.

> G. H. HARDY: I have myself always thought of a mathematician as in the first instance an *observer,* a man who gazes at a distant range of mountains and notes down his observations ... [W]hen he sees a peak he believes that it is there simply because he sees it. If he wishes someone else to see it, he points to it, either directly or through the chain of summits which led him to recognize it himself. When his pupil also sees it, the research, the argument, the *proof* is finished ... [W]e can, in the last analysis, do nothing but *point* ... proofs are what Littlewood and I call *gas,* rhetorical flourishes designed to affect psychology ...

33. A gestalt shift may be facilitated by the judicious selection and arrangement of aspects or elements; or by setting up objects of comparison.

Hence the importance of a text with multiple voices.

> SIMONE WEIL: There is a pitfall here for the human mind, which constitutes the essential difficulty (and which Descartes failed to see) ... If there is a remedy, it consists in substituting *series* in place of *generalizations.*

34. The positioning of resonant particulars to facilitate perception of their attunement, the presentation of other texts or works or things for comparison, constitute lyric arguments.

What is an argument? — An attempt to assist others to see what we (think we) have seen.

> LUDWIG WITTGENSTEIN: You must go right down to the original sources so as to see them all side by side, both the neglected and the preferred.

35. The 'is'— explicit or implicit — of a metaphor is its lyric aspect. For this reason, a metaphor is true to the degree that it is resonant.

> HERAKLEITOS: The fairest order in the world is a heap of random sweepings.

36. A metaphor is an explicit refusal of the idea that the distinctness of things is their most fundamental ontological characteristic.

But their distinctness is one of their most fundamental ontological characteristics — the other being their interpenetration and connectedness.

> CHARLES SIMIC: Metaphor is a part of the not-knowing aspect of art, and yet I'm firmly convinced that it is the supreme way of searching for truth. How can this be?

37. How can we know there are other beings that see the world in roughly the way we do? — Our experience of meaning; our recognition of beauty; because we have been spoken to, pierced by some gesture; because we recognize the symptoms of such experience in others.

The capacity to recognize other beings' gestures *for what they are* — expressions of experience like our own — is the capacity to experience meaningful coincidence of context, the arc of energy released when one context, laid across another, coincides in ways that refract back into the individual contexts.

This capacity — a sensitivity to resonance — is what we call imagination.

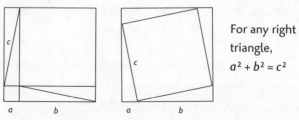

For any right triangle,
$a^2 + b^2 = c^2$

38. "Things are, and are not, as they seem." Fascinated by the 'are not,' we frequently skip over the 'are' — and it is this tendency or impulse that is at the root of metaphysical reductionism, the idea that incompatible appearances must always be the result of a failure, or an inability, to attend to some 'deeper' reality.

    Both Herakleitos and Wittgenstein attempt to resist this impulse. It is not a coincidence that both also write aphoristically. Developed in a certain way, a collection of aphorisms invites a reader to see connections for her or himself. That is, aphoristic writing can be used to cultivate our ability to see-as. We may be puzzled at first — but then we 'get it,' we *experience* the coalescence of a gestalt. It is the experience of the coalescence that is crucial. It is an experience quite other than that of granting the reasonableness of proposition B, given proposition A.

> LUDWIG WITTGENSTEIN: Each of the sentences I write is trying to say the whole thing, i.e., the same thing over and over again; it is as though they were all simply views of one object seen from different angles.

39. Being is the interconnectedness, the resonant ecology, of things.

    The meaning of what-is is the live, metaphorical relation between things and the resonant structure of the world.

    To know the meaning of what-is is wisdom.

> ROBERT HASS: Often enough, when a thing is seen clearly, there is a sense of absence about it ... as if, the more palpable it is, the more some immense subterranean displacement seems to be working in it; as if at the point of truest observation the visible and invisible exerted enormous counter-pressure.

40. To see-as, to hear with a 'musical ear,' is to grasp meaning — it is to see the face in the chaos of lines, to sense the shape of the phrase. And the face and the shape are there, we aren't mak-

ing them up. But because a faculty we've called 'imagination' is involved, and because in reductionist contexts imagining has come to mean making it up; and because for some time meaning has been thought to reside only in non-metaphorical language: we feel that in seeing-as we are confronted with an unusual phenomenon.

But all that confronts us is the world, gesturing at us. The world has patterns, of which our thinking is a part. It makes us feel good to experience these patterns: it is one way of coming home.

> ADAM ZAGAJEWSKI: To defend poetry means to defend a fundamental gift of human nature, that is, our capacity ... to experience astonishment and to stop still in that astonishment for an extended moment or two.

41. Other than pointing and hoping, there are no rules, no algorithms, by which human perception of a gestalt may be facilitated.

But if the perception of such gestalts is the basis of understanding, then it is also the basis of philosophical insight. This means there can be no rules or decision procedures whose application constitutes the practice of philosophy. That practice is better understood as an exercise of attention disciplined by discernment of the live, metaphorical relation between things and the resonant structure of the world.

> SIMONE WEIL: How is it that man becomes a slave to his own method? The essential problem ... The mind is enslaved whenever it accepts connections which it has not itself established.

42. To love wisdom is to find your way home in the protean *phusis* of what-is. It is to embrace the *duende* of language, the emptiness and fullness of things.

43. Without syntax, a lexicon cannot constitute a language.

WHAT IS LYRIC PHILOSOPHY?

The ability to recognize naming activity and to participate in it is necessary to produce human language, but it is not sufficient.

The idea of *logico-linguistic* syntax is the idea that if thinking is to be 'correct' only certain combinations of words will do. Or: that the order of words, or the way they are inflected, matters. Or: that some combinations of (forms of) words don't constitute sentences. Or: that only certain types of associations among, and certain forms of, elements of a lexicon are acceptable — if one violates the rules governing these associations and forms too violently, one ceases to 'make sense.'

The grammar of any given language specifies syntactic classes and subclasses and regulates their interrelations. It also specifies a preferential ordering among three basic elements: subjects, objects, and verbs. (The need to respect preferential ordering is much greater in uninflected languages, such as English, than in inflected languages, such as Greek.) To the extent that 'good order' includes specifically 'logical' relations, a specific type of *sequencing* is involved: that of consequence.

Basic to the idea of syntactic classes in logico-linguistic syntax is the notion of discrete elements. It is their relationships that are governed by syntax. (Such elements are also essential to another notion of consequence, the Newtonian concept of *cause.*)

44. Logico-linguistic syntax is the beginning of system.

If Freud is correct, the neuronal organization necessary for logico-linguistic syntax also gives rise to a phenomenological sense of self.

The ability to see something as an object distinct from oneself is necessary before one can cease to care about that thing sufficiently to regard it as nothing more than an object one can use. The ability to see it in this way does not guarantee that one will cease to care, but it is a precondition.

That is: the experience of self, which is concomitant with language use, is the ground of all technology.

45. If the capacity for technology is fundamental to human beings, then those beings will find completion in *domesticity*.
(I use 'domesticity' here in a way that sets aside connotative
associations with tameness and servility to focus on a much
more abstract sense of home: the attempt, by a human, to
lead a life that is swept up neither in the objectifying project
of tool-use — which includes the use of language — nor in
the impossible goal of sustained lyric attention.)

46. Lyric awareness desires ongoing dissolution of the self in the
resonance of being: it desires this dissolution as the complete
fulfilment of the eros for coherence, its limiting case.
    Lyric thought achieves integrated speech only to the ex-
tent that words are bent to the shape of wordlessness. (The
tension on the bow which gives thought the power to move.)
    But to abandon speech is to refuse to accept the full burden
of humans' capacity for language.

47. A domestic attitude accepts the essential tension between
lyric desire and the capacity for technology.
    It is not so much a static mid-point between these two
contrary moments as it is an active acknowledgement that
the tension between them cannot be resolved.
    To adopt a domestic attitude is an attempt to come home
to ourselves in the presence of that tension.

48. "Isn't that the project, then? Why don't you call it domestic
philosophy instead of lyric philosophy?"
    Because, conceptually, the *immense* problem is to call atten-
tion to the existence of lyric thought. Because I didn't want
the book shelved under 'Household Management.'

49. "Well, find some other word than 'domestic'!"
    The idea itself is old; the name, in English, needs a Greek
or Latin root. The word from the Greek root, 'ecologicity,' is
slightly more of a mouthful. More importantly, the idea of
ecology — in the usual sense of the word — is a crucial ana-

logue for lyric structure. To have used the same root for two
distinct phenomena would have produced confusion.

50. There is no simple recipe for communicating gestalts; or,
rather, there is only the roughest and readiest: point and hope.

51. Wisdom has to do with the grasp of wholes that occupy the
same space, yet are different. This life, as opposed to that.

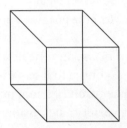

52. To be wise is to be able to grasp another form of life without
abandoning one's own; to be able to translate experience into
and out of two original tongues. To resist, then, translation
that understands itself as a form of reduction.

53. There is a moral aspect here, as well as a talent for seeing-as.
One has to be able to see what *is* there, rather than what one
hopes or expects. This requires a certain sort of strength.

54. Wisdom is a form of domestic understanding.

55. Metaphor, too, is a form of domestic understanding: a perception of deep connectedness can override the distinctness of
individuals, but it will not erase it. The distinctness of things
remains the foundation of their resonant connection.

56. Darkness, absence — the cancelling of being which is the
source of being's value and which is simultaneously inseparable from that-something-is — this is the warp of lyric understanding, as light is its weft.

57. It's true: evaluation of lyric compositions by analytic criteria frequently blocks rather than facilitates understanding. It is not true that lyric is thereby relieved of all responsibility for rigour, exactitude, and concern for truth in its execution.

> CHARLES SIMIC: Ambiguity is the world's condition. Poetry flirts with ambiguity. As a 'picture of reality' it is truer than any other. Ambiguity is. This doesn't mean you're supposed to write poems no one understands.

58. What is truth? — The asymptotic limit of sensitive attempts to be responsible to our actual experience of the world and ourselves in it. (The result of being puzzled and courageous where it might be easier to be cavalier.)

59. Lyric thought is not postmodern in the same way it is not Romantic: it rejects the primacy of words as bearers of meaning and locates meaning's roots in the prelinguistic gestures of music and the resonance of the nonhuman world.

60. If truth is a continent over which we purpose dominion, an appropriate mode of expression will be the tract. But suppose it is an archipelago. Suppose to know is more like to visit or to cohabit than to own.

61. To appreciate how our understanding can be limited by fear, by a will to mastery, by a need to control, is to begin the learning/unlearning that constitutes the practice of lyric philosophy.

Bringhurst's Presocratics:
Lyric and Ecology

The form of the following discussion is a result of my belief that several of the most important things about Robert Bringhurst's sequence of poems "The Old in Their Knowing" can be more clearly shown than said. One of those things is the difference between his way of reading the extant fragments of a number of ancient Greek philosophers and the way those fragments are read by scholars who are not also lyric poets. Another is the degree to which the poems incorporate, rather than make reference to, what most of us would unhesitatingly call philosophical ideas. A third is the way in which the poems are not only preoccupied with ideas but are also preoccupied with the relationships of the minds behind the ideas to the world. A fourth is how this concern of Bringhurst's resonates metaphilosophically with aspects of Presocratic thought itself.

In trying as much as possible to allow the sequence its own voice, I have adopted a form that allows the juxtaposition of various passages and texts against one another. My own commentary is a compromise between simply displaying the relevant texts in the hope the reader will notice what I think is important about them, and trying to say what I maintain is better shown. It is intended as a series of indicators or route signs for a path whose meaning lies in the walking. Section 1 addresses Bringhurst's framing of the sequence as a whole, and Section 2, in the light of that framing, attempts to provide a philosophically congenial context for the remainder. In Sections 3–6, parts of Bringhurst's poem "Herakleitos" are set against Greek fragments on which they draw; interpolated in my commentary are, additionally, portions of other poems in the sequence, other fragments attributed to Herakleitos, and portions of texts by other authors.

For reasons of space, "Herakleitos" is the only poem for which a close reading and commentary are provided. (A summary of textual bases for the other poems in the sequence is given at the end of the notes for this essay.) Section 7 offers a summary of themes exemplified by "Herakleitos," which also run through the sequence as a whole. Section 8 attempts to summarize and extend the discussion, with particular attention to the suitability of a lyric approach for our understanding of a range of ecological questions.

The basic axes of thought in the following pages intersect, rather than repeat or mimic, primary axes of thought in an earlier book, *Lyric Philosophy*. A brief overview of its themes is provided in the essay that precedes this one. This project does represent an extension of *Lyric Philosophy*, but more as a rib represents an 'extension' of a backbone than as the next few miles of track represent an extension of a railroad.

Bringhurst's sequence is written out of material many poets would consider too 'difficult' in a form most philosophers would regard as too 'lax.' But its success as poetry, on the one hand — its beauty — and, on the other, the fact that the philosophical positions that inform it are both coherent and intelligible, together constitute a significant challenge to assumed relationships among lyric thought, philosophy, and poetry. None are identical with either of the others; all overlap in important ways. What I will attempt to do here is to read a particular sequence of poems as philosophy, allowing the poems to teach us how that might be done, and allowing them, in the process, to deepen our understanding of what lyric philosophy itself might be.

HERAKLEITOS

I

Herakleitos says a dry soul is wisest and best.
Herakleitos is undeniably
right in these matters. These
bright tatters of wisdom, cast

over grey welter and spume should at any rate yield
a few visions and reflections, a little light
cutting crosswise like a fin,
splayed against the sea's grain
or annealed on the wave crest.

A dry soul. Dry: that is to say
kiln-dried, cured like good lumber or old Bordeaux,
salt-pork and pemmican, meat of the soul
under the chokecherry,
                              sunlight
and sea-salt arrayed in the grain.

II

Herakleitos says something of concord — not
like a carpenter's clamp or lashed
logs, as in Homer.
Harmony with an arched back,
laminated ash upended like an unlaid keel, the curl
of live flesh in the fire, flexed
like the soul between the muscle and the bone, like
the bow, like the lyre.

III

All things are exchangeable for
fire and fire for all things,
like gold for goods and goods for gold,
or so sings old
                  Herakleitos.

IV

Dead men are gods, men are dead gods, said
Herakleitos. And furthermore,

mortal immortals are immortal mortals,
the breath of the one is the death of the other,
the dying of one is the life of the other:

mortals are deathless, the deathless are mortal,
living in the body the death of the other,
dying into air, earth and fire, siring

the other, the utter
incarnation.

V

Wind stirs his ashes.

◄   I   ►

*   1. "The Old in Their Knowing" by Robert Bringhurst is a sequence of twelve poems based on material drawn from classical and preclassical sources. The titles of the poems are: "Herakleitos," "Parmenides," "Miletos," "A Short History," "Empedokles: Seven Fragments," "Empedokles' Recipes," "Pherekydes," "Pythagoras," "Demokritos," "Xenophanes," "Of the Snaring of Birds," and "The Petelia Tablet."

2. The prose introduction to the sequence in *The Beauty of the Weapons* opens:

A hundred generations, twenty five centuries ago, in tiny sea-coast towns and outports strung through the northern Mediterranean, pinned to the sea's edge by the horned mountains rising close behind, among sailors and farmers and fishermen and potters, lived a scattering of men who knew no distinctions between physicist, philosopher, biologist and poet, and who were, each in his own way, all in one. We call them now the Presocratics. Unlike Socrates, they argued with themselves and not their listeners. Unlike Plato, they were not in business to reorder and convince. Unlike Aristotle, as Aristotle says, they were more interested in the union than the distinction between intellect and feeling.

3. The two earlier versions of the sequence offer instead an epigraph taken from Hölderlin's "Patmos," a poem whose third and fourth lines are the focus of the last part of Martin Heidegger's famous essay, "The Question Concerning Technology." Bringhurst's epigraph reads:

> *Es rauschen ...*
> *Hinziehend da und dort*
> *In ungewisser Meeresebene*
> *Der schattenlosen Straßen genug,*
> *Doch kennt die Inseln der Schiffer.*

†

4. The introduction to the fourth version includes only the passage from Aristotle's *Metaphysics* 1010a with which Bringhurst concludes the introduction in *The Beauty of the Weapons*:

> *They saw moreover that the whole physical world was in motion, with nothing coming true from its continuous transformation, and they decided that nothing at all could be truthfully said about something that was always and everywhere changing. From these conclusions stem the more extreme views of some who claimed to out-Herakleitos Herakleitos. Take Kratylos for example. Finally he stopped talking altogether and only moved his finger. And he censured Herakleitos for saying one could not step twice into the same river. His own view was that one could not do so even once.*

5. The framing of the sequence in all cases is significant. In the first three versions, the introductions invoke knowledge in which sensory intuition and physical skill cannot be prised off conceptual geometry. In the fourth version, this invocation is abandoned in favour of an even more complex gesture.

Aristotle's commentary is, in its entirety, unsympathetic, as the introduction in *The Beauty of the Weapons* indicates. (In the passage Bringhurst has chosen to quote, however, Aristotle does not say he thinks the view is mistaken; he takes its muddle-headedness to be obvious.) Presented in isolation, however, the effect of the passage is to highlight Presocratic claims about ineffable experience. Thus, an arc is established between "The Old in Their Knowing" and another sequence, "The Book of Silences," in which Bringhurst meditates on the work of ancient and medieval Indian and Asian thinkers.

6. Compare Burnet's orientation in *Early Greek Philosophy*:

> *My aim has been to show that a new thing came into the world with the early Ionian teachers — the thing we call science — and that they first pointed the way which Europe has followed ever since, so that, as I have said elsewhere, it is an adequate description of science to say that it is 'thinking about the world in the Greek way.' That is why science has never existed except among peoples who have come under the influence of Greece.*

Or Hargrove's, in *Foundations of Environmental Ethics*:

> *However silly and simplistic the actual ideas offered by these early philosophers may seem by modern scientific standards, they served admirably as preliminary studies that helped make possible physics as we know it today.*

Or Kirk and Raven's, which, although conveyed more subtly, clearly shares the same bias:

> *By no stretch of the imagination could the views of Pherecydes … be termed philosophical. They were, however sometimes directed towards an explanation of the world as a whole, especially of how it came to be what it is; and they reveal on occasion a method not essentially different from that of Thales and the first Ionian philosophers … It was in Ionia that the*

*first completely rationalistic attempts to describe the nature of
the world took place …*

> *Heraclitus' relation of the soul to the world was more cred-
> ible than that of Pythagoras, since it was more rational; it
> pointed a direction which was not, on the whole, followed until
> the atomists and, later, Aristotle …*

> *So far, of course, there is little to distinguish Pythagoreanism
> from a mere mystery religion: the only reliable traces, in the
> evidence so far cited, of another side to Pythagoras' teaching are
> Heraclitus' references … and Herodotus' description of him …
> as "by no means the weakest sage among the Hellenes." These
> passages alone, however, do suggest — what is evident also
> from the fact that in the fifth century the Pythagoreans were
> among the leading scientists — that Pythagoras was interested
> in science as well as in the fate of the soul.*

7. The normative force of Bringhurst's use of Hölderlin is also
   unmistakeable: for *ungewisser Meeresebene* (uncertain plain of
   the sea) read European intellectual history; for *Inseln* (islands)
   read solid epistemological ground. It is the one who is intui-
   tively involved with sea and sky, not the laboratory specialist,
   who knows the way.

8. If the world has physical being — if it is surprising (in motion),
   paradoxical (shot through with extraordinary coincidence
   but not wholly predictable), full of strange beauty as well as
   logico-mathematical structure, capable of both killing us and
   sustaining us — then best to describe it with an instrument
   capable of making sense, like a musical instrument, under
   tension.

9. Our ability to comprehend a thought depends to a significant
   degree on our openness to the passion that informs it.

   It is easy to forget that the passion driving thought is what
   gives thought life.

   Philosophy without passion is bookkeeping in the history
   of ideas.

◄ II ►

1. It is common among twentieth-century students of academic philosophy to regard philosophy as the attempt to articulate the logic of science. Logical analysis of the preconditions of science, most notably of seventeenth-century physics, is taken to be paradigmatic of philosophical activity; the style of such analysis is defining of 'good' English-language philosophical style.

2. To the extent that the Presocratics are regarded as philosophers, the tendency is to treat them as ambitious preschoolers in the playpens of seventeenth-century physics.

   The predominant rhetorical tone is one of condescension.

   That any of the Presocratics might have been proposing a credible alternative to technocracy's world view does not appear to occur to most commentators. To the extent that Presocratic proposals are presented as credible, they are presented as primitive versions of contemporary versions of truth about the world.

3. Although Aristotle's motives were not (exactly) technocracy's, what he says about the Presocratics is, on the whole, congenial to us. "Physicists who attempt to discuss truth, and the way it is accepted, show their lack of training in logical analysis; for when they have arrived at the level of physics, they should already know about these matters and not be still investigating them while attending to their special studies." (*Metaphysics* Γ 1005b)

   That is, it is easy for us to take Aristotle to be marketing a view of 'genuine' philosophical activity that, like our own, assumes a division of faculties, and that places knowledge entirely in the province of the analytic intellect.

4. Aristotle, however, did not believe in either 'Art' or 'Science,' much less in a divorce between them.

5. What we have left of European philosophy before Aristotle is, on the whole, lyric — informed both by profound intuitions of coherence and by the desire for clarity. (Plato often appears to champion a division of faculties — particularly one between sensory awareness and intellectual comprehension — but his insistence on the centrality of *erōs*, and his focus on the robustly physical and emotional character of Sokrates, makes his approach neither Aristotelian nor Presocratic.)

   Aristotle consolidates a shift in philosophical imagination. It is Romanticism, though, that enshrines an Aristotelian picture of philosophy as 'anti-poetic' — that construes philosophy as *essentially* opposed to 'Creativity' and 'Imagination.' (A construal that would not have occurred to Aristotle, nor to most others before the late eighteenth century.)

6. One common contemporary notion of poetry, dominant in North America, has it that poetry is anti-rational — a blowzy rejection of common sense and practicality. But this notion is itself an offshoot of interwoven and not fully distinct ideologies indigenous to post-industrial capitalism — ideologies rooted in notions like 'development,' 'progress,' 'industry,' and 'economic growth.'

7. That is, the anti-rationalism many associate with poetry — though it is currently on the losing political and economic side — is rooted in the polarization of 'Art' and 'Science' proposed by Romantic culture.

   Contemporary versions of that polarization frequently subsume philosophy under 'Science.'

8. What is radical about Bringhurst's reading of the Presocratics is not the triumph of poetry over science, but a rejection of the terms of the disagreement.

9. It is not analysis per se that Bringhurst's reading of the Presocratics calls into question, and certainly not science, but rather

the institutionalization of the intellect in a way that excludes the possibility of its taking lyric form.

10. In the same gesture, Bringhurst calls into question the institutionalization of poetry as an activity that excludes the possibility of conceptual content.

11. Within the domain of lyric thought, the distinction between poetry and philosophy has no meaning.

12. Presocratic thought is not best charted as an adjunct to the mainland of our own culture's self-understanding.

13. Bringhurst's reading identifies the philosophical vision of the Presocratics as lyric.
     This itself is a lyric insight.
     Its coherent expression requires lyric form.

14. I do not wish to suggest that lyric thinkers of the twentieth and twenty-first centuries comprise a unified group that is historically continuous with Greek philosophical culture of the seventh to fourth centuries BCE. Nonetheless, it is possible to think of lyric thought-style as characteristic of an abstract, ahistorical intellectual culture that includes, among others, many of the Presocratics.
     A lyric reading of the Presocratics, then, one might say, has the strengths of a portrait by a member of their own culture.
     An analytic reading has the strengths of a portrait by a member of a foreign — and, in this case, powerful and unsympathetic — culture.

◀ III ▶

FRAGMENT 118: αὐγὴ ξηρὴ ψυχή, σοφωτάτη καὶ ἀρίστη.   †

(augē ksērē psūkhḗ, sophōtátē kai arístē)

A brilliant ray of light, dry soul: wisest and best.

I

Herakleitos says a dry soul is wisest and best.   1
Herakleitos is undeniably
right in these matters. These
bright tatters of wisdom, cast
over grey welter and spume should at any rate yield   5
a few visions and reflections, a little light
cutting crosswise like a fin,
splayed against the sea's grain
or annealed on the wave crest.

A dry soul. Dry: that is to say   10
kiln-dried, cured like good lumber or old Bordeaux,
salt-pork and pemmican, meat of the soul
under the chokecherry,
                    sunlight
and sea-salt arrayed in the grain.   15

1. The tone of the first stanza is important. It invites us to regard
what is being said as a series of discrete, factual observations,
each of which is more or less obvious — a weather report.
But the musical associations of the words out of which this
report is constructed play against this tone (which, of course,
is also dependent on those same words, in that same order):
rhymes, part-rhymes, stress, repetitions, and alliterations
connect images, names, and concepts in a complex web whose
'components' are anything but discrete:

Her a<u>klei</u> tos   –   *line 1*   a d<u>ry</u>
Hera <u>klei</u> tos   –   *line 1*   w<u>i</u>sest
                      –   *line 2*   undeni<u>a</u>bly
                      –   *line 3*   right
                      –   *line 4*   bright
                      –   *line 4*   light – on which the stanza climaxes
                                       rhythmically; and which will be echoed in
                                       'sunlight,' the visual and rhythmic climax of
                                       stanza 2.
                      –   *line 7*   cross<u>wi</u>se (like)
says   –   *lines 1–2*   is
                      –   *line 1*   wis<u>est</u>, b<u>est</u>
                      –   *line 9*   cr<u>est</u>
is   –   *line 2*   is
                      –   *line 4*   wisdom
                      –   *line 6*   visions
und<u>e</u>niably   –   *line 3*   these (twice)
                      –   *line 5*   an<u>y</u>, yield
                      –   *line 8*   sea's (and end of diphthong in 'splayed')
                      –   *line 9*   annealed
these/These   –   repetition within line and line end position both
                           stress immediacy
ma<u>tt</u>ers   –   *line 4*   ta<u>tt</u>ers, cast
                      –   (*line 5*   at)
                      –   *line 7*   cu<u>tt</u>ing
right i<u>n</u> these matters. These / bright tatters – the matter (both
                                       how we are to think of it, and what it is com-
                                       posed of) of a dry soul is 'bright tatters'; the
                                       wise, the best, soul gives off light and is, at
                                       the same time, in tatters (shredded, torn, like
                                       rags; wind-blown, in motion [tonal associa-
                                       tions with 'flutter' and 'scatter']).
                      –   Herakleitos' *being right in these matters* does
                           not exactly parallel, but is woven into *these*
                           bright tatters (brilliant fragments). What he
                           says is true — that is, he may be trusted —
                           because of the consonance between what he

says and its fragmentary mode of expression.
His being right is inseparable from his saying
it in fragments.

   – these bright tatters should yield: visions, reflections, light that cuts, light that is splayed,
light that is annealed. But as bright tatters
they are already radiant and cut, splayed, annealed. What they are born of they (should)
give birth to. (A flash, a ray, of light.)

tatters of wisdom – *line 6*   few visions

few visions, reflections, (little) – echo of visions in reflections

   – *line 7*   fin
   – part rhyme between 'few' and *line 5* 'spume'
   – 'little' alliterates with 'light' and *line 7* 'cutting,'
the two words that immediately follow it.

cutting crosswise – cu/cro (slant rhyme)

   – 'wise' echoes previous long i's (see Herakleitos
above), and, of course, 'wisdom'
   – *line 7*   fin

splayed   – *line 8*   against
   – *line 8*   sea's
   – *line 8*   end of ay diphthong in vowel of 'sea'
   – *line 8*   grain

against   – *line 8*   grain (slant rhyme; compare 'cutting
crosswise' above)

annealed   – *line 9*   on
   – echoes *line 8* sea (and note associations of annealed with heat/fire/light and apparent
oxymoron of these being attached to water)

wave   – echoes *line 5* 'grey welter,' which has also just
been echoed by *line 8* 'sea's grain'
   – *line 8*   splayed
   – *line 4*   wisdom

or   – picks up on open r's from *line 5* (previous image
of waves)

crest   – echoes *line 7* crosswise

– best: full rhyme of first and last lines produces, in
contradistinction to the image of fragments
flung out over the sea, complete closure. The
effect is of something simultaneously in motion and, more deeply, at rest (a description
of what a wave in some sense *is*). Surface
disunity, underlying permanence.

FRAGMENT 12: As they step into the same rivers, different
and again different waters flow upon them.

The stanza — whose subject is Herakleitean philosophical
fragments — is a densely coherent musical structure bound
together along the joint axes of full rhymes with *dry* and *light*,
and full and partial rhymes with *best*. Their pivot is the word
'wisest,' which contains rhymes with both of them. Line 5,
which visually flings itself out over the stanza, introduces a
third, subsidiary, musical axis which through the remaining
five lines carries images of light reflected from the sea on *r*,
ee, and *ay* vowels and a variety of enactive consonantal alliterations. The light in this antiphonal musical axis is, however,
cut, splayed, roughened, and annealed — that is, it is *imagis-
tically* continuous with 'bright tatters' which is the imagistic
focal point of the two primary musical axes. The sea-music
axis is pulled into the second dominant musical axis by the
closing full rhyme.

That is: beneath the apparent semantic discontinuity of
Herakleitos' aphorisms, and Bringhurst's apparently offhand
diction, is hidden a profound (musical) unity connected with
images of light, the sea, being torn apart, and 'what is best.'

FRAGMENT 123: Nature loves to hide.

2. The one significant word that has no significant echo in
stanza I is 'soul.' There is an assonantal connection with 'over'
and a faint aural connection with 'should,' both in line 5. In
the context of this stanza, this constitutes a virtual silence.

3. The stanza's musical closure, while in some sense absolute, is not static — the thought is tonally poised (with its light vowels and tapped consonants) above the deeper music of the second stanza. The imagistic-conceptual theme of the second stanza reinforces this: the best soul requires (real) food and (real) drink: the vehicle of lyric insight is not some disembodied product of Neoplatonic aesceticism, but is sustained by a form of life that respects human dependence on the physical world.

4. Section I, stanza 2: rhymes, part-rhymes, alliteration:

soul	–	*line 1*	say
	–	*line 2*	or, old, Bordeaux
	–	*line 3*	salt, pork, soul
	–	*line 4*	chokecherry
	–	*line 6*	salt
dry	–	*line 2*	dried, like
	–	*line 5*	sunlight
'a *dry* soul *dry* that'	–		the musical structure of the phrase is an arch with 'soul' at its apex
kiln-dried	–	*line 2*	'cured like' (note associations with heat)
dried	–	*line 2*	cured, good, old, Bordeaux
	–	(*line 6*	under)
cured	–	*line 2*	good (near frame rhyme and similar vowel tonality)
	–	*line 2*	lumber (vowel rhymes with *cure*, consonant echoes *d*)
lumber	–	*line 2*	Bordeaux (and pun on 'board')
pork	–	echoes *line 2*	Bordeaux
	–	*line 3*	pemmican
pemmican	–	*line 2*	cured, lumber
	–	*line 3*	meat
meat	–	*line 6*	sea
under	–	echoes *line 2*	lumber
	–	*line 5*	sunlight

sunlight   –   *line 6*   sea-salt; see stanza 1 for connections
                        with *light*
arrayed   –   *line 1*   say
            –   *line 4*   chokecherry
            –   *line 6*   grain
'sea-salt arrayed in the grain' – echoes *stanza 1, line 8* 'splayed
                    against the sea's grain'

5. In stanza 2, the images are images for *dry* but the music repeatedly echoes *soul*. In both stanzas, that music (dominated
   by *o/u* and *r*) is associated with images of the sea.

   > FRAGMENT 36: For souls it is death to become water; for water
   > death to become earth; out of earth water comes, and out of
   > water, soul.

   > FRAGMENT 67: The god — day, night, winter, summer, war,
   > peace, satiety, hunger — changes the way fire does when
   > it is mixed with incense at the sacrifice and is named ac-
   > cording to the pleasure given by each.

6. The second stanza culminates in the claim that sunlight and
   sea-salt are arrayed in the grain of the dry soul, a very close
   echo of the sense as well as the music of the first stanza's claim
   that Herakleitos' fragments yield wisdom in the form of light
   splayed against the sea's grain. 'Splayed' is more violent than
   'arrayed,' but in both cases the suggestion is of something
   spread out, as to dry; displayed, as in clearly visible.

   Not only are the fragments themselves made coherent
   through their connection with light and the sea, light and
   the sea are the visible components of the dry, that is, best,
   that is, coherent, soul.

7. In his commentary on Fragment 118, T.M. Robinson, following Charles Kahn, identifies the substance of Herakleitos' soul
   with the element *air*. However, even Robinson's own trans-

lation — "A flash (or: ray) of light ⟨is⟩ a dry soul, wisest and best (or: most noble)" — does not support his further claim that "[f]or Heraclitus (human) soul is also of course a rational principle (fragments 107, 117), not just the principle of life, and such a *psychē* is for him most 'alive' precisely to the degree that it is most rational." 'Rationality' is a post-Enlightenment term of philosophical art, much narrower in scope than 'noble,' 'wise,' 'comprehending,' or even 'reasonable,' and different in scope than 'perceptive.' Its root is Latin: *ratio*, to calculate or reckon, as in the apportioning of goods or money. It has come to indicate primarily skill in calculative arts such as algebra, economics, and formal logic.

8. In contradistinction to Robinson, Bringhurst reads Fragment 118 as claiming the wisest and best soul is *coherent*. It is dry in the sense of weathered, tempered, cured, a sense that connects it with our colloquial understanding of the Anglo-Saxon 'wise.' It is a sense of 'dry' that, in addition to its opposition to wet (sea), is explicitly associated with the action of salt (sea). For the coherence of these images with Herakleitos' life, we need look no further than the islands of the Aegean.

9. What recommends Bringhurst's reading is its own coherence: its enactive complexity, its intensity. That is, its beauty.

RAINER MARIA RILKE, from "Archaïscher Torso Apollos":   †
  Sonnst stünde dieser Stein entstellt und kurz
  unter der Schultern durchsichtigem Sturz
  und flimmerte nicht so wie Raubtierfelle;
  und bräche nicht aus allen seinen Rändern
  aus wie ein Stern: denn da is keine Stelle,
  die dich nicht sieht. Du mußt dein Leben ändern.

  Otherwise this stone would stand defaced, cut off
  under the shoulders' diaphanous plunge
  and wouldn't shimmer like the pelt of some wild beast;

and wouldn't burst from all its boundaries
like a star: for there is no place
that does not see you. You must change your life.

◀ IV ▶

FRAGMENT 51: οὐ ξυνιᾶσιν ὅκως διαφερόμενον ἑωυτῷ
ξυμφέρεται. παλίντονος ἁρμονίη ὕκωσπερ τόξου καὶ λύρης.

(ou ksuniâsin hókōs diapherómenon heōutô ksumphéretai.
palíntonos harmoníē húkōsper tóksou kai lúrēs.)

They do not apprehend how, pulling apart from itself,
it agrees with itself. A back-stretched harmony, as in
the bow and the lyre.

II

Herakleitos says something of concord — not   1
like a carpenter's clamp or lashed
logs, as in Homer.
Harmony with an arched back,
laminated ash upended like an unlaid keel, the curl   5
of live flesh in the fire, flexed
like the soul between the muscle and the bone, like
the bow, like the lyre.   8

1. Images and music:
   The obvious heavy-handed uniformity of primary consonantal alliteration ('carpenter's clamp,' 'lashed logs') is rejected, along with epic style, as an adequate way of reading
Herakleitos on the subject of ἁρμονίη. The suggestion is that
the treatment must be, by contrast, lyric; explicatory prose
is not an option here. The music of the ensuing lines, while
once again dense, is more complex than that of the opening
alliterations. I will note only a few examples.

Harmony   –   *line 4* 'arched back,' this phrase connecting with
                line 5 'laminated ash'
           –   *line 5* an, echoing 'ash,' and through it 'arched' and
                'harmony'; situated in the centre of the equally
                dense 'upended like an unlaid keel.'

live   –   *line 6* fire, *line 8* lyre. The semantic importance of the as-
            sonance and the full rhyme cannot be overestimated,
            given that the live (flesh) is explicitly compared to
            the soul, that fire is the primordial element for Her-
            akleitos, and that the lyre is exemplary of music and
            therefore concretely instantiates the musical sense
            of 'harmony.'

> KIRK AND RAVEN: Now comes an important addition: there
> is (*sc.* in it, i.e. it exemplifies) a connexion or means of join-
> ing (the literal sense of ἁρμονίη) through opposite tensions,
> which ensures this coherence – just as the tension in the
> string of bow or lyre, being exactly balanced by the outward
> tension exerted by the arms of the instrument, produces a
> coherent, unified, stable and efficient complex. We may infer
> that if 'the hot' ... seriously began to outweigh the cold, or
> night day, then the unity and coherence of the world would
> cease, just as, if the tension in the bow-string exceeds the
> tension in the arms, the whole complex is destroyed.

           –   The rhyme/assonance of fire/live/lyre mimes the con-
                tinuity of the formal principle, harmony (conceived
                as coherence), with being-in-tension. As the primary
                musical axis of the stanza, it connects Herakeitos'
                account of the 'back-stretched harmony' inherent in
                apparent contraries with his more general account of
                the cosmos, and reinforces the explicit comparison of
                'harmony' to the soul.

flesh   –   *line 6* fire, *line 6* flexed (/like the soul). Note also that
            'live flesh in the fire,' given the relationship between

fire and a dry soul, becomes a picture of the body in relation to the soul, as well as in relation to the animating principle of the cosmos.

soul – *line 7* bone, which alliterates with *line 8* bow

like – four direct occurrences in lines 5–8, an echo ('live') in the one comparative clause that does not contain 'like,' and a partial repetition in 'not/like' in lines 1–2. In a poet of Bringhurst's skill, such insistence on simile cannot be accidental. I suggest that its import is that 'concord/harmony' is not simply an abstraction from various concrete examples of concord or harmony, but is, rather, *something*: not a concrete particular – it is distinct from the 'real things' cited in comparison – but it is nonetheless as real. Whether or not Herakleitos believed this, it is in keeping with Bringhurst's own attention to ἁρμονίη in the construction of his own poetry.

2. The images tell us that harmony is not sweet.

Throughout lines 4–7 the image of the rack predominates, reinforced by the musical echo of 'lashed' in 'arched back,' and the part rhyme of 'flesh' and 'flexed.' This is a concord that shrieks. (Herakleitos' own images are less violent.)

The three central images of lines 5–7 echo the images associated with the dry soul in the second stanza of the first section, reinforcing the image of thought produced in a harsher, more sensually immediate world than that inhabited by most twenty-first-century professionals.

The bond between the soul and the body — their mutual interpenetration and inseparability — is the import of the three clauses that associate the soul with, respectively, meat, flesh, muscle and bone.

3. Finally, because of the buried image of the rack in Section II, the connection of the explicit images with images in Section I that are themselves connected with the 'arrayed/splayed' axis of that section, and the involvement of the soul with

flesh, flexing, and images of (context allows *visible*) muscle
and bone, I suggest we are to hear 'flayed' as a deep musical-
imagistic substratum of these two sections. And that we are
to understand that the soul itself is flayed — tattered — as
the price of wisdom, of becoming full of light.

> ROBERT BRINGHURST, *Tzuhalem's Mountain*, § xxi:
>   Bright fish in the shallows
>   breaking their guts to come home to these gravels,
>   their bowels chewed by the unborn,
>   their backs by the eagles.
>
>   The man in the sun, savaged
>   by cats, drags his cloak through the waters
>   and limps up the mountain,
>   his footprints in tatters.

4. The view that a flayed soul may be the price of wisdom has,
   it is true, a Romantic ring. It may or may not have been Herakleitos'. (Indeed, it may not be Bringhurst's. He remarks in
   correspondence that fire unites things, makes things whole
   — anneals them, for instance — as well as reduces them to
   their elements.)
      It is, however, a view that I find suggestive independently
   of the degree to which it appears to be required as a reading
   of Bringhurst's poem.

5. Why might a flayed soul be the price of wisdom?
      Lyric comprehension is of the collective coherence of all
   things, and their individual mortality. If Western European
   society is founded on aspirations to immortality and a conviction that human fate is ontologically distinct from (because
   superior to) the lot of the rest of the world, lyric comprehension will come at the price of unreflective participation in
   dominant social, political, and economic institutions. That
   is, at the price of power.
      Lyric comprehension requires the dissolution of the ego,

that neuropsychological vehicle of our separateness from the
world, the platform of logico-linguistic syntax.

> ROBERT BRINGHURST, "Pythagoras," § 1:
> Remnants: the thirty-nine rules, a sundial
> untied like a shoelace, a theory of number
> dismembered and scattered like dice. And the third-hand
> chatter over the transmigration of souls.
> And a story: Pythagoras wouldn't eat meat
> and his legs buckled under him.
> > Rubble
> of picked-over thought, broken pediments, cracked
> roof-tiles laid up with mortar now gone in the rain.
>
> Seabirds over the high grass,
> nothing erect
> except these pillars:
> the mind of Pythagoras stands on two columns of words.

6. This theme dominates the sequence: the disciplining of the
intelligence by the natural world — a disciplining which is
frequently violent and always conditioned by loss; a world
that European culture (among others) has set out systematically to enslave. And this: the joining (ἁρμονίη) of the mind
and this world in the moment of truth; the joining as what
truth *is*; the moment of truth in some ways indistinguishable
from the moment of death.

> ROBERT BRINGHURST, from "Pherekydes":
> There remains of the mind of Pherekydes:
> the esker and the glacial milk,
> the high spring runoff in the gorge,
>
> and the waterfalls hammered out of cloud
> against the mid cliff,
> vanishing in the hungry Himalayan air.

DIOGENES LAERTIOS, from *Lives of Eminent Philosophers*: As to [Empedocles'] death different accounts are given ... Hippolytus, again, asserts that, when he got up, he set out on his way to Etna; then, when he had reached it, he plunged into the fiery craters and disappeared ...

> ROBERT BRINGHURST, from "Empedokles' Recipes":
> The commentators say that Empedokles'
> hunger is nothing but water.
> And the commentators say
> Empedokles' last formula was for
>
> mind: made in volcanoes
> out of cauterized eyes and vaporized
> muscle, blood and bone.

> ROBERT BRINGHURST, "Demokritos" § VII:
> Thus the earth goes south each summer.
> The mind moults in the north like a widgeon
> and rises, hunting or grazing, in autumn,
> riding the gale,
> the stain of the voice like a handprint at intervals
> in the unravelling rigging.

7. Kirk and Raven read Fragment 51 as a statement by a physicist about the nature of certain equilibria. It would, I think, be incorrect to argue that Herakleitos did *not* have such equilibria in mind — witness the bow and the lyre — but it is at odds with the tone of the collected fragments, the range of their preoccupations, and their linguistically dense ('poetic') Greek, to suppress the fragment's moral-metaphorical dimension. Bringhurst's version emphasizes its continuity with Herakleitos' age, not with our own.

> FRAGMENT 93: The lord whose oracle is in Delphi neither speaks nor conceals, but gives a sign.

◀ V ▶

FRAGMENT 90: πυρός τε ἀνταμοιβὴ τὰ πάντα καὶ πῦρ
ἁπάντων ὅκωσπερ χρυσοῦ χρήματα καὶ χρημάτων χρυσός.

(*purós te antamoibē ta pánta kai pûr hapántōn hókōsper
khrusóu khrémata kai khrēmátōn khrūsós*)

Fire requites all things and fire is their requittal, as goods
for gold and gold for goods.

III

All things are exchangeable for   I
fire and fire for all things,
like gold for goods and goods for gold,
or so sings old
                 Herakleitos.   5

1. One striking feature of these five lines is their sing-song quality. In the first three, the only words that occur once are 'are,'
'exchangeable,' and 'like'; the rest are repeated panlindromic-
ally, except for 'and,' which is repeated as the link between the
phrases. 'Exchangeable' and 'Herakleitos' are, moreover, the
only words in the whole section of more than one syllable.
It is short. The rhyme 'gold/old' (forced into an end rhyme,
first by the reversal of the order of 'goods' and 'gold' as they
occur in the Greek, and then by the setting of 'Herakleitos'
as a one-word drop line), the frame rhyme 'goods/gold,' the
internal rhyme 'things/sings,' plus the choice of the word
'sings' all conspire to suggest we're dealing with a nursery
rhyme. The Herakleitean cosmological equation is — apparently — as simple as ABC.

ROBERT BRINGHURST, from "Xenophanes":
     The earth gives birth to the sun
     each morning, and washes herself in the water,
     and slits the sun's throat every night

with a splintered stone, and washes
herself once again in the water.

Some days the sun, like a fattening
goose, crosses over in ignorant stupor.
Other days, watch: you will see him
shudder and twitch, like a rabbit
caught in the snare — but what
does is matter? One way
or the other, his death is the same.

2. The complication comes with the syllable 'or' in "or so sings old/Herakleitos." My sense is that this is to be read as doubly ironic: "Of course it's just a silly old saying by a silly old man. You're quite right. Not to be taken seriously." — but said in that particularly nonchalant tone we use when we're teasing children: "Oh, yes, it was all covered in chocolate and whipped cream, so I knew you wouldn't have wanted me to save you any ..." The ultimate sense being: it sounds like childish nonsense, but the real fool is the one who doesn't take it seriously.

3. The Greek for the comparative clause is even more heavily alliterative than "goods for gold and gold for goods." That is, Herakleitos' own phrasing is at the very least witty, arguably arch. The sense of play, particularly the nagging suspicion that someone may be having us on — at least at the level where it's 'obvious' that gold is an exchange for goods — is integral to the meaning of the fragment.

4. Fire is heat and light; that is, the medium of cosmological exchange is the substance of the dry soul.

> FRAGMENT 10: Graspings [linkings, connectings, biological conceptions]: wholes and what isn't whole — gathered together, drawn apart, in tune, out of tune: out of all things one; and out of one, all things.

◀ VI ▶

FRAGMENT 62: ἀθάνατοι θνητοί, θνητοὶ ἀθάνατοι, ζῶντες
τὸν ἐκείνων θάνατον, τὸν δὲ ἐκείνων βίον τεθνεῶτες.

(athánatoi thnētoí, thnētoi athánatoi, zôntes ton ekeínōn
thánaton, ton de ekeínōn bíon tethneôtes)

Immortals mortal, mortals immortal, living the others' death,
dead in the others' life.

IV

Dead men are gods, men are dead gods, said   I
Herakleitos. And furthermore,
mortal immortals are immortal mortals,
the breath of the one is the death of the other,
the dying of one is the life of the other: 5

mortals are deathless, the deathless are mortal,
living in the body the death of the other,
dying into air, earth and fire, siring

the other, the utter
incarnation.   10

1. The text of the fourth section of "Herakleitos" is significantly
different in both earlier and later versions. In *Bergschrund*,
the first two lines quoted above are missing and in their place
occur the following three lines:

Herakleitos says something which cannot be put
into prose, though the Bishop Hippolytus quotes
it as though it were prose. Its essence is this:

In *Eight Objects, Cadastre,* and the version in *Arion,* these
three lines also open the section but they are set off as a
separate stanza.

A third significantly different version appears in *The Calling* and *Selected Poems*. It contains minor modifications to the first stanza as it appears in *The Beauty of the Weapons*, and its second and third stanzas are entirely rewritten.

> *Dead men are gods; men are dead gods, said*
> *Herakleitos. Immortals are mortal, mortals immortal.*
> *The birth of the one is the death of the other;*
> *the dying of one gives life to the other.*
>
> *The living are dying. The dead live forever,*
> *except when the living disturb them, and this*
> *they must do. The gods die*
> *when men live forever. Air, earth and fire*
> *die too. Dying, we mother and sire*
>
> *the other: our only and own*
> *incarnation.*

2. What is illuminating about the earlier versions is the explicit emphasis on the essentially lyric character of Herakleitos' work. What is illuminating about the version reprinted at the top of this section is the absence of this explicitness.

> FRAGMENT 54: An unapparent connection is
> stronger than an apparent one.

ROBERT BRINGHURST, "Empedokles: Seven Fragments" § v:
> ... sighting in on the peaks, one after the other, and not just
> talking one straight trail through the understorey words.

3. The later version of Section IV abandons the gesture of piling on repetitions (an enactive image of generations) in favour of direct statement of a theme Bringhurst elaborates in a self-contained poem in *Selected Poems*: "The Living Must Never Outnumber the Dead." It is a potent claim and it is, arguably, implicit in Fragment 62.

But I prefer the version in *The Beauty of the Weapons* because of its subtle connection to Fragment 50, discussed below, and, through Fragment 50, its connection to the magisterial Fragment 1.

> FRAGMENT 1: Of the Logos, which is forever, uncomprehending men turn out to be, both before hearing and once they have heard ...

4. That Fragment 62 cannot, in fact, be easily rendered in English of any sort is apparent from Robinson's translation, which spells out the ambiguities: "Immortals ⟨are⟩ mortal(s), mortals immortal(s), these (the former?) living ⟨in?⟩ the death of those (the latter?), those (the latter?) dead in the life of these (the former?). Or: Mortals ⟨are⟩ immortal(s), immortals mortal(s), these (the latter?) living ⟨in?⟩ the death of those (the former?), those (the former?) dead in the life of these (the latter?)." The rich musicality of ἀθάνατοι θνητοί, θνητοὶ ἀθάνατοι, the multiplicity of meanings filling the same space, are not defects, but indications of Herakleitos' ability to use language to *show* what he meant: that all the various options are simultaneously, inseparably the case. An explicit account of the ambiguities destroys the gestural power of the thought which is (*pace* Donald Davidson, Bishop Hippolytus, et al.) part of its meaning.

   A reader who denies there is a difference in meaning between Robinson's translation and the original is the literary-philosophical equivalent of a person who can't distinguish a pile of ingredients from a baked cake — easy to please, in some sense, but not worth inviting to dinner.

5. In Section IV, the palindromic structure introduced in Section III is echoed and extended. Once again, the lines are a tightly knit complex of full and part rhymes, claiming for the thought a coherence that simultaneously undercuts and underscores the paradoxes that are its explicit constituents.

6. Far from being obscure, Fragment 62 amounts to a fairly straightforward ecological claim: nothing in fact is ever elim-inated from the coherent, living complex that is the world. But what cannot be put into prose is the beauty of this thought, its rhythmic coherence with the coherent music of the world.

> ROBERT BRINGHURST, "Empedokles: Seven Fragments" § VIII:
> They come among the animals as mountain cats
> and among the broadleaf trees in the forms of laurels.

7. Death, gods, humans, life: there is no ontological or moral separation of one from the other. What is permanent cannot exist apart from what perishes, what is spiritual is inextricably bound up with what is physical.
   The way the world means is the way music means.

> ROBERT BRINGHURST, from "Parmenides":
>   ... and suddenly
>   then
>   Parmenides
>   hummed to himself, caught an idea clean
>   in his teeth and bit into it, singing:
>
>   ... *things which appear to be,*
>   *even though they all exist, actually*
>   *have to be there*
>   *always. Everywhere.*

8. Water is conspicuously absent from the elements into which 'deathless mortals' die and out of which they are sired (line 8). This cannot be because Bringhurst has failed to notice that water is part of the overall Herakleitean cosmology.

9. Death as transfiguration (ontologically continuous with life), death as moral extinction (ontologically discontinuous with life): one way of reading Herakleitos, consistent with the extant fragments, is that dying into fire, air, or (and) earth

is the former; and that dying into water is the latter. On this
reading, Herakleitean water is cognate with Pythagorean
darkness, as Bringhurst reads Pythagoras:

> ROBERT BRINGHURST, "Pythagoras" § v:
> Octaves of silence
> do not exist and do not echo. Intervals
> of darkness disassemble
> endlessly. *Do not drink*
>
> *the darkness,* said Pythagoras,
> *the soul cannot become pure darkness.*
>
> *Possibly.* Possibly.

10. The last five words of Section IV are especially important.
The assonantal rhyme separated only by a comma identifies
our incarnation in otherness (our dying-siring relationship
to air, earth and fire) with *the utter incarnation.* 'Utter' must
be read both as 'absolute,' and in its connection with 'giving
audible expression to.' The utterance, which is an incarnation,
is not Herakleitos', but the world's: an incarnation which is
alive, meaningful, characterized by superficial paradox and
underlying coherence: the λόγος.

> FRAGMENT 50: Listening not to me but to the Logos it
> is wise to agree that all things are one.

11. What we understand when we listen to the λόγος then is ἀθάνατοι θνητοί, θνητοὶ ἀθάνατοι, ζῶντες τὸν ἐκείνων θάνατον,
τὸν δὲ ἐκείνων βίον τεθνεῶτες. And it is understanding this
that shreds the syntax of the soul, opens it to light and air,
reconnects it to the body and death.

12. The idea that the λόγος is incarnate, an uttered incarnation,
is the idea of an ontological community of mind and body
— an integrity of intellect and feeling.

ROBERT BRINGHURST, "Empedokles: Seven Fragments" § VIII:
... tumbling in the surf and undertow
of blood, where the thing called thought is. Thought
is, in fact, the blood around the beating heart.

This relation, as Bringhurst reads Herakleitos, is also ἁρ-
μονικός. That is, it is resonant.

The λόγος then is the expression of the lyric order of the
world. This order is both moral and ecological.

13. While Herakleitos is much concerned with things we tend
to regard as invisible or at best obscure, he is concerned with
these things as they are *manifest* in the physical world. They
are not themselves apparent particulars, but they may be
read off apparent particulars. (Compare Wittgenstein on adequately notated propositions and the logical structure of the
world: *Tractatus Logico-Philosophicus* 4.022, 4.121, 4.1212,
5.511, for example.)

As manifest in the physical world, these things — which
are ultimately indisseverable moments in a single thing, the
λόγος — are not articulate in the sense of 'expressed in (a)
language': the λόγος is a pattern of sorts — what the living,
coherent universe hums to itself — but while it is intelligible and not *ir*rational, it is *a*rational, in that it cannot be
adequately captured in syntactically unexceptional words.

LUDWIG WITTGENSTEIN, *Tractatus Logico-Philosophicus* 6.522:
There are, indeed, things that cannot be put into words. They
make themselves manifest. They are what is mystical.

FRAGMENT 55: The things of which there is seeing and
hearing and perception, these do I prefer.

14. Fragment 124 — below — is a testament to the natural order
of the universe, phrased as a trap for the unwary. A koan.

15. There is an astonishing unanimity among lyric writers on the perceptual metaphor of choice for focussed attention to non-articulate beings or aspects of the world: not seeing, but listening.

16. Meaning is not coextensive with syntactic propriety.

> FRAGMENT 124: The fairest order in the world is a heap of random sweepings.

17. Wind stirs his ashes.

◀ VII ▶

1. Moral knowledge is rooted in knowledge of the living — cyclic or reciprocal — interconnectedness of all things.

2. Meaning is simultaneously obvious and hidden. Its obvious and hidden aspects do not exist as layers, one beneath the other, but rather as indisseverable elements of the same whole. In each case, all elements are apprehended, and they are all the same, and stand in the same relations to one another — as in the Necker cube.

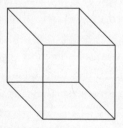

The box presents first one then another of its faces as projecting towards the viewer. It is impossible to draw the constituent lines of the box under one of its aspects without thereby drawing exactly the lines that constitute it under its other aspect — whether that aspect is noticed or not.

3. The prime virtues are curiosity, humility, courage, and a sense of humour. Without the first three, intelligence is wasted; without the fourth, there is no happiness.

4. Oblivion is ever-present. Death is ever-present. Death is and is not oblivion. To die is to change state. There is a form of oblivion that is to disrupt, to step outside, to ignore or reject the moral-ecological order. To experience this form of oblivion is worse than death. It is evil.

5. Beauty is not truth; but it is among the sane human being's tests of truth. Absence of beauty is a sign that something may be missing from the experiment; a sign that something may have been overlooked, some error made.

◀ VIII ▶

1. "The Old in Their Knowing" is a sequence of portraits. Is it philosophy? Its subjects are minds of people who are thought of as philosophers. Its claim as a sequence is that there are certain things these minds share: courage, passion, a lack of urbanity, an intuition of the deep connectedness of things.

2. These poems are attempts to understand the minds of certain thinkers as those thinkers themselves tried to understand the world: lyrically. That is: ecologically. That is: morally.

3. The poems are not for this reason better readings of certain extant Presocratic fragments than readings that view them through the lens of Aristotle, or the lens of technocracy.
   But they are different readings.
   And diversity often fosters stability.
   Monocultures, whether of the land or the soul, frequently precipitate disaster.

4. What makes Bringhurst's readings better is that they respect, rather than condescend to, their subjects.

They constitute a challenge to, rather than an affirmation of, a world view that has led us over the brink of planetary disaster.

The old in their knowing — the old in the *act* of knowing; the act being crucial here, since what is known is not possessed or owned, is not a commodity, cannot be mass-produced for effortless consumption.

These readings are open to the passion of the Presocratics' own thought.

5. These readings argue for an integrity of thought: scientific wonder intertwined with and inseparable from moral wisdom, aesthetic sensibility, and domestic expertise.

Ecology, not seventeenth-century physics, is offered as the paradigm for scientific thought.

Morality is conceived on the paradigm offered by craft — something done, done well, done with the hands, in the physical world — in which beauty cannot be distinguished from fitness, or from harmony and engagement with a larger form of life. (In this, the view has affinities with Aristotle's.)

6. Compare Hargrove:

Because of the general direction that Greek philosophy took from its very beginnings, in Asia Minor, it was virtually impossible for Greek philosophers to think ecologically in any systematic way. To begin with, the Greeks would not have considered an understanding of ecological relationships in nature to be knowledge. Objects of knowledge, like the ultimate objects of reality, were believed to be permanent, eternal, and unchanging. Ecological relationships, in contrast, are concerned with objects that are impermanent, perishable, and in a constant state of change ... [Moreover, Presocratic] philosophers developed no aesthetic appreciation for nature because they were too busy speculating about matter, atoms, and other hypothetical entities that could not be experienced directly by the senses ...

Bringhurst's readings deny the common academic assumption that any understanding worthy of the name will be what Hargrove means by 'systematic.' They deny also that most of the Presocratics believed 'objects of knowledge' to be Cartesian. His readings show that partly *because* the Presocratics themselves would have denied these assumptions, they were able to develop profound understandings of ecological structures. His readings argue that this understanding just is an aesthetic (from *aisthētos*, 'sensible' or 'perceptible') appreciation of nature, and that it is more profound than our own — partly because the Presocratics were perforce, in their lives and daily, sensually alive to the physical world; and partly because their sense of beauty was not heavily mediated by a notion of expensive canvases hung in galleries.

7. Compare Oliver Letwin:

If I teach myself over the course of many years to attend to and act in relief of the pain and misery of others, I am likely, when I see the child run over by the bus, to find myself regarding the situation as one contrary to my preferences: and this unfavourable judgement, if it is manifested in any emotion, will be manifest in sorrow rather than in joy.

The idea of what it is to be human that informs this perspective renders Presocratic thought, and Presocratic conceptions of morality, unintelligible.

8. Bringhurst's readings challenge us, on the one hand, to let the Presocratics be, to perceive ourselves as co-responders rather than legislators. They challenge us, on the other, to test the integrity of their lyricism, to contemplate their conceptual claims as well as to respond to their affective-aesthetic intensity. (Not that these two, in such writing, are fully distinct, let alone separable, from one another.)

9. As the limit of sensitive attempts to be responsible to our experience, truth has a moral dimension. Epistemology is *preceded* by moral choice.

10. A common contemporary notion of poetry as something written out of intense private feeling, which expresses — self-consciously or unselfconsciously — the unique genius of its author, is a caricature of a Romantic conception. It is not a lyric conception, as I have characterized 'lyric.' Lyric awareness is focussed on the cosmos, not the perceiver thereof.

    This does not mean that lyric awareness cannot be subjective — sometimes the best way to the world is through the medium of the self. The trick, and the difference, is to regard the self as medium, a phenomenon in and of the world, not something over and against it, superior to the rest of it, and, in virtue of its linguistic capacities, acting as its much-needed interpreter.

    Lyric thought is characterized by humility as much as by longing.

11. Lyric humility is isomorphic to ecological humility.

    A thing's 'worth' is not directly proportional to its ability to think rationally, but is a function of its contribution to the flourishing of the whole. How do we measure that contribution? What constitutes the flourishing of the whole? What, in any given case, counts as 'the whole'? These are excellent questions. Deciding them will involve wisdom as well as calculative intelligence.

    From a lyric perspective, it is immoral overtly to ignore that the world is an organically integrated complex. One subclass of immoral acts is defined by ecological thoughtlessness.

12. Lyric's *telos* is ecological in form — beauty and stability through integrity. (Aldo Leopold.)

13. Lyric longing is born of a failure of immersion in the living rhythms of the planet. The price of the capacity to manipulate

those rhythms to the extent that technocratic culture manipulates them — the price, that is, of dwelling in a manufactured world of consumer goods — is separation from those rhythms.

This capacity is concomitant with our capacity for language.

The condition of language is the Herakleitean opposite of lyric. That is: they die into one another.

14. To apprehend mind as a living integrated complex of all facets of experience, when such experience is continuous with the larger integrated complex of the living world as a whole, is to apprehend mind ecologically.

Kirk and Raven, despite their overall disparagement of Herakleitos' sophistication, put this quite clearly: "… all things, although apparently plural and totally discrete, are really united in a coherent complex of which men themselves are a part, and the comprehension of which is therefore … necessary for the adequate enactment of their own lives … '[F]ormula,' 'proportionate arrangement' and so on are misleadingly abstract as translations of this technical sense of λόγος."

15. Many philosophers, from Plato to Russell, understand the difference between appearance and reality hierarchically, as the difference between disjoint — obvious on the one hand, hidden on the other — layers of the world. Bringhurst's readings suggest that many of the Presocratics did not understand the difference this way: appearance and reality were ontologically identical for them. As well as distinct.

This, too — this approach to appearance and reality — is characteristic of lyric-ecological understandings of the world.

16. Not all enquiry that goes by the name 'ecological' is, however, lyric in form — much ecological science, for example.

Generally, 'ecological inquiry' denotes thought concerned with complex interdependencies among living beings and their environments.

Some examples of ecological thinking — Herakleitos,' Bringhurst's — are also examples of lyric philosophy.

17. While lyric thought includes work — some of Wittgenstein's, for example — that is not explicitly ecological in its concerns, the ability to think lyrically is nonetheless a precondition for sound ecological thought.

18. Many of the thinkers Bringhurst names in "The Old in Their Knowing" understood the cosmos as an organic whole, understood that reciprocal interdependence characterizes the relations of all beings, animate and inanimate.

19. The theme is one of Bringhurst's own:

> *The bud of light before the sunrise*
> *mated with the dusk,*
> *bore rock and jagged water,*
> *mated with the water, bore*
> *the tidal bore, the overfall, the spindrift and the mist.*
>
> *The starlight seeded earth and mist and water,*
> *germinating slime.*
> *Slime ate into the rocksalt and the darkness,*
> *the seacrust and the metamorphic stone, breeding*
> *nail and nervecord, bone marrow, molar and*
>
> *bones taking root in the darknesses*
> *and darknesses*
> *flowering out of the bone.*
> *Gods and men and goddesses*
> *and ghosts are grown out of this,*
>
> *brothers of the bark and the heartwood and the thorn,*
> *brothers of the gull and the staghorn coral,*
> *brothers of the streptococcus,*
> *the spirochete, the tiger, the albatross, the sea-spider,*
> *cousins of lime and nitrogen and rain.*

20. Unlike Hargrove, Aristotle is quite clear that most of the Presocratics are not proto-Aristotelians (let alone proto-Cartesians):

> *The conclusions reached by these men are rooted in the fact that, while professing to study the nature of reality, they identified reality with the sensible world. But there is in the sensible world much of the Indeterminate [that which exists potentially but not actually]; so that their statements, though plausible enough, are not true.*

21. Nonetheless, Aristotle and, following him, most contemporary commentators (Charles Kahn being an important exception), charge the Presocratics with a staggering linguistic naïvete. (Not quite as staggering in Greek as it is in English, but still remarkable.)

    According to Aristotle, the Presocratics believe that being and absence, death and life, interpenetrate one another simply because they fail to distinguish between subjective opinion and objective fact. So, for example, because you (being 6′6″ tall) find the table low, and some other person (being 4′10″) finds it high, the Presocratics — identifying reality with the physical world — think that the table is both high (and not low) and low (and not high); and hence conclude that it simultaneously *is* and *is not*.

22. Doubtless some among the Presocratics offered dubious, even sophistical, arguments to support their claims. (Nothing new under the sun, especially in philosophy.) But to argue, as Aristotle does, that this is what is *meant* by "the void and the plenum are alike present in any part, though the one is being, and the other is nonbeing" is willfully to misunderstand.

23. In Aristotle's view, the Presocratics also got the true nature of reality wrong because they believed that something could not come from nothing; so, when they perceived contraries (low

and high?) "generated from the same thing," they concluded
that that 'same thing' must have possessed both qualities and
so, falsely, "that contradictories or contraries are compatible
from their observation of the sensible world."

But, again, this is simply to miss the point of a claim like
συλλάψιες. ὅλα καὶ οὐχ ὅλα, συμφερόμενον διαφερόμενον,
συνᾷδον διᾷδον, ἐκ πάντων ἓν καὶ ἐξ ἑνὸς πάντα. (Fragment 10. See v. 4 above, pages 43–44.)

24. Bringhurst's thought is that Herakleitos and other Presocratics are intelligent thinkers entirely capable of Aristotle's
grammatical sophistication — but thinkers whose world view
differs from Aristotle's (and our own) in about the way that
the *Dào Dé Jīng* differs from Descartes' *Rules for the Direction
of the Mind*.

25. Bringhurst paraphrases Aristotle's summary diagnosis of the
problem with the Presocratics: "They had too much faith in
the physical world, Aristotle says, and that is why they contradict themselves."

To have 'too much' faith in the physical world relative to
Aristotle's or our own is to understand that our humanity
depends on an alacritous reciprocity between ourselves and
nonhuman being.

It is to attribute meaning to the somatic and affective power
of well-wrought speech, to trust your nose and your heart as
well as your analytical intelligence.

26. Both lyric and analysis show more than they can say.
But the difference in what is shown is not cosmetic, it is
cosmological.

27. 'Eco' from οἶκος, *house*. Ecology as the λόγος of home.
The passion of the Presocratics is the passion for integrity
in our understanding of humans-in-the-world.

Plato's *Phaidros*: Philosophy as Dialogue with the Dead

Phaidros and the history of *Phaidros* are the problem of written philosophy and its relation to *erōs*, dialectic, and the good life. The problem arises because the dialogue apparently fails to unify its own themes: it closes with an attack on rhetoric and writing which, by rights, should apply retroactively to the inspired discourse on love and the human soul which precedes it. Some commentators are content to regard the dialogue as "broken-backed," in G.R.F. Ferrari's phrase; others struggle to coordinate its disparate topics; yet others, like Jacques Derrida, focus on the final pages — in which, they argue, the dialogue triumphs over its author, undoing itself (and Plato's philosophy generally) in the series of paradoxes that attend any piece of writing that mounts arguments against writing.

Suspicion about the existence of an underlying unity is bolstered by a multitude of tensions: not only intra-textual anomalies, but also tensions between *Phaidros* and other dialogues. It isn't clear whether these tensions are the result of a deliberate effort on the part of its author, or of failures of cross-cultural imagination, or of accidents of transmission — with the result that it is impossible to decide once and for all which tensions to ignore and which to take seriously: the ambiguities extend to the very bottom. I believe, however, that despite these ambiguities it is possible to discern an architectonic — or at least to light the dialogue in such a way that one begins to stand out: an architectonic that is the literary enactment of a philosophical question about the nature of philosophy and writing.

My argument for this claim will rest on a number of assumptions, some more contentious than others. But it begins with a literary observation — that Plato was a gifted and meticulous writer. In this lies one of the most striking puzzles of the dialogue, and a puzzle I think readers are meant to notice. How could someone who takes writing seriously enough to have produced the brilliant literary effects of the first half have been entirely convinced by the critique of writing that is put into Sokrates' mouth in the concluding pages? This question is deliberately rhetorical: I don't think Plato *was* entirely convinced. But nor, I think, was he convinced the critique could be dismissed. It is this dynamic that determines the structure and intent of the dialogue, and integrates its themes.

To make my case, I will need to assume that the views about rhetoric, and particularly the views about writing, contained in the last third of the dialogue accurately represent the historical Sokrates' views; that Sokrates was dead at the time *Phaidros* was written; and that he was someone Plato had loved and conversed with. I will assume that these conversations confirmed Plato in the view that philosophical thought involves a 'bringing forth,' and that it is most effectively pursued in intense one-on-one conversation between an older, more experienced person, and a younger, less experienced one. I will also assume that Plato agreed with a doctrine attributed to Sokrates in *Symposium* as well as *Phaidros*: that true philosophy is grounded in *erōs*; that it is an impassioned desire to understand, which is also a cherishing of the roots of human intuitions of moral beauty. Finally, as part of my attempt to establish an architectonic, I will need to assume that there are two speeches by Sokrates in the first part of the dialogue, corresponding to the use of the dual at 262d1, 265e3, and 266a3, and despite the use of the singular at 265c6, 265d7, and 263d3.

I · RHETORIC AND WRITING: PLATO'S OBJECTIONS

The dialogue occurs between two speakers, Sokrates and Phaidros, and makes reference to two other persons, Lysias and Isokrates: Phaidros, who as far as we know is not a writer himself, is said to regard Lysias, a successful rhetorician and speech-writer, as his

* † παιδικά — his favorite, or beloved; Sokrates, who is not a writer himself, is said to have Isokrates, a young writer-rhetorician, as

his παιδικά. It is, however, Phaidros and Sokrates who carry on
the action of philosophical converse that, in the dialogue itself,
is characterized as the epitome of genuine love. Thus we have
the following strikingly symmetrical arrangement of speakers
and characters:

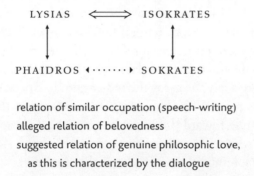

Mapped in this way, it does not seem surprising that the dialogue might be about the relation between good and bad love, on
the one hand, and good and bad writing or rhetoric, on the other.
But Sokrates, in the dialogue, is portrayed as thinking that good
philosophical writing simply does not exist; so we may wonder
whether the symmetries of character are in fact echoed in the
questions the dialogue treats. Is there a genuine question about
the relation between good writing and philosophy in *Phaidros*?
I wish to argue that there is, and that it is put to Sokrates not
by Phaidros — or Lysias or Isokrates — but by the writer of the
dialogue himself. As he develops Sokrates' negative answer, Plato
simultaneously demonstrates his love.

The main discussion of rhetoric occurs at the end of the dialogue:
259e–278e. It is prefaced by Sokrates' recounting of the myth of
the cicadas, who are also mentioned at the outset. This myth is
one of four told in the dialogue, and each is an occasion for conveying a point of central importance. Here, we learn that, singing
and conversing, the cicadas "actually died without noticing it": an
apt description of Sokrates' own life-conduct. (Arguably, Sokrates

did notice his own dying. But according to *Phaedo,* not much. He remained in sustained philosophical conversation to the last, arguing, among other things, that the philosopher seeks to live in a state as close to death as possible, his soul unfettered by his body.) The cicadas' story reminds us that Sokrates is dead, and that he died for 'singing and conversing,' not for promulgating false gods or for corrupting the youth. Once we notice this, it becomes clear why, throughout the dialogue, Plato is at pains to underline Sokrates' passion for discourse and the dithyrambic quality of his speeches; and also why he underlines Sokrates' virtue in precisely the areas the indictment had pretended to question: his respect for the gods; his knowledge of the old myths; his attitude toward the younger generation's ignorance of, and lack of respect for, those myths; and his prodigious ability to resist the temptations of a physical seduction.

The reasons advanced for Sokrates' suspicion of rhetoric — especially the view that the rhetorician typically fails to know the truth about his subject — are familiar to us from *Gorgias* and *Protagoras.* What is unique to *Phaidros* are the objections mounted specifically against writing, and the contrasts asserted between writing's potential achievements and those of dialectic. These topics are the focus of the final few pages, 274b–278e.

The discussion of the 'seemliness' of writing opens with another myth: Theuth, Sokrates tells us, having invented writing (among other things), takes it to Thamous, king of the gods, for his approval. Thamous is not impressed. He thinks that far from being a recipe for memory and wisdom as Theuth claims, writing will lead humans to *cease* to exercise memory — they will no longer "call things to remembrance from within themselves," but will rely on external marks. Thus, Theuth has not provided a means of showing people *how* to remember, he has merely provided them with a way of recording many things without understanding. His invention does not offer humans the wisdom that would allow them to grasp what the things they have recorded *mean.*

After a brief skirmish over the reliability of myth, Sokrates elaborates on the lesson in a series of objections. A written manual, he continues, provides us with nothing "reliable and permanent," no *knowledge*, and it cannot do anything more than "remind one who already knows that which the writing is about." (Let's call this Objection I.) This suggests to him a similarity between writing and painting: their products seem to stand before us as if alive or intelligent, but if we question them they do not respond (Objection II). And, once written, a composition "drifts all over the place," falling into the hands not only of those who already possess the knowledge it records, but also those who do *not* know what it purports to remind them of: "it doesn't know how to address the right people, and not address the wrong" (Objection III). When it is thus inevitably misunderstood and abused, it is helpless to defend itself — and it needs its living parent to come to its aid (Objection IV).

In contrast, Sokrates goes on to claim, there is another sort of discourse, of "unquestioned legitimacy" (as opposed to the bastard, writing) that is "much better" and "more effective." This is living speech: it "goes together with knowledge, and is written in the soul of the learner" (a recasting of Objection I). It "knows to whom it should speak and to whom it should say nothing" (an echo of Objection III); and it is, moreover, "the original of which the written discourse may fairly be called a kind of image" (Objection V).

Thus, Sokrates concludes, writing can be justified only as a pastime or an amusement (Objection VI): a writer necessarily lacks the serious intent of a *dialectician*, who aims to sow the seeds of his words in suitable soil, and who understands that he will have to tend the seedlings for some time before they come to maturity. Objection IV is reiterated, and the words of the writer are said to be unable to "present the truth adequately" (Objections I and II again).

But if writing is regarded as a pastime, it is surely a more honourable one than going to drinking-parties, Sokrates suggests: to write as a pastime is to "[collect] a store of refreshment" both for the writer's own memory in old age, and for those who come after. Phaidros leaps enthusiastically on this point and misses it: what an excellent recreation writing is, he exclaims; how far superior to "the other sort" when it occupies itself with matters of justice and the like! Sokrates steers him back on course: yes, but *writing* about justice and the like is far inferior to the serious pursuit of those topics by the dialectician:

The dialectician selects a soul of the right type, and in it plants and sows words founded on knowledge, words that can defend both themselves and the one who planted them, words that are not sterile but contain a seed whence new words will grow up in new characters, yielding fruit forever, and its possessor the fullest measure of well-being that a human can attain. [276e–277a]

*   In an earlier passage, the art of dialectic has been described as a practice that employs two techniques. The first of these "brings together scattered particulars under a single idea, in order to make clear what is being talked about." The second involves cutting up such an idea into subclasses "along its natural joints, trying not to splinter any of the parts, the way a bad butcher might." Exercised together, these two techniques confer "the power to speak and think." At 266b, Sokrates uses the terms συναγωγή (*sunagōgé* — collection) and διαίρεσις (*diaíresis* — division) for these processes. He says that he follows "as a god" any man "able to discern an objective unity and plurality."

*   After his encomium on the dialectician, Sokrates launches into a summary of the whole discussion of rhetoric, both written and unwritten. If rhetoric is to attain the status of a *technē*, its practitioners, whether they aim to persuade or expound, must:

> ‣ know the truth of the matter on which they discourse; that is, they must demonstrate knowledge of their subject via the method of Collection and Division; that is, they must be able to isolate their subject in definition, and then show its genus-species structure. (277b)

> ‣ know the nature of soul — that which is moved by discourse — and know the type of speech that is appropriate to each type of soul: 'complex' souls must be addressed in a complex style, simple souls in a simple one. (277b–c)

Even if its author fulfills these criteria though, his work will be a disgrace to him if he thinks there is "any great certainty or clarity in it." If, on the other hand, a person embraces the truth about writing, then we may indeed wish to emulate him; and in the final summary of the dialogue Sokrates rehearses the various difficulties that must be acknowledged:

- A written discourse on any subject is bound to contain much that is written merely for amusement. (Objection vi)

- Nothing written, whether in verse or prose, merits much serious attention, nor does declamatory speaking: these aim at persuasion without any questioning or exposition. (Objection ii)

- Writing is, at best, a reminder to those who already know the truth. (Objection i)

- Clarity, completeness, and serious value belong only to lessons on justice, beauty, and goodness, which are offered for the sake of instruction of those listeners in whose souls the lesson is [thereby? or, already?] written. (Objection iii; and perhaps, by implication, Objection vi again)

- The sorts of discourses just described alone constitute a thinker's legitimate children. (Objection v, and, by association, Objection iv)

Sokrates concludes, nonetheless, that a writer, whether rhetorician, poet, or constitutionalist, who knows the truth of his subject and can defend his statements when challenged, and who, in addition, *can demonstrate the inferiority of his writings out of his own mouth* — such a writer deserves the name 'philosopher.' By contrast, the mere poet, speech-writer, or law-giver will "not possess things of more value than the things he composed." He will not possess living truth.

The question is to what degree Plato intends the foregoing as an indictment of the serious intent of his own writing. A few compositional details are worth noting. The first is that except for general references to writing and writers (γραφή, γράμματα, συγγραφεύς), Plato never refers to writing of the kind he does. In *Phaidros* we get τέχνη ἐν γράμμασι (written manual), λόγων γραφή (speech-writing), ἐν πολιτικοῖς λόγοις συγγράμματα (political compositions), ποιητής (poet), λόγων συγγραφεύς (speech-writer), νομογράφος (law-writer) — but Plato coins no term such as διαλόγων γραφή (dialogue-writing) or διαλογο-γράφος (dialogue-writer). Nor does he mention ἡ Σωκράτικων λόγων γραφή (writing of Sokratic dialogues), even though Aristotle refers to Sokratic dialogues as an established literary genre. Not even 'playwright' shows up in either of its common Greek forms, τραγῳδογράφος or κωμῳδογράφος. Also, although the dialogue portrays Sokrates and Phaidros as engaged in the very type of dialectical conversation that Sokrates *contrasts* to written discourse and praises as having none of its defects, Plato very pointedly indicates that it has failed to have the effects Sokrates boasts for it on Phaidros: their dialectical examination of rhetoric has left not a trace in his soul — he remembers nothing of it, though it's only an afternoon old. Thus, either Sokrates, in engaging in spoken dialectic, has misjudged his audience (Objection III); or we have an instance of spoken dialectic's being no better off than written discourse as far as providing "reliable and permanent" knowledge of truth.

Moreover, Sokrates was himself "unfairly abused" on account of a (complexly motivated) misunderstanding of his views; but being able to speak for himself *did no good*. In effect, he was no more successful in defending himself at his trial than a 'dead' discourse.

These observations invite us to consider the degree to which the piece of writing before us, the *Phaidros*, in fact succumbs to Sokrates' objections. Let me recast the criticisms Sokrates lodges against writing as a series of questions:

I *Version* A: Does this piece of writing provide us with a mere record of things we are not also taught how to understand? Are we kept in the dark about how we are actually to do philosophy?

   Version B: Does it, or its author, lack a knowledge of truth, written in his, or its, soul?

   Version C: Does it, or its author, aim at mere persuasion without questioning or thinking?

II If questioned, does this piece of writing fail to respond?

III Does this writing fail to distinguish its audience properly? Or, to put the emphasis where the dialogue seems to invite us to put it: Does it, to a greater degree than a knowledgeable living practitioner of dialectic, fail to make appropriate discriminations?

IV Is it like a child with no acknowledged parent? Is it — any more than a living practitioner of dialectic — helpless to defend itself?

V Is it 'illegitimate' in a metaphysical sense — a mere copy of a living original?

VI Does it contain much that is merely amusing, and therefore lacking in serious intent? Can it, on the other hand, reply to the charges laid against it? Most importantly, can it demonstrate the inferiority of writing out of its own mouth?

I believe we can show that, for *Phaidros*, the answer to each of the questions ranged under I–V, and the first question of VI, is *no*; and that the answers to the final two in VI are *yes*. In attending to the ways the dialogue responds to objections it raises against itself, we come to appreciate the profound coherence, indeed the unity, of its overall design.

II · THE PHAIDROS' DEFENCE

What Sokrates says at 230d4–5 is usually translated: "landscape and trees won't teach me anything, whereas men in the city do." Nehamas and Woodruff strengthen the sense that nonhumans are useless: "landscapes and trees have nothing to teach me — only the people in the city can do that." However, the Greek also permits the sense to shift the other way, with the stress falling not on humans' *capacity* to teach, but their *wish* to do so: "landscape and trees aren't willing to teach me anything, whereas men in the city are." If we do translate the passage this way, ironic possibilities immediately spring into focus.

Sokrates' intent here matters. This remark follows hard on the heels of two interesting exchanges: Sokrates' demonstration that, although Phaidros accuses him of never setting foot outside the walls, he knows more about the geography (and associated culture) of the area than Phaidros — who allegedly walks every day outside the city; and Sokrates' rejection of the current fashion for the rationalization of myths. He explains his distaste by claiming that a complete set of such rationalizations would take too much time to devise; he'd rather spend his time trying to "know himself." But at 275b–c, following the myth of Theuth and Thamous, we get something much stronger. Here, Phaidros doesn't simply ask Sokrates whether or not he thinks a myth is true, he challenges the validity of myths as a form of genuine understanding: "Oh, sure, Sokrates, make up any old story you like." Sokrates' reply, though laced with his characteristic blend of irony and admonition, is nevertheless startling:

Oh, but the authorities of the temple of Zeus at Dodona, my friend, said that the first prophetic utterances came from an oak-tree. In fact the people of those days, lacking the wisdom of you young people, were content in their simplicity to listen to trees or rocks, provided these told the truth. For you apparently it makes a difference who the speaker is, and what country he comes from: you don't merely ask whether what he says is true or false.

Coupled with his chiding tone at 259b, where Phaidros is admonished for claiming to be a lover of the Muses while not knowing the myth of the cicadas, and Sokrates' disparagement of the new, uninformed style of speaking about prophecy at 244c–d, it seems quite clear that Sokrates regards both myth and divine inspiration as sources of genuine understanding, and that he does not believe it impossible that gods, rocks, and trees should truly teach people who know how to listen. (The theme lurking beneath the surface here connects the inability to listen with cultural corruption — the rationalization of myths and the substitution of the pursuit of rhetoric for myths being only two symptoms among many.) The extra-textual irony is almost too thick to cut with a stylus: Sokrates was executed for heresy and corrupting the youth, although he pushed young men to greater integrity through the reinforcement of traditional ways of knowing and honouring the gods.

Phaidros, then, in initial reply to Objection 1, Version A, does not merely record some putative facts about the genesis of philosophic practice in *erōs*, it shows us how we are to begin to acquire philosophically sensitive vision: we must respect the inspiration of traditional myth. It does not *tell* us to do this, but it offers us an intriguing character — clearly intelligent, arguably noble — who pursues this course; and it invites us, through a second character's questions and objections, to consider the worthiness of myth as a guide to truth.

But it also shows us a second way in which philosophy may be pursued: dialectic. The term appears to have been invented with Sokrates or Plato, though its basic lineage is clear: it is from διαλέγεσθαι, 'to converse, talk with, discuss.' And while this indicates why a lover of dialectic such as Sokrates would also be a lover of conversation, and perhaps an advocate of a conversational, question-and-answer style of philosophical inquiry, it does not immediately clarify the connection of dialectic with the method of Collection and Division.

For this, we need to consider the etymology of διαλέγεσθαι itself. Ernest Klein tells us it is the "middle [reflexive] voice of διαλέγειν, 'to pick out, choose,' from διά and λέγειν, 'to pick out, reckon, count, tell, say, speak,' which stands in gradational relationship to λόγος, 'word, speech, discourse, account.'" διά, meaning 'through, throughout,' probably stands for *δισά, Klein suggests, and was formed (on analogy with μετά, 'after') from δίς, 'twice,' hence originally meant 'divided in the middle.' For these reasons, *dialectic* might be best thought of as an account that 'divides itself in the middle,' or into two parts — not only as conversation, but in its method of conceptual investigation: on the one hand, a gathering of instances of apparently diverse phenomena that share some core common characteristic; and, on the other, their sorting into natural kinds according to a purely conceptual articulation of the key idea.

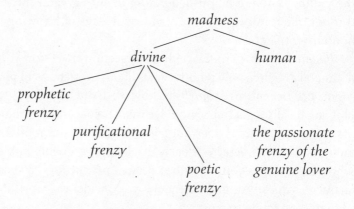

Collection and Division of the concept *madness*:
Phaidros 244a–245c and 249d–e

Phaidros not only describes this second means of acquiring knowledge, it *illustrates* it — both as conversation, and as Collection and Division. It shows us how to do philosophy.

OBJECTION I, VERSIONS A AND C

Does this piece of writing provide us with a mere record of things we are not also taught how to understand? No. Two *methods* of grasping truth are presented: attention to inspired myth, and dialectic.

Both are offered in contexts of challenge: the fashion is to debunk myth, and the tendency is to mistake sophistical rhetoric for dialectical inquiry. Sokrates is made to respond to these challenges, and it is clear that the sympathies of the writer of the dialogue are on the whole Sokratic. But Sokrates is not entirely loveable (he can be infuriatingly coy, heavy-handedly didactic, and righteous by turns); and the dialogue's questions are *genuine* questions. It is impossible for any intelligent reader not to feel prompted by the dialogic form itself to wonder whether Sokrates is *right*; and, apart from being right, whether he has responded adequately. And this last is also the answer to one of the alternate versions of the first question. *Does this piece of writing aim at mere persuasion without questioning or thinking?* On the contrary, it aims to prompt us to search our own souls for what is written there.

OBJECTION III

Does this writing fail to distinguish its audience properly? Or: Does it, to a greater degree than a living practitioner of dialectic such as Sokrates, fail to make appropriate discriminations? The answer to the second question is clearly no. Sokrates was so bad at choosing his audience that he ended up dead. But to take the question in a spirit closer to that of the objection on which it rests: Does this piece of writing offer wisdom that ought, properly speaking, to be reserved for initiates? Does it reveal things that the uninitiated could misconstrue?

This question is impossible to judge. We are in the position of non-initiates, so it is difficult to say what we might understand differently if we were not. There are enough anomalies — strange tensions between this dialogue and others, hints about disguised identities, the insistent suggestion that Sokrates is 'out of place' — to make one wonder if perhaps there isn't some sort of code whose interpretive key was to be provided to students of the Academy. Or if there are matters of secret Pythagorean doctrine related in the myth of the charioteer that Plato would indeed have been mortified to discover had been made public. On the other hand, there are many details — from small, exquisitely

turned ironies to the overarching conception of the dialogue as a
whole — that suggest Plato envisaged it as self-standing. We have
Dionysios Halikarnasseus' testimony that Plato was an obsessive
reviser of small points in his existing written work throughout
his life; such perfectionism is not impossible if that written work
was never intended to be read without an accompanying, legitimating, oral exegesis — but it suggests Plato wanted to get the
writing itself right. Why? On the other hand, in *Letter VII*, the
author says he never commits his profound thoughts to paper;
then again, Plato's authorship of the letter is disputed. We are
left in a state of philological aporia. Ah, but intentionally? As the
result of historical accident? — Meta-philological aporia as well.

OBJECTION IV

Is this piece of writing helpless to defend itself? No. The dialogue is
not merely a statement of doctrine; it is an attempt to elucidate
grounds for any thinking that aims at genuine understanding.
Not only does it raise and attempt to respond to objections about
its own theses regarding the roles of love, sex, rhetoric, and dialectic in the pursuit of a meaning-filled life, it attempts to display
the roots of its own methodology — respect for myth and the
practice of dialectic — so that we may begin to think through
these questions, and Sokrates' answers, for ourselves. Is it possible that this methodology, or its aims, or its conclusions, or the
myths themselves, might be misconstrued? Of course. But the
method, aims, conclusions, and character of Sokrates were also
misconstrued, his ability to defend himself notwithstanding. As
a rhetorical question aimed at forcing us to admit the inferiority
of writing to speech, it is less than compelling.

OBJECTIONS V AND VI (FIRST PART)

*Is this writing a mere copy of a living original? Does it "contain
much that is fanciful," much that is written merely for amusement,
without serious intent?* These two questions, although arising
from allegations presented separately in *Phaidros*, might appear

to be linked. If the dialogue *is* a record of an actual conversation, or conversations, then the degree of its invented content diminishes accordingly. If it contains much that is made up in order to amuse, then it can hardly be charged with being a copy.

But this is again to misconstrue the spirit of the questions. Is this writing a less-than-faithful representation of the thoughts in its writer's soul? Is it full of empty rhetorical flourishes? It is, at least, not *clear* that the answers are *yes*; and it certainly *appears* — from its tone, intensity, and, as I hope to demonstrate, tightly knit conception — that the answers are *no*. The point of the charges of 'being a mere copy' and 'containing much that is fanciful' is to distinguish rhetorically vivid but intellectually confused discourses from *philosophical* treatments of the same topics which employ the art of dialectic. And it is hard to wrestle oneself into a frame of mind in which *Phaidros* appears to be anything but such a serious treatment. The passage that extends this theme has already been quoted above, page 64. Its characterization of the dialectician strikes me as an accurate characterization of Sokrates, and his effect on Plato; but it is also a good description of most of the written dialogues and their effect on subsequent thinkers. We are, it is true, returned to the problematic aspects of the question concerning audience: a piece of writing is unable to 'choose' its readers, in the sense of withholding its words — apart from selecting against illiterates, and those with an insufficient command of the language in which it is written. But to what extent, and in what way, to what end, is the living dialectician better able to select a soul of 'the right type'? — A person not interested in abstract questions about the nature of moral conduct and the philosophical life is not going to bother reading *Phaidros* through. It does discuss physical love, but apart from a mildly salacious reference to what Phaidros has under his cloak, there aren't even any dirty jokes, let alone pornographic encounters. And only a philosopher who could write would be at all concerned with the discussion of rhetoric and writing; and even then might dismiss the dialogue if she failed to see how its rejection of undialectical rhetoric is connected to Sokrates' apparently rhetorical exaltation of love.

*

It is, of course, possible that this reply is still failing to meet the real intent of the question of audience head-on: it may be that what is meant by 'selecting a soul of the right type' involves presupposing some ontological hierarchy of souls in terms of their innate philosophical receptivity, and a faculty of intuitive discernment on the part of some teachers. But unless we can demonstrate that living humans are capable of such discernment, the objection that *writing* is unable to make the necessary discriminations has no bite. Was Sokrates capable of such discernment? If so, he didn't exercise it. He'd talk to *anyone*; and in the end, this was his undoing.

OBJECTION II AND OBJECTION VI (SECOND PART)

There remains the question of the dialogue's status, or lack of status, as an intelligent being. *If questioned, does this writing fail to respond?* Well, what sort of questions? What sort of response? "So, do you think the Flames will take the Oilers?" — Not even Sokrates expects this much. *Does this writing respond to powerful objections raised against its own theses?* Yes. Clearly. Against the contention that *erōs* plays a crucial role in any serious attempt to lead a good life, it offers the speech of Lysias, and the first speech of Sokrates; and against our inclination to accept the second speech of Sokrates as gospel is set the caution that only a god could tell the *true* nature of soul — the myth of the charioteer is a way of conveying a resemblance of the truth. And, we are made abundantly aware that, in Sokrates' culture, myths are not exactly the means of choice for conveying even such approximations. Finally, against an attempt to regard *anything* the dialogue says as being genuinely philosophical, we find the powerful battery of objections we have been considering. There can be no doubt that the dialogue is able to "demonstrate the inferiority of [its] writings out of [its] own mouth." — And that, to this extent, paradoxically enough, it may indeed be entitled to the epithet *philosophos*.

OBJECTION I, VERSION B

But does such a reply perhaps expect too little? *Can we say of this piece of writing: truth is written in its soul?* In what sense could we say this of any writing? In what sense could any piece of writing be alive?

∗

How, indeed, do we distinguish beings with souls from those without?

We look, I believe, to our own souls, to the unpremeditated gestures in them of response. We attend to, as living, as *having meaning*, that which startles us, wakes us up, by which we feel — shockingly, thrillingly, against expectation — both recognized and addressed. Or by that which we sense recognizes and addresses someone else. As Wittgenstein suggests, this 'going up' to someone, this gesture of address, is a crucial part of what we experience as meaning — charged communication — whether the someone gone up to is ourselves, or whether the address is overheard. Does this mean that meaning has nothing to do with content? No; but it may mean that content stands to the live gesture of meaningful address as a museum piece stands to a working tool in the field.

*

In reply to the objection that *Phaidros* has no soul, then, we must reflect on the presence, and power, of its gesture of address. Only a god may be deemed wise, Sokrates says at 278d, but we may call a "lover of wisdom" one who "has done his work with a knowledge of the truth." The work of *Phaidros*, which it can now pursue only as a living piece of writing, is to awaken in us a desire to embrace moral beauty; and this task it still pursues out of deep and passionate reflection, a conviction that it is *erōs* that names the movement toward all genuine insight. To the extent that we are not arrested by this vision, the dialogue has failed. We do not, in the end, have to agree with that vision for the dialogue to succeed; but as human beings with an interest in questions about how to live, we must feel immediately addressed — or hear the power of the dialogue's address to some other.

Recall that the problem of written philosophy is similar to the problem of inspired insight (the medium of Sokrates' great speech on erōs): both are prey to challenges against which they have trouble defending themselves. Written philosophy can't defend itself because, as an inert tablet covered with scratch marks, it is patently unable to respond to questions. Inspiration can't defend itself because its insights are dismissable by the rationalizers. But then someone in Plato's position might formulate the following thought: written philosophy *can* exist and *not* degenerate into mere rhetoric when, but only when, it, too, engages with those who would dismiss it — when it surveys the best available arguments against its existence. That is, when, as written philosophy, it assumes the role of its own interlocutor and its form becomes dialectical.

Where, however, for Plato, would the best arguments against the view just articulated — that philosophy might be pursued in writing — be found? In conversation with Sokrates. But such conversation is, of course, no longer possible, for Sokrates is dead. Indeed, *if* the views Sokrates presents in *Phaidros* are correct, what is there called "the greatest good human understanding or divine mania has to offer" is no longer available to Plato: he can no longer pursue philosophical discussion with his beloved. Unless it were to become possible, somehow, to pursue dialectic with the dead.

But this, I believe, is one way of understanding what *Phaidros* is, and of understanding why it chooses to interweave and set against one another the themes of erōs and writing, in philosophy and rhetoric, enacted through inspiration and dialectic. It is why the picture of the lovers in Sokrates' great speech inevitably conjures the image of Plato and Sokrates, though almost nothing about their relationship is recorded outside the dialogues. And why the myth of the cicadas is located where it is: centrally: at the point where the speaking that is the dialogue divides in two.

To put this another way: given the tremendous symmetry of the characters and 'plot,' what are we to make of the apparent asymmetry of the dialogue's conceptual scheme?

Lysias'	Sokrates'	Sokrates'	conversation
sophistical	sophistical	non-sophistical	about rhetoric,
defence of the	defence of the	defence of the	philosophy,
non-lover	non-lover	lover	and writing

I am suggesting that if we lay it out as I have above, we fail to appreciate the argument's true, self-reflexive scope: that it is the dialogue itself, taken as a whole, that is the written, philosophical defence of the lover:

WRITTEN	NON-WRITTEN	NON-WRITTEN	WRITTEN
sophistical	sophistical	genuine,	philosophical
defence of the	defence of the	philosophical	defence of the
NON-LOVER	NON-LOVER	defence of the	LOVER
		LOVER	
(Lysias'	(Sokrates' first	(Sokrates' second	(Plato's dialogue)
discourse)	speech)	speech)	

By its own lights, *Phaidros* is enabled to be this defence only because, in its concluding conversation, it challenges the viability of writing as a means of doing philosophy. By faithfully developing Sokrates' objections to writing, the dialogue *becomes* the enactment of the principles of erotically driven philosophical discourse as Plato had absorbed them. It becomes the enactment of love for, of philosophical dialogue with, the dead.

⬥

"Wait a minute. I'm not following. What is the connection between the dialogue's gesture of address and the architectonic you've just described?"

Phaidros can have the architectonic I've proposed only if it succeeds in being a written, *philosophical* defence of the lover. But it can be a philosophical defence, in Plato's understanding of philosophy, only if it succeeds in responding, in a very full-blooded way, to the questions and objections Sokrates would have raised had he been alive to raise them. It must somehow offer an adequate and flexible reply to the charges Sokrates lays at the door of any writing with philosophical pretensions. In particular, it must somehow defend itself, qua writing, against the charge that writing is not 'responsive,' not 'living.' One way to understand the metaphor of 'livingness' for writing is through the notion of address. In other words, for *Phaidros* to defend itself against the charge of 'unresponsiveness,' it must constitute a genuine address on Plato's part to Sokrates — or, rather, to the image of Sokrates as that lives in Plato's imagination. *Phaidros*, then, can have the architectonic I've proposed only if it succeeds in being *dialogue* with the dead.

Plato, read this way, is not *asserting* the adequacy of written philosophy as philosophy. He is asking: *Is* it adequate? He knew that something about Sokrates' conversation had been able to change peoples' lives (at least, some peoples' lives). For a prodigiously talented writer, the questions would be urgent: Is it true that writing can't do the same thing? Is there a way to make a piece of writing that might have the same effect? On the one hand, it is difficult to doubt Plato's sincerity in the final pages: he really does appear to think that writing is not the equal of live discourse, and that it can therefore, at best, serve as a recreational adjunct to true philosophy. On the other hand, given his subtlety throughout, it is also difficult to believe that he was unaware of the self-reflexive nature of writing down objections to writing, including that one mark of a true philosopher is the ability to voice objections to writing. (Note that at the climax of Sokrates' encomium on dialecticians, it is unambiguously words that defend dialecticians, not dialecticians who defend words.) And that the dialogue therefore does not *come to rest* with the notion that writing is simply the meek servant of dialectic. Nor does it *come to rest* with its own writerly undoing of arguments against the legitimacy of writing. That is: it does not come to rest.

The momentum of the arguments is countered at every point by the brilliance of their written execution: this wrought counterplay of content and form is itself the *phusis* of the work. Content and form are themselves in dialogic relation, and their tension, instead of blowing the dialogue apart, is its torqued unity, the breathless updraft at its centre that pulls the questions from us.

We feel its address to the spirit of Sokrates because we cannot help but be aware both of Plato's gifts as a writer and of his integrity in challenging writing's usefulness, as Sokrates would have. The words of the dialogue say that the lovers are, in society, the pairs Sokrates and Isokrates, Phaidros and Lysias; and the doctrine of the first part *shows* that, in the dialogue, they are actually Sokrates and Phaidros; but the conceptual interaction of the second part with that doctrine, *in writing,* means that they are, in reality, Plato and the ghost of Sokrates.

III · LIVING PHILOSOPHY

It is not true that those we love always call us to the clearest and most complete speech. But it may be true that their image does. All letter-writers, says Virginia Woolf, "instinctively draw a sketch of the person to whom the letter is addressed … without someone warm and breathing on the other side of the page, letters are worthless." *Phaidros* may lead us to wonder if this is perhaps not true of all writing, including written philosophy.

Not that written philosophy must always be conceived as a gesture of address to the dead — though the dead have frequently been addressed in good philosophical writing other than Plato's. The addressee need not be a single individual, nor even human. Or it can — as it is in Wittgenstein's case — be the writer himself. What, then, does it mean to say that a piece of writing is *alive* only insofar as it is an address? It means that living writing proceeds from *persons* and that, in its imaginative gestures, it establishes other *persons* for whom its questions are a concern. There must be something about which the writer genuinely cares — enough that it prompts speech; and the writer must then conceive the addressee as a being with genuine interests and intelligence, capable of being caught by the discussion, and capable of walking away if the discussion is boring. Or, to put this another way: it is impossible to conceive writing as alive — as what I have been calling a gesture of address — without conceiving it to be driven by *erōs*.

Perhaps all good writing, good conversation, is in this sense philosophical.

"But *erōs* with what object? Doesn't Plato think that philosophic *erōs* is aimed at what he calls 'the Good'? You want to claim that *Phaidros* raises some questions about the nature of written philosophy which are relevant to philosophers today. And, you say, those questions can be framed in terms of whether or not we can discern an 'erotic' stance behind the writing. But either this 'erotic' stance has to be characterized with reference to Platonic metaphysics — and thus is irrelevant to philosophers today, since no one (well, hardly anyone) believes (or will admit to believing) in those kinds of absolutes anymore — *or* your notion of address is *not* informed by a *Platonic* conception of *erōs* — so it's conceivably relevant to contemporary philosophers, but it has nothing to do with what's going on in *Phaidros*."

In other words, how much of Plato's broader view must we accept if we are going to take seriously the suggestion that philosophy should be pursued as a gesture of address?

We need not, I think, accept the ontological apparatus of Plato's metaphysics or epistemology; nor need we accept the view that the method of Collection and Division is 'the' method of philosophy. We must, I think, share Plato's intuition that philosophy is an activity grounded in a longing or yearning for understanding; and we must also accept the view that philosophical thought is sculpted by a demand for clarity, which it is the part of the addressee to help the writer fulfil. But this intuition and this demand are basic to philosophical enterprise across cultures. (Clarity need not foreclose on ambiguity! In some cultures, philosophy's task is understood as the clear delineation of puzzles that cannot be resolved in certain ways.) Plato's insistence that philosophy be pursued 'dialectically' is his *version* of this basic philosophical commitment to clarity. What we must retain from Plato's notion of dialectic then, if the notion of address is to be compelling, is the thought that an attentive interlocutor — imagined or real — is crucial to keeping one's thought alive and responsive, to ensuring that it is, and remains, meaningful.

It is in this way that it is also possible, in keeping with the general outline of Plato's account, to write philosophy as an address to the self. We need not be 'beloved' of ourselves in anything like a romantic way — it would be distasteful if we were. But we must have — as Wittgenstein, for example, did — an *erōs*-driven concern for the state, if not the fate, of our own souls. And on nearly every reading, it is just this that is at the core of the relationship of the lovers in *Phaidros*. Philosophy conceived as an address in this sense, must also be then an address that listens. A maieutic art.

♠

Which returns us to Woolf.

Because we pursue writing alone, whether it is an address to the dead or to a living audience or to ourselves, because we pursue it alone, we address — as Woolf understood — an image. And it is in this sense that all writing requires imagination: not for the invention of fictions or colourful ways of saying things, but to focus the gesture of address, to allow it to complete itself. The image of the auditor calls the gesture from us, and with it, we call to the auditor.

This is how — and why — some words stay alive long after their original utterer is dead: they are infused with the movement of address. They remain in motion toward the image of their auditor, even if that auditor is — as long as it is genuinely — the writer her- or himself.

One way to understand the vision of philosophy that lives in the pages of *Phaidros* is this: thought that through imagination completes itself in a gesture of questioning address; questions focussed and enriched because of love; thinking sustained in its attempt to complete and clarify itself by love; thinking, then, that is alive, and that remains alive, because its questions mattered to the one who framed them; and he believed they would have mattered to the one to whom they were addressed.

♠

"But if it's an image, it's *not* a person!" True. The writing must go up to someone, and to 'make' it do that, the person writing focusses an image of the person addressed. The writer does not focus *on the actual person* or perforce would not be writing. Except in unusual circumstances, such as deafness or physical muteness, if the person were present, one would simply speak. (Or remain silent.)

❧

Tomas Tranströmer, in "Baltics," his long meditation on individual identity, politics, love, and history, writes:

> *The wind walks in the pine forest. It sighs heavily, lightly.*
> *In the middle of the forest the Baltic also sighs, deep in the*
> *   forest you're out on the open sea.*
> *The old woman hated the sighing in the trees, her face hard-*
> *   ened in melancholy when the wind rose:*
> *"You have to think of those out there in the boats."*
> *But she also heard something else in the sighing, as I do,*
> *   we're related.*
> *(We're walking together. She's been dead for thirty years.)*
> *It sighs yes and no, understanding and misunderstanding.*
> *It sighs three children healthy, one in the sanitarium and*
> *   two dead.*
> *The broad current that blows some flames into life and blows*
> *   others out. Conditions.*
> *It sighs: Save me, Lord, the waters are come unto my soul.*
> *You walk around listening for a long time, finally reaching the*
> *   point where the boundaries begin to open out*
> *or rather*
> *where everything becomes boundaries. An open square sunk*
> *   in darkness. People streaming out of the dimly lit buildings*
> *   around it. A murmuring.*

❧

The questions raised by *Phaidros* force us to reflect on the audience for our own writing, and what it is, philosophically, we hope to achieve by publishing. Do we wish merely to convince or persuade, without any real concern for truth? Can we proceed at all, then, unless we have some fairly clear notion of what truth is? Can written philosophy be adequate as philosophy? What might philosophy be, that this question should come up? If it *can* be adequate is this because written philosophy mimics something about philosophical conversation? Its 'aliveness'? What value can there be in an abstract investigation of moral concepts whose outcome has no consequences for how the investigator chooses to live? What is the difference between 'pure conceptual analysis' — about whose results people care in the way they care about winning a game — and sophistry? Even if we disagree with Plato's answers at every point, we must still experience the pressure of these questions; and the difficulty of formulating different answers that are not obviously shallow, uninteresting, or confused.

Indeed, the most powerful, because most consistent, alternatives to Plato's answers are forced to shocking extremes to maintain their consistency. We need not worry about writing because, in fact, there's nothing else — everything we do, if it has 'meaning' at all, is made 'meaningful' by being parsed as some form of text, text which is, in some profound sense, authorless — a mere 'occasion' through which the episteme, or L*A*N*G*U*A*G*E, or the culture of electronic media, manifests itself. At the heart, here, are dual, intertwined nihilisms: not only nihilism with respect to the possibility of ontologically robust acts of referring, but also about the possibility of taking individual responsibility for our own words. But this last is, I believe, the very wellspring of Plato's work: the view that political and moral decay is the product of just such an abandonment of responsibility; a refusal to take ourselves seriously as Woolfian individuals; as persons; as beings capable of experiencing the erotic pull of meaning in the world.

And it may be that if our standard for seriousness is set by what Plato characterizes as sophisticated rationalization — or what, since the seventeenth century we have learned to call rationality — the only fully self-consistent position is that of nihilism. But despite what Fredric Jameson has identified as the "euphoria" attendant on its current forms — both theoretical and cultural — the counsel of abandonment has about it an aura of despair. And despair is what our culture, like Plato's, prepares its members for. Despair is made the path of least resistance by allegiance to a host of measures of intelligibility and truth that, strictly followed out, must lead to skepticism. Plato, like Hume, saw that human beings could not live sanely in the conviction of skeptical emptiness. And he experienced the immense difficulty of proposing an alternative measure of intelligibility and truth. It is clear that, for us, old-style piety towards various imperialisms, academic and otherwise, will not do; and clear also that versions of Plato's views, entering the mainstream of Western European culture centuries after his death, played a part in generating and maintaining some of those very imperialisms. But from this it does not follow that Plato's *example* is not open to us. We may still draw inspiration from what we see across the range of his corpus — a refusal of the path of least resistance, a commitment to the possibility of intellectual integrity.

Phaidros argues that the test of the integrity of a philosophical encounter is its livingness: the degree to which it provokes, in us, *erōs* — a movement toward meaning. A philosophical being's livingness, Plato suggests, is reflected in its ability to respond to questions; and I have suggested that this may be understood as a written text's ability to make *us* respond, to provoke us to questions worth trying to answer. The degree to which we are provoked is the degree to which we find ourselves asking these questions over, and again, until their shape, which is the shape of our desire, begins to come clear — a shape that may be the closest we can get to an answer: thrown up, finally, not as a trick of the light, but as a boundary; the darkening edge around that which is transparent to light.

Dream Logic and
the Politics of Interpretation

I don't believe in any interpretation of dreams. I don't want to believe in dream interpretation. I will not touch this last freedom.
— ELIAS CANETTI, *The Secret Heart of the Clock*

We speak of the interpretation of dreams, and mean by this the process of rendering them intelligible. But this at once presents us with a puzzle. If we are indeed *interpreting* our dreams, then according to one common understanding of the word, we are expounding, explicating, or rendering clear a meaning that they already possess. But why, then, do we need the interpretation? Are we not the dreamers of the dreams? Are they not efflorescences or excrescences of *our* minds? If dreams are indeed intelligible, why do we require an interpretation to reveal this to us?

One answer: we are simply wrong in imagining that dreams are products of our minds. God, or some other agent, sends them to us and constructs them according to a pattern whose logic we must always struggle to comprehend. This is a model of the epistemology and metaphysics of dreams with a long and distinguished history; but as a denizen of Freud's century, I prefer another course. I will begin, then, with premises that echo fundamental tenets in Freud's own theory: that dreams do indeed have meaning, and that they are products of our own minds. I will sketch an answer to the question 'why, then, do they require interpretation?' based on Freud's metapsychology. But I will argue that compelling as Freud's account is, it still doesn't answer the question. My thesis will be that, understood as products of a system of mental organization that Freud called 'primary process,' dreams do not, in fact, *require* interpretation in a conceptual or epistemological sense of 'require.' But the requirement nonetheless remains. I will argue that its root is political. Students of

Civilization and Its Discontents may hear in this claim a further echo of Freud. But I will urge, against Freud, that the political requirement of an interpretation barrier between ourselves and the *logos* of primary process, while perhaps necessary for civilization as we know it, is not necessary for civilization; and that integrity, both in the wider sense, and the sense provided by Freud's metapsychological theory, requires that the wall to some extent come down. I will conclude with a sketch of one of the ways in which I take primary process — the logic of dreams — to be of interest to the pursuit of philosophy.

➤

Freud's thesis that dreams are a meaningful form of human mental activity created a stir in Vienna when it was first aired in 1905. But it was underwritten by a yet more radical conceptual innovation: for Freud, dreams were merely one expression of a basic *form* of mental activity characteristic of a psychical system he called 'the unconscious.'

"Our right to assume the existence of something mental that is unconscious and to employ that assumption for the purposes of scientific work is disputed in many quarters," Freud remarks mildly near the beginning of his 1915 paper, "The Unconscious." He then goes on to mount a muscular defence. The assumption of the existence of unconscious thought is justified, he says, because: (1) "the data of consciousness have a very large number of gaps in them; both in healthy and in sick people psychical acts often occur which can be explained only by presupposing other acts, of which, nevertheless, consciousness affords no evidence"; (2) "the assumption of there being an unconscious enables us to construct a successful procedure by which we can exert an effective influence upon the course of conscious processes"; (3) it is obvious that "at any given moment consciousness includes only a small content, so that the greater part of what we call conscious knowledge must in any case be for very considerable periods of time in a state of latency, that is to say, of being psychically unconscious"; (4) "all the categories which we employ to describe conscious mental acts, such as ideas, purposes, resolutions and so on, can be applied to them"; and finally, (5) the existence of the unconscious is "tangibly demonstrated" by *pre*-psychoanalytic experiments with hypnosis. Now, while these hardly constitute the "incontrovertible proof" Freud at one point claims they do, I think most people — especially in nations as heavily therapized as Canada and the United States — will grant that they constitute substantial *support* for the notion of unconscious thought. In the event we remain unconvinced, Freud has saved his boldest — but, I will argue, most problematic — argument for last: the assumption of unconscious thought is not merely justified, he claims, it is "legitimate" — by which he means that "in postulating it we are not departing a single step from our customary and generally accepted mode of thinking."

That mode, Freud claims, is manifest in our daily assumption that, on the basis of their outward behaviours, beings other than ourselves have minds. "Psychoanalysis demands nothing more," he says, "than that we should apply this process of inference to ourselves also … If we do this, we must say: all the acts and manifestations which I notice in myself and do not know how to link up with the rest of my mental life must be judged as if they belonged to someone else: they are to be explained by a mental life *ascribed to this other person.*" An astonishing claim, indeed; and Freud goes on to note what is obviously wrong with it: what the argument appears to lead to is not "the disclosure of an unconscious; it leads logically to the assumption of another, second *consciousness* which is united in one's self with the consciousness one knows." — And those who resist the notion of "an unconscious *psychical*" are not likely to buy the notion of an unconscious *consciousness* "of which its own possessor knows nothing." Additionally, the processes that appear to characterize unconscious thought "enjoy a high degree of mutual independence, as though they had no connection with one another, and knew nothing of one another" — hence, Freud thinks, we would be logically compelled to admit the possible existence of a third, fourth, indeed an unlimited number of, consciousnesses, all of which we know nothing about — and this is absurd. Most tellingly, he claims that these "latent processes" have characteristics "which seem alien to us, or even incredible, and which run directly counter to the attributes of consciousness with which we are familiar." From all of this he concludes that there cannot exist a second conscious*ness*; rather, we must "modify our inference about ourselves" and say that what is proved is "the existence of psychical acts which lack consciousness."

Here, I think it is appropriate to pause a moment in surprise: isn't the *point* of the exercise to demonstrate a whole realm of mental activity "of which its own possessor knows [almost] nothing"? And if the course of this mental activity — once, somehow, made known — strikes us as "alien," "incredible," and "run[ning] directly counter to the attributes of consciousness with which we are familiar," why *shouldn't* we conclude exactly what Freud tells us we cannot: namely, that it isn't ours? I take it that the arguments cited previously to justify the claim that unconscious mental activity exists still go through, bizarre though that activity may seem. But here another puzzle must strike us. *One* of those arguments rested on the observation that obviously not all conscious knowledge is, actually, at any given moment, conscious. Freud's rhetorical question — *Where, then, does it go?* — masks a genuine tension between this observation and what is asserted about the processes governing unconscious thought. For the force of the observation hinges on our admitting that we're *unaware* of what, at other times, is conscious knowledge — our teaching schedule, our Swiss bank account number — and which we are nonetheless willing to admit is *our* conscious knowledge — when it shows up — because it *seems* like our conscious knowledge: it has all the familiar characteristics. But it is precisely this claim — that unconscious thought has the familiar characteristics of our conscious thought — that Freud denies a few pages later. What is going on? Though our intuitions about the existence and to some extent the nature of unconscious thought may remain with Freud, the argument that would focus these intuitions seems to be disintegrating into chaos.

What these quandaries point to, in good latent fashion, is that in Freud's conception, the *fundamental* distinction between what he calls 'conscious' and 'unconscious' thought is a *structural* one.

There is not an on-off attention-switch involved in the transition from one to the other, but something more like a change of state. Indeed, where there *is* something like an on-off switch — our latent knowledge of our teaching schedule, or our Swiss bank account number — Freud will argue that the form, the pattern of the thought, must be the same as that of conscious thought. Such thought, he appears to have maintained, is nothing more than conscious thought without the gain on the amplifier turned up; *and for that reason* — because of its structural similarity to 'normal' waking thought, *in spite* of its overt affinity with dream-thought in being nonconscious — Freud distinguished it from genuinely unconscious thought by the rubric 'preconscious.' Jokes and parapraxes, on the other hand, are structured like dreams, he argued — *and for that reason,* and *in spite* of the fact that we are demonstrably conscious when they occur, they are to be classed as products of the unconscious. Though I do not wish to deny that we are frequently asleep when we dream, it seems to me the terminology is getting in the way of the insight. The insight is that there are two distinct *logoi* operating in human mental activity, of which we are, at different times and variously, conscious and unconscious. These two *logoi* — the one informing dreams, slips of the tongue, jokes, and neurotic symptoms, the other informing 'normal' waking thought — Freud called, respectively, primary and secondary process.

＊
＊

†

Freud opens Section v of "The Unconscious" with a brief outline of the characteristics of "the so-called *primary psychical process.*" This is essentially a condensed version of material treated in Section E of Chapter vii of *The Interpretation of Dreams.* A rather different, but equally synoptic, treatment of the two processes is provided in the 1911 paper, "Formulations on the Two Principles of Mental Functioning." Fully to understand some of this material, and more importantly to grasp its significance for the unity of Freud's later metapsychological reflections, we would have to return to the earliest and most startlingly original of Freud's psychological writings, the incomplete "Project for a Scientific Psychology."

Drafted and abandoned in 1895, the "Project" constituted Freud's attempt to provide a physically reductionist explanation of consciousness, based on his clinical observations of the clusterings of characteristics that distinguished dreams and hypnotic states from "normal mental life." A full exploration would take us too far afield. What is crucial for the present discussion is that the attempt at reductionism failed, while the clusterings continued to assert themselves. It is to Freud's characterizations of these *logoi* I now turn.

†

                                 ➤

In 1915, in "The Unconscious," Freud writes:

†

By the process of displacement [*in the system* Ucs.] *one idea may surrender to another its whole quota of cathexis; by the process of* condensation *it may appropriate the whole cathexis of several other ideas. I have proposed to regard these two processes as distinguishing marks of the so-called* primary psychical process.

Freud considered them defining, I believe, because of their importance for the "Project's" account of the ontogenetic relationship between primary and secondary process (from which relationship they in fact derive their names). There are, however, a number of other features, on the surface every bit as distinctive as condensation and displacement, that also characterize 'unconscious' thought. These include an emphasis on psychical, rather than external, reality; timelessness; a tolerance of paradox and contradiction; and the capacity to "[exert] on somatic processes an influence of intense plastic power which the conscious act can never do."

*

Secondary process, by contrast, appears to be all that primary process is not: its operation is predicated on a fundamental distinction between self and non-self, as well as consistently observed distinctions between psychic and external reality, and among individual images and perceptions as well. It recognizes, and operates according to, linear orders in space and time, and adheres to the standard inference patterns of basic logic — in par-

*

ticular, it respects the principle of non-contradiction. Judgement, which doesn't occur in primary process, is its central function. Grammatical and logical language-use is its hallmark.

What, then, for Freud constitutes an interpretation of a dream? The closest to a theoretical statement I have been able to find occurs at the beginning of Chapter 11 of *The Interpretation of Dreams*:

> ... 'interpreting' a dream implies assigning a 'meaning' to it — that is, replacing it by something which fits into the chain of our mental acts as a link having a validity and importance equal to the rest.

What is this 'something'? Freud's descriptions of his practice throughout make clear that it is an account, in words, that makes explicit the associations of the various elements of the dream with all other relevant thoughts and ideas, and which then arranges these verbally clothed renderings in a way that "makes sense" — that is, in a way that untangles the discontinuities, compressions, and contradictions produced by condensation, displacement, and the dream-work's tendency to disregard time. An interpretation, then, is a secondary process elaboration and restructuring of material initially presented in primary process: it is, to paraphrase Wittgenstein, the substitution of an expression   *
in one *logos* for an expression in another. The end result of this substitution or replacement is that we become able to understand material that was originally presented "in a manner which is in the highest degree bewildering and [apparently] irrational." This, in interesting and obvious ways, echoes our experience of utterances in languages with which we are entirely unfamiliar. An interpretation, in short, is a translation.

Indeed, the whole point of psychoanalysis in the treatment of neurotic symptoms is to provide a translation in this sense: "the talking cure," as one of Freud's and Breuer's earliest patients described it, aims to take the mute gestures of primary process and attach them to word-presentations in order that we may bring them to 'consciousness.' And because of the peculiarities we've noted in Freud's notion of the unconscious, it turns out that this 'bringing to consciousness' cannot amount to 'becoming *aware* of them'; it must, rather, amount to something more like coming to understand what the gestures (do, already) mean. To understand them through familiar word-presentations, accord- ing to the clinical theory, *just is* to lift repressions and to begin the process of healing. Thus Freud's remark in Section VI of "The Unconscious": "a complete divergence of their trends; a total severance of the two systems, is what above all characterizes a condition of illness." The 'translations' of psychoanalysis are viewed by Freud as one way of re-establishing the link.

There are many things that might strike us as interesting and problematic by turns about this conception of interpretation as translation; I shall focus briefly on two. The first concerns the identity of the 'content' as it passes from one system to the next: if, in order to understand it, we have to alter the *structure* of the thought — change its grammar, as it were — on what grounds can we be confident that, so altered, the thought as represented in the second system *really is* the thought as it came to us in the first? Isn't what-the-thought-is in some important measure a function of the way it is expressed? It is, I believe, no accident that this puzzle is precisely paralleled by a purely literary phenomenon: the alleged impossibility of translating poetry. A poem's mean- ing, it is often maintained by those who read or write poetry in more than one language, is inalienably tied to the language in which it is written. A good poem is dependent on every detail of its articulation — sound play within particular grammatical con- structions, relationships among rhyme, rhythm, and sense, tonal effects supervenient on culturally determined factors reflected in idiom and dialect, and so on. The meaning of a good poem is reflected in a complex lingua-chemical equilibrium; to translate it is to change its state. How could the translated product possibly possess the same meaning as the original?

Well: this is precisely wherein lies the art of the translator. For the fact is, good — even brilliant — translations of poems do exist. And so do good — even brilliant — interpretations of dreams. How this could be so deserves more careful reflection than the subject usually receives — more careful than space here allows. I raise the issue, and draw out the analogy between interpreting dreams and translating poems, to note only that the puzzle points not to the absolute impossibility of translation between primary and secondary process, nor to the need for a reversion to hard-core tone-and-form-insensitive theories of meaning; rather, because our comprehension of poetry shows that sense is, in some measure, a function of tone and characteristics like diction, rhythm, and rhyme, and because translation is still, in some measure, possible, the puzzle points to the need for further reflection on the *relation* between conceptions of meaning that are sensitive to these characteristics and conceptions of meaning that are not. — Or perhaps to the need for a conception of meaning that manages to sidestep the perennially vexed notions of 'form' and 'content' altogether.

The second puzzle on which I wish to focus grows directly out of the first: the one respect in which the interpretation of dreams on Freud's model *cannot* be said to resemble the translation of poetry is the absence of two *languages*. It is, we might argue, precisely the characteristic *absence* of language, primary process's refusal to adhere to basic grammatical rules, that makes translation into secondary process *necessary*. The obvious next question is: In what sense, then, is it *translation*? How can it be translation, except in a metaphorical sense, if language is involved on only one side?

The *Oxford English Dictionary* marks three main divisions in its definition of the verb 'translate.' The second of these is headed by the definition "to turn from one language into another." This, the editors note, is the chief current sense. (The first division concerns movement from one person, place, or condition to another, especially with religious emphasis or connotation; and the third reads, "to change in form, appearance, or substance; to transmute; to transform, alter.") The second definition included under the second main division is the one that interests me most: "to interpret, explain; to expound the significance of … to express [one thing] in terms of another." This definition is prefixed by the abbreviation for 'in figurative use,' and the

examples (unlike those for most of the other definitions given)
date from the early seventeenth century. The short answer to
the question 'how can dream interpretation be translation except
in a metaphorical sense?' is that it is indeed 'translation' *in this
metaphorical sense*. Is this to skirt the interesting philosophical
issue? On the contrary, I believe it points to its heart.

What the 'metaphorical' use of the word allows is precisely
the right set of emphases in the consideration of Freud's account:
it allows that dreams, that primary process thoughts in general,
can be non-linguistic in form, and nevertheless *possess meaning*.
I will return in a moment to the most provocative aspect of this
claim. Here, I wish to proceed directly to the central question
of my discussion: If dreams do indeed have meaning, and they
are our dreams, why do they need to be *interpreted* before we
can find this out? Why do our primary process thoughts *require*
translation into secondary process before we can acknowledge
that they are intelligible?

*   Freud's answer was that the *content* of dreams was dangerous
to civilization — that our dreams express instinctual aggressive
and sexual wishes that, were we to act on them, would destroy
the social fabric. These wishes must be repressed — kept from
our conscious awareness — but still allowed some form of expression, lest the endogenous instinctual energy invested in
them overwhelm the individual. Hence, they are consigned to
our dream life, forced to assume shapes that allow them to pass
before morality's censorious eye unrecognized.

While I think this account may indeed have had merit in the
ferociously bourgeois context of late nineteenth- and early twentieth-century Vienna for whose dreamers and neurotics it was
devised, as a *general* account — say, for our own rather more licen-
tious times — it seems a little thin. My own experience suggests
that some dreams are indeed about subjects that are preoccupying
me but that I'd rather not *admit* are preoccupying me; but a large
number of them are about — apparently — quite unthreatening
matters, most mundane, a few rather more interesting. Why,
then, does the mind cast them in primary process form? — for
indubitably in my own case, *that* part of Freud's account seems

to stand. If they don't *need* to be kept from secondary process awareness, why are they? Why do I need a secondary process translation to find out what I, myself, am thinking?

The straight answer to the question, I believe, is that I don't. Nor do any of us. At least not in the *conceptual* sense of 'need' that Freud's account was originally designed to underwrite. To put this another way: what Freud's account suggests — namely, that our thinking can proceed according to more than one pattern, and that the characteristics Freud grouped under the headings 'primary' and 'secondary process' pick out two such *logoi* — is basically correct. Where I diverge from Freud is precisely the point at which Freud's own account stumbles in its articulation of the notion of 'the unconscious': the connection — or lack thereof — of such *logoi* to awareness. There is, I believe, no coherent argument in Freud that establishes a logically or psychologically necessary connection between consciousness and secondary process thought; nor, then, a convincing argument against the possibility of awareness and unmediated understanding of thought structured according to the *logos* of primary process. There may be physiological considerations in the case of dreams — one relatively distinct subclass of primary process thought — which affect their role in our mental life, and our ability to remember them; but such a possibility, as I presently understand it, cannot weld those features of dreams to their *logic*.

That is: we, or at least many of us, *are* aware of primary-process-structured thought, at least from time to time. Its products marble our daily waking life in the form of slips of the tongue, and jokes — which, unlike dreams, do not tolerate much   †
in the way of secondary process translation. They also apparently visit us when we're tired, or moved, or, often, when we are confronted with certain kinds of spatial problems whose solutions may strike us as evident but difficult to reconstruct in words. And it must be noted that we do, often, remember dreams — not just those that Freud would agree are relatively transparent, but   *
dreams of striking imagistic power that, though difficult to relate, nevertheless haunt us for days. Psychoanalytically inclined scholars like Charles Rycroft have argued that primary process   * †

informs a good deal of the mental activity of conscious persons
making and appreciating what, in this culture, we regard as lyric
art — synchronous, allusive, densely imagistic compositions — in
a range of media. The processes of displacement and condensation are overt structural analogues of metaphor and metonymy,
as these function in both the literary and visual arts; and the
'mobility of cathexes' they are meant to embody echoes nothing
so much as Keats's notion of 'negative capability': "when man
is capable of being in uncertainties, Mysteries, doubts, without
any irritable reaching after fact and reason." There appear also
to be connections with the image- and rhythm-based thinking
of many students of Tao and Zen: not merely their tolerance of
paradox, but their embrace of it; the alleged resistance of their
insights to linguistic expression; their insistence on a mode of
awareness free from the domination of ego and its willing. And
timelessness: again, a feature of the alert awareness cultivated
in a range of meditative practices, and a characteristic of creative
thought attested to by many lyric artists, from Katherine Anne
Porter to Jorge Luis Borges. These observations underline, I believe, what Freud got essentially right: the existence of at least
two broad currents of experience, one dominated by what we
think of as logic, language, and the will, the other characterized
by the *absence* of both ego and language, by timelessness, and
by a profound sense of the extra-logical connectedness of things.

    And, to return for a moment specifically to dreams, we should
note that there are cultures other than our own in which dreams
are understood very much as ours understands poems — as har-
bingers of growing wisdom or as sound reasons to change one's
life — and in which they — dreams — don't stand in need of
the explications we require. "Ah," someone might object, "but
they still often need *interpretation*, don't they, by shamans or
elders, oracles or some sort? And," pressing the objection, "even
you, a good Freudian as far as the metapsychology is concerned,
predisposed to find your dreams intelligible, don't you, at least
sometimes, find them opaque or obscure? Doesn't this show that
interpretation *is* required?" Perhaps. But interpretation in what
sense? Even though we read and speak the language in which

a poem is written, we may have trouble understanding it: this doesn't mean, when we go to the literary critic, that what we're hoping for is a pedantic, heavy-footed prose allegorization. Often, what we need from the literary critic is simply suggestions like: "notice that the music in the line here is harsh and bunched with consonants, despite the apparent subject matter" or "see how the image of the crow is echoed here, and here, and here." Such 'interpretation' — namely, a highlighting of various resonances and juxtapositions, without a wholesale dismantling of the fundamental *logos* — is in many cases all that is required to help us grasp the meaning of a poem. Or a film, or a work of visual art. Certainly, it is about the only kind of 'interpretation' a joke can bear and still remain a joke. It is at least possible that it *may* be all that is required in the case of dreams.

Indeed, if a roughly Freudian model of dream interpretation is correct, then it seems we should at least entertain the possibility of the dream not merely as *interpretand* but as *interpretiens*. — The dream as, in some cases, a restructuring or translation of its own; as a raid on the articulate — language, logic, kidnapped by connectedness, a dense protean vision of the world. Proof that you've understood such expressions is not that you can translate them, or translate them back, into secondary process, but that you are left breathless with the shock of meaning — with the recognition that you've been addressed, or with the sense of "several things dovetailed in [the] mind," as Keats would say.

Still: we do speak of the interpretation of dreams and mean by this, roughly, the process of rendering them intelligible. Let me approach the paradox of their alleged unintelligibility again, and finally, by framing that paradox with direct reference to philosophy.

Metaphilosophically, the paradox looks like this: if, as I have just urged, Freud was right — dreams do have a *logos*, primary process does constitute a way of knowing — why has this not been of more interest to philosophers? Why does A.R. Manser, in his entry on dreams in the *Encyclopedia of Philosophy*, claim that

"Freud's doctrine of the unconscious is important for psychiatry; but he had little to say about the nature of dreams which is of interest to the philosopher"? Why, if I'm right that Freud's right, are this *logos* and its manifestations regarded as acceptable *objects* of (fringe) philosophical study — but the *logos* itself is nowhere regarded as a possible mode of philosophical reflection? If a broad range of our mental activities exhibits an identifiable logic of its own, why, as philosophers, do we not think it is a logic that can be used to find out about the world?

Because it isn't — logical?

What is a *logos*, anyway?

If we attend to Herakleitos' use, and not the letter of the word's etymology, a *logos* emerges in his work, as in the present discussion, as a coherent pattern, shaped by rules or resonances, whose integrity forms the basis of its ability to sustain meaning. However, as we noted above, primary process does not, in fact, constitute a *language*. At least, not a language like first- or second-order predicate calculus — its syntax is imagistic and freely associative, not linear and fundamentally algebraic. And it is this, I think, that is at the root of our failure to accept that dreams are meaningful in the absence of secondary process reconstruction: it is a version of the claim that all meaning worthy of the name is in a narrow sense linguistic, and that apparent non-linguistic instances of meaning — gestures, facial expressions, music, pictures — are *parasitic* on linguistic meaning so understood. Freud was right, I believe, to see grammatically unexceptional language-use as secondary process's hallmark; he was wrong, however, to ignore the evidence he himself uncovered, and to insist that only secondary process could be conscious. Because he did ignore the evidence, *grammatically unexceptional* language-use became, for him, the necessary condition of our *acknowledgement* of meaning, too. Thus, like many other theoreticians over the last four hundred years, Freud rolled meaning, understanding, awareness, and language together into one intra-synonymous ball. Even if we were willing to disentangle some of the threads, though — to entertain the existence of a *logos* that is not a language — could we make sense of the image of philosophy pursued according to its lights?

What is philosophy, anyway?

❧

One way philosophy may be defined, I believe, is as thinking in love with clarity. But note that this is not yet to say what clarity *is*.

Philosophy is also, or in many quarters has also become, a job: an institutionalized practice, a way of participating in a globalized capitalist economy, something to do in one's waking hours to put food on the table, *technique* in a Heideggerean sense — constrained by bureaucracies, by pressures of numbers, by notions of professionalism and, for these very reasons, less immune to fashion, insecurity, and greed than we might wish. And the thing is: however much we may deplore some of these aspects of philosophy's late twentieth- and early twenty-first century academic instantiation, many of us feel compelled to at least partial compliance in order to have any contact with the disciplined clarities of thought with which we first fell in love. But the result, I believe, is that what was once, at the beginning of the seventeenth century, a *proposal* about the nature of philosophical clarity — that it consists in the shackling of imagination (Bacon), and the pursuit of rigorously mechanical analysis (Descartes) — has become enshrined as an obvious truth, one that we have lost the metaphilosophical appetite to question. It is a conception of clarity closely tied to other aspects of the Enlightenment. It permits an assembly-line approach to problems, and it allows the identification of *criteria* of philosophical production — thus engendering what would have struck Sokrates, though not the sophists, as a virtual oxymoron: philosophical career advancement. It is a conception of clarity that is hospitable to technologification — easily seduced by the prospect of digitalization, and by the idea that doing it by machine is doing it better. It is a concept of clarity that allows us to take seriously the idea that the good is utility, and that compassion and love are irrelevant to our ability to perceive what exists and to understand it. I do not wish to suggest that a notion of clarity that stood these various emphases and attractions on their head would be preferable; what I want to draw to our attention is that the question of what constitutes philosophical clarity *is* a *question*. Nor do I wish to hold up the shaggy, galumphing tossed-offedness of many dreams as the quintessence of philosophical enlightenment. I assume that were we to take seriously the idea of a primary-process-structured philosophical reflection, it would have to be primary process burnished and disciplined — in much the way secondary process is burnished and disciplined to produce what we recognize as sound argument. What I do wish to suggest, what I think the facts suggest, is that the reason we don't think dream-logic can constitute a genuine *logos* is political.

It is because we *do* have the capacity to understand dreams that we must *legislate* that we do not — that we require them to speak the lingo of secondary process. In an interpretation, dreams are dragged into the culture of a narrow definition of the intelligible: secondary process syntax. The isolated gypsy in the Tokyo Stock Exchange being asked to explain herself is not a threat but a curiosity.

Civilization's discontent, in other words, is interpretation's self-doubt: the repressed knowledge that it *is* able to understand primary process without translation. The demand for interpretation is thus a gesture of delegitimization; and the eros of interpretation is not simply the exercise of power, but the location of meaning in a structure that creates the idea of power as 'rank in a hierarchy.' The academic apotheosis of this trend is not, as might be imagined, so-called analytic philosophy — which at least suspects the existence of renegade mental activity against which it must be vigilant. It is, rather, poststructuralism — the blithe nihilism of "il n'y a pas de hors-texte" — that most profoundly exemplifies the exclusion of non-linguistic thought from consideration, and is thus most clearly symptomatic of contemporary intellectual malaise. Lyric poetry, on the other hand, emerges as profoundly subversive: it takes the coin of the realm and turns it into jewellery — braids it in its hair, sews it on its dress, shapes it into teeth.

And this, it seems to me, should interest us vastly. We're the anthropologists hereabouts. To take ourselves seriously as philosophers is to be curious about other cultures of thought — not for what we can appropriate from them for the purposes of the culture in which we were raised, but in their own right. We must *ask* if analytic rigour, for example, or the history of the gradual identification of mind with text for another, is indeed synonymous with clear thought.

Why does primary process have the characteristics it does? One reason, which I have been attempting to undermine, was Freud's perceived need for a mode in which instinctually flavoured thoughts could escape detection *as thoughts*. Another, allied in Freud's presentation with the first, was the *proximity* of primary process to somatic sources of psychic energy. Primary process features an associative mobility of cathexes and a tolerance of paradox because the instinctual energies to which it gives expression are themselves highly plastic, and often contradictory. Those energies — instincts, drives — are organic or physical in origin: they swirl and pour ceaselessly out of the cells of our bodies, an expression, simply, of the fact that we are alive. Primary process thought is the point at which the mind emerges from the body, "like a mushroom out of its mycelium" as Freud puts it; and the point at which the body coalesces out of the mind. Emotions in particular — especially physically profound ones associated with instincts or instinctual reactions — are creatures of this frontier.

As I noted earlier, Freud maintained that a complete divergence, a total severance of the two systems is what above all characterizes psychic illness. I believe such a divergence, such a severance, is the condition that the institutionalization of philosophy pushes us toward. If Freud is even partly right about primary process's role as mediator of the psycho-somatic interface, and its phylogenetic openness to emotion, then what philosophy loses if it refuses the *logos* of primary process is the ability to speak to us as integrated entities, beings for whom questions about the good life must, in some measure, have to do with physical and emotional synthesis, as well as acute logical dissection. What philosophy loses if it refuses the *logos* of dreams is, above all, the intelligibility of itself as an *erotic stance* toward wisdom.

What is wisdom? Not, I think, the same thing as clarity. In my informal surveys of students, friends, and colleagues, negative definitions proliferate: "Well, it isn't cleverness. It isn't the same thing as being smart. It's sort of smarts with *depth*." What's depth? — A shrug. The dictionary lists the following as synonyms for wisdom: knowledge, enlightenment, learning, erudition — but we all know Mr Casaubon was not wise. Prudent? Perhaps. But whatever *phronesis* meant to Aristotle, for us it conjures too much the image of the successful banker. The etymology of the word "wise" tells us that it is very old and comes from a generalized Indo-European root meaning to see or to know. Again, not much help. Well, then: how, or of whom, do we use the word? Herakleitos, albeit in translation, says: "The one, the only truly wise, does — and does not — consent to be called by the name of Zeus." The character of Sokrates in Plato's *Phaidros* caps the argument of the dialogue's second half by saying: "[To call a man who writes with a knowledge of the truth, who can defend what he writes when challenged, and who can *make the argument that his writing is of little worth*] — to call such a man wise ... seems to me too much, and proper only for a god. To call him wisdom's lover ... would fit him better." And, of course, there is the famous example from *Apology* where Sokrates characterizes his own wisdom as the knowledge that he did not know. These observations, it seems to me, actually dovetail in an interesting way with the negative definitions ("wisdom isn't just smarts or cleverness"); and they are pointing, I think, to something like the following: wisdom is thought conditioned by an awareness of *limits* to the systematically provable, articulable, or demonstrable. Whence this awareness? Plato, I think, correctly identified one source: ongoing, long-term ravishment by beauty. The Tao hints at another: loss. And the folk tradition to a third: working with one's hands, in silence; attending, through the body, to the rhythms of the earth and one's own mortality. There are other routes.

But for some time now, North American culture has worked to insulate itself against those I've mentioned: the noise, clutter, wealth, speed, and artificiality of late capitalism are as legion as the malls and monitors that are its embodiment. Little beauty in their precincts or among the clearcuts. We find ourselves in this situation because for several centuries we have refused to acknowledge limits. The institution of philosophy, along with everything else, is paying the price.

What has all this to do with dreams? I have been arguing that dream-logic, as Freud characterizes it, is also the *logos* of lyric art, of some forms of religious understanding, of pain and instincts denied cultural acknowledgement, of slips of the tongue, of jokes. And why did Wittgenstein claim to Malcolm that a serious and good philosophical work could be written that would consist entirely of the latter? Because a joke of the sort he had in mind, a 'grammatical' joke, is the irrepressible reflex response of primary process to the pretensions of secondary process to know it all. In *Philosophical Investigations* 111, Wittgenstein says: "why do we feel a grammatical joke to be *deep*? (And that is what the depth of philosophy is.)" Combining Freud and Wittgenstein then, we arrive at the suggestion that the *depth* of philosophy is revealed to us through our capacity for *primary process* reflection on what Wittgenstein called forms of life.

An example:

So, there were these two horses — thoroughbreds, y'know, Kentucky, white-washed stables, the smell of bluegrass hay. Anyway, this one horse is just coming back from a race, all lathered up and sweaty, and he says to the other one, "You'll never believe what happened to me today! It was just amazing! I was set for a terrible race — I dunno, I haven't placed in the last nineteen, I heard 'em talking about the glue factory in the exercise yard the other day — and on top of it all, I broke late from the gate. So there I am, way back in the pack coming around into the final stretch, when suddenly I hear these voices singing. There was a sort of rainbow light in the sky, and then I felt this sizzle at the tip of my tail that zinged up along my backbone — and I just shot ahead, passed everything on the outside and won by a length! Just incredible — haven't had a race like that in years."

"Well, now," says the other horse, "it's funny you should mention that, because just last week a very similar thing happened to me. You know I've been coming off this injury, it's been pretty up and down, mostly down lately, and I know they've been thinking of pulling me for the season. Like you, I broke late, and I could feel that twinge in my right fore, so I wasn't planning on making up for lost time — oh, I must've been sitting eleventh or twelfth going into the last turn — and then — it's just like you said — I heard voices singing and saw this rainbow of light and I felt a huge surge of energy right up my spine — and I shot ahead, flew past the lot, and won going away!"

And this greyhound who's been wandering up the alley between the stalls looks over and says, "You know, I couldn't help overhearing, and you're never gonna believe this, but practically the same thing happened to me. It was nearly three weeks ago. I was figurin' I was done for before they even fired the pistol — I got the burn-out, y'know — about as much interest in that f*****g rabbit as a trip to the vet. Well, anyway, I got myself in a tangle right at the start and was dead last coming into the home stretch. And then — just like you said — this rainbow o' light opened up above me. I could hear these voices singing, and I felt this tingle of electricity startin' at the tip of my tail and zippin' right up along my backbone. Whoo-ee. I tell you, I got my butt in gear then — practically jumped right over a coupla the other fellas I was in such a hurry — didn't just win, either, set a track record into the bargain. They couldn't believe it back in the chow line."

And the first horse turns to the other horse and says, "Would you get a load of that. — A talking dog!"

The joke works (if it does!) because it subverts our understanding of the grammar of narrative relevance. But what does the subversion show? Not that the rhythm of expectations the story sets up is arbitrary: indeed, the joke affirms those rhythms. But it says they are *rhythms,* not theorems, of conversational etiquette;

they carry the meaning of the story, but not as a fully elaborated semantic model does. The joke, if we get it, dissolves, while embracing, the distinction between form and content. It *shows* us that we often grasp semantic relevance as primary process does — as an indisseverable aspect of what we call 'form'; and *at the same time*, it shows us that this is something that no fully linguified notion of coherence as logical consistency can do. To put this another way: 'how to tell a story' is a form of life, and as such, basic to our experience of meaning. From the point of view of secondary process, such forms must remain arbitrary: why *can't* you change the subject here? — There's no convincing answer that points to anything like conceptual necessity. But the joke would not be *funny* if the form of narrative relevance *really were* arbitrary. The joke shows us we know it isn't arbitrary, but that we also know there is no secondary-process-acceptable line of argument that would establish this. To the extent this joke reveals 'the depth of philosophy,' what it reveals are the *limits* of articulable, secondary process thought. The awareness of such limits, I have suggested, is the foundation of wisdom.

And to love wisdom in this case would not be simply to love knowledge, but to cherish the judicious discernment of the limitations of *styles* of knowing: for example, to know (in the sense of acknowledge) that we do not know (in the sense of have an articulate account).

                              ✦

We speak of the interpretation of dreams. I have argued that in practice, this amounts to more than the naming of an epistemological procedure; it also describes a culturally specific act of marginalization. To acknowledge and cultivate the *logos* of primary process in philosophy would, I believe, lead not only to a fuller appreciation of a number of existing works of philosophy and an expansion of our conception of the discipline: it would enable, I hope, a reconnection with the roots of our discipline, and a greater integrity of thought. In the final chapter of *The Interpretation of Dreams*, Freud remarks:

There is often a passage in even the most thoroughly interpreted dream which has to be left obscure; this is because we become aware during the work of interpretation that at that point there is a tangle of dream-thoughts which cannot be unravelled and which moreover adds nothing to our knowledge of the content of the dream. This is the dream's navel, the spot where it reaches down into the unknown. The dream-thoughts to which we are led by interpretation cannot, from the nature of things, have any definite endings; they are bound to branch out in every direction into the intricate network of our world of thought.

So, too, philosophy. So, too, the gestures through which we bind, and let go of, our lives.

Oracularity

Oracularity is a charge frequently levelled at thought couched in aphorisms. — Not, it's true, in literary contexts, where the term often can occur simply as a descriptive adjective, without pejorative connotations. But in philosophical contexts, to pronounce something 'oracular' is, almost without exception, to condemn it to the slag heap of intellectual irrelevance. Why might this be so? Are philosophers justified in their disregard for oracular utterance? What is it about oracularity that makes it so suspect?

The word itself is a straightforward construction from 'oracle,' whose roots extend through the Latin *oratio* into ancient notions of speaking, beseeching, prayer, and praise. It frequently connotes expressive intensity or pithiness, and can indicate, variously, (divinely) inspired, veiled, ambiguous, enigmatic, mysterious, or obscure utterance. In North America, it has also come to suggest speciousness:

… *2. Assuming to deliver opinions or statements as indisputable or authoritative* without proof *and* with an air *of superior wisdom and knowledge.* [Funk & Wagnalls New Standard Dictionary, *1944, my emphasis*]

… *2. giving forth utterances or decisions* as if *by special inspiration or authority.* [Random House Dictionary, *1973, my emphasis*]

Philosophy, since its self-designated inception, has understood its love of wisdom to be intimately bound up with clarity of thought. Given this, it is evident why 'oracularity,' understood as ambiguity or obscurity, might be a problem. But this does not yet explain why oracular writers should come in for special censure while Hegel in the Preface to the *Phenomenology* or Kant in the Third Critique continue to be upheld as paragons of philosophical penetration. Thus, it would seem, it is the allegation of *speciousness* that is at the root of the problem. Readers take it that oracular philosophical writing — that of Herakleitos, for example, or of Wittgenstein — assumes a rhetorical posture designed to create the *impression* of special access to truth, meaning, or understanding where no such access is, or could possibly be, available.

So, I believe, the question of oracularity in philosophical writing is actually two:

1. Are 'oracular' philosophical writers always trying to put one over on us? — passing off portentous phrasing as insight, in lieu of the hard work needed to make a genuine philosophical point?

2. *In precisely what sense* are oracular pronouncements obscure?

I will urge that there are good reasons to think that the answer to the first question is *no*: there is a way of understanding oracularity that reveals its appropriateness for the expression of certain kinds of philosophically interesting insight. And while this, if true, would not obviate the possibility of abuse — there are in philosophy, as in every profession, con artists — it *would* mean that we must learn to distinguish cases in which the 'oracular tone' is allied with philosophical understanding from cases in which it isn't. But the possibility of 'justified' oracularity in turn suggests that the notion of obscurity with which oracularity is associated is the negative image of a conception of philosophy that countenances, without sufficient reflection, an excessively narrow understanding of itself.

LYRIC AND ORACULARITY

In *Anatomy of Criticism*, Northrop Frye, listening to the beginning of Claudio's speech in Act III, Scene i of *Measure for Measure* notes:

But we can also, if we listen to the line very attentively, make out still another rhythm in it, an oracular, meditative, irregular, unpredictable, and essentially discontinuous rhythm, emerging from the coincidences of the sound-pattern:

> Ay:
> But to die …
> > > and go
> > > we know
> > > > not where …

Just as … semantic rhythm is the initiative of prose, … so this oracular rhythm seems to be the predominating initiative of lyric.

Frye, of course, is concerned with lyric as it figures in our grasp of literary, rather than philosophical, genres; but his observations are pertinent here, as the language of lyric philosophy is governed by the same eros that informs lyric literature. Frye calls the eros an "initiative" and describes it as an impulse to tonal and rhythmic association among words. I think we can, and ought, to go further. Construed broadly, lyric's eros may be understood as a drive to coherence in multiple dimensions — the interfolded responsiveness of all aspects of a composition, the mutual reflexivity and interdependence of 'form' and 'content,' of 'material' and 'thought,' resulting in a whole that consists of an integration that is neither additive nor systematic. But even this is misleading since the identity of those parts is in fact derived from their dependence on the whole. The densely associative sound patterns of lyric utterance are thus an aspect, and also an embodiment and enactment, of this drive to coherence.

But that's lyric. What has this to do with the oracular? Frye wants to contend that in getting at the sonority characteristic of lyric expression, we are in fact investigating the oracular. While this strikes me as insightful, I also think the situation is more complex than it suggests. In particular, I do not think the oracular is the 'ground' of lyric: the two are, I will urge, different species

of the same genus. Nor is that genus 'sonority,' though sonority
is crucial to how each achieves what it does. The fundamental
point of connection between lyric and oracular utterance is, rather,
to be found in their relation to a certain type of insight — one
that perceives a radical but non-systematic integrity in some
phenomenon. It is this, I will argue — their *mode* of understanding — that is the source of the importance of sonority for each.
— And also, ultimately the source of their rejection as genuine
forms of philosophical expression.

THE EPISTEMOLOGY OF ORACULAR INSIGHT

The Gestalt school of psychology early in the twentieth century argued that *insight* is "the name given to the perceptual
reorganization of the visual field confronting the learner." Two
things are crucial to this definition: the idea that the focus of
understanding is the 'field-as-a-whole,' rather than its component parts; and the claim that insight — a form of knowing — is
a kind of perceiving. The epistemology that I wish to propose is
not an epistemology of sense perception; but, with the Gestalt
school, I think that there is a phenomenon analogous to the
grasping of a perceptual gestalt that operates on concepts, and
on concepts-in-conjunction-with-percepts. This kind of understanding is phenomenologically akin to seeing, hence the appropriateness of the term 'insight' for these (re)organizations
of what we might call the conceptual or conceptual-perceptual
'field.' *What* we understand when we understand in this way is
a complex whole of some kind, a whole that is not merely the
simple additive sum of its parts, but is rather an integrated and
integrating product of their interactions.

The crucial point here for the epistemology of oracular utterance is that sometimes, just as with lyric utterance, we do not
elaborate *as such* (even sketchily) the whole that is grasped in
understanding. Instead, we gesture to it. As Herakleitos puts it,
"The lord whose oracle is in Delphi neither declares nor conceals,
but gives a sign." Oracular utterance, I wish to claim, is a kind
of figurative pointing, a form of expression that aims to get us

to see a conceptual gestalt — but which proceeds, we might say, by fingering a contour rather than by providing a full frontal photograph. (Why this is so is an important question to which I shall return later.) The comprehension of such utterance involves grasping — even if only dimly and inarticulately — what is being pointed at and *that* it is being pointed at. But how?

An analogy: Imagine that you have before you what appears to be a partially filled-out crossword puzzle. You are cudgelling your brains over 24 Across when the gnomic librarian passes behind you and, glancing over your shoulder, mutters, "Contiguous." But 24 Across is already intersected at several points by solutions to several Down clues that make this an impossible response. Ah: but then you notice that there are, in fact, solutions to those Down clues that are quite other than you had thought, and that do indeed fit with 'contiguous.' Of course, if you redo those Down clues, you'll have to redo many of the other Across bits you thought you'd worked out — but, well, yes, it looks as though it *is* possible to proceed that way ... And then, in a flash, several of the other clues that had been intractable suddenly become clear; and finally — or, rather, simultaneously with this last recognition — you realize that all the words in the solved puzzle are linked not just physically, but that they all belong to a famous passage in literature. — Except some words are missing: if you read first all the Across answers and then all the Down answers, for every horizontal or vertical space separating those answers in the configuration of the puzzle, a word has been left out. That is, the puzzle does not contain the contiguous words.

Imagine, now, not a crossword puzzle but the world, and ramifying lists of questions — ethical, psychological, political, scientific — whose patterns of codependent answers (to the extent we have any) constitute our best effort at making sense of the whole. In this world-puzzle, oracular utterance works like the keyword dropped by the librarian: it realigns vision by forcing consideration of alternative linked responses, which in turn substantiate, deepen, and elaborate the realignment itself.

The test of an oracular claim's truth, then, will simply be its adequacy to experience, its ability to save the phenomena. The difficulty is that it often manages to save them, at least in part, by a reconceptualization of what the phenomena *are*. Thus the oracular utterance tests us, too: we must be willing to hear, to do the critical, dismantling, imaginative, and synthetic work that it demands. We must measure the claim against our own experience and what we know of the experience of others; think how the world would appear if it were true; ask whether there is a way of looking at the phenomena that would reveal them to be as the utterance says they are — as though the world were a complex crystal and a claim had been made that in spite of its present dull brown irregular (or scintillating blue hexagonal) appearance, there *is* an orientation in which a very different colour, geometry, or reflective character will become apparent.

Of course, there may be no such orientation. The oracular utterance may be false. And because of the complexity of the task, we may never be sure whether the problem does indeed lie with the utterance or with us. Oracular utterances have the *form* of empirical generalizations; but because they are concerned with the stance toward phenomena *from which we judge* the truth or falsity of various empirical claims, pointing to an apparent counter-instance will not always serve to show them false. Not only must there be a bad fit between the apparent counter-instance and the orientation of vision on which the oracular utterance insists, that bad fit must *disturb* us — it has to strike us as so significant that we are willing to give up on or reject our original orientation of vision. In this, oracular utterances resemble the articulation of fundamental scientific paradigms more than they resemble empirical generalizations. An oracular utterance is more like the claim "The earth goes around the sun," spoken in 1542, than it is like the claim "All swans are white," spoken either then or now. Then, as now, it's obvious to anyone with eyes that the sun goes around the earth; but this, we have since learned, does not entail that the contrary world view fails to save the phenomena.

Further, the rejection of existing scientific paradigms and the acceptance of new ones appears to be the result of the interaction of many factors, such as comprehensiveness, elegance, and cultural or social context, as well as the sheer accumulated weight of

confirming or disconfirming evidence. Indeed, many have argued
that because our understanding of what constitutes confirming
or disconfirming evidence in individual cases is itself bound up
with the acceptance of a given paradigm, we cannot intelligibly
talk about the 'truth' or 'falsity' of such paradigms if we intend
anything more by those terms than 'accepted' or 'rejected.' I do
not wish to engage that debate here. Suffice it to say that the
occurrence of similar perplexities in the evaluation of oracular
utterance is a function of the similar role of such utterances in
determining contexts of understanding. To reiterate: it is indeed possible for an oracular utterance to be false — but in just
the sense, and to just the extent that, one believes it is possible
for a scientific (or philosophical) paradigm to be false. As with
scientific paradigms, the falsifiability of the oracular utterance
may be *undecidable* with respect to the available evidence. And,
just as with scientific paradigms, its acceptance or rejection will
depend — wholly or in part, depending on one's view — on tem-
perament and sensibility. These are the individual analogues of
cultural and social context, and determine not only degree of
effort and fineness of observation, but also willingness to change
in the face of what one observes.

Just as we may distinguish oracular utterances from con-
textualized empirical generalizations, we may distinguish them
from old saws and epigrams, which in many respects they also
resemble. Old saws — for example, *Mackerel sky, not twenty-four
hours dry* or *A happy woman has no history* — are what I will call
'straightforwardly' falsifiable, for they purport to be contextual-
ized empirical generalizations. Like oracular utterances, they are
confirmed or disconfirmed by our experience, but, importantly,
old saws are typically conservative of cultural expectations. They
do not require — and usually militate against — a reorientation of
a 'standard' perspective on experience. They have (or are meant
to have) a single transparent reading, and do not invite us to
work in order to comprehend them. Epigrams — for example,
Wilde's "The egotist is a person of no taste: he likes himself better
than he likes me" — may appear less culturally conservative than
old saws; but unlike oracular utterances, they tend to play with

standard social conceits by reversing their objects or satirizing them, rather than undoing their foundations. Epigrams, in other words, are jokes whereas oracular utterances are metaphors. (The attempt to falsify an epigram is not so much to undertake a life's labour as it is to miss the point.)

This sketch of a taxonomy is not meant to be complete or exhaustive; nor am I suggesting that its categories do not overlap. There are a number of 'oracular' fragments attributed to Herakleitos, for example, that look suspiciously like old saws, and many that have an epigrammatic twist. 'Aphorism' is a term that seems to embrace them all, while perhaps including other utterances that do not have the hallmarks of any. The pressing question, and the one that will eventually lead us back to Frye, concerns the distinction between oracular utterance and lyric.

Like oracular utterance, lyric utterance is concerned with the communication of a gestalt — both aim to comprehend a whole in a single gesture. Unlike oracular utterance, however, lyric utterance is often not *literally* singular; its unity springs from the dense interconnectedness of its frequently multiple sentences. Lyric utterance touches the world in several places, typically by focussing on particulars; oracular utterance grips it in one, and is usually configured as a general or an abstract claim. Lyric utterance holds the world up to the light *in* a particular config-uration by saying, "This; and this; and this." (Woolf's novels; the poems of Tomas Tranströmer; the casidas and garcelas of Lorca.) Oracular utterance by contrast identifies an armature of insight in relation to which other observations fall into place. In understanding lyric utterance, the work is seeing the face in the leaves: grasping the whole that the selection and attunement of particulars suggests. In comprehending oracular utterance, the work is seeing both the whole the claim necessitates and, simul-taneously, that particulars, reconfigured, do indeed confirm that whole as a way the world is.

This suggests a reason for the apparent dissimilarity between oracular and lyric utterance with respect to tone. Lyric utter-ance enacts the conviction that the relevant particulars (and, in some cases, patterns or structures) are, so to speak, right there in front of us — we need only recognize them as such. Its aim, then, is to get us to 'see' a whole that is not, in fact, hidden — to overcome blindness or inattention, to make sense of what may appear chaotic or random. Oracular utterance, on the other hand, is concerned with a *reorientation* of vision. It construes itself as a challenge to an existing epistemic alignment. Lyric's rhetoric, as a consequence, is basically assertoric; though its emotional colour — for reasons to do with its relations to language — is predominantly elegiac, sometimes ecstatic, and often both. Oracular utterance, by contrast, often has a provocative edge; we have the sense, even if only distantly, of a gauntlet being thrown down. Although it *can* take on an elegiac colour, characteristically, we have the sense of its having been purged of sentiment, of insight having been shocked, blown through the other side of emotion, by the force of its recognition. There is something primitive, almost 'pre'-emotional, in the energy of oracular insight; and where this does not come to us, however faintly, as a whiff of terror, we sense it as laughter.

But although the differences are important and even, to a degree, striking, they are by no means sharp or mutually exclusive. The identifying characteristics of oracularity and lyric constitute interpenetrating centres of gravity. Oracular utterances can, frequently do, occur within lyric compositions — Woolf's novels, again; many poems. There are even some lyric compositions — what we have of Herakleitos' book for example, Wittgenstein's *Tractatus,* for another — that are composed predominantly of oracular utterances. These are unusual cases precisely because their constituent sentences make abstract or general claims, rather than focussing on particulars; but they are, in the cumulative disposition of those claims, essentially lyric.

SONORITY

The common genus to which lyric and oracular utterance belong, I've been urging, is that of expressions whose aim is to help us discern some radically integrated pattern, structure, or whole. In the case of lyric, this expression itself takes the form of a radically

integrated — more particularly, a *resonant* — structure. One feature of the linguistic expression of such structures is their overt
sonority, their characterization by some or all of the following:
aural repetitions, echoes, inversions, and homonyms, patterned
sequencings of vowels and consonants, alliteration, rhyme, part-
rhyme, slant rhyme, and a pattern or patterns of rhythmic stress.
With this observation, we return to issues raised at the outset
by Frye's remarks: To what extent does sonority play a role in
the constitution of oracular utterance?

The rise of English as a language of philosophy closely parallels the development of systematic analytic-argumentative
thought. It should come as no surprise, then, that examples of
oracular utterance in the canon of English-speaking philosophy
are rare. But I shall begin, perversely enough, with an English
translation of a text that survives only in Theophrastos' prose
† paraphrase. Herakleitos, he tells us, says, σάρμα εἰκῆ κεχυμένον ὁ
κάλλιστος [ὁ] κόσμος: "Refuse [or: a sweeping] at random massed
together [or: dissipated] [is] the most beautiful [in] [the] cosmos."
One fully 'Englished' version of this thought might be: "The most
beautiful arrangement of [things-in-]the[-]universe is constituted
by a pile of refuse" — a grammatical sentence, yes, but no more
than that. A more compelling translation, Charles Kahn's, runs:
"The fairest order in the world is a heap of random sweepings."

And this sentence *is* more interesting. It breaks into two essentially iambic lines — the break occurs after 'world' — in which
key concepts occur as parallel trochees: fairest order/random
sweepings. (This trochaic voicing gives the images force: the
flow of iambs reassures the ear; trochees make a point.) In the
first line, 'order' and 'world' constitute a part rhyme and 'fairest'
contains an echo of the rhyming syllable. (Compare, for effect,
the weak sonority of 'most beautiful arrangement.') In the second
line, 'heap' and 'sweepings' also rhyme with one another. But the
adjective 'random' consists of syllables that rhyme with nothing
else in the sentence — it belongs to no pattern.

A different but equally brilliant translation might have found
a trochee meaning 'random' that rhymed with 'heap' and 'sweep,'

but I haven't been able to uncover one. (That place in the line has to be held by a trochee — quite apart from the integrity of the line as a whole — so that the phrase '[stressed syllable] [unstressed syllable] sweepings' will parallel 'fairest order.') Note that 'world' (unlike 'cosmos' or 'universe') and 'heap' (unlike 'collection') are monosyllables. It is important, I would argue, to the strategy of this particular oracular utterance that its two lines share the same rhythmic impetus, but that the intra-linear rhyme is *not inter*linear. There must be a contrast — some opposition — between the two characterizations so that they remain in tension, while also being unified. The connection is deep, but it is also back-stretched. In short, the utterance is indeed sonorous, and its sonority is not unconnected to its meaning.

Here are some other examples in other languages:

道可道非常道
Dào kě dào fēi cháng dào.
Tao called tao is not tao.

συλλάψιες. ὅλα καὶ οὐχ ὅλα, συμφερόμενον διαφερόμενον,
συνᾷδον διᾷδον, ἐκ πάντων ἓν καὶ ἐξ ἑνὸς πάντα.
[*Sullápsies: hóla kai oukh hóla, sumpherómenon diapherómenon, sunáidon diáidon, ek pántōn hen kai ex henos pánta.*]
Conceivings: wholes and what isn't whole — gathered together, drawn apart, in tune, out of tune: out of all things one; and out of one, all things.

Die Welt ist alles, was der Fall ist.
The world is all that is the case.

Wovon man nicht sprechen kann, darüber muß man schweigen.
Whereof one cannot speak, one must be silent.

The last two examples, the opening and closing sentences of Wittgenstein's *Tractatus Logico-Philosophicus*, constitute variations on a single ontological theme. The interplay between sonority and meaning in each is remarkable. The first of these, Proposition 1 in Wittgenstein's numbering, articulates a claim of sweeping generality, one that many philosophers will find problematic; but it simultaneously insists that, at root, its truth is simple, uncontentious, and familiar. It has the short two-foot line and sing-song quality of a nursery rhyme. Thus, at the outset of the *Tractatus*, we are invited to register a certain skepticism about the efficacy of complex metaphysical speculation. The second, Proposition 7, the only one that stands entirely on its own in Wittgenstein's numbering system, also contains two major periodic movements — though both are more complex than those that comprise Proposition 1. The first of these periods itself consists of two parts, so that we have:

> *Wovon man | nicht sprechen kann, ||*
> *darüber muß man schweigen.*

Within this periodic structure, there exists a dense weave of interlinear parallelisms and recurrences: in the first (double) period, the rhythmic stress occurs on the rhymed 'man' and 'kann,' which are picked up by the *un*stressed repetition of 'man' (echoed, however, in the final consonance) in the second period — where the rhythmic stress (and the dominant stress of the sentence) occurs on an entirely new vowel. 'Man' and 'kann' are doubly engulfed in silence.

    I conclude that there is good reason to think sonority is a basic feature of utterances that we intuitively recognize as oracular. The examples further suggest that this sonority, insofar as it varies from utterance to utterance and lacks rules that would allow its precise nature to be predicted in any given case, corresponds to Frye's 'oracular rhythm.'

RESONANCE AND THE ONTOLOGY OF ORACULARITY

I've been attempting to show not only that oracular utterances are sonorous, but that their sonorities are strategic: that important aspects of their physical construction echo, even if only faintly, important themes in the resonant wholes to which they point. Their literal sonority is thus an aspect of their philosophic meaning. Hence, we may say, one answer to the question of the role sonority plays in oracular utterance is that it is — as it is in lyric utterance — enactive. It aurally traces the body of its vision.

In other words, oracular utterance is *resonant*. It displays a fundamental attunedness of thought and expression; and it is not understood unless this attunedness is perceived (although it may not be perceived consciously). Charles Kahn, in discussing Herakleitos, uses the term this way: "By *resonance* I mean a relationship between fragments by which a single verbal theme or image is echoed from one text to another in such a way that the meaning of each is enriched when they are understood together." As I use it, the notion of resonance is somewhat broader: it characterizes not only different expressions of similar themes, but also similar (or overtly contrasting) expressions of different themes. Like Kahn, though, I wish to claim that the similarities (or in some cases, overt oppositions), whether of 'content' or 'expression,' invite us to consider the words or sentences together (or in juxtaposition); and that when we do so, the meaning we then discern extends beyond what could be captured in a straightforward summary in language. (It's conceivable that, in some cases, a couple of pictures or diagrams might do the trick.)

Relations among aspects of a resonant thought structure need not ignore standard semantic and syntactic associations; indeed, such features are usually prominent among those aspects of an utterance that are set in resonant relation. Where standard semantic or syntactic associations appear to have been thrown to the winds, the gesture is almost always deliberate and self-aware: their rejection is one of the elements being set in resonant relation with others. What is crucial to the notion of a resonant thought structure is the idea of meaning relations that are, or are *also*, other than straightforwardly logical.

Here is yet another example, a poem by Tomas Tranströmer (translated by Robert Bly) that is, I would argue, a lyric description of the phenomenology of oracular insight:

TRACK

2 a.m.: moonlight. The train has stopped
out in a field. Far off sparks of light from a town,
flickering coldly on the horizon.

As when a man goes so deep into his dream
he will never remember that he was there
when he returns again to his room.

Or when a person goes so deep into a sickness
that his days all become some flickering sparks, a swarm,
feeble and cold on the horizon.

The train is entirely motionless.
2 o'clock: strong moonlight, few stars.

The orientation that is realigned is, as the title suggests, that of the 'traveller on life's highway' (here metamorphosed to train tracks), and the key to the realignment is the vision of lights flickering on the horizon. In the Swedish original, the words Bly translates as 'flickering' and 'horizon' — *flimrande* and *synranden* — rhyme. That is, the poem says, in deep dreams or severe illness, we are given a perspective on our own mortality: we both *see* it — comprehend it — and see that it is at the limit of our understanding. The limit of our vision and the brilliant-but-unsustained nature of our days are brought together — are, in fact, made variations on one another. Had Tranströmer been inclined to state the oracle, rather than describe the phenomenon of grasping it, he might have said, in Swedish: *Life flickers coldly at the limit.* As it is, he is concerned to argue that the power of such insight throws us a great distance from that life: we are frozen — astonished and paralyzed — in the cold terror of our own oracular gaze.

Although in this example the key words literally rhyme, the 'attunedness' of concepts in a resonant conceptual structure may also take any of a number of less overt forms. Their expression may, for example, involve imagistic or etymological echoes, or it may involve a structural rhyme of some sort, like the mirroring relation of the first and last propositions of the *Tractatus*. This is not to say that sonority is an expendable feature of lyric and oracular utterance. Rather, it is to emphasize that it is one aspect of the linguistic expression of resonant thought; and that such thought typically possesses non-aural dimensions of resonance as well. What is fundamental is that the *meaning* of such utterances just is their resonant integrity; and the ontology of this integrity is non-systematic. What oracular utterance does is to point to such a structure; it does so, in part, by setting the resonant whole of which it is a part, in motion — much as a chord — the right one — can evoke an entire piece of music.

And here, I think, is one source of contemporary philosophical difficulty with the oracular: much in our modern intellectual inheritance predisposes us to seek *dis*integrative understandings. With the possible exceptions of some claims of sense experience and allegedly self-evident axioms of logic and mathematics, we believe that a claim cannot be said to be *true* or *known* in the absence of both argument and criteria of evaluation. We take the presence of (good) argument and/or criteria to be both necessary and sufficient conditions of philosophical *justification*. But what is argument? What are criteria? Most generally, arguments and criteria are intended to supply reasons for a claim. In practice, though, only a narrow set of what might actually *be* the reasons for a given claim is taken to be philosophically respectable: *real* reasons, we say, must be *logical* — and in spite of the fact that our best logicians and philosophers of logic have repeatedly pointed out that logic is ultimately an intuitive notion, we believe that reference to it constitutes reference to an authority that is both absolute and utterly perspicuous. Logic's perspicacity, we feel, lies in its analytic structure — its algorithmic manipulation of fully discrete semantic atoms. Thus, among the things we have made of our inheritance from Bacon and Descartes, is the idea that philosophic clarity is to be achieved by systematically breaking down assertions into their constituent atoms and then building up knowledge through a process that employs a small, explicit

*

set of rules. Knowledge, this model tells us, *is* additive: there is a hierarchy of (necessary) principles and (expendable) details; and the world it is knowledge *of* is a machine — with fully detachable, and fully replaceable, parts.

My object here is not to argue that analysis never reveals anything helpful or useful about meaning. I believe that in some contexts, it can be very useful indeed. What I wish to call to our collective attention is the consequence of *requiring* analytic structure for any claim or view that aspires to philosophic status. The consequence is that visions of the world (or visions of aspects of it) that insist on the intimate connectedness and interdependence of things — and which understand this connectedness as coherent but not formalizable, intelligibly patterned but not reconstructible according to an articulable set of criteria — such visions will tend to strike us as suspect. If, to gain them credence, they are expressed in systematic-analytic prose, they will deny, in the very gestures of that expression, what they seek to maintain, and we will sense their lameness. But if they seek the resonant, deeply associative mode of expression that the integrity of their vision demands, we will dismiss them as unserious — 'merely' poetic, philosophically unfounded, 'oracular.'

Now, all this would still be of merely literary, or perhaps anthropological, interest if we knew for a fact that the world is not a non-systematically integrated whole. But we don't know this. The intuition that it does (or that at least significant parts of it do) 'hang together' not only informs lyric art, but drives a good deal of investigation in natural science. Whether and how the world hangs together are, arguably, the fundamental issues in metaphysics. Science, granted, frequently takes the world's unity to be systematic; but it does not always do so. And the arts almost universally do not. The philosophical interest of oracular claims is thus suspect only if we are sure, before we look at the evidence, that any glimpse of non-systematic unity *must* be an illusion.

To put this another way: to find oracular utterance philosophically significant, we must be prepared to entertain the kind of metaphysics that informs it. Oracular utterance, in each instance, points to, without fully articulating, a way of understanding the world as a whole. An oracular utterance is true, then, if that pattern — that ecology of non-systematic resonant relation- ships — really exists *in* the world. Lyric and oracularity under- stand truth, as do argument and systematic science, as a form of semantic coherence with a context (which, for some, is the way the world is, and for others, is the way the rest of language is). But unlike argument and systematic science, they understand semantic coherence to be resonance of embodied expression, as the possession of gestural integrity. "Is it true?" for oracular utterance thus becomes: "Is there a gestalt with which this claim is fully resonant?" That we are sometimes unable to answer this question, or that we sometimes turn out to have answered it incorrectly, are not, in themselves, grounds for rejecting it out of hand for all possible epistemological contexts — any more than mistakes in, or uncertainties about, deductive reasoning constitute grounds for rejecting out of hand the possibility that, at least in some contexts, truth is appropriately understood as that which is transmitted by valid argument.

Another analogy: the mystery story. The lyric utterance is the arrangement, in clear view, of all the significant particulars, including the fact that the dog did nothing in the night-time. (Lyric *ability* is, among other things, a capacity to see what the significant particulars *are*.) The oracular utterance is the Great Detective's citation from Herakleitos, pronounced with no other *overt* indications, beside the muddy corpse: "Dogs bark at those they do not recognize." And now suppose there are two basic hypotheses available: one, that it was an inside job; two, that it was done by an anonymous intruder. The Shocked Relatives' refusal to countenance the first possibility will be reflected in their rejection of the Great Detective (in either her lyric or or- acular mode); they will dismiss the pronouncement about dogs as irrelevant nonsense, and demand investigative donkey-work with fingerprint kits and house-to-house interviews. (And that donkey-work may well turn up a stranger who ran into the neigh- bour's shrubbery on the evening of the crime.) What we need to notice — what, as schooled readers of mystery stories we *will* have noticed — is that the Shocked Relatives' insistence on in-

vestigative donkey-work is part and parcel of their interest in
pursuing a particular solution to the crime. Likewise in philosophy: allegiance to analytic method is often not fully separable
from a commitment to disintegrative metaphysics.

   Disintegrative metaphysics instantiates, it *enacts,* the part-
whole relations suggested by the etymology of the word 'analysis': 'throughout to loosen, unfasten, or set free.' Cognates
in other languages mean to perish or destroy. The metaphysics
allied with analytic method is a metaphysics that conceptualizes
wholes as — at most — additive. In such a metaphysics, the parts
of the world are, in some *fundamental* sense, non-interdeter-
mining; they are understood to bear external but not internal
relations to other parts and to (aggregate) wholes. (Indeed, in
extreme cases, analytic metaphysics asserts that there can be no
intelligible notion of an 'internal' relation.) The metaphysical
stance that informs oracular utterance suggests otherwise. The
possibility of its truth points to ways of understanding the world
in which non-systematically resonant pattern is ontologically
fundamental, and in which parts are grasped only secondarily
as heuristically identifiable, but non-ontologically separable,
aspects of those wholes.

   Finally, if we look again at the negative connotations of the
term 'oracular,' we see yet another way in which sonority is important to oracular utterance. The 'air' of superior understanding
which makes oracular utterance seem "as if [the product of] …
special inspiration or authority" comes, I suspect, from the somatic response to rhythmic impulsion, enactiveness, and rhyme.
Sonority literally moves us; we respond with an involuntary
adjustment of various somatic rhythms and attitudes; we *move
to* the sound — it attracts us, we dance. This can be dangerous, as
Plato understood, because it can make false proclamations harder
to resist. But it can be beneficial when it provides an impetus to
a reorientation that yields genuine insight. To take the sonority of oracular utterance seriously is to take seriously our own
embodiment, that is, the embodiment even of our philosophic
understanding; and the idea, then, that the body may, in some
instances, help us to truth.

In addition to its enactive attributes, sonority *encourages* us in our efforts to understand oracular utterance. Such utterance is notoriously difficult; the presence of sonority acts as an initial assurance of the presence of meaning. A sonorous linguistic gesture makes immediate physical sense to us in a way that a non-sonorous articulation does not. If Herakleitos had said, "The most suitable arrangement of entities in the universe would constitute a homomorphism with the set of relations obtaining among a random selection of atoms," his fellow Greeks might have taken a moment to assure themselves that the sentence really was making the screwball claim it appeared to be; but having done so, it is unlikely they would have bothered to record even a paraphrase for posterity. Sonority quickens our intuitions of meaning; it places the somatic apprehension of intelligible recurrence on the mind's tongue; and thereby provokes us to, and sustains us in, the work of trying to understand.

LYRIC AND ORACULARITY, AGAIN

Oracles employ the form of utterance they do because they need a form of expression whose presuppositions don't do violence to their intuitions of non-systematically coherent wholes. But what this doesn't yet explain is why oracular utterance has the *deeply* riddling character it so often has: why, that is, oracles don't simply use lyric utterance. Lyric shares the relevant epistemological and ontological presuppositions, and importantly, it does say more. (Not much more, in some cases, but at least a little.) It calls our attention to particulars in a way that oracular utterance does not. Given this, wouldn't it be in everyone's best interests to proscribe oracularity as *excessively* obscure?

In part, this question may be asking about the appeal of puzzles and riddles of all sorts. Why are mystery stories so universally popular? Since we *know*, by the rules of the genre, that we will eventually be presented with a solution, and that we will also, in the course of the story, be presented with all the evidence that establishes it, why doesn't a summary — "It was the butler, in the pantry, with the candlestick, because ... " — appeal?

Why do we *like* to try to discern the pattern for ourselves? This is a deep, and deeply interesting, question whose answer lies in the evolutionary neurobiology of gestalt perception. I will not pursue the discussion here, but simply note that I am convinced that the allusiveness of oracular utterance has deep-seated psycho-biological appeal.

Charles Kahn suggests that, in Herakleitos' case, oblique and provocative utterance is philosophically strategic:

> [*The*] *parallel between Heraclitus' style and the obscurity of the nature of things, between the difficulty of understanding him and the difficulty in human perception, is not arbitrary: to speak plainly about such a subject would be to falsify it in the telling, for no genuine understanding would be communicated. The only hope of 'getting through' to the audience is to puzzle and provoke them into reflection. Hence the only appropriate mode of explanation is allusive and indirect: Heraclitus is consciously and unavoidably 'obscure.'*

Here I believe we are returned to contemplation of the philosophical significance of tone. There is, in the challenge of much oracular utterance, a provocation that is absent from lyric utterance. To grasp the meaning of a resonantly integrating whole — of which the world, according to most oracular utterance, is the foremost example — is, in part, to grasp that its structure of intelligibility is *other than* the structure of intelligibility that informs 'ordinary' or 'semantically and grammatically unexceptional' human speech. Lyric, too, enacts and embodies this recognition, but, unlike oracular utterance, it does not demand that that recognition be conscious.

Why does oracular utterance insist on it? My hypothesis is that it has to do with oracular aspirations to wisdom. Wisdom does not, it seems, have to do with the accumulation of significant amounts of factual or technical knowledge — we do not always regard those who are sophisticated, smart, and widely read as wise, and we sometimes do so regard those who are illiterate. And wisdom does, it seems, have to do with the integrity and depth of vision that oracular and lyric insight share. But it has also to do with the recognition that there are things knowable by humans that are, in their ontological structure, epistemically resistant to 'linguistically unexceptional' thought: wisdom is the acknowledgement of the limitations, as well as the strengths, of such thought.

This, then, is the point of oracularity's 'excessive obscurity': in the understanding appropriate to oracular utterance is not only the grasp of a resonant whole, but a *conscious awareness* of the inadequacy of 'semantically and grammatically unexceptional' language to effect this grasp. Both lyric and oracular utterance gesture; but lyric comprehends and embraces its insight where oracularity insists and points. Lyric will not, cannot, provide a systematic disintegrative characterization; but it does *direct* vision: "Notice these things simultaneously; or notice them in this order; notice all of them." And so understanding may be achieved *without phenomenological awareness* of the difference between the epistemological structures accommodated by lyric and those accommodated by 'plain speech.' One need not notice that a 'standard' way of understanding is undone in lyric comprehension — one simply *sees*, in lyric mode. Oracular utterance, by contrast, demands that one dismantle, by oneself, various common presuppositions about the world, and then that one come to see, by oneself, the whole to which the oracular utterance points. In this is the pleasure of the puzzle, yes; but also the difficulty of wisdom. For it is in the struggle to see for oneself that one comes to relinquish the universal adequacy of 'plain speech' — in either idealized or demotic incarnations — as a means of expressing what one knows about the world. In the seeing *is* the relinquishing. If the vision were made manifest, as it can be in lyric utterance, one would not have to accomplish the *work* of letting go. But it is in this work, in *awareness* of the shift of vision demanded by oracular utterance, that wisdom is achieved.

ORACULAR PHILOSOPHY

Hume's mistake, Kant said, was to equate analytic thought with a priori thought and synthetic thought with a posteriori thought.

In so doing, Kant claimed, Hume had deprived reason of its "most important prospects" by failing to note that the a priori and the synthetic do not exclude one another.

Whatever one wishes to make of the analytic-synthetic distinction, there is a lesson to be learned here about the philosophical imagination. While there have always been outriders, the mainstream of Western European philosophical thought has impoverished itself by insisting on a false identity: philosophy must avoid carelessness in thinking — and good argument, or good systematic thought, is one way to pursue this goal; lyric and oracular utterance, on the other hand, frequently employ linguistic gestures common to poetry — and poetry is almost never argumentative in a systematic sense. *From this it does not follow* that argument is to be identified with care in thinking, and lyric and oracular utterance with intellectually irresponsible 'poetic licence.' Lyric and oracular utterance can indeed be pursued responsibly, and *are* so pursued when they carefully, thoughtfully, in meticulously crafted language (or some other medium), seek to help us to grasp a resonant whole. They are subject to revision, and to the recognition (by their author or auditors) that they are not achieved — that they fail to measure up to the vision that they attempt to comprehend or point to. Oracular utterances, like scientific paradigms, aim at truth; and a thinker working in the oracular mode can take this commitment very seriously. (Wittgenstein, arguably, took it as seriously as any philosopher in the twentieth century.) Lyric and oracular utterance, I have argued, are, further, necessary to the expression of certain ideas about the nature of the world and human relations to it, ideas that fall squarely within the ambit of the traditional conception of metaphysics (though not many of its current English-speaking versions).

When we ask about the 'meaning of life' or the 'meaning of the world' we are seeking gestalts — gestalts for phenomena so complex that there may be no understandings at once true and sufficiently comprehensive. We may believe we have glimpsed or heard a unifying pattern, but it disappears as soon as we try to focus our argumentative gaze. We feel this may have to do not so much with the illusoriness of our initial impression as with the act of focussing on it, not with the absence of meaning but with our attempt to grasp meaning in a certain way.

A final analogy: When I was a child, we had a dog. She was a mutt, but looked as though she had a lot of spaniel in her: soft hair, basically black and brown, with gold eyebrows and gold feathery fringes on her sides and tail. If you went out walking with her at night, she was dark enough to pretty well disappear. If she had her collar on, you could hear her dog tags jingling; and she'd hold her tail up so you could catch those gold feathers in your peripheral vision. But only in your peripheral vision. If you looked right at her, she was gone. Oracular utterance understands the meaning of the world like this: the world's meaning exists, it says, and is detectable, but not by the mind's argumentatively focussed eye. The oracular — in its obliqueness, its startling leaps, its paradoxes — is the undoing of that gaze. It is the trace in speech of our scotopic awareness of the world-as-a-whole. In recognizing that oracular utterance does constitute a genuine mode of philosophical expression lies, indeed, one of philosophy's most important prospects: the contemplation of intelligible world-orders that traditional argument is incapable, coherently, of conveying to us.

Mathematical Analogy
and Metaphorical Insight

I · A QUESTION ABOUT METAPHOR

My interest in this topic grows out of a long-standing, hands-on engagement with the discernment of metaphors. As a poet, and as an editor and reader of poetry, I have often been struck by the power of good metaphors to change my stance in the world, to alter in a profound and, it seems, permanent way how I look at things. Whence this power? And further, how is it that we are able to distinguish such 'good,' world-altering, metaphors from metaphors that are merely *outré* or arcane — surprising linguistic constructions that lack, or seem to lack, genuine ontological depth?

It is difficult to provide examples without quoting whole poems or paragraphs. A metaphor is like a depth charge: if you know nothing about the material in which it is embedded, it can be difficult to evaluate what it's telling you. Some very powerful metaphors can speak to us without context; but often metaphors in the shallow and mid-ranges won't yield up their full meaning on their own. As a consequence, almost any candidate for a shallow metaphor that I might offer without context can appear as a challenge to invent a context in which it would appear effective.

With this caveat, let me offer without further commentary the following: "the eyes are the windows of the soul" (a good or strong metaphor); "the table fizzed like a platypus" (a weak or shallow metaphor); "the river/Is a strong brown god" (good); "the luggage resembled/godly" (weak); "the road was a ribbon of highway, perfect for Pekinese" (weak); "If I have exhausted the justifications I have reached bedrock, and my spade is turned" (good). My interest, as I say, is in what appears to be an intuitive capacity many of us have for being *struck* by certain metaphors, and for being left cold by others. What is involved in the comprehension of good metaphors? *How* do metaphors mean?

In reflecting on these issues, three things struck me more or less simultaneously. The first was obvious: that metaphors involve what Wittgenstein called 'seeing-as,' a seeing of one thing in terms of another. (I should note here that I am using the term 'metaphor' broadly to cover any linguistic expression of focussed analogical thinking. Thus, what we would strictly regard as a simile is also 'metaphorical' in the sense I am concerned with.) The second thing was that, as a working poet, I find that understanding a metaphor *feels like* understanding certain kinds of mathematical demonstrations: I am aware of features of various figures or expressions, or various images or ideas, being pulled into revealing alignment with one another by the demonstration or the metaphor. The final observation — or, in this case, idea — was that 'seeing-as' involves a kind of re-cognition, and, as such, is what we mean when we say we *understand* something. This last claim is essentially empirical in nature. If we ask "When do people *say* that they 'understand' or 'get' or 'see' or 'grasp' something?", it turns out that the experience of 'getting it' seems to involve a reconfiguration of an initially problematic array or scenario — a redirection of emphasis that somehow affects the overall shape of the problem. And the emergence of this new way of looking at things is often accompanied by a feeling of astonishment, or of things falling into place, of their coming home.

In sum, I began my investigations with the intuition that both metaphors and certain kinds of mathematical demonstrations are species of analogical *reasoning*: both say, in effect, "Look at things like this, if you want to understand them." But how close is the connection between mathematical analogy and metaphor? (And here I should perhaps emphasize that my use of the phrase 'mathematical analogy' is intended to be at least as broad as my use of 'metaphor' — it embraces everything from certain visual proofs of the Pythagorean theorem to Euler's conjecture about how to find the sum of the reciprocals of the squares.) Mathematics clearly involves reasoning — but poetry? Aren't literary metaphors simply inventions — airy nothings, loose types of things, fond and idle names? Can understanding in mathematics really be compared with understanding in literature? These are the questions I wish to explore in what follows. First, I will offer more detailed testimony from mathematicians and poets to support the claim that there is an important correspondence between metaphors and analogies in mathematics. Then I will look briefly at two points of apparent non-correspondence. I will conclude by suggesting that the answer to our initial questions about the power and recognizability of good metaphors lies with the phenomenon of what we might call *metaphorical insight*: to grasp a good metaphor is, like understanding a fruitful mathematical analogy, to experience the significance of a newly seen alignment for what the figure, concept, or thing actually is. Or, to put this another way, a good metaphor changes the way we see the world because it is not a mere linguistic fiction, but is in some sense — a sense analogous to that which attaches to mathematical demonstration — true.

II · EVIDENCE FOR A CORRESPONDENCE
BETWEEN MATHEMATICAL ANALOGY AND METAPHOR

Because of the third idea mentioned above — that 'seeing-as' is at the root of our experience of *understanding* — I was led to the work of Max Wertheimer, one of the leading figures in the development of gestalt psychology. There I found elegant and thoroughly researched descriptions of the phenomenon of 'getting it,' couched in terms of re-arranging 'internal' structural relations — in effect, re-seeing an initial configuration in a different way. For example:

In this square with a parallelogram strip across it the lines a *and* b *are given. Find the sum of the contents of the two areas. One can proceed thus: The area of the square is* a², *in addition that of the strip is...? But suppose instead that one hits upon the idea:*

$[Sc1 =] \ (square + strip) = (2 \ triangles, \ base \ \text{a}, \ altitude \ \text{b}) \ [= Sc2]$

$$[Sc2 =] \ldots \ldots \ldots = \left(2 \, \frac{ab}{2} \right) = ab \ [= P].$$

The solution has thus been attained, so to speak, at a single stroke.

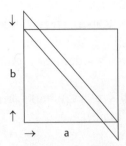

Indeed, most of Wertheimer's examples were drawn from elementary geometry or arithmetic, a few from music — and none from poetry. But his summary characterization precisely captured central features of the experience of grasping a metaphor:

In general we see that in [trying to discern whether S is [S']], the object (S) ... is given as [something defined by a certain set of characteristics] — but there is no direct route from S to [S'] ... It frequently occurs that [seeing] the required relationship to [S'] is only possible when [S] has been re-formed, re-grasped, re-centred in a specific way. And it is not less frequently the case that to effect this process a deeper penetration into the nature and structure of S is required.

And subsequently, in Poincaré, I found descriptions of the process of mathematical creation that appeared to echo the process of actually *making* metaphors.

To create consists precisely in not making useless combinations ... [in choosing to study facts] which reveal to us unsuspected kinship between other facts, long known, but wrongly believed to be strangers to one another.

Among chosen combinations the most fertile will often be those
formed of elements drawn from domains which are far apart. Not
that I mean as sufficing for invention the bringing together of ob-
jects as disparate as possible; most combinations so formed would
be entirely sterile. But certain among them, very rare, are the most
fruitful of all.

This could easily be Robert Hass, talking about metaphor:
"Metaphor, in general, lays one linguistic pattern against another. It can do so with a suddenness and force that rearrange
categories of thought."
But it was ultimately Kepler's remarks on analogy that seemed
to me most suggestive of all:

The geometrical voices of analogy must help us. For I love analogies
most of all, my most reliable masters who know in particular all
secrets of nature. We have to look at them especially in geometry,
when, though by means of very absurd designations, they unify in-
finitely many cases in the middle between two extremes, and place
the total essence of a thing splendidly before the eyes.

The phrase "by means of very absurd designations" seems
designed to invoke the image of metaphor, which, of course, in
its strict sense depends on an 'absurd' designation. Kepler's claims
that mathematical analogies "unify infinitely many cases" and
"place the total essence of a thing splendidly before the eyes"
both underscore the connection with gestalt thinking and are
echoed in the remark of poet Anne Michaels that "metaphor uni-
fies separate components into a complex whole, creating something greater than a sum of parts." (Kepler does not explicitly
say that the "total essence" that is placed "splendidly [*luculenter*]
before the eyes" is something other than a mere sum of parts,
but the rhetorical construction here suggests he experiences it
as something other than a computed arithmetical average or
simple mean.) And I believe Kepler's sense of what analogy *does*
is also surprisingly close to poet Jane Hirshfield's sense of what
metaphor does: both are, in Hirshfield's words, "central devices

for ordering the plenitude of being." Finally, Kepler's suggestion that these mathematical analogies "know all secrets of nature" could be a paraphrase of poet Charles Simic's claim that, surprising though it sounds, metaphor is "the supreme way of searching for truth." And in this connection, we should note that Kepler is not alone in thinking analogy is of vital importance to discovery in mathematics. Eberhard Knobloch points out that both Johann Bernoulli and Leibniz made similar claims. More recently, George Polya has argued that analogical thought is fundamental to both mathematical insight and pedagogy.

A final point of correspondence between metaphors and mathematical analogies concerns an awareness on the part of practitioners that they can lead us astray, but a refusal to cede pride of place either to analytic description or logicist investigation. Both Kepler and Leibniz explicitly acknowledged the potential of analogies to mislead, yet remained advocates of analogical reasoning. Polya, though one of its most vigorous champions, notes that it is "hazardous, controversial, and provisional." (Their attitude is nicely captured in Samuel Butler's observation that "though analogy is often misleading, it is the least misleading thing we have.") The poet Charles Wright is speaking of a similar difficulty in literary composition when he discusses the discipline of learning to distinguish between true and false images; Simic also alludes to it in discussions of the epistemology of poetic composition.

III · APPARENT POINTS OF NON-CORRESPONDENCE

But no one is seriously going to maintain that mathematical analogies and metaphors are essentially the *same thing*. There are several obvious points of non-correspondence, of which I'd like to discuss two. My aim here is to concede differences, while arguing that the most significant among them need not damage our impression of fundamental similarity. Indeed, I wish to suggest that these apparent differences point to deeper connections we have not considered, and will help us begin to formulate answers to our original questions about metaphor.

The first dissimilarity arises as a direct consequence of consideration of the last point of correspondence mentioned above. Precisely because analogical reasoning can be misleading, in mathematics one often does construct 'analytic' or 'logical' proofs to back up one's analogical or visual intuitions. One's reasoning remains suspect until one can produce the four-lane axiomatic deduction that leads to the same destination as the leap of gestalt imagination. There seems no comparable procedure or demand in the case of metaphor. Books of poetry do not usually come organized like Euclid's *Elements* or with appendices that parse and defend every metaphor in the body of the text. Indeed, while we can imagine providing such explanations or elaborations, they would seem to be anti-requisite if the metaphor is to remain literarily pleasing or effective. In this, metaphors closely resemble

*   jokes, as Ted Cohen has pointed out.

The second point of non-correspondence focusses on the relations between metaphors and mathematical analogies and the world. Mathematical analogies are in some robust, though perhaps intuitive, sense *true,* and are perceived to be so, even by members of the general public. This is an honour rarely, if ever, accorded to metaphors except by poets themselves. Polya, for example, suggests that poets "feel some similarity [when they compare a young woman to a flower], … but they do not contemplate analogy. In fact, they scarcely intend to leave the emotional level or reduce that comparison to something measurable or conceptually definable."

I agree that most poets would resist attempts to quantify or schematize their metaphors, but I think Polya is just wrong to suppose that poets don't 'contemplate' analogy. The points of correspondence, and the cited testimony, point to a genuine concern with truth on the part of many poets. The key question, I think, is how we can best make sense of this concern — and how our intuitions about truth in mathematics can assist us in making sense of it. To this end, let me first suggest ways of accounting for the points of apparent non-correspondence in which the disanalogy with metaphor does not appear so severe. Then I will return briefly to the issue of the nature of necessary truth which is, I believe, at their root.

With respect to Apparent Disanalogy No. 1 — the absence of linear or 'analytic' proof in metaphoric contexts — it is important to reflect a moment on how analogies function in mathematical contexts. Guldin, in his discussion of Kepler, comments: "I consider [his] analogies to be useful for the invention of things more than for their demonstration." That is: the analogy expresses the insight; the proof, by contrast, establishes the incontrovertibility of the insight. It is a sentiment one finds echoed in various implicit and explicit forms throughout the literature on analogy and proof. Interestingly, it appears to repeat the first point of non-correspondence and then collapse it into the second: no proof, no truth. But in so doing it points once again to the deep *similarity* between mathematical analogies and metaphors. True, there is nothing corresponding to linear or algebraic proof in metaphoric, i.e., literary, contexts — but this absence (and its corresponding presence in mathematical contexts) is a feature of the *context*, not of metaphor itself. And what Guldin's (and Polya's, and, arguably, Kepler's own) view underlines is that the same holds for mathematical analogies: they are vehicles of insight, not proofs themselves.

This leads directly to a question about the nature of proof: how is it that a proof *establishes* the incontrovertibility of an insight? Isn't its 'incontrovertibility' precisely what makes us call something an *insight* in the first place, rather than a guess or a hypothesis? (Even when we're wrong? — And note that we can be wrong about proofs as well as analogies.) What, exactly, is a proof anyway?

As with most fundamental notions in most disciplines, the answer is unclear. For myself, I am inclined to follow Hardy, who argued that a proof is an attempt to direct others' attention to something. He took mathematicians to be observers, gazing out on a range of mountains and taking notes. A proof, he said, is their way of gesturing at a summit they've seen, in the hope that others will see it, too. When others do see it, Hardy claimed,

... the research, the argument, the proof *is finished.*

The analogy is a rough one, but I am sure that it is not altogether misleading. If we were to push it to its extreme we should be led to a rather paradoxical conclusion; that there is, strictly, no such thing as mathematical proof; that we can, in the last analysis, do nothing but point; *that proofs are what Littlewood and I call* gas, *rhetorical flourishes designed to affect psychology; pictures on the board in the lecture, devices to stimulate the imagination of pupils.*

But if Hardy is right — if a proof is a "rhetorical flourish" designed to get other people to see what you see — then there is a clear parallel with poetry: as proof is to mathematical analogy, so the poem is to metaphorical insight. The poem itself is a 'rhetorical flourish' that positions its reader or auditor in such a way that she or he sees what the poet saw.

An example may be helpful. Consider the claim "The human heart is a red pepper." Yeah, okay, we say: it's about the right size, is in roughly the right colour range (assuming the heart is alive or relatively fresh, and has been exposed to the air). But at first blush, this looks like one of those mid-range or even overtly shallow observations — it's not that interesting. Here, however, is its full context, a poem by Sue Sinclair:

RED PEPPER

Forming in globular
convolutions, as though growth
were a disease, a patient
evolution toward even greater
deformity. It emerges
from under the leaves thick
and warped as melted plastic,
its whole body apologetic:
the sun is hot.

Put your hand on it. The size
of your heart. Which may look

like this, abashed perhaps,
growing in ways you never
predicted.

It is almost painful
to touch, but you can't help
yourself. It's so familiar.
The dents. The twisted symmetry.
You can see how hard it has tried.

The analogy becomes more and more resonant as we proceed through the second and third stanzas, the final line 'explaining' the deformities observed in the first stanza and clinching the bewilderment, the almost-pain and the odd familiarity of the second and third. (That the claim, as articulated above, is not fully explicit in the poem is a feature of what I'd like to call the gestalt-rhetoric of much lyric poetry. An exploration of this phenomenon would take us too far afield; but it is worth noting that we also see such implicitness from time to time in mathematical proofs, as for example in Bhāskara's twelfth-century visual demonstration of the Pythagorean theorem.)   *

"But still," one may wish to protest, "isn't it the case that Kepler's analogies, or Polya's analogical presentation of the Pythagorean theorem, express TRUTHS, in a way that metaphors never do? Aren't metaphors creatures of the imagination rather than delineations of reality?" Here, I think a couple of assumptions, one about literature and one about mathematics, dovetail to produce questionable prejudice. I'll address the literary side of the matter first.

Note that the phrasing of Apparent Disanalogy No. 2 includes the phrase "are perceived to be [robustly true] *even* by members of the general public." This is one clue that we are dealing with a phenomenon conditioned by, perhaps even expressive of, culturally determined levels of literacy and numeracy. My suspicion is that if, as members of either the general or expert public, we were all equally and highly literate and numerate, we would be less inclined to imagine all mathematical demonstrations were ˙

transparently true and more inclined to be struck by the profundity of certain metaphorical claims. The poem as 'proof' — that is, rhetorical flourish that positions its reader or auditor to see what the poet has seen — works by a subtle interplay of rhythm, assonance, denotation and connotation, much of which our schooling does not prepare us to pick up. Just as we are rarely informed in grade school of the existence of contested proofs, or that mathematicians themselves debate the *nature* of mathematical truth.

I do not wish to deny, however, that most of us at some time or another have been struck by what I called earlier the incontrovertibility of some mathematical demonstrations. Consider the visual proof that Plato offers in *Meno* that a square double in size is built on the diagonal of a given square. I have taught this proof countless times, mostly to students who are less interested in lifting it off the page of Plato's prose than they are in the socio-political drama of Sokrates' interrogation of a slave. But the proof, once drawn on the board, is easily grasped:

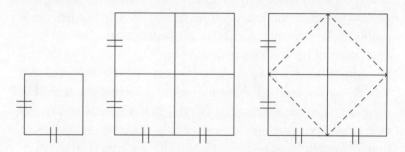

The square double in size is built on the diagonal of the original.

It is also elegant and very powerful. And time after time, there is someone in the class who experiences it with a physical shock — an audible gasp or an involuntary "Oh!" as the light dawns. What underlies this experience, I think, is not only 'getting' that the square double in size is built on the diagonal, but that this *has* to be the case. What impresses is not simply the claim's truth, but its *necessity*.

This — *necessary* truth — would seem to be something a metaphor cannot possess. Metaphors, we think, are creatures of linguistic play, not deductive logic; surely there is nothing *conceptually* necessary about a claim like the heart is a red pepper. But let us think hard about this for a moment. Good poems — including poems like Sinclair's "Red Pepper," which elaborates a single metaphorical insight — are notoriously difficult to teach: ask any poet or sensitive English professor. You can build a tolerable lecture around a mediocre poem, which often requires lots of external information to make it comprehensible; but one often has the sense with a good poem that everything that *can* be said *has* been said, and perfectly, in the poem itself. Either you get it or you don't. In this, it seems to me, good poems resemble the simple visual proofs we try to teach students in ancient philosophy classes. Yes, there are some who grasp the *Meno* proof with a gasp; but there are others who don't see it the first, or even the second, time. If they don't get it, there's little I can do but say the same thing — walk through the demonstration, read the poem — again. And *when* they get the poem, grasp its central metaphorical insight, there is often an expression of astonishment just as there is with the theorem: a sudden stillness in the room, occasionally tears. These are not in all cases the *same* acknowledgements of necessity as we find in mathematics, but that is nonetheless what I believe they are. Their differences stem from the nature of the necessities compassed by the two domains: mathematics, I believe, shows us necessary truths unconstrained by time's gravity; poetry, on the other hand, articulates the necessary truths of mortality.

IV · WHAT THE CORRESPONDENCE BETWEEN MATHEMATICAL ANALOGIES AND METAPHORS SUGGESTS

It is time now to return to our initial questions: Whence the vision-altering power of some metaphors? And how is it that we are able to distinguish between such metaphors and arresting, but mere, linguistic confections? Metaphors, I wish to suggest, can be insightful in just the way that mathematical analogies can: they reveal to us "unsuspected kinships" between "facts long known, but wrongly believed to be strangers to one another." And, as in mathematics, "the most fertile will often be those formed of elements drawn from domains which are far apart." This does *not* mean, as Poincaré notes, that we simply bring together the most disparate objects we can think of — such a tactic can produce surprise, but it is surprise without depth, "sterile," in Poincaré's word. It means that, as in the case of mathematical analogies, metaphorical power is a product of *discernment*, to borrow again from Poincaré.

But discernment of what? I wish to propose that the correspondence between metaphors and mathematical analogies suggests that we distinguish between profound and shallow metaphors along the lines of a mathematical distinction between important or fruitful mathematical conceptions and unimportant ones. Here, it is helpful to note that even a realist like Kepler, who believes that good mathematical analogies reveal truths about the actual universe, argues that the *value* of analogy lies in the "most spacious" field of invention that it opens. In other words, discernment in mathematics, and, as part of this, the development of 'true' analogies, consists in perceiving connections that point the way to yet other connections. The power, the value, of an analogy lies not in a definitive mapping of some territory, but, paradoxically enough, in its freeing of the imagination for further discovery. To put this yet another way: a fruitful or important analogy is one that establishes a deep field of resonance.

It might be objected that this proposal clouds the issue more than it clarifies it. The notion of a fruitful or important conception is so contested in mathematics that it cannot usefully form the basis of a parallel account of good and weak metaphors. For underlying questions about which conceptions will prove fruitful or important is a debate about the nature of mathematical creativity: is it a form of discovery, or a type of invention? Couched in metaphysical terms, the question is whether mathematical entities and truths have an existence independent of the human minds that eventually discover them, or whether they are — as metaphors are often supposed to be — simply constructs of human discourse and imagination. Neither argument nor experi-

ence has yet been able to settle the issue. As Demidov notes, the   *
experience of the working mathematician supports both claims.

It is not my intention to settle the debate here. My aim is to suggest that, rather than rendering the comparison between powerful metaphors and fruitful mathematical analogies problematic, it may point yet again to a fundamental similarity, obscured yet again by literary prejudice we are disinclined to examine.

For what the existence of the debate between realism and constructivism in mathematics should suggest to us, given the correspondences we have noted, is that a similar debate might be joined with respect to metaphorical insight. It may be that the world does exist independently of human activity and discourse, and that writers whose metaphors are consistently strong are not just good at manipulating language, they are good at perceiving the way that world actually *is*. Yet, as noted earlier, we tend to think it is obvious that metaphor has no purchase on what I have previously called a 'robust' conception of truth — that (to paraphrase Nietzsche) metaphor's self-conscious use marks a *liberation* of the human understanding from the stultifying effects of naïve (or even sophisticated) realism. If, however, there is reason to construe the power of metaphors along the lines of the importance or fruitfulness of mathematical conceptions, there is reason to think the realism-constructivism debate might be a live one for metaphorical insight. But in that case, we must accept that we have been given grounds for a radical reconstrual of the role of metaphor in our lives: we must take seriously the possibility that metaphors are not invented but are perceived, and that the true ones among them limn the structure of a resonant, mind-independent universe.

Plato as Artist

The purpose of this essay is not to adumbrate a new theory about
Plato, nor to develop a new approach. Plato is old; he is famous;
my Greek is sketchy — there is nothing revelatory I am compe-
tent to say. And yet I wish to say something; in particular, I wish
to say something about *Meno*. Years ago, I became convinced
that it was as close to a philosophical jewel as anything was
likely to get. It sparkled; it had, I sensed, a kind of geometrical
perfection that I couldn't quite put my finger on. I turned to the
commentators, and learned much. But I also learned that no one
was quite as impressed with the dialogue as I. Many thought it
significant, some thought it central, but none, it seemed, was
convinced it was a work of philosophic art — a complex ecology
of argumentation, a survey of Plato's central views in very small
compass, an exquisitely nuanced report of both his idealism and
his despair. And, like other works of art, provocative, ambiguous, tantalizing. The purpose of this essay, then, is simply that:
to record my astonishment at the beauty of this made thing; to
praise; to express my delight, wonder and gratitude; and to attempt to clarify, for myself, what continues to perplex me, and
perhaps must continue to perplex us all, now that there is no one
who speaks Plato's Greek as fluently as he.

❧

"Can you tell me, Sokrates, is virtue teachable?" the dialogue
begins — no scene-setting, no contextualization, as bald and un-
adorned an opening as the most anti-literary reader could wish.
It's not unlike the opening of Brahms's Third Symphony: the most
cursory of upbeats, and we are plunged into the main theme. Or
no: almost immediately, via a confession that Sokrates cannot

answer since he cannot give an account of the subject — virtue, or human excellence — we are turned to a second, and surely more important question: What *is* human excellence? But then, because it turns out Meno cannot give a Sokratically satisfactory account either, we are led to a third question: How do we search for what we do not know? Here, Sokrates is suddenly willing to admit he is on solid ground: priests and priestesses have convinced him that we search for what we don't know by looking inside ourselves. Our disembodied souls have "seen all things" before birth, and, "as all nature is akin" (συγγενοῦς), we have to remember only one piece of what we saw, and it will all come back. Meno, astonished, requests evidence that this is so, and Sokrates obliges by walking one of Meno's attendants, an uneducated slave, through a visual proof that a square that is double the size of a given square is built on the given square's diagonal. (It is difficult to express this thought clearly in a succinct sentence. Yet what we mean is not difficult to *see*.) Meno tentatively, and without really committing himself, accepts that Sokrates seems to have shown that the boy knew something that he wasn't taught, and Sokrates, for his part, retreats from his claim to have proved we have epistemic access to truths we (think we) do not know, repeating something he has said before: that he is convinced we are "better, braver and less indolent" for engaging in the search. In sum, an inquiry into the nature of human excellence has led us deeply into mathematics, and the experience of mathematical truth has confirmed our commitment to becoming more virtuous human beings.

The dialogue might well have ended here,

OED: *Anamnesis* ... [Gr. ἀνάμνησις remembrance, n. of action f. ἀναμνα- stem of ἀνα-μνή-σκ-ειν to remember, f. ἀνά back + μνο- call to mind, f. μέν-ος mind] The recalling of things past; recollection, reminiscence.

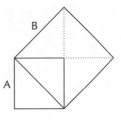

Square B is twice the area of Square A.

but it doesn't. Meno, apparently having forgotten that the point of the demonstration with the slave was to convince him that he and Sokrates should search for a satisfactory account of excellence, pushes for a return to the original question, "Is virtue teachable?" Sokrates, after a complex reproof that plays on the reversal of the traditional roles of pursuing lover and pursued beloved* ("But you do not even attempt to control yourself, so what can I do?"), agrees to discuss the teachability of virtue. He begins with a sketch of something he calls "the method of hypothesis" (which, because it echoes key moves in *Republic* and is nowhere given a full treatment, has much exercised the commentators). Its aim seems to be to establish an equivalence between teachability and knowability. The question thus becomes "Is virtue knowable, that is, some kind of knowledge?" There follows a brief, somewhat technical argument reminiscent of *Protagoras*, which — no surprise, given Plato's apparent commitments elsewhere — concludes that virtue is knowledge (and therefore teachable). But almost before the words are out of his mouth, Sokrates *retracts* this, the expected conclusion, on the empirical grounds that there are demonstrably no teachers or pupils of virtue. Since virtue is valuable, if it *could* be taught, presumably it would be. Thus, on the previously assumed equivalence between teachability and knowability, it follows that virtue can't be knowledge. (The passage is famous for its dramatic details: Anytos, one of Sokrates' accusers in 399 and a friend of Meno, has joined the conversation. Sokrates riles him, it seems deliberately, with talk of sophists — Anytos misses various ironies — and also by casting aspersions on the ability of "Athenian gentlemen" to raise gentlemanly sons.) Well, but if it isn't knowledge, what can it be? Sokrates asks and immediately proposes that it must be true opinion — hearsay that happens to be right, a lucky guess, in short, a gift from the gods. Meno, perhaps, perhaps not, made as dizzy as the reader by the sudden shifts in argumentative direction, happily concurs. And so the dialogue ends.

What in all this is there of jewel-like perfection? It sounds more than a little chaotic — thematically disjointed, argumentatively distracted, philosophically inconclusive. And the dialogue is indeed routinely classed among Plato's 'early' aporetic works. But this picture is the result of focussing in the mid-range — on the outlines of the philosophical plot, as it were — and neither on the dialogue's overall gestalt, nor on the fine details of its composition, the way the individual sentences carry, display, express, and challenge their overt 'content.' Those details confirm that we are meant to notice several things: that the question "What is teaching?," though philosophically central, is never explicitly asked; that Sokrates is, in a way, toying with Meno in the second part of the dialogue — "You want to play it your way? Okay, we'll play it your way"; that Meno does not notice this, nor does Anytos; and that, most importantly, we are in fact given an array of tools for tackling and ultimately answering the core questions posed by the dialogue. There is much that is unvoiced in the writing; but it is latent, as a conclusion is latent in its premises. When we regard Plato not only as a purveyor of arguments but as a consummate philosophical artist, when we take every move, every sentence to be carefully and deliberately crafted to support the dialogue's thematic preoccupa-

OED: *Aporetic* ... [a. Fr. aporetique ... ad. Gr. ἀπορητικ-ός, f. ἀπορέ-ειν to be at a loss, f. ἄπορ-ος impassable, f. ἀ priv. + πόρος passage.] Inclined to doubt, or to raise objections.

tions, when we therefore regard every detail as worthy of our concentrated philosophical attention, the work's essential unity begins to emerge. When we focus on how the dialogue is *made*, we are led to ask the right questions. When we ask the right questions, its meaning springs to life.

❧

The very first question we might want to ask is why Plato wrote dialogues. The basic insight here, I believe, has been ably articulated by Martha Nussbaum*: for the Greeks, drama was traditionally the medium of ethical discussion. If we want to identify Plato's genius and originality as a moral philosopher, we should look for what distinguishes him from Aiskhylos, not from Mill or Kant. Thus character, and characterological response to challenge, are essential elements of his vision; they are at the centre of what we are supposed to attend to, particularly in the suite of dialogues — *Meno, Euthyphro, Apology, Crito,* and *Phaedo* — that are concerned with events leading up to Sokrates' death. We are meant to observe not only the noble intelligence and heroic calm of the protagonist, but also the actions and attitudes of lesser characters. What is human excellence? It centrally involves the wish to be free of delusions about the worth and certainty of our intuitions; and acting on this wish requires a multiplicity of forms of courage, as well as intelligence. (Openness, the ability to listen, resolve, the ability to coöperate.) How would we ourselves react if challenged by Sokrates? How might we wish to behave? I disagree with Nussbaum that Plato's dialogues are emotionally bare, "crystalline theatre[s] of the intellect." Grief, rage, and fury do not pre-

* "Interlude I: Plato's Anti-Tragic Theater" in *The Fragility of Goodness*, Cambridge and New York: Cambridge University Press, 1986: 122–35.

dominate, but they are there (*Phaedo, Gorgias*, Book 1 of *Republic*), as are insolence, revelry, and lust. We are spared terror and horror, and in this the dialogues are certainly distinct from tragedy. But they contain a wealth of reflective feeling in the form of respect, admiration, and friendship, as well as a great deal of defensive emotion in the form of haughtiness, swaggering, posing, self-congratulatory ease, and vanity. They show us, repeatedly, that our emotional attitudes are crucial to learning to think well, and to changing our lives in light of what we learn.

And so we must imagine the studied casualness, the air of sophistication, with which this rich and well-connected young foreigner (70a–71b, 78d) proposes a subject of conversation with Sokrates — that aporetic wizard, whose reputation Meno wishes to test. (It will emerge later that the two have met on the previous day [76e], but — we deduce — did not pursue a philosophical conversation at the time [80a].) "Can you tell me, Sokrates — is virtue something that can be taught? [a slight pause, a shift to catch the light better on his hair or his robe] Or does it come by practice? Or is it neither of these, but men possess it by nature or in some other way?" Read: I want to see for myself this legendary skill in debate. Here's a chestnut: we both know how it goes. I'm too rich really to *care* how it comes out; but I'm socially curious.

And Sokrates replies with an artfully artless speech — apparently complimentary of Meno and deprecating of himself. "How rich you are! And smart! And confident and dignified! How handsome! I can't compete — I'm just a dumb Athenian schmuck. Unlike you, I have no idea what human excellence is." (Imagine Peter Falk as Columbo, chatting up the guy he knows is the murderer.)

Meno is seduced: "You're right [admiring his own manicure — noting that what people say is true, his fingers really *are* beautiful!] — no one could know how gorgeous I was unless they'd met me. But enough about me! I really *am* curious: are you *actually* as dumb as you say?"

Sokrates: "Yup." And plays him, sinking the hooks in deeper, stirring up his competitiveness. "I don't know what virtue is, and I've never met anyone who did, either." Is this true? We can confirm that over the course of the dialogues, Sokrates never encounters anyone who can give what, at *Meno* 98a, he will call a "causal" account — a *logos raisonné* — of virtue; and that he is himself unwilling to give one. But is he actually incapable? Or, to be precise, is *Plato* incapable?

This is a very good question. In some sense, it is the overarching question concerning Plato's work as a whole. And it is certainly a question on which *Meno* sheds complex light, although we need to read on in the dialogue before attempting an answer. The reason the question comes up here is twofold. In the first place, Sokrates clearly does have views: virtue is all he thinks about, and his life betrays a greater possession of it than most. Are we really to believe that he (that is, his author) can't even *begin* to give an account of the sort he keeps pressing others to supply? Secondly, a couple of lines after Sokrates claims not to know what virtue is, we are offered what readers of Plato's work as a whole must recognize as a piece of disingenuous irony: Meno, incredulous, has asked if Sokrates has not heard and approved of Gorgias' account of virtue — and Sokrates, responding with an elegant and untranslatable rhyme on Meno's name, claims that he does not entirely recall (71c8) if he approved or not; Meno had better remind him of what Gorgias said. Or, if Meno likes, why doesn't he tell what he himself thinks, since he probably shares Gorgias' view.

Now there is a sense in which Sokrates might generally be said 'not entirely to recall' things. But it is a quasi-technical one with which Meno (though not Plato's audience at the Academy) would be unfamiliar: Sokrates, like all human beings — according to the doctrine propounded later in this dialogue, and in *Phaedo* and *Phaidros* — forgot, when he was born, at least some of what his soul had seen in its disembodied state. But he has, as we know from other dialogues, remembered more than most; and for details of what people have said (poets, sophists, other philosophers, teachers, interlocutors) he has, in general, a mind like a steel trap. (See, for example, his recollection of Gorgias' views on Empedoklean natural philosophy in this very dialogue, 76cff.)

So: it appears that, here as elsewhere, he offers an opaquely ironic disavowal — in effect, he lies — in order to provoke his interlocutor into stating his own views. And this may be, *at least in part,* what we are to understand him to be doing when he says he doesn't know what virtue is. It is true that in *Republic* his disclaimers about his understanding of the Good sound more genuine than his disclaimers about his understanding of virtue here; but the Good is there said to be well 'beyond' any of the specific virtues, and, it turns out, Sokrates does in fact have a surmise (506d–e), which he then declines to state! He implies, in *Republic,* that he has gone the long road toward grasping the nature of the soul (435d); in *Symposium,* the circumstantial evidence is overwhelming that he has climbed Diotima's ladder; and here, in *Meno,* it becomes clear that he thinks virtue is a form of wisdom and that we come to it by recollection. Is Plato incapable of giving a 'causal' account of the sort he has Sokrates require? Perhaps. (Perhaps not. See Aristoxenos' suggestive account, below, pages 175–6.) In any event, Plato has Sokrates refrain from giving even an outline, I think, because — whatever else — he *does* know that no explicit sketch, let alone account, will provide an otherwise undisciplined and uninitiated interlocutor with *insight.* Thus Sokrates is made to remain mute, putting clues in our way, hoping we'll stumble over them.

"So tell me what you think virtue is, Meno." And Meno is only too happy to oblige.

The next section of the dialogue — the refutation of Meno's first two attempts to define virtue — is straightforwardly what it appears to be. Behind Sokrates' insistence that Meno provide him with an account of that which makes individual virtues "all the same" (72c) is Plato's commitment to 'forms' or 'ideas' as the *explanans* of meaningful communication. The thought is roughly this: Unless we have 'the same thing in mind' when we're talking, we are not actually communicating. Do we actually communicate? All but the most frighteningly alienated among us know that the answer is uncontroversially yes. Apart from routine success buying bread and getting a turn in the shower, most of us have experienced deep and powerful moments of contact, virtually transparent understanding, with members of our own or other species. When you start to think about how this happens, though, you pretty quickly realize there is much for which Newtonian physics cannot account. (Either that, or you reject your phenomenological experience in order to save Newton. — And perhaps it is a surprising capacity for such rejection that is selected for by institutional philosophy.) Plato's metaphysics is indeed strange; it may, in the end, be unworkable. But it represents a direct and sincere attempt to save fundamental — and, to our culture, fundamentally mysterious — phenomena.

In suggesting that a commitment to the metaphysics outlined in *Parmenides* and *Phaedo* also underlies *Meno*, I am relying on a synoptic reading of Plato's work, as I was when I suggested Sokrates was effectively lying when he disavowed being able to recall what he thought about Gorgias' teachings. Such readings are currently unfashionable, though they have not always been. It is indeed possible to point to inconsistencies and tensions in the corpus; and I don't wish to ignore these or pretend they don't exist. But to use them as an excuse for resisting a comprehensive view of Plato's thought, or for denying that he is steadfast in a number of his commitments, is to read against the texts. The right use of philosophical imagination depends on discerning the difference between a legalistic prosecution of technicalities and genuine philosophical rigour.

Apart from the implicit metaphysics, we should note two other things between 71e and 75a. First, for all his polish, Meno is not a quick study (72d, 74a); and second, here, early in the dialogue, Plato introduces an analogy using geometrical concepts (73e). And perhaps we should note a third: the unmistakably ironic colour of Sokrates' response to Meno's confession at 74a that he is "not yet able … to follow [Sokrates'] search and find a single virtue common to all." "It's likely," Sokrates replies — Εἰκότως γε. ("I'm not surprised," Guthrie translates.) "But I shall do my best to get us a bit further if I can." It's a remark partly for the camera — that is, the audience of young Pythagoreans taking their lessons at the Academy — and it tells us Sokrates knows he's working with damp wood. But it is a double entendre, not simply a *sotto voce* slight: it also tells us that Sokrates believes the investigation to be intrinsically difficult, *and yet* that he is willing to work with unpromising material. This in turn confirms our sense that it's not true that Sokrates knows nothing at all about the subject under discussion — minimally, he knows it's difficult, and it is hard to imagine his not having given thought to why this might be so. And it shows his generosity — his willingness to devote energy to a project that he must suspect is going to go nowhere.

Then, starting at 75a, we get a very interesting exchange. It looks at first like a digression, an excursus on definition whose point, if it has one, is completely incidental to the main line of investigation. One could cut from 75a5 — the interlocutor imagined by Sokrates saying, "Don't you see that I am looking for what is the same in all of them?" — directly to 77a7: "Stop making many out of one, as the humourists say when somebody breaks a plate. Just leave virtue whole and sound and tell me what it is." No one would notice that anything was missing. This, according to the method of reading I am recommending, is a sure sign not that we can ignore these two pages, but that we must pay the closest attention to them. If they don't need to be here, why did Plato put them in?

⁂

Meno, at a loss intellectually, reverts to charm. He is childlike, coquettish. Sokrates asks him to try to define shape — since Meno says he sees what sort of definition is required — and he says,

"No, you do it, Sokrates." (Eyelashes sweeping his cheek.) Sokrates, after a pause, and with a sly smile, pretending the part of a hotly pursued youth: "You really want me to give in?" Meno (more eyelashes): "Yes. I do." The double entendre is again clear, but this time Meno is fully awake to it. Thus Plato maneuvers Sokrates into providing the first of three definitions of shape. (The precise significance of the number I cannot guess. Triples abound in Plato's work, as they do in most Indo-European texts; and in this passage, Sokrates' three definitions, best to worst, inversely mirror the three definitions, worst to best, that Meno gives of virtue. Aristotle tells us that three was the Pythagorean number for marriage, but I see no straightforward connection here.) "Let us define [shape]," Sokrates says, "as the only thing which always accompanies colour [ὅ μόνον τῶν ὄντων τυγχάνει χρώματι ἀεὶ ἑπόμενον]." Translating even more literally: *the sole thing belonging to the class of existents that happens together with colour always next in order.*

What, exactly, does this mean? I don't know. Guthrie's "accompanies" makes for clear, comprehensible English. Grube's "follows" is closer to Plato's Greek, but, like the Greek, it is ambiguous. Does Plato mean that shape "follows," that is "[merely] accompanies," colour in being somehow less important? Because Plato was a rationalist and a geometer, this seems unlikely. Does he mean it is "next in order" logically? Or, better, *ontologically*? Are we, in other words, dealing with a claim about the relation of the Form of Shape to the Form of Colour? I suspect something of the sort, and have tried to imagine how it might work in terms of Collection and Division, the heart of the dialectical technique

F. M. CORNFORD: ... Plato's language seems to show that he did not imagine eternal truths as existing in the shape of 'propositions' with a structure answering to the shape of statements ... Dialectic is not ➤

alluded to and glancingly demonstrated in *Phaidros*, *Sophist*, and *Statesman*. Could Plato be intending that we see that one of the following conceptual orders holds?

Formal Logic, but the study of the nature of reality — in fact Ontology, for the Forms are the realities (ὄντως ὄντα).

The problem is that neither of these alternatives seems plausible. In the first proposed division, we can imagine things that are not coloured which are nonetheless shaped: bowls of water, or the shape I draw in the air with my finger, engaging your mind's eye. And, as I suggested above, it is unlikely that a rationalist would put colour 'above' shape in any ontological hierarchy.

However, the second proposal appears to fare no better. For we can imagine things that are coloured that are not shaped: the sky, for instance. — Ah, but did the *Greeks* think the sky was unshaped? They did not — they thought it was shaped like a bowl. So perhaps something of this sort — Shape as the Formal genus "next in order" above Colour — is what we are to understand?

This possibility is obliquely but tantalizingly reinforced by a strange comment Sokrates makes in the course of the upcoming demonstration of *anamnesis* with the slave boy. After the slave's first incorrect guess at the answer, Sokrates abjures Meno: Θεῶ δὴ αὐτὸν ἀναμιμνησκόμενον ἐφεξῆς, ὡς δεῖ ἀναμιμνήσκεσθαι.

PHAIDROS 249b–c: For to be a human, one must gain understanding form by reasoned form, gathering the form into one as it comes [to the mind] from many perceptions. This process is *anamnesis* of ➤

Lamb translates, "Now watch his progress in recollecting by the proper use of memory"; Grube, "Watch him now recollecting things in order, as one must recollect." Wherever the emphasis falls, a proper order or a proper order-of-doing those things that our soul once saw when it was travelling with god, disregarding the things that we now say 'exist,' and rising instead to what is truly real. [My emphasis.]

MARY CARRUTHERS: Particularly in *De memoria*, Aristotle emphasizes the importance of order for storing the phantasmata in the memory, and recommends an alphabet-based mnemotechnique ... In a crux ... clarified by Richard Sorabji [452a17–26], Aristotle describes the advantage of using the order of the alphabet to organize material in the memory. If one assigns a separate letter of the alphabet [that is, says Sorabji, an *image*] to distinct pieces of information, then one can move from one bit to the next using the rigid order of the letters to organize ... material. In recollecting, one can start with Alpha if one wishes ... Or one could begin with Zeta and move easily to its 'neighbours,' Eta or Epsilon. It is the orderliness of the 'places' that makes it possible to 'read' what is 'written' in the 'shapes' stored in memory.

is at stake. This echoes the suggestion of order in the shape definition passage here, as it does the explicit mention of it at *Symposium* 210e. Order was, of course, central to the mnemonic technique of the Greeks, as it was for the medievals. But it was also central to Plato's conception of dialectic, as we are shown in the exercises offered in *Sophist* and *Statesman*. The key terms of both mnemonic technique and Plato's dialectic are 'collection' and 'division.' The evidence is mostly circumstantial — the Greek of the one apparently explicit discussion, in *Phaidros*, is notoriously difficult — but I believe that what it says is this: Plato viewed dialectic as a technique for recollecting the ontological relations among Forms.

All speculation about the content of Sokrates' definition of shape aside, it is unequivocal that it possesses correct definitional form. Plato has Sokrates say (after a little more erotic byplay), "I should be content if your definition of virtue were along similar lines." In other words, a proper definition of virtue is going to have the form: "Virtue is the only thing that always accompanies/follows/comes after ____." (If the Formal reading I've proposed is correct, in such a definition virtue will be identified as either a proper species or a proper genus of something else.) The overwhelming circumstantial evidence from other dialogues, and indeed this one, is that what goes in the blank is 'wisdom.'

But Meno objects to the definition's form. "It's naïve!" he exclaims. What if somebody doesn't understand the second term? They'll be no better off than when they didn't understand the first! "What sort of answer have you given him?" (75c)

"A true one," Sokrates insists, directing our attention back to the definition. And then he is made to offer a set piece, familiar to us from other dialogues, contrasting combative argumentation with friendly question-and-answer investigation. "If you were an eristical and disputatious questioner, I should say, 'You have heard my answer [again directing our attention to the definition, reaffirming his commitment]. If it is wrong, you must take up the argument and refute it.'" But since he and Meno are friends, Sokrates must give a reply "more conducive to discussion. By which I mean," he says, "that it must not only be true [implying, again, that his own definition is], but must employ terms with which the questioner admits he is familiar." (75c–d)

What? Meno really *does not know* what τὸ χρῶμα means? Sokrates is going to go on to define 'end' by offering synonyms — 'limit', 'boundary', 'termination' — and by waving his hands: *you know what I mean.* Could he not easily have done the same with colour? Colour is what you get when you lay on pigments, or dye something — "that's all I mean, nothing subtle" (75e). Or is it, rather, that Plato is suggesting to his audience that Meno, like myself, doesn't understand the terms of the definition because Sokrates is employing Form-talk — a way of using terms, and meanings, with which non-initiates are not familiar? (By the phrase 'Form-talk,' I do not mean to imply that Plato employs a technical vocabulary. He doesn't, and in avoiding it, his practice is consistent with the text of *Letter VII* [whoever wrote it].*) Nonetheless, talk of Forms, and of notions associated with them, tends to involve a certain repertoire of rhetorical gestures. It seems, wherever I think I detect it, to be highly elliptical, and it gives the impression, if not of code, then of allusiveness. I believe it was intended to draw the

PHAIDROS 277b–c: Second, you must understand the nature of the soul, along the same lines; you must determine which kind of speech is appropriate to each kind of soul, prepare and arrange your speech accordingly, and offer a complex and elaborate speech to a complex soul and a simple speech to a simple one.

* See the so-called epistemological digression, 340a–345c. For a discussion of the authorship of *Letter VII* see Harold Tarrant, "Middle Platonism and the Seventh Epistle," *Phronesis* 28 (1983): 75–103.

STATESMAN 263a–b:

Young Socrates: Quite right; but this very thing [the key to dialectic, which you are trying to teach me] — how is one to see ... that class and part are not the same...?

Eleatic Visitor: An excellent response, Socrates, but ... [w]e have already wandered far from the discussion we proposed ... let's go back to where we were ... However, there is one thing you must absolutely guard against, and that is to suppose you have heard from me a plain account of the matter.

attention of initiates and leave the rest of us — if we sense something is going on — faced with a blank wall. We know what *colour* means as much as we know what a *limit* is. But we don't know what it means to say shape is "that thing alone which happens together with colour, next in order." The possibility that this definition involves an unexplicated allusion to a Formal hierarchy accounts for Sokrates' repeated insistence that his definition is correct, for its slightly odd turn of phrase, for its overall simplicity, and for the suggestion that nevertheless Meno can't be expected to understand. (And I believe we are going to get further confirmation of this quite soon.)

At any rate, Meno accepts Sokrates' definition of *limit,* and says he knows also what *surface* and *solid,* as they are used in geometry, mean. (But isn't this surprising? Could you, o reader, right now, without further thought, provide a geometer's definition of *surface* and *solid*? And without using terms that Meno might not know?) So Sokrates says, "Well then, you'll understand this definition just fine: shape is 'that in which a solid terminates, or more briefly, it is the limit of a solid'" — εἰς ὃ τὸ στερεὸν περαίνει, τοῦτ᾽ εἶναι σχῆμα· ὅπερ ἂν συλλαβὼν εἴποιμι στερεοῦ πέρας σκῆμα εἶναι. (76a7)

"And how do you define colour?" Meno replies.

It is an extraordinary moment. Meno's failure to engage, his apparent insouciance thrown lightly over the abyss of his inattention, is breathtaking. There is, I think, a pause. A long one.

Then Sokrates (smiling a bit, looking at the ground) says, "What a shameless fellow you are, Meno. [Another pause.] You keep bothering an old man to answer, but refuse to exercise your

memory and tell me what Gorgias' definition of
virtue was." An admission, in some sense, that
he has been defeated: Meno is such damp wood
there is no teasing him into even a flicker of interest in reality.

More flattery of Meno's good looks; but now
Sokrates' tone is cold, edged. Meno must be
handsome indeed since he behaves like a spoiled
child, a tyrant. But Meno does not register the
insult: he preens. And then Sokrates agrees to
give a definition of colour "in the manner of Gorgias" — one that Meno will "easily follow" (76c).

It is an empiricist's definition, based on Empedoklean physics: things give off effluvia, some
of which fit some channels of sense perception,
some of which fit others. So we may define colour as "an effluvium from shapes which fits the
sight and is perceived" (76d). Meno thinks this
is an excellent account. Sokrates shrugs. "It's the
sort of thing you're used to, something in the
high poetical style [τραγικἠ] — that's why you
like it better than the earlier definition of shape."
(Which one? 76e4 employs the singular — but
there are two definitions that Meno has rejected,
one perhaps appealing to Forms, the other explicitly to mathematical objects.) Meno avers
that he does like it better.

And now, yet another extraordinary moment.
Sokrates, the man who knows only that he does
not know, who serves only as midwife to others'
thoughts, offers, directly, his opinion:

"But it is not [better], son of Alexidemous;
I think the other is." There is no sense Plato is
playing with us here, there is not even a whiff
of irony. We are intended to register and respect
Sokrates' claim; and, I believe, to ask why the first

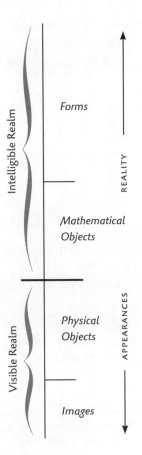

THE DIVIDED LINE,
Republic 509d–510b.

REPUBLIC 510b: In the
[top] subsection [of the
Line], [the soul] makes
its way to a first principle ... proceeding from a
hypothesis ... using forms
themselves and making
its investigation through
them.

REPUBLIC 533d: There-
fore, dialectic [ἡ διαλε-
κτικὴ μέθοδος] is the only
inquiry that travels this
road, doing away with hy-
potheses and proceeding
to the first principle itself,
so as to be secure ... From
force of habit we've often
called [these crafts associated with dialectic] 'ways
of understanding' [ἐπι-
στήμαι] ... but they need
another name, clearer
than opinion [δόξα],
darker than understand-
ing itself [ἐπιστήμη].

* For a brief description
of what is known of the
Mysteries, please see the
Appendix, pages 208–10.

PHAEDO 97b–d: One day,
however, I heard someone
reading an extract from
what he said was a book
by Anaxagoras, to the
effect that it is Mind that
arranges all things in order and causes all things;
now there was a cause
that delighted me, for I
felt that in a way it was
good that Mind should be
the cause of everything;
and I decided that if this
were true Mind must do
all its ordering and arran-
ging in the fashion that is
best for each individual
thing. Hence if one ➤

definition (or the first and the second together) is
better. But hard on the heels of this remarkable
gesture and its attendant puzzle comes another.
Sokrates continues: "And I think you would believe so, too, if you did not have to go away before the Mysteries as you told me yesterday, but
could remain and be initiated." (76e) The remark
is tossed off conversationally, and Meno replies
conversationally, and the interlude moves to a
seamless close, as Meno is brought round to his
third attempt at a definition of virtue.

But before we ourselves continue, let us focus
clearly on what has just happened. Plato, I believe, is *telling* us that the first definition embodies correct definitional form, and also that
that it does would be impressed on anyone initiated into the Eleusinian Mysteries.* This is an
astounding claim. What could be the connection
between correct definitional form and the Mysteries? As we reflect on these startling remarks,
we should, I believe, sense them being ghosted
by the argument in *Phaedo*. There, too, Sokrates
is made to reject empiricist science, saying he
prefers accounts that "assume the existence of a
Beautiful, itself by itself, of a Good and a Great
and all the rest [and that if] you grant me these
and agree that they exist, I hope to show you
the cause as a result, and to find the soul to be
immortal" (100b). That is, Forms and reincarnation theory are a package deal; and our grasp of
either precipitates (or may be precipitated by) a
rejection of empiricist science.

➤

Meno, unlike the Pythagorean initiates who sur-
round Sokrates in *Phaedo*, does not understand
what he has been told. His reply to Sokrates'

comment about staying for the Mysteries suggests he imagines what he'd learn would be more
Empedoklean science. But such is the power of
the Mysteries, that even mention of them has a
salutary effect. For as Sokrates returns the discussion to its initial trajectory — requesting that
Meno keep his promise to define virtue now that
he, Sokrates, has defined shape — what Meno
produces contains the kernel of a correct Platonic
response. He says: "Virtue is to desire beautiful things and have the power to acquire them."
(77b)

It is clear, of course, what Meno has in mind:
an excellent human being is visibly wealthy
and has lots of political clout. But the tireless
Sokrates sees his chance. He gets Meno to agree
that 'beautiful' means 'good,' and then pursues a
standard analysis of the epistemology of desire.
It is impossible, he argues, to desire what we
believe will (merely) make us (genuinely, fully)
miserable; thus desire, of necessity, is for what
we believe is in some relevant measure good.
We can be mistaken about what the good is, of
course, and so can end up desiring what is *in fact*
bad; but a lack of wisdom should not be confused with warped appetite. There is, there can
be, no such thing. Thus Meno's definition must
be revised: Virtue — human excellence — is the
power of securing good things.

No Platonist would disagree! We just have to
get clear on what good things are. Plato underlines this with what appears to be a conversational aside: "Let's see if what you say is true,
then, for you may well be right." (78c) In this abstract formulation, 'good things' uninstantiated,
the definition *is* right. Of course, we all know
that Meno doesn't mean by it what Plato means.

wanted to discover the
cause for anything coming
into being or perishing or
existing, the question to
ask was how it was best
for that thing to exist or to
act or be acted upon.

Nonetheless, we can see the audience of the Academy leaning forward in its collective seat.

Sokrates says, casually, "By 'good things' you mean, oh, say, health? And [the tone here indicates a suppressed "naturally"] wealth?" Meno is eager: "And also acquiring gold and silver and public honour and position." Sokrates, after a little pause: "Nothing else?" Meno, a little puzzled, thinks a moment. (What could the old guy have in mind? Where's the trap? Hmm! Does he mean sex? I bet he does; but he's not going to get me on that one. We don't usually respect someone just because he gets laid.) "No," he says, "just those things." Another, longer pause. Sokrates: "Very well." And in the tone of a public announcement (which it is, to the Academicians): "According to Meno, hereditary guest friend of the Great King [read: one of the most publicly honoured and influential men around], virtue — the highest thing a human being can aspire to — is the acquisition of gold and silver." (78d) He turns around, looks at Meno with raised eyebrows. Meno, thinking he has sidestepped the trap, and that the great Sokrates is proclaiming him a penetrating intellect, gives an emphatic nod.

REPUBLIC 533d: ... when the eye of the soul is really buried in [the Orphics'] barbaric bog, dialectic gently pulls it out and leads it upwards, using the crafts [τέχναι] we described to help it and cooperate with it in turning the soul around.

Why doesn't Sokrates give up? When we read Plato simply for the arguments and assumptions, one of the things we don't notice is how hard Sokrates *works* in these dialogues. He is truly an extraordinary teacher. As long as his interlocutor remains interested, he stays in the ring. Meno is not intelligent; he is no Thrasymakhos. So chances are he won't have thought his way through to a full-blown Nietzschean skepticism. If he hasn't, he will unreflectively salute standard mores, and Sokrates can pit those undigested opinions against Meno's undigested opinions about 'good things,' force another definitional circle, precipitate a collapse, and so place Meno in a position whence he might — if Sokrates is lucky — be willing to reach for a genuine intuition. This is indeed what happens. Meno confirms that grabbing gold and silver any old way does not constitute virtue — he is quite pious in his agreement that one must grab it justly. (Whew.) But justice is a part of virtue. Thus Meno is offering a definition of the whole in terms of an undefined part: "Excellence is acquiring gold and silver in one of the excellent ways." Sokrates hammers the point home, in one of his longest speeches to date. He concludes: "Do you not think you should face the same question again, or do you think one knows what a part of virtue is if one does not know virtue itself?" (79c) This time Meno is silent. Wow, this guy is as good as they say; he's really pinned me this time, and I didn't even see it coming. "I do not think so." Sokrates senses the honesty of the reply; he presses the point yet again: "Remember when we were defining shape? We agreed that circular definitions aren't on." Meno, after another pause, shakes his head: "We were right to think that, Sokrates." And yet again Sokrates pounds him — I make it the sixth iteration between 79b4 and 79e4 — trying to force the crack wider. He succeeds. Meno is broken open. "I think what you say is right," he finally says. "Then answer me again from the beginning," Sokrates replies. "What do you and your friend say virtue is?"

It is a ringing climax. We can imagine the audience again on the edge of its seat. Meno is ready now to reach for truth. Will he?

A very long pause.

No, he won't. Or at least not yet. He must first digest his astonishment at having been so completely beaten at a game he thought he knew how to play; he is reflecting honestly, but his focus remains himself and his social position. "Sokrates, I'm speechless. You've put a spell on me. I feel like I've been stung by a torpedo fish: I'm numb. I don't have an answer. Which is amazing, since I've made many speeches about virtue before large audiences, on thousands of occasions. And thought they were really good. But now I can't say a thing." Pause. "I think you should stay in Athens. If you went anywhere else, they'd

say you were a sorcerer." Another stunned shake
of the head.

It's not exactly an epiphany, but it will do.
Meno is experiencing a classic *aporia*, the dissolution of his unexamined expertise. While he
has not yet begun to remember what his soul
saw in its disembodied state — and since he has
been reincarnated as a human being, he must
have seen more than many — at least the scales
have fallen from his inner eye. With assistance,
he might yet be enabled to see.

PHAIDROS 249b: But a
soul that never saw the
truth cannot take a human
shape ...

Sokrates is immediately kind, joshing. He
once more compliments Meno on his looks.
(Bad cop, good cop — keep the kid soft, off balance.) But the compliment is odd, complicated.
As with the excursus on definition, the passage
that contains it could be cut, and the transition
would be seamless: "'... they'd say you were a
sorcerer.' Sokrates: 'My dear Meno, if the torpedo
fish is numb itself and so makes others numb, I
resemble it; but otherwise not ...'" So, given its
apparent awkwardness, why is it here?

This is how the compliment goes. Sokrates
has jestingly accused Meno of comparing him
(Sokrates) to a torpedo fish in order to get
Sokrates to draw an image of him (Meno) in return. (But it is *quite* clear that this was not Meno's
motive; he's too stunned. And his response to
Sokrates' joshing — "Huh? What?" — shows him
to be still reeling.) Sokrates says: "One thing I
know [*sic!*] about all handsome people — they
delight in having-a-likeness-drawn [εἰκαζόμε-
νοι]." Grube misses the emphasis and, in what
follows, represents Plato as sounding the theme
of image versus reality. But Lamb's translation
is, I think, closer to the mark: "... they delight
in being compared to something. They do well

over it, since fine features, I suppose, must have fine similes."
This is like trying to make a kid who's scraped his knee feel
better by saying "I know why you were running on the gravel!
You were drawn to it, like that genius geologist who first correctly identified the dates of the last interglacial by her surveys
of Arctic drumlins!" — It's weird. It makes a kind of sense, but
is obviously excessively complicated for the social situation.
(And, of course, Sokrates knows it is. He's playing Bugs Bunny
to Meno's Elmer Fudd.)

Again, I believe the passage has been written for the ears of
initiates. It brings to mind the discussion at *Phaedo* 73c–76b, in
which Sokrates is made to argue that just as our lover's possessions remind us of our beloved, likewise material things stir us
to remembrance of the Forms. "[R]ecollection is occasioned by
things that are similar or dissimilar [to the original; but] when
caused by similar things ... one is forced to consider whether the
similarity is deficient or complete." (74a) And from this, since
of course perception of material things always falls short of vision of the Forms, we are led, at 76a, once again to affirm the
immortality of the soul. How else could we be put in mind of
"the Beautiful itself by itself" having merely been exposed to a
summer's day? (If the answer seems obvious to you, think again.)
In other words, analogic ontology and reincarnation theory are
also a package deal. This is the chord I believe Plato is sounding,
remotely, in Sokrates' convolute joke.

There follows the remark about being numb himself — he's
as perplexed about virtue as Meno has become. Nonetheless,
he wants to examine the question together with Meno and seek
an answer.

"But how will you look, Sokrates, if you don't know what
you're looking for?" Meno asks — and I believe undesignedly,
in genuine puzzlement. It's a good question. I remember being
astonished in Grade Two when the teacher told us that if we
didn't know how to spell a word, we were to look it up in the dictionary. I had recently learned to read the word 'know,' which, on
my first encounter, I had pronounced "kuh-now," and, of course,
didn't recognize. If I didn't already know 'know' was spelled with

a silent 'k,' how on earth could I look it up? And
if I did know, why would I bother? The strategy
was a mystery to me. It's a mystery to Meno,
too, though Sokrates feigns concern over the
sophistical potential of Meno's question: "Oh, I
see where you're heading! Do you realize what
an eristical argument you've introduced?" Meno
acknowledges that he sees the problem, but denies eristical intent. He really wants Sokrates to
explain how you can search for something about
which you know nothing.

Sokrates' answer is startling — unless one
has been attending to the various Pythagorean
gestures positioned in the dramatic landscape.
He says he has heard wise people, both men
and women (the emphasis on the inclusion of
women is clear), talk about divine matters …
and he breaks off. Meno, intrigued, presses him;
and he continues; but I think we should hear
the expansion preceded by a real silence. What
he heard was, he thought, both beautiful and
true. The speakers were both priests and priestesses, who had studied so as to be able to give a
"reasoned account of their ministry" (81a). Pin-
dar and other divine poets say the same thing.
"What do you think, Meno, is what they say
true?" What they say is that the soul is immortal, never perishes, but is reborn after dying. He
quotes poetry — Persephone's release of souls
from the underworld after nine years, following
requittal of their *penthos*. Because it is immortal, "has seen all things here and in the underworld," there is nothing the soul has not learned
[*sic*] — about virtue and everything else. So it's
not surprising that it can recollect what it knew
[ἠπίστατο]. And since all of nature is akin, you
just need to remember one little piece to get you

REPUBLIC 455d–e: Then
there is no way of life
concerned with the
management of the city
that belongs to a woman
because she's a woman
or to a man because he's
a man, but the various
natures [φύσεις] are dis-
tributed in the same way
in both creatures [ζῴω].
Women share by nature
in every way of life just as
men do, but in all of them
women are weaker than
men.

started: the rest will follow if you are brave and don't get tired of the search. And that's why it's possible to search for what you (think you) don't know — you actually *do* know it, and what we call 'learning' is really just remembering! Don't listen to that eristical skepticism — it just makes people fainthearted. This other account makes them keen and energetic. He, Sokrates, puts his trust in it, and is ready to search with Meno for what virtue is.

We must note several things here. First, that there is no irony or doubt: this is a profession of profound faith. Secondly, it *is*, overtly, a profession of faith, not a bad or weak argument. Thirdly, to the extent that justification is provided, it is phenomenological and aesthetic, and moral: the account, says Sokrates, struck him as true and beautiful; and trusting it makes us better persons. There is no attempt to provide logical or empirical grounds for belief. Finally, there is its philosophical psychology: Plato is clearly advocating a method that looks distressingly like brainwashing. First you beat them up, disorient them, break them down, and then, when they're at their most vulnerable, you slot in the belief system you want them to adopt. Why should we call any of this philosophy?

An interesting question. Interesting because of what it reveals about our own preconceptions and then because, once we see what it reveals about us, we realize Plato is miles ahead of us. For there are arguments in Plato as penetrating as any in Aristotle, and as sophistical as any in Gorgias. There is no question he is an adept in the elenctic and eristical arts. And there is no question that he believes both are skills essential to the practice of philosophy.* Why, then, this

OED: *Æsthetic* [mod. ad. Gr. αἰσθητικ -ός, of or pertaining to αἰσθητά, things perceptible by the senses, things material … also 'perceptive, sharp in the senses'; f. vb. stem αἰσθε- 'feel, apprehend by the senses'…]

* See, for example, *Phaedo* 97d or *Phaidros* 261d *ff.*

undefended mumbo-jumbo? Why its placement
at such a critical psychological juncture? Isn't
the point that Meno should learn to think for
himself?

Yes. That is precisely the point. What Plato
has understood, and what the current culture of
professional philosophy has not grasped, is the
relationship between thinking and skepticism.
Thinking — as Pyrrhonians and poststructural-
ists well know* — *leads* to skepticism: that is its
only defensible result. (This is why Plato's interest in Thrasymakhos is so intense: the kid has
real intellectual talent.) But it is not an acceptable result — not only can it precipitate cynicism
and its attendant lassitudes, it cripples thinking
itself. It deprives it of objects, and so it turns on
itself, where its effect is utterly corrosive. Some
— Sextus Empiricus, for example — take this
corrosion to be the goal of thought: the peace
of mind that is achieved when the impulse to
think is destroyed. But this, it seems to me and,
I speculate, seemed to Plato, is like promoting
the self-digestion of the stomach because one is
offended by the workings of the bowel. Thinking
is the acid that the mind uses to digest the world;
it is one of the most fundamental ways in which
we are nourished. The aim, then, must be to learn
to contain thinking, while keeping it alive. And —
Plato's insight — it turns out that life-sustaining
thinking is impossible without hope. Hope is
what keeps it turned towards reality.

Meno has been started on the path. Sokrates
has produced a collision between the socially
acceptable notion that power and wealth must
be acquired nicely, and Meno's intuition that
they are the only things that really matter. In
the silence following the crash, Meno has begun

* For a compelling discussion of the relationship
between contemporary
and ancient skepticism
see Martha Nussbaum,
"Skepticism about Prac-
tical Reason in Literature
and the Law," *Harvard
Law Review* 107 (1994):
714–44.

to wonder. One of the cruellest things Sokrates might do to him would be to abandon him — especially if he has reason to suspect Meno lacks the emotional, spiritual, and characterological resources to bootstrap himself out of thinking's inevitable dead, or deadening, end. It is critical, then, in the aftermath of his defeat that support be provided. "You're right. None of it makes any sense. It's hard to know where to turn. But try trusting *erōs.* What draws you, what undeniably pulls you, in this chaos? Here's something that, in moments like the one you're experiencing now, has incontrovertibly drawn me."

Having noted the structural similarities with brainwashing, it is crucial that we also note the differences: instead of *telling* Meno what to believe — adding him to a contingent of mindless cult followers, as it were — Sokrates *invites* him to stand beside him. His tone is not inflated, merely enthused: "I was told this; I thought it beautiful; I have chosen to trust it. What do you think? Do you find it beautiful, too?" not "Look deeply into my eyes: you will now swear eternal obedience to the Dog, god of the Egyptians, and know yourself born again." Philosophy depends on distinguishing between these two attitudes, just as it depends on distinguishing between critical reflection and nihilism. It breathes in the space between unreflective acceptance of dogma and the dizzy paralysis of skepticism. It opens the path of the examined life.

At 81e, Meno is caught up: for the first time, he is genuinely interested in the discussion itself; he has forgotten himself. "Yes, Sokrates," (in response to Sokrates' claim that he trusts the story

PHAIDROS 249d–250b: Now this takes me to the whole point of my discussion of [*erōs,*] the fourth kind of madness — that which someone shows when he sees the beauty we have down here and is reminded of true beauty ... This is the best and noblest of all the forms that possession by god can take for anyone who has it or is connected to it ... As I said, nature requires that the soul of every human being has seen reality; otherwise, no soul could have entered this sort of living thing ... Only a few remain whose memory is good enough; and they are startled when they see an image of what they saw up there. Then they are beside themselves [ἐκπλήττονται, *Cornford:* lose their self-possession], and their experience is beyond their comprehension because they cannot fully grasp what it is they are seeing.

and is willing to try with Meno to remember what virtue is),
"but how do you mean that we do not learn, but that what we
call learning is recollection? Can you teach me that this is so?"
(81e) Sokrates cannot have missed the tone here, but once again
accuses Meno of trying to trip him up by getting him to teach
him something, when he's said there's no teaching but only recollection. Meno apologizes: "No! No! I didn't mean it — really:
if you can show me, I want to be shown."

So: Sokrates has sparked attention in a very unpromising
subject. Meno is not yet willing to search for virtue, but he *is*
willing — truly willing — to be convinced he ought to try. This
is a remarkable piece of psychagogy on Sokrates' part, and the
work now is delicate — to keep the spark alive, to stabilize Meno's
interest without challenging him so much that he lapses into
boredom or, in panic, is thrown back onto his Gorgian rhetorical
haunches. For if Meno, too, were to come to trust — not cult-
ishly, but freely, reflectively — that learning is (or even might
be) recollection, this would indeed be the beginning of his acquisition of excellence. This trust, as I have argued, is, for Plato,
the foundation of hope; hope, in turn, allows thought to sustain,
rather than eviscerate, the life of the mind.

Thus we come to the physical and intellectual centre of the
dialogue, the famous slave boy demonstration. Before he begins,
Sokrates asks Meno to watch closely to see whether the slave is
recollecting, or learning from Sokrates [ἢ ἀναμιμνησκόμενος ἢ
μανθάνων παρ' ἐμοῦ] (82b56–7). My own reaction, when I first
read the dialogue as a student, was that *obviously* Sokrates was
teaching the kid. The whole 'demonstration' is a set of leading
questions to which the slave has given the expected answers. He's
a *slave*, after all — supposing he did start to think for himself, or,
more likely, supposing he didn't really see Sokrates' point, is he
going to let on? But to approach the intellectual drama in this
way is, I have come to think, to miss Plato's point. Two crucial
things are going on in this encounter, neither of which is affected
by the slave's political position or Sokrates' rhetorical technique.

The first I have already mentioned: the slave boy demonstration would, for an alert Athenian audience used to the rote learn-

ing of the *paideia,* invite the question "What is teaching?" Clearly Sokrates is doing something; but he's equally clearly not simply telling the boy the theorem and asking him to memorize it. And then we notice that in Meno's original question there are, of course, two undefined concepts: human excellence and teaching. And as soon as we notice that teaching is undefined, we realize that there is a difference between *imparting information* ("the Greek word for fish is spelled *iota psili, khi, theta, upsilon oxeia, sigma*") and *assisting someone towards understanding.* To say that someone has learned or been taught something is ambiguous with respect to these alternatives. And then, on yet a little more reflection, we realize that it is not that difficult to define — or at least to give an example of — imparting information, but that it is considerably more difficult to say in what the enabling of understanding consists.

Which is where the second crucial aspect of the demonstration comes in. There is no question that Sokrates' questions are leading, but there is equally no question — when we imagine the scene played out with living human beings — that the slave boy is engaged by the puzzle. He is neither listless nor cowering; he doesn't shrug when his initial intuitions are shown to be false — he is surprised. He answers directly, and with some resolution, whenever he can. When, at 84a, he is finally forced to admit his intuitions have run out, he is again surprised, rather than sullen. (For contrast, compare Thrasymakhos at *Republic* 351e8 or 352a11: Plato can convey disengaged 'yea-saying' beautifully when he wants to.) And as Sokrates leads him towards the solution, drawing the double-sized square at 85a, the slave at

LUDWIG WITTGENSTEIN: Let us imagine the following example: A writes series of numbers down; B watches him and tries to find a law for the sequence of numbers. If he succeeds he exclaims: "Now I can go on!" —— So this capacity, this understanding, is something that makes its appearance in a moment...

Or again, B does not think of formulae. He watches A writing his numbers down with a certain feeling of tension, and all sorts of vague thoughts go through his head. Finally he asks himself: "What is the series of differences?" He finds the series 4, 6, 8, 10 and says: Now I can go on.

... —Or he says nothing at all and simply continues the series. Perhaps he had what may be called the sensation "that's easy!" (Such a sensation is, for example, that of a light quick intake of breath, as when one is slightly startled.)

first does not understand; but as Sokrates talks him through, he *gets* it. And this is the crucial thing. He *grasps* that the square of the right area is based on the diagonal, he *sees* it, pointing to it and exclaiming "Most certainly, Sokrates!" when Sokrates spells out what his gesture commits him to.

In a sense, it doesn't matter that the slave sees it; what matters is that we do. Repeatedly, when I have taught this passage, someone gasps or even cries out. The impact of the proof is unquestionable. We see that it *has* to be so — that it is not a matter of convention, or custom, or even an empirical fact. It is seeing *this* — that it *has* to be so — that is at the heart of the passage, and the dialogue, and, I believe, Plato's lifework. The slave has not merely received and memorized the information that the square double in size is built on the diagonal: he has — at least for the moment — *understood* it. And this is deeply mysterious.

It is so mysterious that to this day there is no universally accepted account of what constitutes a proof. Yet, not only do we know one when we see one, we can distinguish better and worse. When I reflect on my own experience, it is clear that the perception of necessary truth involves a kind of intellectual *phenomenology* — that necessary truth has a distinct *feel,* especially when it is given elegant and economical expression. This is what prompts the gasps, or the involuntarily raised eyebrows, in the classroom. It is what comforted Arthur Koestler in his Spanish prison. It is why allusions to geometry and geometrical concepts abound in Plato's work.

For it is the *feeling* for necessary truth that was, I believe, the litmus of philosophical talent

SYMPOSIUM 200a:
Instead of what's likely, said Socrates, ask yourself whether it's necessary [ἀνάγκη] …

MARJORIE WIKLER SENECHAL: Paul Erdős, the great twentieth-century mathematician who loved only numbers, an atheist, claimed that God has a book in which the best proof of every theorem is written. Erdős never listed the criteria a proof must satisfy to be inscribed in God's book: he didn't need to. Though no one has seen the book or ever will, all mathematicians know that Euclid's proof of the infinitude of primes is in it, and no mathematician doubts that computer-generated proofs, the kind that methodically check case after case, are not. The proofs in God's book are elegant. They surprise. In other words, they are light, quick, exact, and visible.

for Plato. Once you admit that there's a phenomenological difference between memorized
information and mathematical proof, you're done
for: you'll end up as a mathematician or a philosopher or both. What must be going on in the
mind in order for this difference to exist? Any
non-skeptical answer leads immediately to great
puzzles in metaphysics. (Indeed, one understanding of skepticism sees it as a characterological refusal of this challenge.) Plato's answer — which is
that since it *feels* like seeing, it *is* a kind of seeing,
with the mind's eye, of non-physical Forms —
has generated millennia of dispute. But because
no counter-proposal has managed to solve all
the apparent problems either, we are led back
and again to reflect on the tally between Plato's
account and our experience of thinking in the
world.

LISTER SINCLAIR: ...
Is simple the same as
elegant? Is the best proof
a simple proof?

JOHN CONWAY: I'd
hesitate to say it's the
same, but it's very closely
related, isn't it?... There's a
funny feeling I get some-
times ... everything's as it
should be.

LISTER SINCLAIR: ...
That sense of rightness,
of everything falling
beautifully into place.

JOHN CONWAY:
... fitting.

But what has mathematics to do with virtue?
For Plato, a number of things. The context of the
demonstration is, of course, Meno's request for
some evidence that Sokrates' astonishing claim
about recollection is true. Both Sokrates' summary comments, and his allusion to Meno's torpedo fish image in the course of the demonstration, make it clear that it is to serve as a model for
the investigation of virtue. First, we use elenctic
techniques to rid ourselves of faulty beliefs or
intuitions; this produces *aporia*, which in turn
precipitates a longing to know what we now *realize* we don't know. Then, if we're lucky, Sokrates
comes along and asks us leading questions ("Did
you think Theaitetos behaved virtuously when
we saw him the other day? Why? Now, can we
generalize the case in this fashion?") so that our

PHAEDO 73a: When
people are asked
questions, as long as the
questioner questions
well, they tell everything
the way it is ...

KRATYLOS 390C: And the
man who knows how
to ask and answer [the
right] questions you call a
dialectician?

buried memory of the Form of virtue (or perhaps
the Form of justice or piety) springs back into
focus. We will then be in the position of the slave
boy with respect to the proof he has just grasped:

*These opinions [will] have been stirred up [in us]
like a dream, but if [we] were repeatedly asked
these same questions in various ways ... in the
end [our] understanding [ἐπιστήμη] ... would
be as precise as anyone's ... And [we] will know
without having been [given information], but only
questioned, and [will] find the knowledge [ἐπι-
στήμη] within [ourselves] ... And is not finding
knowledge within oneself recollection?* [based on
Grube, 85c–d]

Meno concurs in the case of the slave and
the proof, and it is clear we are meant to concur
in the case of virtue. Sokrates presses the point
at 85e, getting Meno to repeat that the slave has
not been taught (*viz*, told), and asserting that
the boy "will perform in the same way about all
geometry, and *all other [forms of] learning*" (καὶ
τῶν ἄλλων μαθημάτων ἁπάντων, my empha-
sis). Sokrates draws the conclusion that dove-
tails with the Mysteries: If the opinions [δόξαι]
are in him, and no one put them there, then he
acquired them at some time when he was not a
human being.

PHAIDROS 247d: On the
way around [heaven, the
soul] has a view of Justice
as it is; it has a view of
Self-control; it has a view
of Knowledge [ἐπιστήμη]
— not the knowledge that
is close to change ... [but]
the knowledge of what
really is what it is.

*If then, during the time he exists and is not a hu-
man being he will have true opinions which, when
stirred by questioning, become knowledge [ἐπι-
στῆμαι γίγνονται], will not his soul have learned
[μεμαθηκυῖα ἔσται] during all time?... Then if
the truth about reality is always in our soul, the
soul would be immortal so that you should always*

*confidently try to seek out and recollect what you
do not know at present* [ὃ μὴ τυγχάνεις ἐπιστάμε-
νος νῦν] — *that is, what you do not recollect?*
[Grube, 86a–b]

Or: Our experience of necessary truth is
explained by the Eleusinian package deal; and
that package deal gives us reason to hope we can
understand virtue, too.

But I believe further that, for Plato — for all
Pythagoreans? — it's also the case that our experience of virtue gives us reason to believe in
the Eleusinian package deal. My hunch is this:
not only was Plato alert to the phenomenology
of necessary truth, he was also deeply impressed
by the phenomenological *similarity* between our
experience of necessary truth and our apprehension of moral beauty.

Consider first the intensity of his preoccupation with moral beauty as it appears in the
figure of Sokrates, yet his unwillingness simply
to sign on as an acolyte. We feel everywhere
in Plato's work both his astonishment at moral
beauty and the *press* of inquiry: *How could this
be so?* Consider also the striking juxtapositions:
here, in *Meno,* the invitation to model an investigation of virtue on a search for mathematical
truth; or Aristoxenos' account of his lecture
on the Good as an exposition of mathematical
ideas; or in *Republic* VI, the way the analogy of
the divided line (the insistence on those pro-
portions, the insistence on a method involving
'hypothesis') follows on the heels of an attempt
to characterize the Good; or the climax of the
argument in *Gorgias* in which Kallikles' moral
skepticism, the *pleonexia* he substitutes for virtue, is laid at the door of his neglect of geometry

ARISTOXENOS: Aristotle
was wont to relate that
most of those who
heard Plato's Discourse
(ἀκρόασις) on the Good
had the following experi-
ence. Each came thinking
he would be told some-
thing about one of the
recognized human goods,
such as Wealth, Health ➤

or Strength, or, in sum, some marvellous Happiness. But when it appeared that Plato was to talk on Mathematics and Numbers and Geometry and Astronomy, leading up to the statement that the Good was Unity (ὅτι ἀγαθόν ἐστιν ἕν), they were overwhelmed by the paradox of the whole matter. Some then pooh-poohed the whole thing and others were outraged by it.

SYMPOSIUM 215e & 216b: ... I swear to you, the moment [Socrates] starts to speak, I am beside myself: my heart starts leaping in my chest, the tears come streaming down my face ... and, let me tell you, I am not alone ... like the Sirens, he could make me stay by his side till I die.

(508a). The writing in these passages does not suggest excited speculation; it is expressive of deep conviction. But what could the grounds for such conviction be? Plato's culture, like our own, was riddled with suspicion of moral certainty; the default position for intellectuals was moral relativism. Plato was not a naïf; and he had an extraordinary ability to perceive and represent human character. Depravity, turpitude, culpable innocence, untempered idealism, recklessness, banality — all these spring to life in his pages. The notion that mathematical truth and moral insight were connected was not itself the result of immature idealism, nor of geeky tinkering in the workshop of nutty ideas. Plato must have seen and experienced the connection in a way that could not be gainsaid by his acute observation of the human pageant.

We experience moral beauty ourselves whenever we are moved deeply — and by relativist lights, inexplicably — by another's courage or generosity or integrity. We are moved not because they have done the 'right' thing, the culturally required or acceptable or expected thing, the thing we would understand in the circumstances — we are moved because often they have acted *against* cultural or circumstantial requirements. And sometimes the gesture is quite small; almost always it is unselfaware. But the tears start involuntarily in our eyes, and, like Alkibiades, we sense the touch of something that could, if we let it, claim our whole lives. It seems to go deeper than culture, and it feels, at the same time, both simple and very pure. These are characteristics the phenomenology of moral beauty shares with the phenomenology of certain elegant mathematical proofs. I don't here wish to insist that we adopt Plato's account — immortal Forms apprehended by immortal souls — but only to suggest why the Eleusinian package deal might have appealed to him. And to record that I am myself struck by the phenomenological resemblance between moral and mathematical beauty that I believe struck him.

Meno, for his part, has appreciated the force of Sokrates' account of the Eleusinian package deal, but doesn't know quite what to say. He has responded to many of the rhetorical questions in Sokrates' summary at 86a–b with standard eristical hedges: "It appears so" or "Likely so." But the *tone* seems genuine. Plato does not show Sokrates put on his guard. We should then, I think, imagine Meno using stock phrases partly out of habit and partly because he's actually trying to think through what he's seen and what Sokrates has said. Now, at 86b5–6, he says: "What you say seems [right] to me, Sokrates, I don't know how." Sokrates senses that the flame is still lit, but wavering, and replies that he can't claim complete confidence in all aspects of the argument he's offered — the immortality of the soul, the recollectability of knowledge — but there is one thing for which he is "determined to do battle, as far as [he is] able, both in word and deed" (Lamb 86c). This is the claim with which he started, namely that "we will be better men, braver and less idle, if we believe that one must search for the things one does not know, rather than if we believe that it is not possible" (Grube 86b). He offers, in other words, a reiteration of the initial moral defence. We *become* virtuous by believing what the mathematical demonstration suggests but does not prove; we awaken excellence, actually produce it in ourselves, by

PORPHYRY: It is said that Dionysius at one time wanted to test [Pythagorean] mutual fidelity under imprisonment. He contrived this plan. Phintias was arrested, and taken before the tyrant, and charged with plotting against the tyrant, convicted, and condemned to death. Phintias, accepting the situation, asked to be given the rest of the day to arrange his own affairs, and those of Damon, his friend and associate, who now would have to assume the management. He therefore asked for a temporary release, leaving Damon as security for his appearance. Dionysius granted the request, and they sent for Damon, who agreed to remain until Phintias should return ... those who had first suggested the experiment scoffed at Damon, saying he was in danger of losing his life. But to the general surprise, near sunset Phintias came to die. Dionysius then expressed his admiration, embraced them both, and asked to be received as a third in their friendship ... they refused this, though assigning no reason therefore.

PROTAGORAS 358d: ... no
one goes willingly toward
the bad or what he be-
lieves to be bad; neither
is it in human nature, so
it seems, to want to go
toward what one believes
to be bad instead of to
the good. And when he is
forced to choose between
one of two bad things,
no one will choose the
greater if he is able to
choose the lesser.

SCHOOL OF PLATO:
ἐπιστήμη (epistēmē),
knowledge: conception of
the soul which cannot be
dislodged by reasoning;
ability to conceive one or
more things which cannot
be dislodged by reason-
ing; true argument which
cannot be dislodged by
thinking.

rejecting skepticism about it. Skepticism, in
blunting philosophical desire, makes us morally
unattractive. It is a very surprising turn and must,
I think, affect our sense of Plato's overall project.
In contemporary North American philosophy,
we often imagine that the correct epistemology
and metaphysics will provide the foundations for
an adequate ethics. Plato suggests otherwise: we
must choose our metaphysics and epistemologies
on the strength of their moral outcomes. This
choice requires unencumbered *erōs* — unfettered,
it only ever desires the good.

The final observation that we are invited
to make about virtue in the light of the mathematical demonstration is related to the buried
theme concerning the nature of teaching. If virtue is knowledge that is recoverable by an initial scouring away of received social opinion
followed by an attempt to pick up the scent of
necessity, it cannot be construed as a kind of information. It must be acquired through 'seeing'
or understanding; and its convictions must be
unshakable, themselves 'necessary,' the sort of
things one could not change one's mind about
even if one wanted to. And further, I suspect the
idea would be that we are put in mind of those
unshakable convictions, clear to us though we
cannot give a full account of them, by their traces
in the physical world — the equivalent in human gestures of the lines Sokrates draws in the
sand, an uneducated slave pointing excitedly at
something that must have the length √8, an irrational number, a concept whose existence taxes
the comprehension of the most skilled experts.
The proof of the theorem is not those lines; they
are simply an imperfect sketch of what we hold
in our mind's eye. Let everyone die who has seen

such lines, the theorem remains a theorem, and chances are it will be recognized again some day. Let the person who best embodies human excellence vanish, let everyone who knew him vanish as well, chances are what he embodied will manifest itself again, and will be recognized as such.

◆

We enter now on the third, final, and most dramatically complex section of the dialogue, its denouement. As I have indicated, Plato has already given us the tools to address the main questions posed by the dialogue: Can virtue be taught? What is virtue? How can we search for what we do not know? We know what a good definition of virtue will look like; we know how and why we ought to pursue it; we have been invited to reflect on the ambiguity implicit in the notion of teaching, and have seen that — whatever we call it — a technique that produces understanding rather than memorized information is liable to be essential to virtue's manifestation in human lives. We have seen that all this, in Plato's view, is bound up with a belief in reincarnation and the idea that in its nonembodied existence, the soul is exposed to immutable truths whose imprint it retains even when it is not consciously able to recall them. Why now do we take up Meno's question again and argue via two extraordinary reverses to a conclusion that capitalizes on none of the foregoing? The answer, I believe, has to do with character, and Plato's sense of its fundamental importance to genuine philosophical endeavour.

We have had the moment of approximate confession, Meno's "you're right, I don't know how," followed by Sokrates' "forget the details,

PHAIDROS 250a: But not every soul is easily reminded of the reality there by what it finds here — not souls that got only a brief glance at the reality there, not souls who had such bad luck when they fell down here that they were twisted by bad company into lives of injustice so that they forgot the sacred objects they had seen before.

just take heart." And Sokrates, trying to establish a flagging Meno
at the trailhead, to drive a tent peg, says: "Since we are of one
mind — since now both of us trust that it makes sense to try to
find out what we don't know — shall we, together, try to find
out what virtue is?" It is, as it were, the proposal at the altar, the
moment of intellectual wedding.

But Meno's courage, as we sensed it would, fails him. "By
all means. But still, Sokrates, for me, what I'd like *best* [a little
smile, coy, but nervousness underneath] would be to go back to
the question I asked first, you know, the one about whether virtue can be taught? Maybe we can pursue our joint investigation
around that, whether it is teachable, or a natural gift, or whatever." Sokrates is, of course, disappointed — a silence. But he's
not altogether surprised — so the silence is short. "It's not how
I'd do it, Meno. But since you have no self-control, confusing
its absence with freedom, and since you try to rule me — and
are successful — I'm at your mercy. I'll yield to you — what else
can I do? So: we must ask what *sort* of thing it is, when we don't
know *what* it is at all ..." (86d–e).

What does Sokrates mean, Meno is successful in ruling him?
Once again, in the rhetoric, we're dealing with a reversal of the
standard seduction tropes of gay Athens; but surely, at this point,
it's clear that this is entirely a game. Sokrates does not find Meno
particularly attractive and he can, in fact does, command the
discussion. So why not insist that they pursue the nature of virtue — as everything so far has prepared them to do? — Because,
as he has just demonstrated, Meno is not ready. He has had a
glimpse, the flame has riffled along the edge of his intelligence;
but it has not caught. Meno's timidity, his retreat into the familiar, shows that he can't cope with real discussion. As Sokrates
keeps insisting, such discussion requires courage.

Thus, Meno chooses the path. As ever, though, Sokrates determines how they will walk it. He suggests that Meno "relax his
rule" enough to allow them to investigate virtue's teachability "by
means of a hypothesis" (86e). He says he means *hypothesis* in
the geometer's sense, and gives an example that both translators
and commentators struggle to make sense of. I can't make sense

of it. But I don't doubt that the Academy's audience, and perhaps Pythagoreans elsewhere, knew precisely the problem or proof to which Sokrates is made here to refer by way of example.

Meno is not given the opportunity to get a word in edgewise, but it is difficult to imagine that he understands. Maybe he does. He has enough geometry to have seen, at 82e10, that in proposing to build the double-sized square on a line twice as long as the original base, the slave *certainly* did not know the answer. (Οὐ δῆτα! he exclaimed in response to Sokrates' query.) If Meno himself had been seeing the proof for the first time, his reply at that stage would not have been as quick or confident. And Sokrates clearly expected him to know the answer. So, maybe the proof was part of a gentleman's education? Maybe Meno was known by Sokrates to have had some contact with the Pythagorean brotherhood? Both seem implausible. (The proof, as just noted, when worked with a square two units on a side, produces a diagonal of length $\sqrt{8}$, which was a cutting-edge mathematical concept at the time. And Meno's character, as it is revealed in this dialogue, is nothing like that of the intelligent, restrained, courageous Pythagoreans we meet in *Phaedo*.) But if Meno is well versed in mathematics, it's a puzzle that Plato does not make more of the tension between his possession of such knowledge and his characterological difference from the Pythagorean ideal. And if he is not, then Sokrates' gesture here, the unintelligibility of the example, constitutes a kind of bullying or interlocutory contempt. — It would appear that his interior patience has finally snapped.

For it turns out that conceptually it doesn't matter for the line of argument as a whole that the example is unintelligible. As soon as Sokrates switches to talk of virtue rather than inscribed triangles and rectangles, it is clear what he has in mind. Which then raises the question: Why is the mathematical example — which is presented too sketchily for non-initiates to make sense of — here? As with the discussion of good definitions, there is a seamless transition if it is left out: "please relax your rule a little bit for me and agree to investigate whether it is teachable or not by means of a hypothesis ... and say this: Among the things existing in the soul, of what sort is virtue, that it should be teachable?" (86e2–5/87b5–6) Because I cannot untangle the example, I cannot say precisely in what its significance lies. But its presence, and its sketchiness, are evidence that the intended audience for the dialogue did consist of mathematical adepts of some kind; and that this should condition our reading throughout. It is my *guess* that it is also evidence that Sokrates has essentially abandoned the project of converting Meno to the philosophic life: throughout the remainder of the dialogue, Sokrates aims the discussion and a good deal of irony well over Meno's head. He clearly doesn't expect Meno to pick up and seems at times to be *displaying* Meno's ignorance — almost as though he were conducting a circus act. For whom? — The same audience that would have recognized at once the example he was using to illustrate the 'method of hypothesis.'

As the setting of the question with reference to virtue illustrates, the move Plato has in mind has a Kantian cast: we are investigating the grounds of the possibility of teachable things. Sokrates quickly draws the conclusion that for a thing to be teachable it must be knowledge, to which he then adds the reverse conditional, making the connection between teachability and knowledge into a biconditional: "if virtue is a kind of knowledge, it is clear that it could be taught" (87c). Meno, confidently, nods. But note that Sokrates has slipped in a startling aside to which Meno does not respond: "In the first place, if [virtue] is something dissimilar or similar to knowledge, is it teachable or not — or, as we were just saying now, recollectable [or not]? *Let's not quibble* about which term we use — is it teachable?" Wait a minute. Let's not quibble about which term we use? Yet how many times

REPUBLIC 511b: Then also understand that, by the [top] subsection of the intelligible, I mean that which reason itself grasps by the power of dialectic. It does not consider these hypotheses as first principles but truly as hypotheses — as stepping stones to take off from, enabling it to reach the unhypothetical first principle of everything.

in the course of the demonstration with the slave did Sokrates insist on the distinction? "I'm not teaching, he's recollecting!" I count four explicit underlinings: 82b, 82e, 84c–d, 85d. What could Plato have in mind here? How can it now, suddenly, not matter?

One possibility is that Plato is inviting us to observe whether or not Meno is awake. He's not. Even if we imagine Sokrates' aside occasioned by a raised eyebrow, when Sokrates gives him a chance to speak, Meno does not venture a query, let alone voice a protest. Another possibility is that Sokrates is making the point that both information and 'recollectable understanding' are *things that can be known,* and that it is the genus here that is of paramount importance. This, of course, accords with Plato's view elsewhere, but it sits in surprising tension with the conclusion of the dialogue, if that conclusion is taken at face value. We know that Sokrates thinks we should trust that virtue is recollectable; this aside means, I believe, that we are meant to understand that he *therefore thinks we should trust that it is something that can be known.* For virtue to be teachable or recollectable, it must belong to the genus knowledge. It cannot, then, be his view that virtue is a matter of 'true opinion' in the sense of a 'gift from the gods.' And now we note that in the closing speeches in which this conclusion is drawn, Sokrates twice makes it contingent on the soundness of the reasoning that has led to it. Reading with foreknowledge of those warnings, knowing that Sokrates thinks the question Meno has insisted on is misguided, we should, I believe, be on the lookout for slips in reasoning in what follows — perhaps even slips that Plato cues as such.

Having concluded that for virtue to be teachable *or* recollectable it must be a form of knowledge, Sokrates says that the next question must be whether it *is* a form of knowledge, or something else.

But isn't this — more or less — the investigation Meno has declined, into the nature of virtue? In a way; but from the point of view of dialectical hierarchies, it's coming at it from the wrong end. Meno is not attempting to "recollect in order, as one must." It's as though a field naturalist were to leap to reflection on the

genus of some plant, without looking carefully
at its species characteristics: Will this thing grow
in boggy territory? — Well, yes, if it's a *Vaccin-
ium*. But what is it? A blueberry, a huckleberry?
Or is it actually a saskatoon? — No, says Meno,
I don't want to look at it carefully and find out,
I don't want to *see*; let's stick with the question
whether it'll grow in a bog.

In pursuance of their generic question,
Sokrates introduces another 'hypothesis,' that
virtue is good. (And in so doing, invites the
question: What are the grounds of the possibility that this is so? What must be the case for
human excellence to be a good thing? What an
extraordinary question.) Thus the issue becomes
the conceptual or ontological relation between
goodness and knowledge: We proceed on the
hypothesis that virtue is good; if it turns out to
be impossible for something to be good without
its being knowledge, then (on the hypothesis that
virtue is good), virtue is knowledge. What an
extraordinary claim. Isn't it patently obvious that
there are good things that aren't knowledge? —
Love, for example; life; a glass of cold water on a
hot day. But look at these examples: Plato would
challenge them all. Love is not good until it has
climbed Diotima's ladder, or at least embarked
on the project — which is, essentially, a discipline that enables one to see love's proper object
(*Symposium* 212a). Life, we are told in *Phaedo*,
is — or should be — simply practising for death
(64a), a condition in which the soul can hope to
be released into perfect understanding. A glass
of water on a hot day may or may not be a good
thing, depending on one's constitution or condition; and to the extent that it constitutes a kind

PHAEDO 101d–e: And
when you must give
an account of your
hypothesis itself you will
proceed in the same way:
you will assume another
hypothesis, the one
which seems to you best
of the higher ones until
you come to something
acceptable ...

REPUBLIC 509b: ... the
good is not being, but
superior to it in rank and
power.

of satiation of mere bodily appetite, we know that, for Plato, it's not even on the radar as a potential candidate for goodness. — In other words, what we have here is one of the *planks* in the Platonic position: the equation of goodness with knowledge. And, not surprisingly, the argument does not proceed by way of an attempt to prove this general claim; its focus is in fact much narrower. It attempts to convince us that humans cannot be excellent in the absence of prudence or good sense.

It is an argument reminiscent of the one that closes *Protagoras*. Indeed, we should note the striking similarity between this section of *Meno* and *Protagoras* as a whole: here, we start with an argument that, because of the way capacities or temperaments or inclinations ("things of the soul" — κατὰ τὴν ψυχήν) are managed by excellent humans, human excellence is knowledge (φρόνησις throughout, until Meno's summary at 89c, which employs ἐπιστήμη); and we follow it with an argument that since such excellence is apparently not reliably transmissable, even from father to son, it cannot be taught. In *Protagoras*, these arguments are mounted in reverse order, and in between them is placed (among other things) a discussion of the relation between something's being good and its being "beneficial" (ὠφέλιμος), a theme that is woven into the first argument in *Meno*. Courage, in both dialogues, is the specific virtue that receives fullest treatment. *Meno*, I believe, was composed to be read or experienced after *Protagoras*. *Protagoras* clearly precedes *Meno* in the historical sequence of events that culminates in Sokrates' death. So we are, I believe — in the full unfolding of Plato's corpus — intended to come on the first argument in *Meno* having heard a version of it before, and knowing, as it were, what comes next. Nor is it an accident that the arguments occur in reverse order. Perhaps their construction reflects historical facts about two of Sokrates' conversations, but if so that is not why Plato has preserved it. The reversed order, I think, constitutes a deliberate challenge. We are not to read 'virtue must be knowledge but it appears it can't be taught' nor 'apparently, virtue can't be taught, although, when you think about it, what can it be but knowledge.' Rather, standing back from both dialogues, I believe we are to hear: Virtue is knowledge *and* it is not transmissable: what are the grounds of possibility of this state of affairs?

The gist of the argument that virtue is knowledge in *Meno* is this: virtue is that by which, or through which, we are good. What makes something good is that it benefits us. Thus (here I gloss the sense, not the actual moves, of the argument) virtue, in our souls, will be that whereby the 'things of the soul' are made to benefit us. Consider ἀνδρεία. (We usually translate this into English with the word 'courage,' which makes it very hard to see — particularly in the wake of Aristotle, or, indeed, the concluding pages of *Protagoras* — how it could be harmful. But that it can be harmful is key to the argument. And Liddell & Scott's *Lexicon* notes that there is both good and bad ἀνδρεία. I suggest, then, that we translate it as *manly spirit*, which can play both ways.) Consider manly spirit. If you give it free rein, without thinking, it can get you into trouble. Only when it is disciplined by good sense, a kind of wisdom, does it benefit you. And it's the same with all 'things of the soul' (self-control, intelligence, etc., etc.), indeed, it's the same even with external things like wealth: directed by wisdom they bring happiness, but, in the absence of wisdom, they bring its opposite. In sum, "about everything: all other human activities depend on the soul, and those of the soul itself depend on wisdom [φρόνησις] if they are to be good [ἀγαθά]." (88e) So, virtue, the thing through which we and the things of our soul are made to benefit us, is wisdom. (The conversion from φρόνησις to ἐπιστήμη is yet to come.)

The argument is, by contemporary analytic lights, shoddy. It has holes you could toss a textbook on informal fallacies through. But Aristotle thought well enough of it to put a version of it at the heart of his own account of the virtues. I believe that Plato would readily have assented to the accusation of sketchiness, but not to the suggestion that the argument couldn't be fleshed out into something wholly compelling. The defeat of Protagoras at the hands of a detailed version of the sub-argument on courage, the emphasis throughout Plato's work — from *Apology* through *Ion* to *Phaidros* — on wisdom as the key to excellence of any kind, suggests to me that we are meant to regard the conclusion as true. In other words, although the argument seems suspect to contemporary ears, I do not think that it is here that we are to look for the errors in reasoning that lead to the view that virtue is merely true opinion.

Meno has been nodding agreement throughout. Now he says, "It seems to me that what you say, Sokrates, is excellent!" (89a) So Sokrates has scored at least a partial victory. We still can't give a full account — we have not penetrated to the conditions of possibility of the conclusion — but we have provided a generic answer, as it were, to the question "What is virtue?" It is the wisdom that directs all things in the human soul and in human affairs.

Why isn't this the high point of the dialogue, then, its rhetorical peak? Because the *fact* is nothing if it is not *understood*, if we don't *see* it, grasp what *has* to be the case for it to be true and thereby take it into our souls. Sokrates' project is psychagogic, and it is clear that Meno's soul is not, at this point, going to be led out. The Academic audience is in on all this. Its members accept that virtue is innate wisdom, akin to the mathematical understanding elicited from the slave boy. It is to that audience that Sokrates now plays.

"Given that what I've said is excellent, Meno, then good men are not good by nature." (Of course, this doesn't follow. Virtue is wisdom, but, according to Plato, the wisdom is innate. The audience knows this; so its members are watching Sokrates set Meno up.) "I don't think they are!" Meno says. "Right. Because if they were ..." — and now Sokrates rehearses the educational strategy of *Republic*, based on the myth of the metals, and echoing the reincarnation story he tells in *Phaidros*. It is a complicated move. Superficially, he appears to be suggesting that if good men were good by nature then this strategy would be heartily endorsed by the state; obviously it isn't; so obviously the good aren't good by nature. But unless *all* of *Republic* is ironic (a possibility, but a remote one), it is an educational strategy in which Plato fervently believes: he really thinks there are 'gold' souls that saw and are capable of remembering more of their disembodied journey at the

PHAIDROS 247b-d: But
when the souls we call
immortals reach the top,
they move outward and
take their stand on the
high ridge of heaven,
where its circular motion
carries them around ...
while they gaze upon
what is outside heaven.
  The place beyond
heaven — none of our
earthly poets has ever
sung or ever will sing its
praises enough!... What
is in this place is without
colour and without shape
and without solidity, a
being that really is what
it is, the subject of all
true knowledge, visible
only to intelligence, the
soul's steersman ... [the
soul] is delighted at last
to be seeing what is real
and watching what is
true, feeding on all this
and feeling wonderful,
until the circular motion
brings it around to where
it started.

rim of heaven, and that they ought to be given special treatment; they are a state's real national treasures, and should be sequestered and trained as befits its future philosopher-rulers. Even if one has not read *Republic* II and III, the rhetoric of Sokrates' speech here in *Meno* suggests that something is up: Sokrates spells out the consequences of thinking that the good are good by nature in beautiful and reverential detail; it reads like a prayer. If Meno had even the beginnings of a real rhetorical ear, he would hear the shift in Sokrates' tone. Instead he accepts the superficial invitation to condemn an educational policy we can tell Sokrates reveres. — And Sokrates shrugs, ever so slightly, for the audience's benefit. Or perhaps he winks.

It follows, he says, that since the good are not good by nature (that is, that there is no innate understanding of the sort Meno saw in action just a few minutes ago), that they must be good by education (that is, that the knowledge you agree virtue is, Meno, must be information). Meno is confidently effusive: "Necessarily, I think, this is how it is! And plainly, Sokrates, on our hypothesis, if in fact virtue is knowledge [ἐπιστήμη] it can be taught." (89c) The shift, at this point, to ἐπιστήμη is interesting. There is no question that the connotations of the word are different from those of φρόνησις, which usually indicates understanding permeated with or sustained by experience; and it's equally clear that commentators with better Greek than mine think the differences don't matter. As I've already mentioned, we have good reason to think that Plato was not interested in developing a technical vocabulary. And, as noted above, he uses forms of ἐπιστήμη throughout his summary of the slave boy dem-

onstration. Yet in *Protagoras,* there is a similar
shift. The argument there is carried out with reference to σοφία (another word with connotations
having to do with skill, and frequently translated
with the English word 'wisdom'); but its conclusion is again couched in terms of ἐπιστήμη.
Elsewhere, when Plato uses ἐπιστήμη he seems
to have in mind *secure* knowledge* — what the
slave boy sees, for example, or the results of ap-
plying 'the dialectical method.' These connections
with mathematics and method have led some
commentators to translate ἐπιστήμη as 'science.'
This makes good sense in Aristotle's case, but in
Plato's, its suitability is less clear: one connotation of 'science' is *ordered* knowing, which does
indeed echo Plato's conception of dialectic; but
another is *data,* or what I've been calling *information* — and this, as I've been arguing, is one
of the things Plato thinks that virtue isn't. In the
crucial passage at 87b–c, where Sokrates says
it doesn't matter whether you say it's taught or
recollected, the 'it' is something "similar to" ἐπιστήμη. But the passage concludes unequivocally:
"nothing other than ἐπιστήμη is taught to men."

Here's my guess: the shift from φρόνησις and
σοφία to ἐπιστήμη is significant, and if you catch
it, you've picked up on one of the things central
to the debate. Information is, paradigmatically,
teachable, that is, *tellable.* — Well: but look at that
sentence. *"Information?"* The etymology points
in exactly the direction I am trying to avoid, to
something taken into the soul, something that
permeates and structures thinking from within.
"Tellable?" As anyone experienced in storytelling
will tell [!] you, there is a fundamental difference between reciting something and actually
telling it; and the word 'tell' is etymologically

* See previous quotation from the School of Plato, page 178.

related to the memory technique of Collection and Division, the heart of Plato's dialectic. As we search for adequate vocabulary here, we realize how many of the old words involve making or invoking an interior impression or state. The idea that knowledge is like a photocopy — a superficial adhesion that does not penetrate its carrier — is one that is hard to express cleanly. I venture Plato also found it difficult.

Information — in the sense of data, facts — is paradigmatically teachable — in the sense that it can be conveyed by techniques that do not alter the character of the knower. Wisdom, however, is not paradigmatically teachable *in this sense* — even though, for Plato, a full grasp may require the ability to *demonstrate* one's understanding through a dialectical, 'causal' account given in terms of Forms. You acquire wisdom by doing (in the case of carpentry, say) or by recollecting (in the case of mathematics or philosophy). Understanding the theorem; virtue; 'philosophicalness' — all these *show up as* skill.

Importantly, it is possible to inculcate skill, especially where there's talent or an inborn knack. And, as the slave boy demonstration is meant to show, *anamnesis* can be facilitated by someone who either knows, or has a nose for, the right questions. As *Phaidros* argues, we often fall in love with images of what we need to remember, and all three of *Phaidros, Republic,* and *Symposium* claim that a lover's highest calling is to be brought to virtue by his beloved. In this sense, or these senses, wisdom *is* teachable — another person can be fundamental in the recovery of insight.

Whether or not Plato's vocabulary is significant, there is, I have urged, a crucial distinction

PHAIDROS 252e & 253b: Those who followed Zeus, for example, choose someone to love who is a Zeus himself in the nobility of his soul ... Hera's followers look for a kingly character ... And so it is for followers of Apollo or any other god: They take their god's path and seek for their own a boy whose nature is like the god's; and when they have got him they emulate the god, convincing the boy they love and training him to follow their god's pattern and way of life ...

between the kind of knowledge that can be recollected and the kind of knowledge that can be said. (The 'theorems' of virtue can, of course, be articulated, rehearsed, and memorized — "Courage is manly spirit disciplined by wisdom" — but such theorems have as much meaning in the absence of understanding as mathematical theorems which are memorized but not understood.) The distinction is at the heart of the relationship between the argument just concluded and the one on which Sokrates now embarks. Virtue is knowable — its objects exist and, with skill, can be accurately perceived by the mind's eye — but it cannot be conveyed as data — as facts, obvious or discovered, about the world.

➤

"But perhaps, Meno, we weren't right to agree to this?" — that is, to Meno's conclusion, on the basis of Sokrates' argument, that virtue can be taught. Meno expresses surprise — on what grounds does Sokrates doubt that virtue is ἐπιστήμη? Sokrates explains. He says he still thinks they are right to maintain that *if* virtue is ἐπιστήμη, it is teachable; but his worry is that there are no teachers. Meno has concurred that if something is teachable, of necessity there must be teachers and learners.

If my guess above is correct, Sokrates' contention here — that he and Meno are right to maintain that if something is ἐπιστήμη, it is teachable — is highly ambiguous. 'Mere' ἐπιστήμη, in the sense of undigested data or the words that constitute the 1,023rd line of the *Iliad*, is teachable in the rote sense. 'Full' ἐπιστήμη, in the sense of recovered interior vision supported by a 'causal' generative account, is *also* teachable, in a Sokratic fashion. There was, remember, that crucial equivocation on teachable and recollectable — or not equivocation, *assertion* rather that 'teachable' was to cover both — at the top of the argument. But 'full' ἐπιστήμη is *not* teachable by rote; and nor can Sokratic questioning be considered teaching if we say that teaching is paid instruction by someone who sets himself up as a possessor of expert knowledge. The diaresis of these key concepts leads to a luminous disambiguation. In its absence, we can expect muddle.

Just at the moment Sokrates announces his worry that there

are no teachers, Plato introduces a third character: Anytos, who, with Meletos, will bring the charges that lead to Sokrates' trial and execution. "You know, I've often tried to find out whether there were any teachers of virtue, and I keep coming up empty-handed.* But look, here's Anytos! Just when we need him! He's got a great reputation — good businessman, good son, good father — he's just the sort to help us figure this out. Sit down, Anytos, give us a hand." (89e–90b) Anytos doesn't get a word in edgewise; before he can even say hello, Sokrates has launched into a classic epagogic argument, designed to show that if you want to make someone expert at something, you send him to self-professed experts in that field, who have shown themselves willing to teach whoever is willing to pay. (Doctoring, cobbling, and flute-playing are given as examples.) Thus, the question with which Sokrates then baits Anytos: To whom should one send a young man who wishes to become expert in virtue — that is, in how to run a household or city, how to take care of their parents, etc.? Isn't it clear we should send him to people who profess to be teachers of such virtue, and who exact a fee for their services — the sophists?

Anytos, sound, conservative businessman that he is, explodes — as it's clear Sokrates knew he would. (His rhetoric has been too pointed, the shafts too deftly aimed.) Anytos' view is not, in fact, that far from Sokrates', that is, Plato's, own: Sokrates might not concur that the sophists are a "manifest plague" (91c, Lamb); but he does think the effect of their teaching is bad. How could it be otherwise? They are not experts in virtue, but only in rhetoric — see Aristophanes' portrait in *Clouds*, or Plato's own in *Protagoras* or *Gorgias* —

* See *Apology* 21b–22e for a full account.

so they make people persuasive speakers, without inculcating moral substance. But Sokrates
is all wide-eyed innocence. "You astonish me,
Anytos! How then could they have gotten rich
(which they have)? You mean for forty years no
one in Greece has noticed that they send people
back in worse condition than they received them?
And you're suggesting they may be doing this
deliberately? How could those deemed wise be
so mad as that?" (91c–92a, with elisions) Again
Anytos replies with a view that's close to Plato's own: "It's not the sophists who are mad, but
those who pay their fees. The cities should drive
them away, strangers and citizens alike!" In other
words, if you're *not* a sophist, citizen or stranger, you don't want Anytos mistaking you for
one. But this is, of course, just what Plato alleges
happened: Sokrates, who charges no fees, who
professes ignorance, is arraigned as a corrupter of
youth, someone who teaches them how to make
the worse argument the stronger. (*Apology* 18b
and *passim*.)*

    Sokrates might at this point (92b), as he
will at 92d, simply ask Anytos to whom, then,
he thinks Meno should be sent. ("Sokrates!
Sokrates!" the Academicians — in their role as
live television audience — might shout.) But he
doesn't, and the exchange that follows is important to the epistemic design of the dialogue as well
as to Plato's attempt to defend Sokrates' good
name. "Has some sophist wronged you, Anytos,
or why are you so hard on them?" Anytos replies
that he has never met a sophist, would never allow any of his people to have contact with one,
and is — thank God — entirely without any experience of them. Plato can now place the key
question squarely in front of us: Sokrates asks,

* Why we might have
some doubts about
Plato's account is
explained in Eric
Havelock's "Why Was
Socrates Tried?" *Studies
in Honour of Gilbert
Norwood* (*The Phoenix*
Supplementary Volume
No. 1), ed. M.E. White,
Toronto: University of
Toronto Press, 1952:
95–109.

"How then can you know whether there is any good in their instruction or not if you have no experience of it?"

Anytos' answer, that he knows "what these people are" regardless, of course explains how he came mistakenly to figure Sokrates among their number: having no experience of their teaching, or, by implication, Sokrates' own, relying on hearsay in both cases, fearing — correctly — for Athens' future, he got his hands on what he thought was the homegrown source of infection. (Of course, it helped that Sokrates — as we're about to see — trounced him in argument, insulting him into the bargain. [Isn't that just what they say those sophists do? No respect! They have no respect!])

But as well as foreshadowing the events of Sokrates' trial, the question foreshadows the discussion of true opinion which will occur at the end of the dialogue. What distinguishes true opinion from knowledge there is *absence of experience* (97a–c). Anytos, by Academic lights, has *true opinion* about sophists; and yet Sokrates dies. It is also true that he had (according to Plato) false opinion about Sokrates' own teaching. But, as Plato has Sokrates suggest in *Apology*, he's got it from the same sources as he's got his true opinion about sophists. It's a very murky business, opinion. There can be little question that we are being invited to reflect that had Anytos had *understanding* of sophists, Sokrates might never have been charged.

And there is yet more. Sokrates' question also shoots a conceptual arrow back through the entire dialogue, hooking the demonstration and discussion of *anamnesis* en route and nailing it, along with Anytos' disavowal, to the question first announced at the very beginning: "If I do not know what something is, how could I know what qualities it possesses?" (71b) Here, in Sokrates' challenge to Anytos, we have both a reminder of Meno's mistake, and a covert reference to the core argument for Plato's Eleusinian epistemology: If you have no experience, you have no understanding; but if you have understanding, you must have experience; and if your understanding did not come from experience in this world, then how or where did your experience occur? It is a moment of consummate literary artistry — a remark in the course of what appears to be a casual conversation, which draws the attention of neither Anytos nor Meno, but which serves simultaneously as Plato's capsule explanation of Sokrates' indictment, and reveals to us, twisting like steel under the dialogue's verbal skin, the skeleton, the axis, the conceptual DNA, of Plato's most deeply held views.

There ensues now the discussion that gets Sokrates in trouble: but again, it's clear Sokrates has seen the conclusion from the beginning, that he has in fact steered towards it from the moment Anytos (the perfect foil) was invited to join the conversation. Anytos states the obvious (we can imagine him: bluff, brusque, beefy, mildly irritated that Sokrates needs to have it spelled out): *Of course* you send Meno to any Athenian gentleman. (Meno, in the background, mugs oo-la-*la*!) And now, the argument familiar from *Protagoras* (319b–320c). Sokrates does not doubt that there have been many Athenians exemplary in their virtue; but he does doubt that they've been able to teach it. He cites several cases of virtuous fathers with louts or layabouts for sons. He notes that the fathers paid good money to have the sons educated in horsemanship, gymnastics, wrestling, what have you, and so obviously cared about them, but they failed to pass on, at no cost, what — were it teachable — they would most have wanted their sons to have: human excellence. This, Sokrates claims, must show that such excellence cannot be taught. ("Send him to Sokrates! Send him to Sokrates!" the audience hollers.)

Anytos (as Sokrates explicitly notes) becomes angry. He advises Sokrates not to slander people and drops out of the conversation. (If he doesn't leave [99e leaves the matter open], we should imagine him gruffly stalking over to the bar and tackling a plate of canapés.) Plato lays on the irony and the foreshadowing with a thick brush: Sokrates prophesies to Meno, and, we might imagine, Anytos' turned or departing back, that if Anytos "ever realizes what slander is [read: as Sokrates will realize it at Anytos' hands], he will not cease from anger [read: as Plato and the Academicians for whom this line is written have not ceased]." Then the moment is over, and Sokrates returns, in an apparently light mood, to conversation with Meno.

Meno, too, is in a light mood. (But then, a valley boy often is.) In response to Sokrates' query, we get a portrait of Gorgias that tallies with the one Plato draws in the dialogue bearing his name. Does Meno think the sophists, who profess to be teachers of virtue, *are* teachers of virtue? "I admire this *most* in Gorgias, Sokrates, that you would *never* hear him promising this [imagine the emphases a little excessive] and he ridicules the others when he hears them promising it. *He* thinks one should make people clever speakers." (95c) There it is. Exactly: the sophist is, in fact, quite honest, and the real disease courses in the veins of the body politic that is willing to accept clever speaking as a substitute for moral excellence. So Meno doesn't think the sophists teach virtue, then? — Meno isn't sure; sometimes he thinks so, sometimes he thinks not. There ensues discussion of this very confusion as it seems to appear in the work of a poet — yet another echo of *Protagoras,* but here carrying different freight.

It is signficant, I think, that Plato's presentation of 'the poet's view' occurs in the lead up to the discussion of virtue as true opinion. Here, as elsewhere (*Republic* I containing the most striking example), 'the poet' announces a view that is in essence Plato's own. Frequently, as in *Republic* I, the poet Plato cites is Simonides, but in this case it is Theognis. Sokrates quotes Theognis first to the effect that the company you keep affects the behaviour and understanding you will come to possess — "you will learn goodness from the good." But then, exclaims Sokrates, he contradicts himself! For elsewhere he says if virtue could be taught, whoever could do it would collect large fees, but this won't happen for "not by teaching will you ever make a bad man good"! (96a)

Once again the apparent tension trades on the ambiguity of the concepts *teaching* and *learning.* We know Plato doesn't believe the tension is real: the fundamental argument of *Republic* assumes a division of labour based on the soul's innate nature, and Plato is clear there that cultural influence can profoundly affect one's ability to realize or manifest that nature. Not only that, it is clear that good men, like Sokrates, draw the *desire* for goodness to the surface in all of us, their actions reinforce our dim dream-like intuitions and their conversation may even start us on the path to philosophy. But the soul that did not see much, or whose body has got the better of it (*Phaidros* 248a ff), whose eye is deeply sunk "in a barbaric bog" (*Republic* 533d), is not going to benefit from a photocopied handout. The poet does not contradict himself — but because he is merely uttering what has come to him through inspiration as in a dream, because unlike those priests and priestesses he has not "studied, so as to be able to give an account" of his intuitions, his words can be manipulated by a clever speaker to give the appearance of contradiction. Meno, of course, falls for it.

Sokrates summarizes: So we have the professed teachers on the one hand, who we often think aren't teachers, and who are regarded as not even understanding virtue; and on the other, we have worthy men (you, dear Meno, and, of course, Anytos) who, like Theognis, are utterly confused about its teachability. Neither of these, then, are promising candidates for teachers of virtue. Sokrates concludes by rehearsing the main syllogism: if no teachers, then not teachable; no teachers; therefore, not teachable.

❧

"Apparently not," Meno echoes, and launches what becomes the final section of the dialogue with a Gorgian flourish: "I certainly wonder, Sokrates, whether there are no good men either, or in what way good men come to be." (96d)

There is the skeptical card — just a flash, but it's where failure to attend to the epistemology of necessary truth leads. Attention to that epistemology, on the other hand, shows that all the equipment necessary to say how good men come to be is in fact before us. Genuine virtue,

SYMPOSIUM 216d–e:
I wonder... if you have
any idea what a sober ➤

and temperate man [Socrates] proves to be once you have looked inside. Believe me, it couldn't matter less to him whether a boy is beautiful. You can't imagine how little he cares whether a person is beautiful, or rich, or famous ... But once I caught him when he was open like Silenus' statues, and I had a glimpse of the figures he keeps hidden within: they were so godlike—so bright and beautiful, so utterly amazing—that I no longer had a choice—I just had to do whatever he told me.

virtue that will remain steadfast, is a kind of understanding: it is that which limits — that is, both disciplines and shows forth — desire, that which alone of existing things always follows wisdom. Whence this wisdom or understanding, this skill that can give an account of its origins? It is retrieved from the soul's latent memory-store, what it saw during its disembodied circuit of heaven, and now, without consciousness, retains. Through reflecting repeatedly on the conceptually necessary answers to questions put by a skilled director, one can recover these memories. Sokrates: the original practitioner of the talking cure.

Indeed, how close philosophy is to psychotherapy, in Plato's conception of it. It's all there: neurosis, transference, the importance of being able to give a generational account, the importance of tailoring the cure to the patient, the fundamental role of *erōs*, even the juxtaposition of dawning insight and dream. This is not, I think, because Freud read Plato and saw in his work a creation that he then revamped and presented as his own — the emphases are too disparate. Freud does not share Plato's view of the radiant source of those dream-like insights; contrary to Plato, Freud believes that the disciplining of *erōs* is the root of human unhappiness not the foundation of enlightenment; etc. Rather, I think both Plato and Freud, independently, recognized the existence of the phenomenon of unconscious thought and memory — they saw its traces everywhere, grasped its tremendous influence on behaviour, and sensed its connection to inexpressible desire. Plato, the optimist, still in touch with a live shamanic tradition, focussed on its importance for spiritual integrity; Freud, the pessimist, lodged in a desacralized culture, focussed on the way in which it acted as a repository for the socially taboo. Jung grew from Freud and found his way back to Plato's roots.

Unconscious awareness, though not described as such, frames the discussion in these final pages. We have just seen Sokrates quoting Theognis (with whom Plato agrees). And in the final few speeches, intuitions of which we can give no account yet which appear to be genuinely inspired, are said to be the source of true utterance about virtue by poets, prophets, and soothsayers alike. But inside this frame, the core of the discussion concerns non-knowledge of a different sort. Sokrates begins by invoking two sophists: "We're poor specimens, I fear, Meno, you and I. Gorgias has not adequately educated you, nor Prodikos me." (96d) There's no question this is ironic: Plato is not suggesting that Prodikos has taught Sokrates anything significant about virtue. But why then is the line there? There are any number of ways the transition might have been effected. Plato sets Prodikos' name at the head of the discussion, I think, as an imagistic warning, an indication that what's coming involves a nice distinction, but one that will prove philosophically empty.

Sokrates continues: "So first of all, we must attend to ourselves, and find someone who will have some means of making us better." (96d–e) Another sentence that does not need to be there, and, on the face of it, oddly undoes itself. It is, I suggest, yet another remark aimed not at Meno but at Plato's Academic audience, meaning roughly: We know why the Gorgiases and Prodikoses must always fail — we must look within for the answer, and hope to find someone who, with insightful questions, can speed us on our anamnetic way.

"I say this," Sokrates says, "in view of our recent investigation, as it's ridiculous we didn't see that it's not only through the guidance of knowledge that men succeed in their affairs — and [this is] equally why the knowledge of how good men come to be escapes us." (96e) "How's that?" Meno asks. Sokrates explains: You don't need knowledge to ground excellent conduct. It's entirely possible for *true opinion* to provide the requisite 'beneficial' guidance.

Suppose you've never been to Whitehorse. But someone who has says, "It's easy! You take a plane to Vancouver, and then another plane straight there." You, without checking with the airlines, believe this and, as it happens, you're right to do so: there is in fact a direct flight each day. You tell someone else, in Winnipeg, say, who (very peculiarly) does not check your information, but hops on the next morning flight to Vancouver and, sure enough, phones you again from Whitehorse that night. You didn't *know* how to get to Whitehorse — not in the way you would have if you'd actually done it — but your true opinion, based on hearsay, served as an adequate guide.

Right! says Meno — and then, surprisingly loquacious, adds that there's nonetheless a difference: the one who *knows* will always get it right, whereas the one with true opinion will some-times get it right, sometimes not. (Think of Anytos, getting it right about the sophists, getting it wrong that Sokrates was one of them.) — But how could that be? Sokrates asks; if the opinion is *true,* won't it always guide you correctly? — Yes, I guess so, Meno replies. But then why is knowledge thought to be better than true opinion, and why are the two even thought to be distinct?

Good question! By the standards of twenty-first-century epis-temology, one of the best. And Sokrates provides what, in outline, looks like a twenty-first-century answer. True opinions, he says, are like the statues of Daidalos: beautiful possessions, but liable to fly off or run away unless they are fastened down with "causal reasoning ... [which] process, friend Meno, is *anamnesis,* as we previously agreed." (Lamb, 98a) That is, it appears that Sokrates thinks what many contemporary North American philosophers think: that knowledge is justified true belief.

But what is this "causal reasoning" — αἴτιος λογισμός? Grube translates: "an account of the reason why" — which, in English, connotes something a bit more general, a bit less philosoph-ically self-conscious than 'causal.' Here, I think Lamb is right to draw attention to the vocabulary of *Phaedo,* where Sokrates describes his conversion to ontological explanation by way of Forms. There, Sokrates says that he was delighted when he first encountered Anaxagoras' view that Mind "directs and is

the cause of everything" (97c) because he believed that this entailed that the 'cause' of a thing
amounted to 'the best way' for it to be or act or
be acted upon.* But he was then disappointed
to discover that Anaxagoras did not rise to the
demands of his own theory: "the man made no
use of Mind, nor gave it any responsibility for the
management of things, but mentioned as causes
air and ether and water and many other strange
things" (98b–c). Thus Sokrates was forced to
develop the "mixed" way of proceeding (τϱόπον
εἰκῆ φύϱω) that is now his own (97b). (Grube
translates "confused," Hackforth "hotch potch,"
and Tredennick "haphazard," but none of these
makes a lot of sense. "Mixed" does, if you see in
Sokrates' 'way of proceeding' the rationalist element of Anaxagoras, played out in Pythagorean
and Parmenidean tropes.) According to this way
of proceeding, what it "befits a man to investigate
is, only, what is best (though, inevitably he will
also know what is worst for this is part of the
same knowledge)" (97d).

    How, exactly, does one proceed? Apparently
by some method involving hypotheses, and
their justification by higher hypotheses (100a,
101d–e).* Sokrates admits this isn't very clear,
but all he means is what he has never stopped
talking about: he *takes as secure* [ὑποθέμενος]
"the existence of a beautiful that is in and by
itself, and a good, and a great and all the rest,"
and "proceed[s] from them" (100b). It appears,
he says, that "if anything else is beautiful besides
the beautiful itself the sole reason for its being so
is that it shares [Grube] or participates [Hack-
forth] in that beautiful" (100c). He doesn't want
to fuss about the vocabulary or metaphysics of
this 'participating' (100d); it's apparent to him

* See previous quotation
from *Phaedo*, pages
160–1.

* See previous quotations
from *Republic* and
Phaedo, pages 182 and
184.

(and he repeats this) that this way of thinking
about things is "the safe course" (100e). In other
words, the cause of the way things are is 'what is
best'; and 'what is best' are the Forms — however
their presence 'in' things comes about.

This "way of proceeding" seems, then, to be
what Sokrates is referring to as the αἴτιος λογισμός in *Meno*: the "causal reasoning" we must
generate in order to "make fast" our true opinions
("which process ... is_ *anamnesis*"*). On closer
inspection, it doesn't look anything like the pro-
vision of empirical evidence or argumentative
reasoning that we now tend to associate with
justification. It looks more like a cross between
hope and conviction, an attempt to orient ourselves in the way that will make us most available
to interior anamnetic illumination. Indeed, I believe that what is at the core of Sokrates' 'way of
proceeding' is not actually a worked-out method
of some sort, but rather an attempt to honour
the phenomenological experience of necessary
truth: the experience of *seeing*. Once we have had
such an experience, and can reproduce in memory what caused it, our conviction becomes unshakable. (Note that it is unshakable in a different way — it produces a fundamentally different
posture — than opinionated blustering that has
its roots in arrogance or fear.) When we have not
had an experience of necessary truth, though, we
remain open to argument, to the suggestion we
may have been deceived, or confused, or weren't
looking at things from the right perspective. It is
this availability to rational reconsideration that,
for Plato, is the hallmark of opinion — even true,
'justified' opinion — as distinct from ἐπιστήμη or
knowledge in the sense of understanding.

Whether or not the preceding reconstruction

* See previous quotation
from *Phaedros*, pages
155–6.

is correct, Sokrates ventures that it is because understanding is "fastened" — buckled in to our souls, guaranteed to be present — that we value it more than true opinion. Meno says that "it seems to be something like that"; and Sokrates concurs that he, too, is just speculating. However, *that there is a difference* between ἐπιστήμη and true opinion he is sure of. He reminds us that he claims to know very little; but this, he says, he does.

Meno has been assenting enthusiastically to all this, notwithstanding his apparent failure to grasp anything else that would follow from his acceptance of Sokrates' account of *anamnesis*. Sokrates, as we've come to expect, starts to summarize:

Since then it is not only because of knowledge that men will be good and beneficial to their country (when they are), but also because of right opinion; and since neither of these comes by nature to men, [being] acquired —

and breaks off (98c–d). Apparently it has just occurred to him to grill Meno a second time on whether he thinks goodness is innate. We can imagine him turning directly to Meno, as though to address an afterthought: " — or do you think either of these comes by nature?" Why does he do this? Meno missed it the first time (89b–c); and it is, let us say, unlikely that Sokrates has forgotten this. My sense is that the audience is being invited, a final time, to witness Meno's stupidity. Sokrates has just, yet again, handed him the whole pie, plus a fork, on a platter. He has made *direct reference* to the slave boy demonstration by mentioning *anamnesis*, and he has stated that it is relevant to the difference between knowledge and true opinion. Meno remains oblivious. "Not I!" he responds. Sokrates carefully and very explicitly draws the conclusion, repeating the premiss about knowledge and true opinion: "Then *if they do not come by nature,* good people are not so by nature either." "Indeed not," Meno responds, not even adding that they agreed on this before. *And — since — they — do — not — come — by — nature …."* — Sokrates repeats the phrase a third time! We should imagine the words being spoken quite deliberately: here is where the error in reasoning is made, here is the wrong turn in the argument ["Class, you all (except Meno) see this? Good"] — "… we next inquired whether virtue could be taught" (98d7–8). "Yes," Meno concurs.

And everything else discussed in this third and concluding section of the dialogue flows from this. Sokrates does, now, provide a very tight and succinct summary of the argument from 87c to 98d, the point at which he broke off to re-question Meno about whether knowledge or goodness comes by nature. As he works towards this conclusion, Sokrates again seems to be offering Meno a chance to recant his claim that knowledge is not what makes men virtuous. In the space of fifteen lines (ten lines, if we leave out Meno's brief interjections), Sokrates says *five times* that their conclusion was (or some other conclusion followed because they agreed) that virtue was not knowledge or wisdom. (Read: not *innate* knowledge or wisdom.) It is via this claim that they have come to the view that "[a]s regards knowledge, [statesmen] are no different from soothsayers and prophets" — who are inspired, but can give no causal account of the truths they utter (98c).

"And so, Meno," Sokrates asks, "is it right to call those men divine who, without understanding, are successful in many of the important things they do and say?" ("No!" we can hear the live television audience roaring, "SAY 'NO,' MENO!") "Certainly," Meno says.

"We'd be right to call divine those soothsayers and prophets we just mentioned, and all the poets; and especially we can say of the statesmen that they are divine and enraptured, as they are inspired and god-possessed when their speeches lead to success in many great matters, though

PHAIDROS 249c–d: For just this reason it is fair that only a philosopher's mind grows wings, since its memory always keeps it as close as possible to those realities by being close to which the gods are divine. A man who uses reminders of these things correctly is always at the highest, most perfect level of initiation, and he is the only one who is perfect ... He stands outside human concerns and draws close to the divine; ordinary people think he is disturbed and rebuke him for this, unaware that he is possessed by god.

they have no idea of what they are saying."
(99c–d) But this is ridiculous. (Anytos enraptured and god-possessed? No.) It is the point at
which, if Meno were as intelligent as Thrasymakhos, he might blush — he might feel shame that
his argument has led to a conclusion that not
only mocks the possibility of a genuine politics,
but renders the sophists' version unintelligible as
well. Even Gorgias, Meno's *teacher*, has told him
that making fine speeches that sway the crowds
has nothing to do with virtue; Meno 'admires'
this view, but is incapable of registering the most
simple of its consequences.

We are near the end. Sokrates next remarks
— as though offering support for Meno's view
that virtue depends on a passing fit of inspiration — that "women too call good men divine,
and the Spartans, when they eulogize someone,
say 'This man is divine'" (99d7–9). The gesture
is extraordinarily complex. In the first place, the
remark is a non sequitur. Women and Spartans
may indeed say good men are divine, but this
tells us nothing about *why* they say this. They
might say it because they think what Sokrates
does, namely that goodness is a manifestation
of innate wisdom and wisdom is the hallmark of
the divine. Meno should catch the non sequitur,
but he doesn't. Secondly, even if what women and
Spartans say is that virtue is not a manifestation
of knowledge but rather the result of momen-
tary possession, to present this as though it were
an argument from authority is socially prepos-
terous. Few Athenian males would regard the
opinions of Spartans as counting for much — a
fact Meno acknowledges in the next line ("Anytos here might be annoyed with you for saying
so!") — and few Greek males would have given

APOLOGY 31d–32a: Be
sure, gentlemen of the
jury, that if I had long ago
attempted to take part
in politics, I should have
died long ago, and bene-
fited neither you nor my-
self... A man who really
fights for justice must lead
a private, not a public, life
if he is to survive for even
a short time.

a fig for what women thought. Finally, though, Plato himself, on the evidence of *Republic,* was a Spartaphile and, by the standards of the day, a feminist. So there is here a double reverse: the view that Plato espouses — that virtue as the manifestation of innate wisdom does merit the epithet divine, and anyone who recognizes this is worthy of intellectual respect — is presented 'positively,' but in such a way that any socially alert Greek (male) visitor to Athens who had not grasped the point of the slave boy demonstration ought to protest vigorously. Meno, we are forced to see, not only lacks the courage to think his way through to the socially unacceptable truth, he lacks the presence of mind to recognize that what he assents to here is incompatible with everything he has been taught. Like Anytos, he in a sense gets the words right: "Virtue is a manifestation of something divine," "What the sophists teach is corrupt." But what he means by them — if he means anything at all — is roughly the opposite of what Plato believes to be the case. The lesson echoes the epistemological digression of *Letter VII** very precisely: words alone cannot deliver us to insight. The portrait of Meno that goes with this complex gesture is also precise. And savage.

We have arrived at this intensely ironic state of affairs because of "the way in which [Sokrates and Meno] spoke and investigated through the whole discussion," 'discovering' that human excellence "is neither inborn, nor taught, but imparted to us by divine dispensation without understanding" (99e). It is a view of which Plato is contemptuous. As an indication of the direction a correct argument would have gone,

* See previous reference, page 157.

PHAEDO 101e: ... you will not jumble [higher and lower hypotheses] as the debaters do by discussing the hypothesis and its consequences at the same time, if you wish to discover any truth. This ▶

Sokrates again rehearses a view familiar to his audience and to us from *Republic*. "If there *were* [a statesman capable of making another into a statesman]" — we recall Plato's attempts with Dionysios of Syrakousai —

he could be said to be among the living as Homer said Teiresias was among the dead, namely, that "he alone retained his wits while the others flitted about like shadows." In the same manner, such a man would, as far as virtue is concerned, here also be the only true reality, compared, as it were, with shadows. [100a]

This is, of course, an encomium of Sokrates, couched in images that expand, in *Republic* VII, to become that most famous of Platonic tropes, the Parable of the Cave. Here, in *Meno*, Plato speaks to us directly, confirming, if we were ever in any doubt, that he thinks Sokrates does bring people to virtue, by assisting them in their attempts to recall inborn wisdom.

In the last lines of the dialogue, Sokrates connects "the result of our reasoning" — that virtue is not innate, is not teachable, but is a gift from the gods — to their failure to proceed by inquiring directly what virtue is in and of itself (αὐτὸ καθ' αὐτό — familiar Form-talk). The phrasing is not direct. He says certainty with respect to their present conclusion will be available only when they investigate not as they have been, but as he keeps recommending they should. Meno, and anybody else who has not been paying attention, may infer that Sokrates thinks proof is at hand; whereas Plato's audience would have grasped that the statement itself — the reality of virtue

they do not discuss at all nor give any thought to, but their 'wisdom' enables them to mix everything up and yet to be pleased with themselves ...

as something that can be apprehended αὐτὸ καθ᾽ αὐτό — *means* that no confirmation for Meno's sophistical shadow-conclusion can be forthcoming.

And with these deeply allusive gestures, Sokrates takes his leave. The flute-girls have arrived perhaps, or a crowd of drunker, noisier guests — a scene much like that which concludes Sokrates' recounting of Diotima's wisdom in *Symposium*. Plato speaks to us a last time, obliquely, in his own voice.

Convince your guest friend Anytos of those very things of which you have been convinced, so as to put him in a gentler mood: for if you can persuade him, you will also do a good turn for the Athenians.

A few lines earlier, Sokrates has said that he does not mind if Anytos is annoyed by his reference to the Spartans: he, Sokrates, will be talking to him again. The remark is made in passing, but anyone who knows the story must sense its chill. Plato has shown us plainly that Meno has not understood. Anytos will be unpersuaded.

The indictment will be served.

    🐚   🐚   🐚   🐚   🐚

APPENDIX:
THE ELEUSINIAN MYSTERIES

One of the most surprising things about the Eleusinian Mysteries is that we know so little about them. For at least a thousand, perhaps as much as two thousand, years they were celebrated at Athens and nearby Eleusis, and embraced an unusually broad range of initiates: men of all classes, women, foreigners, children, and at least some slaves. (You needed to be able to speak Greek, to be uncontaminated by bloodguilt, and, according to an oration attributed to Demosthenes, to have a wealthy sponsor — or be able to put up the required money some other way.) Yet — to

the best of our knowledge — no clear record of their central
rites survives. The punishment for breaking the required oath
of secrecy was death; but not only do we not know the contents
of the Mysteries, there are few records of alleged executions.
Aiskhylos, it is said, came close to saying too much — but in
the end survived.

What we know is this. There was at Eleusis a sanctuary dedi-
cated to Demeter and Persephone, at which were celebrated rites
connected with the story of Persephone's abduction by Haides,
Demeter's grief, and Persephone's eventual return. The Homeric
Hymn to Demeter is the canonical text for this story, but there
is overwhelming circumstantial evidence connecting the rites of
Demeter with much older agrarian, fertility, and Great Mother
cults throughout the Mediterranean. A common view has it that
the Eleusinian Mysteries proper date from the fifteenth century
BCE and are of Mykenaian origin.

The celebration of the Mysteries took place over nine days
in what is now late September. There was a procession from
the temple at Eleusis to the sanctuary of Demeter in Athens;
following this, three days of purification and sacrifice; and then
on the fifth day, a formal procession back to Eleusis. At Eleusis,
initiates and celebrants rested and further purified themselves
through fasting; it is commonly believed that they broke their
fast with a drink called κυκεών (kukeón), containing barley meal
and perhaps a psychadelic substance, in imitation of Demeter
(see Homeric Hymn to Demeter, lines 208–11). Finally, initiates
entered the initiation hall or τελεστήριον — large enough to
accommodate three thousand people — where the mysteries
were revealed. It has been suggested that participants may have
re-enacted Demeter's agonized search for Persephone or that
they may have been led through a dark and terrifying imitation
of the underworld. Some have suggested — and others have hotly
denied — that the celebrating hierophant and high priestess engaged in a sacred marriage, which culminated in the symbolic
birth of a son (perhaps Iakkhos, a personification of Dionysos).
It is commonly asserted that the climax of the initiation involved

a blaze or flashes of light in which sacred objects, the ἱερά, were revealed. Whatever the actual events, the import of the ritual seems to have centred on death and rebirth, and to have been connected, actually or historically, to fertility rites.

On the closing days of the Mysteries, initiates poured libations to the dead and then dispersed.

Connections with Orphic and Pythagorean doctrine are clear, but exist only in outline, owing to the secrecy surrounding both Pythagorean and Eleusinian practice. There are also clear points of continuity with the rites of Thesmophoria, a festival celebrated only by women in what is now late October, involving sacrifice to earth deities.

With the rise of Christianity, the popularity of the Mysteries declined, but there were still adherents. The sanctuaries were finally closed late in the fourth century CE by Theodosius I, and, shortly after, the precincts were destroyed by Alaric I.

For an overview with an extensive scholarly bibliography, see Chapter 12 of Mircea Eliade's *A History of Religious Ideas*, Vol. 1: *From the Stone Age to the Eleusinian Mysteries* (Chicago: University of Chicago Press, 1978). Walter Burkert's *Ancient Mystery Cults* (Cambridge, MA and London: Harvard University Press, 1987) offers compelling insights into the experience and meaning of the Mysteries, and points to connections with numerous passages in Plato's texts. Burkert makes one observation in passing that is, I think, especially telling in this context. Once initiated, a person could return for a subsequent celebration of the Mysteries. One who did so, who returned for more, was known as an ἐπόπτης — *epóptēs*. The etymological origin of the prefix is uncertain, Burkert says, but there is no doubt about the stem: οπ- or *op-*, referring to the eye, the root of our English word *optic*. The most advanced initiate, then, the one whose commitment was deepest and most real, was neither one who had a mission nor one who believed, but one who had seen.

Why Is Diotima a Woman?

There is more in a culture than is inscribed in its rational decisions.
— GIORGIO DI SANTILLANA

I · PROLEGOMENA: WHY ASK

Why is Diotima — the professor of erotics at the centre of Plato's *Symposium* — a woman?

Well, one might respond, why not? What's so surprising about casting a woman in the role? To which the straightforward answer is: the notoriously patriarchal character of fifth- and fourth-century Athenian culture. The city is often lauded as a participatory democracy; what we tend to mention less frequently is how few people actually got to participate. Athenian society was heavily stratified along class lines. To vote, you had to be a male citizen — that is, someone legally entitled under the constitution to own land. Foreigners — *metics* — who were numerous, could participate in commerce, and often served in the army — but they could not hold property and therefore had no political voice. Slaves constituted a third class: they were, of course, themselves a kind of property and had neither economic nor political power although their numbers outstripped those of citizens and metics combined.

Women, especially in the citizen class, were not so numerous — exposure of female infants was common. But, like slaves, citizen women were virtually powerless. Their 'citizenship' consisted in their capacity to transmit citizenship to their offspring — as long as the father of their children was also their husband and himself a citizen. Women in the land-owning classes could not themselves own land, and therefore could not vote; they required the approval of a supervising male relative for any significant economic transaction; they were often uneducated; and they were subject to a social ideology of seclusion. Even if this last

*

was more repressive dream than actual practice, the fact remains that we have little evidence that women occupied positions of cultural authority, and plenty of evidence that they were constitutionally debarred from nearly all state offices. In contemporary terms, it would be like someone writing a play in which Willard van Orman Quine's logic teacher was represented as a talking cow — well, not quite. No one would have found the idea of a talking woman surreal, although their cultural role *was* that of breeding stock, and many — though not all — male writers of the period appear to have believed they had the mental capacities to match. In one respect, a citizen woman's situation was even more extreme than that of a cow: she was supposed to be invisible. In public, respectable men refrained even from mentioning the names of living respectable women other than priestesses or foreign-born queens. In such a context, it looks like the question we should ask is how could Plato even have *imagined* a woman as the teacher of the young Sokrates.

This question does in fact have answers; for Diotima's situation turns out to be a little more complex than the outline I've just given might suggest. First, it is possible that at the dramatic date of the dialogue, she was dead; and secondly, she is said to be from Mantineia and is therefore a foreigner. On both counts, it would not have been considered overtly bad Athenian manners to discuss her and her views in public. Additionally, the symposium was not a fully public institution like the assembly, but more like a men's club. Things one would be careful never to put on record might plausibly be joked over with the boys after work. But none of this yet explains why or how Sokrates could have considered Diotima as a candidate for a teacher. The thought that perhaps Sokrates took his lessons someplace else, Sparta maybe, where the restrictions on women were not as severe, won't help. He had to have taken them in Athens because he is famous for never having left the place.

Plato is clear in other dialogues that people who taught things — like rhetoric or music — did so as a profession: they got paid for their work. The first piece of good news is that as a *metic*, Diotima would not have been subject to the full range of economic restrictions that Athenian women faced. It would have been legal for her to charge enough to make the exercise worth her while. Moreover there is evidence that the *kind* of expertise she professed did fall within the province of women. When Plato introduces her, he has Sokrates say the following:

I'll now go through the speech about Eros that I heard from a Mantineian woman, Diotima, who was wise [σοφή] about this and about many others things (once she told the Athenians what sacrifices to make for the plague, delaying the sickness ten years); and indeed it was she who taught me about erotics. [Symposium 201d]

Many have applied the epithet *priestess* to Diotima on the basis of this passage, and this is a profession that was both public and revered, even for Athenian women. Is this the explanation? Not quite; for 'priestess' is not actually what Plato says. Not only does he not use the word ἱέρεια, he makes no reference to a cult, or to cult beliefs, with which Diotima is associated.

    What he tells us is that she has knowledge of how to keep the ill will of the gods at bay; and that she is not from Athens, but the Athenians are willing to take her advice. This suggests more the figure of an itinerant μάντις — a seer or diviner. Such people were indeed generally men, but we have records that attest to women in this role. We also have evidence that some respectable women had specialized *professional* knowledge of birth and procreation — they were midwives. Sokrates' own mother, we will recall, was among them. And there were the *hetairai* — also members of a professional class, also with specialized knowledge pertaining to sex, and often, like geishas, well educated. But they were not, of course, respectable. Still, this does not stop Sokrates from consulting them — in the allegedly Platonic dialogue *Menexenos*, the alleged *hetaira* Aspasia, Perikles' consort, is portrayed as Sokrates' teacher of rhetoric; in Aiskhines' Sokratic dialogue *Aspasia*, she was represented as Sokrates' teacher, and as expert in matters of moral and political excellence; and Xenophon represents her as someone Sokrates regards as an expert on marriage. Was Diotima a *hetaira*? I do not think so; we have no attestations of *hetairai* who were also μάντεις. The absence of such attestations does not prove the point; but given religious preoccupations with the purity of purifiers, I take it to be highly unlikely.

At any rate there are, in fact, precedents — both for the idea that a woman might be a professional authority on spiritual matters and for the idea that she might be professionally knowledgeable about pregnancy and childbirth. But a general problem remains: these precedents are not numerous enough to make the choice of a female professor natural or obvious. It is possible to grasp how Plato could have imagined the scenario, but it remains difficult to understand why, or in what way, or by whom, he expected it to be taken seriously.

That is, given the general cultural situation, one would anticipate that the effect of putting a woman in a position of pedagogical authority over a male would have been comic — as is the depiction of women wielding political power in Aristophanes' *Lysistrata*. (The play is funny precisely because women's only access to power is through sex. There is no tragic version of this premise. If you try to take it seriously, you get not theatre but revolution.) It is apparent, however, that comedy is not Plato's intent. The rest of the discussion — until Alkibiades shows up draped over a flute girl — is, as it is throughout nearly all of Plato's work, an entirely masculine affair. It is also entirely sober: although it is a party of sorts, it is a strange one — Plato makes a point of sending away the flute girl Agathon has hired and putting a lid on the drinking before the speeches start. There are comic episodes — Eryximakhos is a colossal self-preoccupied bore, and would be completely upstaged by Aristophanes' hiccups and feather-tickling in any actual performance of the dialogue. But it is nonetheless clear that we are to take the *content* more or less at face value. Aristophanes' speech, which one might expect to be pointedly satirical and laced with off-colour jokes, is, in fact, an exquisitely humane account of the tragedy of the sexed human condition. In case anyone is inclined to mistake Agathon's Hallmark sentimentalities for genuine charm or grace, Sokrates' cross-examination shows them up for the chillingly vacuous blather that they are. The account of the lesser mysteries of Eros is characterized by the impatience of its argumentation, the bluntness of its biological references, and the accuracy of its phenomenology of love. The higher mysteries are conveyed in language of great intensity and reverence. There is nothing in any of this to laugh at.

The more closely we look at the dialogue, the more our puzzlement must deepen. The culture is patriarchal, Plato is not writing a spoof. Why, then, is Diotima a woman?

The question has been addressed by a number of commentators over the last century. Among these, David Halperin has provided the most lengthy, as well as one of the most erudite, discussions. The 1990 version of his essay — also entitled "Why is Diotima a Woman?" — includes a survey of responses extant in the literature. The following list provides a brief overview of that survey, which I have in places updated.

Diotima is a woman because Plato has his eye on the literary-philosophical unities — if Sokrates' erotics instructor were male, this would strongly suggest the possibility of a paederastic affair between them, and so undermine the principled argument for so-called Platonic love, or it would cloud the rationale for Sokrates' rejection of Alkibiades' proposition later in the dialogue; or, yet again, the dialogue's design demands, in Sokrates' speech, a balance between male and female. Or: Diotima is a woman because Plato was gay, and so, unlike Xenophon, was not threatened by the possibility of female authority; or because, as a homosexual, he was subject to pathological fantasies of male pregnancy and needed a projection of the feminine to embody them. Or: Diotima is a woman because Plato was a closet heterosexual and sought to dignify relations between the sexes; or because he was a proto-feminist. Or: Diotima is a woman because the events in the dialogue actually occurred — that is, because she *was* a woman; or because she was a historical personage although the dialogue, like the dialogue *Parmenides*, is a historical fiction. Or: Diotima is a stand-in for Aspasia; or she is a 'Zeus-honouring' bodiless mistress for Sokrates (her name might be translated as *Zeus's honour*), to parallel Timandra — Alkibiades' 'man-honouring' bodily mistress (whose name might be translated as *honour* [*towards a*] *man*). Or: Diotima is a woman because Greek men knew about physics (Anaxagoras was Sokrates' teacher in *Phaedo*) and Greek women knew about sex. Or: Diotima is a woman because putting the rebuttal of Agathon in the mouth of a woman spares him complete humiliation. Or: Diotima is a woman because the special quality of erotic experience hints at connections with mystery religions and Plato wants to avoid the Aristophanic charge (*Clouds* 140 *ff*) that Sokrates is a fake mystagogue; thus he needs a representative of the Eleusinian Mysteries; and this has to be a woman. Or: Diotima is a woman because through the image of philosophic discourse as male and yet also as a mimesis of pregnancy, maternal power is appropriated by the patriarchy that disinvests it — *Symposium* enacts a symbolic cultural matricide. Halperin's own view is complexly Foucauldian: Diotima is not a woman but a 'woman' — that is, an image that embodies a male idea of the "reciprocal and (pro)creative erotics of (male) philosophical intercourse." To put this slightly more concretely: Diotima is a woman because Plato is trying to model a particular conception of what it is to do philosophy: one in which intellectual conversation, construed as reciprocal intimacy, allows participants to express new ideas that are growing inside them. The notion that this conception of philosophical activity is best modeled by using the image of a woman involves, Halperin suggests, a male idea — a Greek male idea — of what it is to be a woman.

Halperin is undoubtedly correct that stereotyping was as much a problem for fourth-century Athenian thought as it is for our own. He is also correct that it is a problem we must take seriously. Indeed, a version of this issue could be raised in connection with several of the other suggested answers as well. But for this reason, *as an answer to the question at hand,* it seems to me less interesting than the good old modernist 'content' on which it is erected. The additional quotation marks ultimately leave our curiosity unappeased. "So Diotima's not a woman, she's a 'woman.' Fine. *Why?*" I am interested in Halperin's answer to this question because I agree that Plato *is* trying to sketch a picture of what it is to do philosophy, and, like many of the arguments and observations throughout his corpus, this picture is rooted in phenomenology: genuine intellectual intercourse can *feel* extraordinarily intimate; we *feel* like we are teeming with thoughts; we *feel* like we do when we're in love — obsessed, excited, elated, frustrated, despairing. Plato's picture helps explain all this. Whether or not the picture explains why Diotima has to be a 'woman,' Halperin is right to focus our attention — however briefly — in this direction. The intimate, abstractly erotic *experience* of engagement with intellectual beauty — its life-changing nature — is clearly at the core of what Plato wants to communicate in this dialogue.

Does that experience require a 'woman' to model it? Halperin argues that because Athenians believed only women both gave and received pleasure in sex, a male, giving lessons to Sokrates, could not represent the excitement of reciprocal philosophical exchange. Boys were supposed to be inertly passive objects, completely unexcited by their older male lovers; it was inappropriate for them to become active participants in lovemaking. Their adult male lovers, by contrast, were styled as sexual predators, excited because they were making a conquest, exercising dominance. Moreover, Halperin argues, we find Diotima articulating the idea that sexual desire does not involve 'having' an object, but is, rather, an experience of one's own fecundity and need to give birth. This, he suggests, means "Plato's theory of erotic procreativity … is oriented around what his contemporaries would have taken to be a distinctively feminine order of experience."

But is Diotima a stereotypical woman? Not if we judge by the extant literature of the period. Is she excited by Sokrates? Is the exchange between them reciprocal? It does not seem so: her engagement is with Beauty, not her pupil. She berates him, is frequently exasperated by his thoughtlessness, says she is unsure if he is capable of grasping the revelation on which genuine philosophical illumination depends. She sounds more like his mom than his lover. Her theory of sex does indeed identify birth, rather than sexual possession, as its point. But the other key element in it — that we *start* by being pregnant, and require

beauty in order to excite us to give birth — is one that no Greek
would have imagined any female of any species could represent.

In other words, the question still stands: Why is Diotima a
woman? She is not a stereotypical woman; her theory of sex,
while not stereotypically male, is not stereotypically female
either. If Plato intended the dialogue for a public audience, why
did he risk the laughs, the possibility of misinterpretation? If
it was a teaching tool, and Diotima's presence was intended to
model respect for women's intellectual capacities, why doesn't
he exploit her character more frequently or develop other female
characters in other dialogues? If the dialogue was intended as an
entirely private *aide-memoire* (following an extreme reading of
Phaidros 276d), then, given the general absence of female characters in the rest of Plato's work, the question still arises — only
now in an unanswerable form about the peculiarities of Plato's
personal psychology. The truth is, we do not have enough information to decide the matter. At best, we can guess. And that
is what I, too, am going to do.

My excuse for doing so is that there are pieces of literary
evidence whose collective significance has been overlooked. The
evidence does not so much obviate other guesses as allow us to
push deeper, both into the fabric of the dialogue and into Plato's
philosophical culture. Diotima is a woman, I believe, because
Plato is — at least in some respects — a Parmenidean. Seeing
how this might be so will affect our understanding both of the
Greek philosophical tradition and of Plato's own project.

II · PLATO AS PARMENIDEAN:
THE HARD LITERARY FACTS

The evidence for significant Parmenidean echoes in *Symposium*
falls into two categories: hard facts about the two texts in question; and circumstantial evidence. I'll start with the hard facts.

At the climax of her speech on the higher mysteries of Eros
— which is one of two climaxes in the dialogue as a whole —
Diotima describes the end toward which all the hard work of the
initiate has been directed: it is a vision of something "at once as-

tonishing and beautiful" (210e). Plato's Greek is dense, emphatic, the sentences run on, as though delivered in a rush, groping for their subject. And — the first piece of hard evidence — the key characteristics of this intensely beautiful and astonishing thing are remarkably similar to those ascribed to Being in that scrap of Parmenides' poem we now call Fragment 8. Here is Plato:

First, it always is, neither coming to be nor passing away, neither waxing nor waning; next, it is not beautiful this way and ugly that way, nor beautiful at one time and ugly at another, nor beautiful in relation to one thing and ugly in relation to another; nor is it beautiful here but ugly there, as it would be if it were beautiful for some people and ugly for others. Nor will the beautiful appear to him in the guise of a face or hands or any other part of the body. It will not appear to him as a particular discourse or a particular kind of knowledge, nor as existing somewhere in some other thing, as in an animal or in the earth or in the sky or in any other thing, but itself by itself with itself, singular, it is, all other beautiful things participating in it in such a way that, though they are coming to be and perishing, this does not become greater or smaller or suffer change. [210e6–211b5]

And here is Parmenides:

*… Being is ungenerated and imperishable,
whole, single, unperturbed and without end.
It never 'was,' nor 'will be,' since it is, now, all in the same place
one and together. What birth will you seek for it?
how and whence did it grow?…
Justice holds it fast: it cannot come to be
nor perish …
Nor is it divisible since it is all alike,
not clumped more here more there — which would prevent it
clinging to itself — but it is all full of being,
it is all one thing: Being wedded to Being.
Motionless in strong moorings,
without origin, ceaseless …*

Itself in itself it remains by itself
perpetually stable in place. (Fr. 8.3–30)

The passages are not identical. Plato is not simply quoting.
But the *thought* is very close, particularly on these points: the
emphatic, insistent present tense that attaches to the 'it,' the absence of coming-to-be or perishing, the absence of change, the
way the 'it' is "itself in — or with — itself by itself," its singleness,
the absence of relative aspects or appearances, that it cannot be
divided up, and is continuous or homogenous. There are, I believe, only two significant points of difference, neither of which
undermines the force of the similarities. First, Parmenides' subject
is Being — τὸ ὄν — while Plato's is Beauty — τὸ καλόν. Secondly,
Parmenides' characterization is laced with argumentative rhetoric and insistence that there is no other possible way to think
about the matter. (I have omitted much of this in the preceding
quotation in order to focus on what he is arguing *about*.) In this
connection, he mentions all of Justice, Fate, and Necessity, who
bind or fetter Being so that it *must* be as it is. Plato's initiate, by
contrast, arrives at his vision of Beauty by means of a discipline
or practice over time, not through immediate reflection on the
meaning of 'it is.' (Plato does, however, stress logical necessity,
using the same word as Parmenides, not in this passage, but in
Sokrates' initial exchange with Agathon (200b2). Then, in the
famous ascent passage, the so-called Ladder of Love (210a–e),
Diotima is made to prescribe the 'correct' steps for progressing
from love of some individual's body to a vision of the Beautiful,
all in terms of what the initiate *must* do if he wants the right
result. It's not clear that logical necessity is intended, but it is
certainly clear that she is articulating constraints.)

We might be tempted to insist on a third difference between
Plato and Parmenides, namely that Plato appears to be concerned
with the relationship between Beauty and particular beautiful
things, while Parmenides betrays no parallel concern with particular existent things. Except, of course, Parmenides does. That
preoccupation — and with it, a distinction between what's *really*
real and what merely seems real to mortals — surfaces at the

end of Fr 8, after the description of Being. The distinction itself is familiar to every reader of Plato; but what is more, the question of *how* particular things 'participate' in what is really real "in such a way that, though they are coming to be and perishing, [the really real] does not become greater or smaller or suffer change" — this question is presented, in just these terms, as an unresolved puzzle in Plato's dialogue *Parmenides* (130e4–135c7). In other words, there *is* a parallel between Plato and Parmenides on this point; and Plato's sharpest presentation of the problem it raises appears in Parmenides' mouth in a dialogue bearing his name. Here, though, the trail runs out: we do not know how Plato viewed his relationship to Parmenides on this matter. This is partly because the dialogue *Parmenides* appears to be composed as a series of riddles; and partly because we have lost so much of the rest of Parmenides' own poem. What I hope to have established is only this: on the crucial matter of the *natures* of Being and of Beauty, the parallels between the texts are striking. The natures have different names, and the path to vision is different (in Plato's case, a practice; in Parmenides,' an out-of-body chariot ride followed by a philosophical lecture) — but the *sort* of thing that is grasped in each case is, essentially, the same.

Which brings me to the second piece of hard evidence. In Intro Philosophy, we usually skip over the opening of Parmenides' poem, the scene-setting, the Heliadic charioteers and the horses, the gates of day and night, avenging Justice, etc., etc. The significant discourse, we seem to assume, starts in Fragment 2, with the Ways of Persuasion and Truth. But listen for a moment to the proem:

The mares were taking me, the ones that carry me as far as
    longing can reach,
once they had brought me onto the many-voiced path
of the daimōn, *she who carries unharmed through everything*
the one who knows — and on I was carried,
as the mares, who knew just where to go, kept
carrying me, straining at the chariot and young women led the
    way.

The axle in the naves was shrilling like a pipe, blazing,
pressed on by the whirling wheels at either end,
as the young women, daughters of the Sun, rushed on, taking me,
having left the House of Night for light, stripping back their veils
    from their faces with their hands.
There stand the gates on the paths of Night and Day,
and they are held at top and bottom by a lintel and a threshold
    made of stone,
and hang, gigantic, in the fiery air.
Justice, much-avenging, keeps the keys.
Softly coaxing her, the kourai *then persuaded her that she should*
    push the locked bar back at once,
especially for them. And so the doors — pinned, riveted — swung
    wide,
one, then the other, bronze posts turning in their sockets,
and a vast gulf opened in the frame. Straight through
the kourai *drove the chariot and mares, straight down the road.*
And the daimōn *kindly reached her right hand out for mine,*
and welcomed me.

The mares, the female *daimōn*, the mares, and young women
leading the way, daughters of the sun, who persuade Justice, her,
to push back the bar, and the young women driving the mares
straight through, so that our hero, far from the paths of humans,
may shake the hand of, and be instructed by, a female divinity.
The youth is male, but every other living, mythic presence in the
proem is female, including Night, Day, and the spirit, Themis, of
right order among things, whereby it is "fitting" that the youth
should have travelled so far to learn what he has to learn. This
completely feminized context is, I submit, remarkable in a clas-
* † sical philosophical text. There are no parallels, except the episode
of Odysseus' instruction by Kirke, and in the Sokratic dialogues
that portray Sokrates being taught by Aspasia and Diotima. And
only in the dialogue with Diotima is a young man — like the
youth in Parmenides' poem — *initiated* into a rare and uncommon
understanding, an understanding that will make its possessor

unsurpassable in judgement (Fr 8.60–1), or bring him to genuine excellence (*Symposium* 212a2–7).

There are two further details worth noting. The first is the authoritative tone of the two female instructors. This may be wholly an artifact of Greek pedagogical ideals: real teachers *teach*! And from a *daimōn*, we might expect a commanding attitude (though Parmenides stresses that she is kind [Fr 1.22]). But Plato's portraits of other teachers — Gorgias, Protagoras, indeed Sokrates — show him capable of shadings of attitude and character; and Diotima, in her directness, in her lack of any wish to please, her refusal of all rhetorical blandishments, resembles no other teacher in Plato's dialogues as much as she resembles Parmenides' *daimōn*. Perhaps Plato needed to portray her in this way because he had chosen to make her a woman. But then our original question — why go to the trouble? — returns full force. Either way, the resemblance is interesting.

The second detail worth noting is this: the path on which the initiate is drawn is described in line 2 of Parmenides' poem with the surprising adjective πολύφημον — "many-saying" or "many-voiced." Bringhurst translates "straight up the track that passes through everyone's voices." Suddenly, the extraordinarily nested structure of *Symposium* appears in a new light: an unnamed friend (along with the reader) listens to Apollodoros describe the account of Aristodemos, who relates what five other symposiasts said, en route to recounting Sokrates' recital of what he was told by Diotima. There are clues that one of the things Plato may be doing with this structure is offering us an image of the way 'mortal' speeches replace one another, how copies achieve a kind of immortality for the original speech the way offspring achieve a kind of immortality for parent animals (cf. 207d–208b). In this, oral transmission is unlike writing, which is unchanging, and thus eternal in a different way. (It is a theme Plato also addresses in his other dialogue devoted to love, *Phaidros*. There, the conclusion is the opposite of the one hinted at in *Symposium*: in *Phaidros*, writing is anything but divine.) In *Symposium*, the issue is deeply buried; it appears as an imagistic resonance rather than an explicit conceptual motif. Or rather, it is the *structural* connection with Parmenides' odd epithet that strikes me as significant: *Symposium* — uniquely in Plato's corpus — *enacts* a process in which the listener is drawn "through many voices" to the still centre of truth.

To summarize: The hard textual evidence for my claim that Diotima is a woman because Plato is a Parmenidean is as follows: In *Symposium*, as in Parmenides' poem, but in no other surviving document of the period, there is a youth who undergoes initiation in a feminized context. He is instructed in a no-nonsense fashion by an authoritative — one might even say imperious — female individual. And what he is brought to 'see' in both cases has the same nature: something that sits uneasily in plain human speech, itself by itself, it is: deathless, birthless, unchanging, indivisible, in all respects the same: the substance of truth, the wellspring of human excellence.

"Well and good," a friendly devil's advocate might object, "but what does it all *mean*? You've established two unusual parallels — a vision of the nature of the real, and a feminized context for its communication — which don't seem to have anything to do with one another. That independence is, itself, evidence of a Parmenidean presence in *Symposium*: it's the easiest explanation of an otherwise genuinely odd, and genuinely substantive, coincidence. But — philosophically speaking — so what? 'Diotima is a woman because Parmenidean-style philosophical enlightenment requires a female mouthpiece.' This doesn't tell us much until we know *why* it requires it. Or, to frame the question from *Symposium*'s perspective on Parmenides: What's love got to do with it?"

The answer, I believe, is quite a lot. But here we must leave the land of hard evidence and wade into the murky waters of conjecture.

III · RESONANCES:
THE CIRCUMSTANTIAL EVIDENCE

The waters are made murkier by the fact that the text about which I wish to conjecture — Parmenides' poem — is, in the words of Giorgio di Santillana, "without doubt, one of the most impressively obscure affirmations in the history of thought." The commentaries are legion; the translations numerous; there is no firm consensus on what would seem to be the most basic issues. Is Parmenides a metaphysical monist? Is he an epistemological monist? What does he mean by the notorious Fr 3: *for it is the same to know* (or is that *think*? or is it *mean*?) *and to be*? Perhaps something Idealist? Something mystical? Something empirical? Something scientific? How should we translate the transition from the allegedly monist, so-called Way of Truth to what appears to be the second part of the poem, the apparently cosmological, so-called Way of Seeming or Way of Opinion? Does the *daimōn* mean that what follows is a *lie*, or that it's a *riddle*? And does that apply to the words she uses, or to what her words are pointing to? What, exactly, is the crucial mistake that mortals make in their efforts to understand?

†

I don't know. My aim is not to decide among the competing translations or approaches: each interpretation has its reasons. Like every other reader who has made a serious attempt to come to grips with the poem, I have my hunches. Of the extant commentaries, Cornford's (regarding the Way of Truth) and Burnet's (regarding the Way of Opinion) articulate most clearly and most comprehensively what I myself find in the lines that have come down to us. It would be on their philological expertise that I would rely if I were pressed to defend my sense of what the lines mean. But, as I say, my aim is not to sift the evidence for competing claims, nor to advance an interpretation of the poem as a whole. What I wish to pursue are further connections between *Symposium* and Parmenides' poem that emerge if we follow one extant interpretation of the central figure of the poem: the unnamed *daimōn* of Part II.

*

It may, at first, sound odd to claim that it is this figure — one
I haven't so far mentioned — who is the poem's central presence.
Isn't the first *daimōn*, she who welcomes our hero and imparts
the ontological and cosmological goods, the presiding genius?
In a way, yes: she's the talker. But if we reflect for a moment, we
realize that that's really all she is: an ambassador, the front-of-
house woman, "Hypsipyle" as Proklos styles her, she who belongs
at the High Gates. This *daimōn* describes not only the nature
of being, but repeatedly draws our attention to the activities of
other *daimōnes* — Justice, Fate, Necessity — as the ones who've
made it the way it is; and in Part II, her focus shifts: she wishes
to inform the initiate about — it seems — some features of the
natural world, especially the heavens, and also about a mistake
or mistakes humans make in their approach to these features

† or this realm. In particular, she wants to alert him to a problem
to do with naming or perceiving two things or aspects where
there is only one. But at the centre of the arrangement — which

∗ both Cornford and Santillana argue we must regard as a serious
contribution to cosmology, whatever the cosmos's ontological
status — is the second *daimōn*, also a female, who, according to
Fr 12 runs the show:

In the midst of [rings of fire and darkness] is the daimōn *who
    steers all things.*
Everywhere it is she who is the origin of sex and horrifying birth,
*Sending female to join with male repeatedly, and male with
    female.*

Who was this *daimōn*? A less secular age might say, "Don't
† ask! There's a reason Parmenides doesn't name her, and you
mistreat his meaning if you poke and pry like an insensitive
adolescent." I will attempt not to poke and pry. And I would like
to acknowledge at the outset that focussing on a single name will
indeed queer the pitch to some extent: one of the core features
of the Greek conception of goddesses, gods, and spirits is their
multi-facetedness. Nearly all of them have several faces or aspects; and each of these aspects can, itself, have more than one

name. Further, I'd like to acknowledge that it is often important not to speak to or of deities using *any* of their actual names, but to invent indirect ways of referring to them; to approach obliquely, deferentially, with the verbal equivalent of downcast eyes. (Addressing a goddess is not unlike saying hi to a grizzly bear.) In other words, I agree, that we cannot give the figure of the *daimōn* a single unequivocal name without distorting Parmenides' meaning. But I also believe we lack vast amounts of essential cultural knowledge — not only about how, when or if to name goddesses and gods, but also about the simplest matters of *who they were*. It is my guess that Parmenides would have expected anyone who was willing to be taught by his poem to have recognized, in their peripheral vision, who he was talking about. We don't have that peripheral vision; it is available only to persons steeped in the common knowledge of a culture. We need to get the *daimōn* at least briefly in our focal vision before we can get her out of it.

Who, then, is Parmenides gesturing towards? There is evidence, as good as any, that she is Aphrodite Ourania — "Aphrodite of the Heavens." I hardly need to state the significance for *Symposium*: if the ontological views Plato expresses there are connected with a tradition concerned with Aphrodite in *any* of her manifestations, Plato's focus on erotic love in the same dialogue is immediately explained. And this account of the identity of Parmenides' *daimōn*, I will argue, also allows us to knit together some of the rumours about Parmenides' biography better than other proposals — a slender recommendation, to be sure, but a recommendation nonetheless. (Not exactly support for the platform, but something like a penny that, placed under a leg, effects greater stability of the whole.)

❧

But who was Aphrodite Ourania? What's the evidence? Here I follow Santillana, who builds on the work of Albert Rivaud.   *

We met her in Fr 12. From Fr 13, we learn:

> First of all the gods she contemplated Eros.

It's not a lot to go on, but we can discern at least a few things. To begin with, this *daimōn* must be old — pre-Olympian. This in itself would constitute a reason for giving her a nameless *thematic* presence, connected with the natural order of things. It would also be a reason her representative — the welcoming *daimōn* — might be so preoccupied with Justice, natural law, Necessity, and Fate, themselves pre-Olympian manifestations of the order of the world. In this connection, it is perhaps worth noting (though it is by no means conclusive) that Parmenides refers to her as a *daimōn* or divine being, not as a *thea* or goddess — a word he might plausibly have used if she were one of the standard Olympians. How can she be an aspect of *Aphrodite* if she is pre-Olympian? Here, I can only point to a general characteristic of pantheistic thought: that theogonies generally occur in dream time not Newtonian time. Time exists in the mythworld, but time's arrow usually does not.

At any rate, there is evidence that she is very old. Then, because a paraphrase of Fr 12 occurs in Aetius in the context of an astronomical cosmogony, and this passage from Aetius appears also to summarize the content of other genuine Parmenidean fragments of an astronomical nature, we might venture that she is a sky-goddess. We note also that she is immensely powerful — she steers or pilots all things; and she is origin, *arkhē* — that from which, through the agency of Eros, sexual union and birth arise.

One might think that the references to her primordial involvement with sex and Eros cinch it: she *has* to be Aphrodite. But matters are not so simple. Earlier, I mentioned the multifaceted nature of most Greek divinities. One consequence of this complexity is that, for those of us with only focal vision, there appears to be a degree of redundancy among the divine managerial functions. Aphrodite is not the only goddess who can take a hand in situations where childbirth and sexual union are concerned. Guthrie, for example, looks at the same evidence, connects it with the myth of Er in Plato's *Republic* (616b–617d), and concludes that the *daimōn* is Hestia, keeper of the hearth, the fire within the earth. This is by no means an impossible identification, and because of the parallels with the Er myth, it has the

same penny-under-the-table quality I will be urging for my own
hypothesis. More: Rivaud himself suggests Hestia is one of the   *
faces of Aphrodite Ourania. I do not think Guthrie's guess can be
shown to be wrong, then; indeed, I am prepared to believe that
from some perspectives, it is highly illuminating. My claim is
only this: If we *miss* that one of the *daimōn*'s fundamental aspects
is Aphrodite Ourania, we miss something crucial to the tradition
to which both Parmenides' poem and Plato's dialogue belong.

Among my reasons for thinking this is what Francis Walton   *
says in his entry on Aphrodite in the *Oxford Classical Dictionary*:

APHRODITE, *Greek goddess of love, beauty, and fertility ... To
Homer she is "the Cyprian," and it was probably from Cyprus, in
the Mycenaean age, that Aphrodite first entered Greece, though
the Hellenic goddess doubtless owes something to earlier Aegean
divinities, such as Ariadne, whose cults she absorbed. Greek tradition consistently pointed to an eastern [pre-Homeric] origin for
Aphrodite ...*

*Primarily, she is a goddess of generation and fertility, and in
poetry often seems little more than a personification of the sexual
instinct and the power of love ... The title Urania ... seems frequently a mark of the Oriental goddess, and was a cult name at
Cyprus, Cythera, and Corinth. It was also applied to various foreign
goddesses (e.g. the Scythian Argimpasa, Hdt. 4.59 ...) ...*

*Apart from Hermes, Aphrodite has no strong associations in
cult with the major Hellenic gods ...*

That is: the very idea of Aphrodite is old — pre-Hellenic. She
is not much of a personality. She had a Scythian sister — who,
presumably, knew how to ride a horse.

Santillana believes that the two *daimōnes* are in fact the intellectual and physical aspects of a single figure, and thus that
features of the proem are relevant to her identification. He works
through Hesiod's *Theogony* and suggests Themis, Hekate, and
the Oracle of Night as "homologues ... here concentrated in one
figure which is also given total cosmic power in the Second Part
of the Poem"; but this, even if correct, still tells us little except

that she is old, and is associated with the night sky and with order
or natural law. If Rivaud's guess that she is Aphrodite Ourania
is correct — and Santillana (extending his list of homologues)
believes it is — we can say a little more. Specifically, we can add
that she was in tradition "the oldest of the Moirai" or Fates. The
Moirai's parentage varies but frequently includes either Themis —
Natural Law — or Ananke — Necessity: so again, an association
with cosmological or metaphysical order, and one whose terms
are explicitly mentioned, more than once, in Parmenides' poem.
In the Orphic tradition, the mother of the Moirai was Night, and
they were thus sisters of the Erinyes. A scholion to *Oidipous at
Kolonos* confirms the astronomical associations of Aphrodite
Ourania, telling us that she was associated with the Dawn, the
Sun and the Moon; and also with the Nymphs — the spirits of
wild places — and Mnemosyne or Memory. The same scholiast
adds: she was worshipped with rites of wineless libation.

    Suddenly an odd detail of *Symposium* is set ringing: the gath-
ering is convened as a drinking party — at which nobody drinks.
Plato underlines this; he spends several exchanges on it (176a–e);
it is, in fact, the *reason* for the speeches praising Love — the erst-
while symposiasts have nothing else to do.

    Then we note that Moira, in the not-uncommon singular, is
mentioned by Diotima at one of the cruxes of her argument — the
importance of contact with beauty for giving intellectual birth.
She says: Μοῖρα οὖν καὶ Εἰλείθυια ἡ Καλλονή ἐστι τῇ γενέσει
— "Moira thus and Eileithuia Beauty is in (or at) birth" (206d2–
3). Nehamas and Woodruff disentangle this as: "Therefore, the
goddess who presides at childbirth — she's called Moira [as well
as] Eileithuia — is really Beauty." Or: reading a connection between *Symposium* and Parmenides' poem, reading Parmenides'
cosmic *daimōn* as Aphrodite Ourania, and following the tradition
that identifies Aphrodite Ourania with Moira, Diotima would
be claiming that what wants to make us give intellectual birth
— write a big poem about the nature of being, say — is actually
a *vision* of the *daimōn*. Whether or not one has a taste for this
sort of "high speculative terrain," there can be no question that
Being is repeatedly subject to the constraining activities of Moira,

Dike, and Ananke. And that control appears to be one of the main functions of the cosmic *daimōn* in the poem's second part.

And another curious fact: Aphrodite Ourania is mentioned *by name* twice in the opening speech of Pausanias, he whose idea it was to have an evening of speeches devoted to Love. At 180d, he tells us that she is the elder of two Aphrodites (the other being Aphrodite Pandemos or 'Popular Aphrodite'), and that she is the motherless daughter of Ouranos, the god of the Heavens; and then, at 181c, he says that her age and the fact that she "participates" only in the male mean that she is not wanton, and that those inspired by her Eros are themselves attracted to the male — that is, to what is more vigorous and has more mind or intelligence. Alone, these two references might not seem to   †
amount to much — the topic is, after all, Love; Pausanias wants to construct a case for the nobility of paederasty. However, when we note that Aphrodite Ourania is mentioned by name in only two other works *of the entire period* — Herodotos' *Histories* (1.105,   †
131; IV.59) and Xenophon's own *Symposium* (8.9–10) — the fact that there are two references to her in the opening pages of Plato's *Symposium* assumes greater significance. Especially if she *is* Parmenides' cosmic *daimōn*.

Is she? The final piece of circumstantial evidence I would like to bring to bear also originates in an observation made by Santillana (which he develops in the course of elaborating his view that we must understand Parmenides as an *astronomikos* and *phusikos* — someone concerned with physical nature — as well as a mystic and metaphysician). Although its connection to Parmenides' poem can only be surmised, there is nothing speculative about the observation itself. It is an astronomical fact,   *
independently corroborated. It concerns the heliacal risings of the planet we call Venus — a planet the Greeks regarded as an embodiment of Aphrodite, her manifestation in the night sky. If the heliacal risings of this planet — that is, the times when it becomes visible above the eastern horizon *just* before sunrise — if these points are plotted out on the zodiac conceived as circle, a shallow cylinder, the pattern they trace out across the centre of the circle repeats with extraordinary regularity every eight years.

There is a mere 2.4 degrees of rotation through each cycle. And, of course, its heliacal settings will trace out the same repeating pattern, shifted somewhat along the zodiac. Of all the planets, Aphrodite's is the most regular. Its period is also the shortest: eight years, compared to 46 for Mercury, 59 for Saturn, and over 70 for both Jupiter and Mars. Thus it is a regulator, one might say, of the heavens, a "time-keeper … of planetary periods" as Santillana puts it, and, in the reliable unvarying repetition of its path, a moving image of eternity. Its position on its path changes, but the path itself remains the same. Now it is Fr 2 of Parmenides' poem that suddenly becomes resonant, although we do not know if the speaker is the initiate or the welcoming *daimōn*. Is that speaker describing the lineaments of being, or Aphrodite of the Heavens, when he or she says:

†

> *It is all the same to me*
> *where I begin: for to that place I shall come back again.*

And what is the path that Aphrodite Ourania marks out so steadily every eight years, bound by, or *binding,* the circle of the zodiac? —— It is a pentagram, the emblem of the Pythagorean sect.

Amid the plethora of questions that this observation raises, I wish to stress this: that we now have a very clear reason to associate "Aphrodite of the Heavens" with a principle of regulation, order, and absolute reliability. As Santillana remarks, connecting the astronomical pentagram to alleged Pythagorean doctrines, the "image of the pentagram in the sky [indicates] how position was divinely given by the order of time, and how points [as units] having position could be imagined as generating things in their turn. Time, it has been known from ever, brings all things. But time means essentially rhythm." It is in this respect that we may understand Parmenides' cosmic *daimōn* as a being who "steers all things" — one whose representative might plausibly promise her initiates that they

*

> ... *shall also know the encompassing heaven*
> *whence it grew, and how Necessity both led and bound it,*
> *mastering the stars.* (Fr 10)

As for the Pythagoreans ... We know that Plato admired some of them enough to set them to watch over and converse with Sokrates in his final hours. He corresponded with Arkhytas, one of their most famous and accomplished proponents. Geometry and mathematical proportion, as well as alleged Pythagorean precepts (like the basic equality of women with men and a belief in metempsychosis) appear at crucial moments in many of the dialogues. And Parmenides ... There are those rumours that I mentioned earlier. Diogenes Laertios, that gossip columnist of the ancient intellectual world, writing some 700 years after the fact, tells us that Solon says Parmenides studied with Ameinias the Pythagorean. If this is so — and it is not unlikely — his resolute rejection of the Pythagorean view of the fundamentally dual nature of reality, and his insistence on the monadic nature of being, suggests someone in lively conversation with his teachers. Diogenes Laertios also reports that Theophrastos says that Parmenides, not Pythagoras, was the first to state that the earth was spherical; and that Speusippus says that Parmenides wrote laws for his city. And, says Diogenes Laertios, Favorinus tells us that Parmenides was also much interested in the Morning and Evening stars. If the rumour is true, it was he, and not Pythagoras, who was the first Greek to proclaim publicly that humans were mistaken in naming and perceiving two different bodies, where there was only one.

*†

What is it to be a Parmenidean? What are the defining commitments of his thinking? The tattered text that has come down to us does not permit a comprehensive answer to this question. But even the fragments that we have constitute a document that is unparalleled, not only in the surviving record of the West but in the surviving record of the intellectual history of the world. For this much is clear: It is a written account of an initiation journey whose vision of being has none of the secondary hallmarks of a mystical revelation. The *daimōn* warns of some problem, associated with her own speech or — and? — with mortal naming, in the second part. But the knowledge about being imparted in Part 1 is not secret, it is not ineffable, there are no prohibitions on its publication — quite the contrary, it would seem — and despite its impressive obscurity neither the initiate nor the *daimōn* *says* that he or she is struggling to find words. Neither resorts to paradox. The vision of being is in fact an argument. It is an argument to the effect that we are constrained by the meaning of 'to be' to assert the indivisible, atemporal nature of reality. There are indeed many accounts of mystical experience that make a similar claim. But to the best of my knowledge there are none that combine both the frame of a vision quest *and* the attempt to argue the point. These, then, taken together are candidates for identifying features of a 'Parmenidean' view. To this list, I believe we can safely add a feminized context for the initiation and the delivery or experience of insight. And somewhat less safely, but still defensibly, a central preoccupation with *erōs* and love. I speculate further that we should expect to find some suggestion of constraint or order inherent in that love or *erōs*.

All these elements are present in *Symposium*. Diotima refers to her lessons as an initiation in 'erotics'; she attempts to guide Sokrates through both lower and higher mysteries (209e5–210a3). The prelude to the initiation is an argument about the core nature of Eros — that it desires the beautiful and therefore is not, itself, Beauty — in which Sokrates goes out of his way to underline the "necessity" of this observation (200a8–200b2). Diotima's lessons then proceed by way of argument. The lessons are about, the initiation is into, the nature of Eros and the *correct* way of pursuing it. The vocabulary of requirement and constraint is one of the most striking features of the so-called Ladder of Love (210a–e). Its culmination is a vision of the Beautiful that has many of the hallmarks of Parmenidean being, including, above all, an atemporal, indivisible *isness*. And: the initiation occurs in a feminized context: Diotima is a woman.

Why does it occur in a feminized context? What is it about

knowledge of the natural order of love that belongs to women? Why did first Parmenides and then Plato associate such knowledge with atemporal being? Beyond what is suggested by the image of Aphrodite Ourania as an eternal timekeeper, I do not know. The explicit combination of ideas may be original with Parmenides. Perhaps it points to the influence of some strand of Orphism. Or it may be the remnant of an archaic pre-Hellenic fertility cult of which there were other scattered remains in fourth-century Greece. To my mind, though, the absence of an obvious explanation makes the feminized philosophical context in the two documents even more surprising.

To be clear: there are important methodological, literary, and conceptual differences. I do not believe they are sufficient to overwhelm the similarities, but I would like to summarize them, too, so that they may be set in the balance against my guess. First, Plato's focus is Beauty, not Being; second, the initiation occurs in a mundane context — there is no chariot ride, there are no non-human spiritual guides; even more importantly, I believe, there are no horses. Most importantly, there is no separate, second part of Diotima's discussion in which Love and Eros appear for the first time, and as controlling forces in a natural physics; her talk is all of Eros from the start. And yet, and yet ... There is one last remarkable structural echo of Parmenides' poem in the overall compositional strategy of *Symposium*. True, there is no 'secondary physics' that takes up the appearances of the natural world. But there *is* a second part. There is Alkibiades — who, changing the tone and direction of the talk completely, attests to the physical Sokrates' immutable moral beauty, and describes for us the intensities of *particularized* philosophical love.

I conclude from this what is obvious: that Plato is not a mere acolyte. He is his own man: an original thinker of breathtaking imagination and depth. It is distinctly possible that the unique combination of features in Parmenides' account — the *argument* for the meaning of the mystical vision, located in a transmundane frame — reflects Parmenides' position on the cusp of Greek literacy, a position and experience Plato could not share. What seems to me clear is that even if we choose to emphasize Plato's originality or Parmenides' unique cultural perspective, the resonances between the two documents won't go away. Once heard, I believe those resonances reflect back into our reading of Parmenides himself; and they allow us to discern that in both philosophers, there is a conception of *what philosophy is* that is very different from our own. If I am correct, both Plato and Parmenides understand philosophy to have deep, live roots in the mythworld. More specifically, they view philosophy as a practice whose culminating visions spring from a fundamentally feminine province of that mythworld. To read or to teach either of them otherwise is to do them a serious intellectual disservice.

What Is Ineffable?

Is there anything that is genuinely ineffable? If so, how is it possible to think about it or to understand it?

It is fashionable in some philosophical circles to express impatience with these questions. The word 'ineffable,' some will urge, is itself a predicate — one that obviously cannot be predicated of anything on pain of self-contradiction. Others, content to dismiss the paradox as a minor metalinguistic knot, nonetheless assert that ineffability claims are uninteresting: language, they maintain, or some language-like structure, is involved in all human cognition and thus, by definition, nothing *genuinely* ineffable could ever claw its way over the horizon of human consciousness. Part of getting with the program of analytic philosophy has been adopting the agenda of positivist science — and although science, in many quarters, has moved on, many analytic philosophers still feel there is something more than a little disreputable about the very idea of ineffability.

I propose at the outset to dismiss these dismissals. The paradox is indeed superficial: ineffability claims — at least the ones I'm interested in — mean something like 'no words seem right or adequate here.' And the hypothesis of a 'language of thought' is just that: a contestable, and contested, theoretical reconstruction of the evidence. In what follows, I will be developing a few contestable hypotheses of my own, coming at the issue of ineffability from the other end, so to speak. I propose to take serious ineffability claims seriously, and to see what they suggest about the nature of the world. In doing so, I hope that my approach will be recognizable as a kind of inductive science — that is, an activity that the ghost of Xenophanes might recognize as continuous with his own.

By 'serious ineffability claims' I mean ones in which people really appear to be driving at something — they're not just being flip, or witty, or feeling frustrated by the complexity of some situation. What would have to be the case for such ineffability claims to be true? The question is difficult because we are immediately confronted by an empirical puzzle that cannot be easily dismissed: often, we make a serious ineffability claim but then don't fall silent. We keep trying to communicate, or articulately wishing that we could. The *desire* to communicate is still manifestly present. The ineffability claim itself can be an expression of this desire.

The intensity of the pressure to communicate is, I believe, key to the phenomenon as a whole. To focus on it is to focus in the right direction. It tells us that meaning is at stake.

I · A FIRST HYPOTHESIS

What sorts of things do we say are ineffable? Frequently, what we feel we cannot talk about adequately is an experience — a complex of perceptions, feelings, thoughts, and memories, something we undergo. So-called mystical experiences obviously comprise a large subclass here; but often experiences of the natural world are described as ineffable, as are experiences of love, both sexual and nonsexual. We also often have difficulty conveying dreams in words, and our experiences of art, especially of music, are frequently said to be 'wordless' or indescribable. And on occasion, we want to claim that the art objects or the rocks and trees themselves are ineffable. I have chosen the examples that follow with an eye to themes and characteristics that occur repeatedly across cultures, while avoiding accounts that impose doctrinal religious interpretations. Such interpretations tend to deflect attention away from the raw phenomenology that should be our initial focus. For there are commonalities among accounts of ineffable experience *in addition* to ineffability claims. These commonalities can be discerned across cultures and also in accounts that make no overt reference to religious conviction. Forthwith, the examples.

Suzanne Langer:

[I]t seems peculiarly hard for our literal minds to grasp the idea that anything can be known which cannot be named … The real power of music lies in the fact that it can be 'true' to the life of feeling in a way that language cannot … Hans Mersmann … wrote: "The possibility of expressing opposites simultaneously gives the most intricate reaches of expressiveness to music as such, and carries it, in this respect, far beyond the limits of the other arts." Music is revealing, where words are obscuring … [Its meanings exist] outside the pale of discursive thinking. The imagination that responds to music is personal and associative and logical, tinged with affect, tinged with bodily rhythm, tinged with dream, but concerned with a wealth of formulations for its wealth of wordless knowledge, its whole knowledge of emotional and organic experience, of vital impulse, balance, conflict, the ways of living and dying and feeling … [Its meanings occur to us in] a flash of understanding. The lasting effect is … to make things conceivable rather than to store up propositions. Not [propositional] communication but insight is the gift of music.

Bernard Berenson:

It was a morning in early summer. A silver haze shimmered and trembled over the lime trees. The air was laden with fragrance. The temperature was like a caress. I remember — I need not recall — that I climbed up a tree stump and felt suddenly immersed in Itness. I did not call it by that name. I had no need for words. It and I were one.

R.M. Bucke:

I was in a state of quiet, almost passive enjoyment, not actually thinking, but letting ideas, images and emotions flow of themselves, as it were, through my mind. All at once, without warning of any kind, I found myself wrapped in a flame-colored cloud. For an instant I thought of fire, an immense conflagration somewhere close *by in that great city; the next, I knew that the fire was within my-self. Directly afterward there came upon me a sense of exultation, of immense joyousness accompanied or immediately followed by an intellectual illumination impossible to describe. Among other things ... I saw that the universe is not composed of dead matter, but is, on the contrary, a living Presence; I became conscious in myself of eternal life ... I saw that all men are immortal; that the cosmic order is such that without any peradventure all things work together for the good of each and all; that the foundation principle of the world, of all the worlds, is what we call love, and that the happiness of each and all is in the long run absolutely certain. The vision lasted a few seconds and was gone but the memory of it and the sense of the reality of what it taught has remained during the quarter of a century which has since elapsed.*

It's noteworthy that these passages are articulate. They make it clear that the experience *can* be described, can be described in some detail, at least insofar as we are required to *say what happened*. We can recount events that occurred, in the correct sequence; we can describe the impressions they made on us; and in the case of music, we can describe, or even write out, the sequence of notes.

The problem, then, seems to be that listing a series of notes, giving a run down of events, indeed, simply speaking — in any way — can feel wrong. It is as though such speaking involves a distortion or misrepresentation of some kind; we feel it fails to capture what *matters* in the experience, or that it does not adequately convey what we grasped or understood.

This leads me to my first hypothesis:

HYPOTHESIS ONE: *It is the* meanings *of certain experiences that are ineffable.*

This would explain why we seem to be able to say so much about the experiences themselves, while continuing to insist that they are indescribable.

But what is meaning? Meaning, I would like to say with Robert Bringhurst, is what keeps going. It is what keeps going right through us, transforming us as it does so. Or, with Simone Weil, I could say meaning is the 'mystery in reading':

*

Two women each receive a letter, announcing to each that her son is dead. The first, upon just glancing at the paper, faints, and until her death, her eyes, her mouth, her movements will never again be as they were. The second woman remains the same: her expression, her attitude do not change; she cannot read. It's not sensation but meaning that has grabbed hold of the first woman ... Everything happens as if the pain resided in the letter and sprang up from it into the reader's face. As for the sensations themselves, such as the colour of the paper or of the ink, they don't even appear.

†

Weil herself is quick to state the difficulty with this idea of meaning:

It is in this way that at every moment of our life the meanings we ourselves read in appearances take hold of us as though from outside. We can therefore argue endlessly about the reality of the external world. Because what we call the world are the meanings we read — it isn't real. But it grabs hold of us as though from outside — so it is real.

But Weil does not see this difficulty as a difficulty with our characterization of meaning. That characterization does precipitate an old, apparently insoluble, dilemma. But the problem, Weil suggests, is that we want to resolve the contradiction rather than allowing it to lead us into what is genuinely mysterious. This is a bold suggestion, but I believe she is right. Weil herself construed the mystery in Platonic terms; but it can also be stated as a puzzle about the relation of certain kinds of wholes to their constituent parts. For example: *Even if we grasp it incorrectly,* what happens when we hear or read a sentence is different from what happens when we attend piecemeal to its individual phonemes or syllables. (Weil asks us to consider the difficulty we have proofreading a familiar text.) The same difference is at play when we hear a melody rather than perceive first one tone, then another tone, then another. (Quickly: what is the interval between the first and seventh tones in "Row, Row, Row Your Boat"? You will have to sing the *melody,* slowly and deliberately counting on your fingers as you go, to find out what the seventh note is. And by then, unless you are a musician, you will probably have lost track of the first tone. But both are there in your memory, if the melody is. Why can't you just hum one and then the other?)

    To put the point generally: what Weil terms *les significations,* Max Wertheimer calls *Gestalten.* The mystery of *la lecture* then is not how we learn to form correct gestalts, nor how to construct an epistemology that could coherently evaluate their correctness; the mystery is that we form gestalts at all. And that they matter to us far more than the collections of elements into which we are capable of analyzing them. They matter to us so much that we reserve expressions that show we've really *understood* something — "now I get it!" or "oh, I see how it goes!" — exclusively for situations that involve the grasp of gestalts. This is what Weil is suggesting is involved in 'reading' the world: not an accumulation of impressions of discrete particulars — an *m,* as it were, followed by an *e,* followed by an *a,* an *n,* an *i,* another *n,* and a *g* — but a non-sequential grasp — sudden and complete — of an integrated whole. To grasp such a whole is to experience meaning.

II · HOW COULD THE MEANING OF AN
EXPERIENCE BE INEFFABLE? HYPOTHESIS TWO

Why can it feel wrong to use words?

    In some cases, it appears that the intensity of an experience, or the intensity of our emotional reaction, is beyond words. The use of language is perceived to have a dampening effect, as though we'd turned the volume down or washed out the colour. But as the examples I've given illustrate, overwhelming affect is not always the issue. In the most striking cases, the use of language is felt to distort, or to be at odds with, the meaning of the experience as a whole. The meaning can include the emotional intensity of the experience but is not restricted to it.

This immediately suggests a second hypothesis:

HYPOTHESIS TWO: *The* structure *of some meanings is different from the structure or structures of language.*

This, as it stands, is vague. In a first attempt to refine the hypothesis, I have looked not only for common features among reports of ineffable experience, but also for an *independently* plural epistemology — that is, an epistemology that, without reference to ineffability claims, sees reason to suppose that there are at least two structurally distinct ways of knowing the world and that at least one of these ways does not involve the use of words.

Common features that crop up in conjunction with ineffability claims are these:

- a sense of at-oneness with the environment, or an absence of a sense of self;
- a sense of timelessness, or eternity, or that time has been suspended;
- an awareness of opposites that do not exclude each other;
- a sense of being flooded with love or joy, often awe or astonishment, occasionally horror.

Other features appear in individual accounts, and many accounts lack mention of one or another of the characteristics mentioned. But a broad survey of ineffability claims suggests that these form the core.

As for the plural epistemology: there are any number, but the one culturally closest to hand, and which I have found most suggestive, is Freud's — the theory of mind and knowing usually referred to as his metapsychology. It is outlined in papers and sections of books that span his entire career; and one of its summary statements is what made him famous: the idea that in addition to a conscious mental life, each of us also possesses an unconscious, a realm of mental life that functions independently of and in ways foreign to conscious thought.

   In appealing to Freud's view, I do not mean to suggest that I think it is in all particulars correct; nor that I believe that, even in outline, it is uncontroversial. It is hotly contested in many quarters and for many different reasons. In this respect, it is not unlike the theory of the cosmos published in 1543 under the title *De revolutionibus orbium coelestium*: Copernicus' theory, too, faced stiff opposition, and in some cases for good reason — there were both conceptual and empirical problems. As we know, one key feature (retained from the Ptolemaic system) — the premise of the planets' uniform circular motion — turned out to be incorrect; to reconcile this premise with astronomical observations, Copernicus also had to retain epicycles and eccentrics; and he was unable to provide adequate replies to obvious objections — such as why, if the earth was moving at speed, everything on it didn't fall off. But there was one thing that Copernicus got *hugely* right; and I think something similar is true in Freud's case. What Freud got right is this: there is coherent, meaningful mental activity that cannot be adequately modelled with standard logical and causal structures. We know that Copernicus was not the first to think the earth moved around the sun, and Freud was not the first to think that humans have more than one way of knowing. But he was the first European to try to amass evidence and to put the case to an intellectual culture deeply conditioned by the Enlightenment. This is a cultural circumstance in which we still find ourselves. The history of Enlightenment culture's refusal to take dreams seriously is matched, if not superseded, by its contempt for ineffability claims. I believe these facts are connected, and that Freud's theory — or a version of it — can explain why this is so. In showing how a revised version of Freud's account can explain a second, apparently unrelated, phenomenon that it was not designed to address, I hope both to legitimize interest in ineffability claims and to strengthen Freud's fundamental insight.

   In overview: there are striking correspondences between the core characteristics of ineffability claims and aspects of Freud's metapsychological theory of the structure of dream thought. Reflection on these correspondences suggests the following refinement to Hypothesis Two: *Conscious awareness of what Freud called primary process thought underlies at least some ineffability claims.*

III · PRIMARY AND SECONDARY PROCESS: A REVISION OF FREUD'S VIEW

Freud's idea that the life of the human mind comes in at least two distinct forms arose from his attempts to understand how dreams could impress us as having meaning — indeed could have powerful effects on our lives and serve as important guides in unravelling the psyche — while at the same time appearing to be a kind of nonsense. 'Primary process' was his term for the 'unrestricted' psychic play that characterizes dreams, and 'secondary process' was the name he gave to the organization of 'normal' waking thought — 'secondary' because it constituted a developmental inhibition of primary process.   †

Although Freud thought primary process was uninhibited, he did not think that it lacked structure. He proposes "condensation and displacement of cathexes" as its "distinguishing marks." The sense of esoteric science conveyed by the vocabulary is deceiving. The examples Freud gives show that condensation and displacement are simply metonymy and metaphor in epistemic guise. What is crucial about them is their shared logic: patterns of connection that are broadly associative rather than narrowly conceptual or causal. (Elsewhere, Freud makes it clear that he would not, himself, dignify these patterns with the epithet 'logic.' In primary process, he says, thoughts are linked by associations "of a kind … scorned by our normal thinking and relegated to the use of jokes.") These associative and alogical connections are not the only features of primary process, though. In other passages, Freud tells us that it is also characterized by timelessness and   *
by a tolerance of paradox and contradiction.   *

Secondary process not only avoids puns and poetry, it recognizes, and operates according to, causal orders in space and time, and adheres to the standard inference patterns of basic   * logic — especially the principle of non-contradiction. It inhibits primary process in accordance with what Freud called the "reality principle": the organism's recognition that, if it is to survive, it cannot hallucinate the satisfaction of basic needs, but must reach out, grasp, and then manipulate features of the external world. In order to do this successfully, Freud speculates, the organism must make correct judgements about what is external to the self and what is internal to it; it must, as well, draw distinctions in space and time, and among individual images and perceptions. Language, he says, is the tool that secondary process develops to pursue this task.

This, so far, sounds promising as a theory of mind that could be used to account for ineffability claims. It distinguishes two modes of thinking, aligns language, logic, and a sense of self with one of them, and aligns timelessness, multiple associative connections, tolerance of contradiction, and, by inference, *absence* of both language and a sense of self, with the other. The difficulty is that Freud attached yet another set of contrasting characteristics to primary and secondary process: only secondary process, he claimed, only thought "linked with word-presentations," can become *conscious*. Primary-process ideation, he maintained, remains essentially *unconscious*. If this is so, then of course primary process cannot be what is involved in our conscious awareness of ineffable experience.

Freud's view that primary process cannot be conscious is, in fact, a version of his notion that it constitutes a refusal of reality. At its root is Freud's belief that dreams are *nothing more than* hallucinated fulfilments of unacceptable desires, and that they have the structure they do *in order* to prevent them from reaching conscious awareness.

But there is overwhelming evidence, much of it in Freud's own observations, that this cannot be the whole story. In the first place, we remember dreams. And we tell jokes, and, while using language, make slips of the tongue — conscious phenomena that, according to Freud, are also structured by primary process. Charles Rycroft, one of Freud's ablest commentators, has argued that dream-like thinking is characteristic of conscious literary

artists, and that, in addition, such artists frequently do not experience "impermeable ego boundaries" between themselves and
other things. (It would not be difficult to expand his observations
to include painters, sculptors, composers, and dancers.) The arts
in general frequently exploit paradox, and many artists have
testified to an experience of timelessness in connection with   * †
their compositional activity. In the case of puns, our awareness
of primary process may indeed be slight. But in other cases, it is
more significant. The at-oneness characteristic of mystical experience, I propose, involves a sense of the profound extralogical
connectedness of the world, of the world comprehended as a
whole, sudden and complete. It is, in other words, an immense
gestalt of multiple, interlocking gestalts.

Not only is there a link, then, between what Weil calls meaning and what Wertheimer calls gestalts; there appears to be a link
between gestalt thinking and what Freud calls primary process.
The evidence for this connection is circumstantial, and a thorough
exploration would constitute a major study. Here, I will simply
sketch a few of the reasons for thinking it is real.

Gestalt shifts function like metaphors; that is, they operate
according to what Freud called displacement. In fact, metaphorical
understanding is a species of gestalt shift: an internal structural
relation is perceived between two disparate entities; they are
connected by a deep, underlying structural unity — the same
ontological 'shape,' as it were. These internal structural relations   †
cannot be understood by the "traditional piecewise methods of
logic ... and science," according to Wertheimer. Konrad Lorenz
describes them as "ratiomorphic," intending by this a contrast
with what he calls "rational processes." Rational processes, he
implies, are focused on "exact" perception of objects; they are
quantitative, and generate statistics; from their perspective, gestalt comprehension appears to be "marred by utterly incomprehensible epistemological illogicality." One of the most striking
characteristics of gestalt perception, according to Lorenz, is its
incorrigibility — this, he points out, can make it dangerous; but
we can, he says, compensate for this danger either by increas-
ing the range of perceptions on which the gestalt is based or by

"collect[ing] data from another 'point of view.'" I am struck by
two things here: first, the oft-reported incorrigibility of mystical
experience; and second, the precise echo of Weil's remarks on
how to discriminate between the real and the illusory in "inner
life." Nearly all discussions of gestalt comprehension emphasize
its sudden, timeless, and involuntary nature. Both Arne Næss
and Lorenz also emphasize the way in which gestalts evaporate
under the press of "rationally controlled attention to … details."
Michael Polanyi distinguishes "two kinds of awareness" — one
characterized by gestalt comprehension, and the other by the
referential word–thing gestures of linguistic thought. In sum,
gestalt comprehension appears to possess versions of the defining
characteristics of primary process; diverse thinkers contrast it
with a 'scientific,' 'objectifying,' 'piecemeal' mode of awareness;
and, like primary process, gestalt comprehension has for the
most part been derided and marginalized when it has come to
the attention of post-Cartesian European intellectuals.

All this suggests that the basic scenario is simpler than Freud
himself imagined: human beings can think in at least two structurally different ways, one of which is good at handling phenomena piecemeal according to Aristotelian logic and Newtonian physics, another of which is good at making associative
connections, disregarding distinctions, and binding experience
into a unified whole. These structures can, often do, reach for
constituents formed by the other logic. The boundary between
the two systems is not impermeable, and features of one may
occur in mental activity that is dominated by the other — thus,
for example, self-focussed and lucid dreams, thus gestalt thinking
in mathematics and the sciences.

Poetry presents an especially intriguing case, as it seems to be
intimately involved with both modes of thought. While it displays
paradigmatically most of the features of primary process, it seems
in one crucial respect to be emblematic of secondary process:
far from being ineffable, it is *made* of words. There is, however,
an interesting sense in which poetry *is* ineffable: it is often said
to be untranslatable, and it is famously resistant to paraphrase.
That is, it is made of language, but in an odd and peculiar way: it

consists of words, but only and exactly *these* words, in precisely *this* arrangement. Its meaning is uncapturable — in its original tongue — by any other use of language. Translators of poetry often describe their activity as an attempt to 'recapture' this meaning in a 'new' poem in another language — as though the meaning were something like the effect produced by a chord on one instrument, which feeling could be reproduced by a somewhat different chord on a different instrument. A translation of the *words* of the original poem won't work. (We sense immediately that we are once again dealing with gestalts.)

It is, I believe, Freud's tight and relentless focus on dreams and the phenomenon of repression that prevented him from seeing the wider implications of his view. And he was right that there was a connection between repression and primary process in his own culture. But it was not that primary process structure somehow prevented thoughts from becoming conscious; rather, because primary process was *itself* denigrated, it was able to become a virtually exclusive home for culturally unacceptable ideas. If you create an epistemological ghetto, then you can toss things you don't want to think about into it. In cultures in which primary process thinking is not denigrated — in which dreams are regarded as sources of publicly valuable knowledge; in which poetry, sculpture, painting, and dance are central means of archiving intellectual wealth; in which everyone *knows* that shamans don't talk about what they can't talk about — in such cultures, there is not, as far as I know, anything that corresponds to turn-of-the-twentieth-century, bourgeois, Viennese neurosis.

IV · WHAT IS INEFFABLE? HYPOTHESIS THREE

To summarize: to take ineffability claims seriously is to accept that there are experiences whose meanings are distorted or compromised when they are put into words. For this to be the case, I have proposed, the form or structure of such meaning has to be distinct from the form of linguified thought. Freud's metapsychology offers a suggestive first approximation to a distinction between ineffable and 'effable' knowing: it delineates two types of mental functioning, one characteristic of dreams, the other characteristic of waking thought. The first has additional characteristics — timelessness, absence of a sense of self, tolerance of paradox and contradiction — that echo other core features of ineffable thought. I have proposed a revision of Freud's account that emphasizes the obvious — that we are often aware of primary process ideation. This, in turn, reveals what is structurally essential about Freud's account: human beings experience (at least) two modes of interpenetrating awareness. Ineffable thought is characterized dominantly by the intensely associative, conceptually nonsequential mode.

Crucially, both modes can be completely conscious. Primary process characterizes dream thought but also characterizes many waking experiences, a number of which we describe as ineffable — attempting, within secondary process, to gesture to their primary process structure. I think Freud is right about what secondary process is for: it is for conceiving the world as a collection of discrete physical objects that we must learn to manipulate, alter, and control if we, as discrete physical organisms, are to survive. But if Freud is wrong that primary process is simply the dumping ground for culturally unacceptable instinctual energy, then what is *it* for? I believe that if we don't assume that secondary process is the only way to access reality, then the answer springs out at us: primary process, like secondary process, is a way of knowing the world.

† Just as there are species of sequential thinking — proofs in logic appear to be different from chains of causal reasoning in science — so there are identifiable species of primary process ideation. Dreams constitute one subclass; what this culture calls mystical experience constitutes another; and I suspect we could argue that jokes, slips of the tongue, poems, each of the other arts, flashes of mathematical insight, and sudden inductive inference in the sciences, constitute yet other distinguishable species. And there are further divisions within each: anxiety dreams are distinct from numinous dreams, experience of at-oneness with the natural world is not the same as experience of at-oneness in which sensory awareness fades completely. Et cetera. Some

instances of primary process ideation are simple and fleeting —
slips of the tongue, for example. Others are complex and life-
changing — Bucke's mystical experience or Langer's appreciation
of Mozart. It is such complex experiences of primary process
ideation that appear to precipitate ineffability claims; and in the
interests of focussing on them, I would like to suggest a taxonomy
that cuts across many of the divisions I've just suggested. Some
primary process ideation, I propose, is simply associative — a
word that alliterates with the one we're reaching for may be the   †
one that comes out of our mouths; and it may have been close
to the surface of our mind because of some chance event that
occurred earlier in the day. But in other instances, the associative
connections are multiple and involve a number of dimensions
simultaneously. The result is a complex integrated gestalt, rather
than a series of associations.   †

Consider, for example, the brief chorale that concludes Bach's
cantata "Nun komm, der Heiden Heiland," BWV 61 (overleaf).
Note the complex polyphony that surrounds the descending
G major scale in the soprano line in the last seven bars. Note
also the text set to that scale: "I await thee with great longing"
(*Deiner wart' ich mit verlangen*). The scale, announcing our
longing, is that about which everything else in the composition
turns. But the scale itself does not 'long'; it steps very securely
down into a cadence on the tonic. Its musical gesture, then, is an
aural image of faith. So, together, the words and music say that
the world turns about our faith, which is the foundation of our
longing.

The notion of a complex integrated gestalt is a rough and intuitive characterization — that is, it is a preliminary gestalt. But
to imagine that it is therefore unsuitable for philosophical work
and reflection is to forget that *logic* and *causality* are themselves
similarly imprecise notions. Their vague boundaries and lack of
rigour do not prevent them from being immensely powerful in
our philosophical conceptions of the world. Ineffable experience,
I wish to suggest, is a species of primary process ideation that
involves complex, integrated gestalts. It is the multiplicity and intensity of the non-logical, non-causal connections informing such

gestalts that cannot be communicated adequately in language. For language is the medium of secondary process thought, whose aim is to block gestalt comprehension and to foster awareness of the world as a collection of discrete entities whose relations are ordered in causal and logical sequences. Of course, the world *is* such a collection of entities; but to take ineffability claims seriously is to open oneself to the suggestion that the world *is also*

an integrated whole, whose structure is reflected in the structure of primary process thought.

Is language *necessarily* the medium of secondary process thought? I believe that this is a question like: *Are saws necessarily tools for cutting wood?* To which the answer is: *Well, no: you can use saws to make music and you can cut wood with an axe.* But to leave it at this is to neglect the extraordinary functional fit between saws and woodcutting. The question about language might, then, be recast as: Did language evolve in conjunction with secondary process thought? Or is it literacy that has produced, in our own culture, an *experience* of language as the tool of analysis? Or perhaps literacy reinforces — allows us to *see* — something basic about the nature of language? These are excellent questions. I do not know their answers and I am not sure that we have, at this time, the means to answer them.

What we do know is that language is now, in our culture, a fundamental means whereby the discreteness of discrete entities is emphasized and reinforced. And in the wake of the suggestion that the world as given in secondary process thought — the world of discrete entities — is not the only world, I would like to offer one further extension of the hypothesis as it now stands. That hypothesis is that conscious awareness of primary process is at the root of many serious ineffability claims. In amplifying this idea, I have suggested that what Freud calls displacement and condensation are themselves species of highly integrative non-sequential associative connections, and these connections also structure what I have referred to as gestalts. Let me now offer a simpler and less esoteric term, and with it, an ontological version of the hypothesis. What numinous dreams, mystical experience, unparaphrasable lyric poems, a great deal of music, and the natural world all share, I believe, is *resonant form*.

HYPOTHESIS THREE: *It is the experience of resonant form that is ineffable.*

What is resonant form? Form that is the result of an attunement or integration of multiple aspects, constituents, or parts. (Does talk of constituents here mean that secondary process awareness is ontologically basic? No. The notions of 'constituent' and 'part' imply reductionism only when their use is itself informed by a reductionist context.) In the physical case of a resonance body, a vibration in one component will set off vibrations throughout the structure. And a perfectly tuned chord offers us a paradigmatic example of resonant form. In a resonant ideational structure, images, sounds, word meanings (if there are words) and connotations, etymologies, emotional associations, tone, colour, et cetera will be attuned in this way: attending to one aspect of the meaning will quicken other aspects, too.   +

The image is profoundly aural, but it has a rough visual analogue. Imagine the world as a geodesic sphere in which every node is connected to every other node not by steel bars, but by elastic bands. Any change at one node will effect a change at all others. Imagine that the various nodes, like individual beings in the world, are in movement. And now imagine an abstract version of this sphere: the nodes shrink to dimensionless points. 'They' are nothing but the constantly changing sets of relata that define any given point. Abstract further: eliminate visual representation: what-is is a wholly resonant structure. Aspects of this structure are experienced as resonant structures themselves, but what sounds through them is, ultimately, the resonance of all that is.

Such structures, with their simultaneous quickening of multiple aspects, are precisely what the language of metaphysical judgement, of logical and causal sequence, cannot deliver. Language of its nature holds things still, distinguishes them, allows us to pick through them piecemeal without interference from other things or the world as a whole. And then to bind, glue, or hammer them together in arrangements at least partially of our own choosing. The aim of secondary process thinking is just this: to block the perception of resonance, and thereby to make technology possible.

But if Weil is right that the experience of grasping a gestalt — that is, the perception of resonant form — *is* the experience of meaning, then we get a very surprising and counter-intuitive result. For the aim of secondary process thinking is then also this: to block the experience of meaning.

Let me be immediately clear about two things: I am not saying that all linguified thinking is without meaning, nor am I saying that it is impossible to experience meaning in connection with words. Weil's paradigmatic example of the grasp of a gestalt — reading — belies both possibilities.

'Meaning,' as analytically trained philosophers well know, is a word that speakers of English tend to throw around with some abandon. I would like, then, in good secondary process fashion, to draw some distinctions. If, with Weil and Wertheimer, we reserve the word 'meaning' for what we experience when we perceive resonant, atemporal, non-sequential complexes, then it turns out we cannot, without confusion, use it of what we communicate in grammatically unexceptional prose about de-contextualized, linguistically parsed, logically and causally se-quenced ideation. I suggest we use 'information' for the latter. It is not an etymologically ideal choice, but it reflects something of the contemporary spirit of the word, that is, its current cultural gestalt. It also allows us to capture an important aspect of how we already use the word 'meaningful': we *don't* use it when we are confronted with a mass of mechanically sequenced data. We save 'meaningful' — when we use it sincerely — for a special class of experiences: those in which our perspective is significantly altered. We use it, that is, when we understand a complex in a new way, when we experience a shift in gestalt.

In reserving 'meaning' for what fully analyzed prose sentences don't have, instead of what they do, I am indeed flying in the face of a nearly 100-year-old tradition in English-speaking philosophy. I do, however, take myself to be keeping company with the later Wittgenstein. One of his fundamental insights was that, in using language meaningfully, we *make gestures* that are themselves inextricably embedded in what he called a "form of life." Language is meaningful, on this view, when its words and sentences are aspects of a resonant gestalt. It is only when it has been denatured — when it has been cut off from living engagement with the living world — that language becomes meaningless.

In making this claim, my aim is not just to close ranks with Wittgenstein against the positivists in philosophy. It is overtly political in a wider sense. I will turn to a full discussion shortly. Before I do, though, I wish to take up two final epistemological points.

The first concerns the nature of our awareness of resonant form. While I have argued on empirical evidence that we are

obviously awake and attentive on many occasions when we experience resonant form, it seems equally obvious that we do not always attend with care and precision either to that form as a whole, or to its aspects. Consider, for example, what happens when we are sensitive to music but listen without training; or read a poem and are moved but can't say anything about why. If training leads to an exclusive focus on details, it can depress our ability to perceive resonance; but in many cases, it can heighten   *
it. Our experience becomes richer and we become, we say, more articulate about it. This points, I believe, to one of the important ways in which primary process and secondary process awareness interact: we use secondary process thinking to sharpen our perception of aspects of resonant wholes, bringing those aspects into distinct focus. And then, typically, we form new gestalts of these more focussed aspects — and then focus aspects of that gestalt,   †
and form a new gestalt again. The richest experience is of the most precise and therefore most multiply re-envisioned form. It is comprehension in which the unhealthy division between what this culture calls science and what it calls art is erased: the flower of deep and real attention.

The second point on which I wish to touch in passing concerns the role of emotion in the perception of resonant form. Earlier, I noted that we sometimes say that an experience is ineffable when we are overwhelmed with emotion; and I distinguished this kind of ineffability claim from the structural ineffability claim that we make when we sense that the use of language distorts resonant meaning. Here, I wish to offer an observation and register a question. The observation is that Freud's description of secondary process, with its references to bound or restricted energy flow, suggests that a large amount of psychic energy, such as may be associated with very intense emotion, could not be 'contained' by secondary process. I do not know enough about neuropsychology to comment on the plausibility of this suggestion, but it is my impression that Freud's 'hydraulic' model of the changing patterns of electrical excitation in the brain has not yet been entirely disconfirmed. The question I would like to raise is metaphysical   *
in nature, but it too perhaps has neuropsychological aspects.

It is this: Is emotion itself — or are some specific emotions — resonant in structure? Or perhaps emotion is, or some specific emotions are, to primary process, what analysis is to secondary process: a way in which we *think* about the world-as-resonance.

V · THE POLITICS OF INEFFABILITY

Earlier, I admitted to flying in the face of the tradition in English-speaking philosophy in which I was raised: the view that meaning is quintessentially, and in some originary way, possessed by words and strings of words. Meaning, I have suggested, is instead a function of resonance, and is possessed by anything with resonant form. What we analyze when we analyze sentences — specifying their grammatical structure, the referents of their nouns, their truth conditions, and their propositional forms — is the structure of information. Such analysis is not irrelevant to meaning: information can be fundamental to making aspects of resonant form precise, and it too can be communicated. But in and of itself, analysis is a tool for the control of meaning. Analysis tames resonance, mutes it, proscribes it; it insists not only on aspects but on elements — that is, it claims individual things or parts are ontologically fundamental. An analytic synthesis is a sum, not an integration, of its parts.

What allows analysis to be the tool that it is — the teeth of the saw, as it were — are the distinctions maintained through non-resonant uses of language. The explicit codification of grammatical rules and the development of formal logical languages for the pursuit of linguistic analysis are, in part, intensifications of the agenda of control. (They are also, in part, an expression of humans' curiosity and their fascination with games — *can this be done?*) The idea that intelligence itself consists of rule-governed sequences of zeroes and ones is one apotheosis of this agenda. At its heart is the conflation of clarity with mechanism.

The root of the English word 'clarity,' according to Ernest
* Klein, is *klā-* or *kal-*, a proto-Indo-European base meaning to shout or to resound. The old image, then, is not one that evokes control, either by the hand or the intellect; it is not even visual.

It is an aural image — of sound as a physical force, by which we are literally moved or shaken, *with* which we move *together*.

And when the base becomes a Latin word, *clarus*, some sense of this physical impact is retained, although the sense modality shifts. *Clarus* does not mean transparent or invisible: it means radiant, shining, glorious — the visual analogue of aural resonance.

Clarity and meaning, then, do go together. And language can indeed possess both, despite the fact that it is the ambassador of the particulate, manipulable world. The physical stuff of natural languages — most often sound, sometimes gesture (and in the case of mathematical languages, written notation) — is capable of resonance. This resonance is literal, in the case of sound, and of a visual-echoic nature in the case of gesture. (It is possible, for example, both to rhyme and to pun in American Sign Language.) And as I indicated earlier, thought structures are capable of resonance that involves ideational as well as physical aspects: a word sounds like what it signifies, or it sounds like its opposite, or a phrase moves with a rhythm commensurate with the tone of the image it evokes, or its rhythm cuts across that tone; and these and other similar aspects stand in resonant relation to one another, informed by the meaning of the whole. We no longer teach rhetoric in the schools, but every great orator has understood either instinctively or through study how to move an audience by exploiting language's capacity for resonance. What happens when language becomes locally resonant is, as Freud noticed, sometimes a joke or sometimes a slip of the tongue. But when its resonance is wide and deep, enacting the resonance of the world, language becomes literature. (When such linguistic resonance is repossessed for purposes of control or manipulation, it becomes advertising. This is why many people dislike advertising: they correctly sense it as a kind of blasphemy, a debasement of something that matters, namely, meaning.)

To summarize again: what is ineffable is resonant form. This is the form of meaning. And so what is ineffable is also, ultimately, meaning itself. What then is language for? It is the means, the enabler, of practical thought — thought that aims to control and manipulate. Language enables such manipulation by allowing us to image the world as a machine, something that consists of wholly distinct but interacting parts. In its role as stabilizer of the world of discrete contents, language refers but it does not resound; it does not communicate movement; it dis-integrates. Language does come to mean, however, when its gestures are complexly resonant. They can be made so deliberately in a work of literature; and they are naturally so when they issue from and embody a form of life.

Meaning, then, and with it ineffability, is not an all-or-nothing affair. Our experience ranges from the ontologically galvanizing to the ontologically vapid, as does what we say, and how we say it. An experience is unlanguageable *to the extent that* it is an experience of resonant form. To the extent that we remain immersed in a culture of human talk and linguistic excess, we may nonetheless feel compelled to find words for such experiences. 'Ineffable,' I have been arguing, is one of the most accurate.

Primary process is, like secondary process, a way of knowing what-is.

One thing ineffability claims will teach us, if we let them, is that the world is not *only* a mechanically organized collection of objects. The notion that it is, is a culturally specific idea. That idea has resulted in vast, almost incomprehensible, damage, and it has been opposed at virtually every point by outriders in its home culture and almost universally by the civilizations colonized by that culture, many of which have been destroyed. It is time to set this idea aside. Yes, the world is an aggregate of objects; but it is, also, a deeply unified whole, a complex of associated and interlocking gestalts, better comprehended as a piece of polyphonic music than as heaps of lumber piled around the workshop door.

These two visions are not compatible from a secondary process perspective. Nevertheless, what ineffability claims teach us is that they occupy the same space. It is this metaontological perspective that we must negotiate if we are to find a way out of the various cultural crises we have manufactured. They are one crisis: the loss of meaning — which occurs both through cultural marginalization of the products of primary process thinking and through the subsequent atrophy of the capacity to comprehend resonant form. Symptoms of this loss include tendencies to regard all dreams as merely private fantasies, to regard the arts as entertainments, to derogate visual thinking in mathematics and the sciences, and to regard ineffability claims as spurious or as, at best, effusions attaching to delusional states.

Ecological science teaches us that things are distinct but not separate. Ontology teaches us that things are distinct *and* that nothing exists but a radiant net of relations.

The world, therefore, is the aggregate of distinct individual things; but it is also resonance.

Its internal relation to itself has the structure of metaphor.

To grasp this, a human being must both possess language and let language go.

In the guise of language, the world is usable; in the guise of resonance, it moves us — to love, to gratitude, to awe. We, too, become resonant.

Moral systems founded on utility, on rights, on duties to beings that demonstrate secondary process awareness, are just that: systems. They are rooted in a truncated epistemology that enshrines a truncated ontology.

To be moral is to find one's fit with the world.

Epistemology is politics. This is not because what humans think is coextensive with what-is. It is because to understand what-is is to be trued by the real.

Imagination and the Good Life

I · THINKING IN IMAGES

1. A.R. Manser writing in the *Encyclopedia of Philosophy* opens the entry on imagination with the following sentence:

Imagination is generally held to be the power of forming mental images or other concepts not directly derived from sensation.

The *Random House Dictionary of the English Language* offers the following:

1. the action of … forming mental images or concepts of what is not actually present to the senses.

The *Oxford English Dictionary* confirms this sense and makes explicit its negative connotation:

1. The action of … forming a mental concept of what is not actually present to the senses … the result of this process, a mental image or idea (often with implication that the conception does not correspond to the reality of things, hence freq. vain (false, *etc.)* imagination).

Subsequent definitions, and Manser's discussion, make reference to the reproductive imagination, which involves accurate memory of previous sense experience; and the *Random House Dictionary* notes that the creative imagination — inventing new images — can be used in problem-solving.

None makes reference to thinking in images.

2. Philosophy is understandably suspicious of a faculty whose conceptions "[do] not correspond to the reality of things." Philosophy is interested in truth; and its current English-speaking academic instantiation believes truth is a property of propositions, or perhaps sentences — certainly something linguistic, and secured in some fashion by logic.

   It is no accident that the single entry on imagination in the *Encyclopedia of Philosophy* is two and a half pages long, while the entries on logic run to 151 pages, dozens more if we include the sections on formal systems and the entries on individual logicians and their most famous results. (The entry on imagination is, however, almost identical in length to the entry on The Good.)

3. The *Routledge Companion to Epistemology* mentions imagination twice, first in a passing reference to Arthur Pap in the article "a priori/a posteriori," and then in two paragraphs at the end of the entry on Hume. (There is no discussion of it in the entry on Kant nor in the article on apperception.) By contrast, the index lists 34 discussions of logic, logical positivism, and logicism, some of which take up several pages.

4. There are, of course, significant philosophical discussions of imagination: in Aristotle's *De anima*; in Hume's *Treatise*; in Kant's first *Critique* (and later, building on Kantian themes, in Coleridge, in Collingwood, and in Croce); in Blake's prophecies; in Ryle's *Concept of Mind*; in Sartre's *L'Imaginaire*. But, with the exception of Kant and Blake (and the remarks in Hume from which, perhaps, Kant drew inspiration), these discussions construe the imagination as a faculty that deals in *what is not there*. (And the Idealists deal in general with a world that, apart from our perception of it, is not there.)

5. It is ethically incumbent on philosophers to avoid epistemic anthropocentrism; we must choose an epistemology that does not place human consciousness before the being of the world.

KONRAD LORENZ: [My view that what we perceive corresponds to a mind-independent reality] rests on the realization that our cognitive apparatus is itself an objective reality which has acquired its present form through contact with and adaptation to equally real things in the outer world ... The 'spectacles' of our modes of thought and perception, such as causality, substance, quality, time and place, are functions of a neurosensory organization that has evolved in the service of survival. When we look through these 'spectacles,' therefore, we do not see, as transcendental idealists assume, some unpredictable distortion of reality which [may] not correspond in the least with things as they really are, and therefore cannot be regarded as an image of the outer world. What we experience is indeed a real image of reality — albeit an extremely simple one, only just sufficing for our own practical purposes; we have developed 'organs' only for those aspects of reality of which, in the interest of survival, it was imperative for our species to take account, so that selection pressure produced this particular cognitive apparatus ... Yet what little our sense organs and nervous system have permitted us to learn has proved its value over endless years of experience, and we may trust it — as far as it goes.

6. I am concerned with the imagination in relation to *what-is*, independently of specifically human consciousness.

❧

7. We can think about what is immediately present, and do this without resorting to words. A carpenter building a cabinet, a tailor cutting and stitching a garment, anyone successfully following Ikea assembly instructions, is thinking in images. They are not translating what they see, what they feel with their hands, into words, then grasping the meaning of those words, then realizing what 'follows' and proceeding on that basis.

They are seeing and feeling, they are picturing some result; they are making.

ERNEST KLEIN: **poet**, n. — … fr. L. *poēta*, fr. Gk. ποιητής, 'one who makes …,' fr. ποιεῖν, fr. I.-E. base *$q^w ei$-, 'to make' …

8. Jazz musicians do this with aural-kinaesthetic images. Baseball outfielders, apparently, do it with aural-visual images. Painters do it with images in paint on canvas.

9. The Latin root shows that the European conception of imagination has been constant over millenia: *imāginārī* means 'to picture to oneself, imagine.' But Klein's *Comprehensive Etymological Dictionary of the English Language* says that this root itself is "prop[erly] a loan translation of Gk. φαντάζεσθαι."
    φαντάζω, which means *make visible*, or *present to the eye or mind*, has its own root in φαίνω, *to bring to light.*

10. The deep etymological root, then, includes perceiving, recognizing, knowing, seeing; it also suggests that this seeing or knowing replaces an absence of some kind, rather than depending on it.

11. Liddell and Scott's *Greek-English Lexicon* is clear that the sense of φαντάζω (*phantázdō*) as "fancy" — the *re*-presentation of images derived from sensation — is contemporary with this perceiving-knowing sense; but it is distinct.

12. Let us preserve this distinction. Let us contemplate thinking in images as a way of understanding the real.

II · SEEING-AS AND SEEING-INTO

13. The philosophers and encyclopedias are to this extent right: thinking in images *can* involve comparing an existing situation with an image of a *non-existent* ideal, and seeing how to get from one to the other. (Civil engineering in this way depends fundamentally on the imaginary.)
    But we are also thinking in images when we see that a given piece of jigsaw puzzle fits just so; when we see the

family resemblance between a child and its parent; when we recognize a series of drawings as a proof of a mathematical proposition; when we feel the power of a metaphor.

These are all instances of what, with Wittgenstein, I call 'seeing-as.'

14. Seeing-as is always an experience of understanding: "Oh!"

Theorem: $\frac{1}{2} + \frac{1}{4} + \frac{1}{8} + \ldots = 1$
Proof:

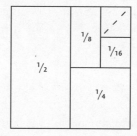

15. "Now I get it!" "Hey, we could do it like this!" — we often use such expressions when we grasp, without verbal intermediaries, a connection between things, situations, or concepts. When we see how parts that are intrinsically related to one another in one context are differently, *but also intrinsically,* related to one another in a different context.

16. The *experience* of this connectedness is the experience of meaning.

17. It is also the experience of a gestalt. Where understanding involves a movement between two images, each grasped more or less clearly, we speak of a gestalt *shift.*

18. In what follows, for the sake of concision, I will often speak simply in terms of gestalt shifts. But these should be understood to include cases where the initial situation is not, properly speaking, a gestalt — where it is too vague, for instance, or too chaotic; where we feel we have no 'grasp' — and the arrival of understanding is the shift *to* a genuine gestalt.

19. A note on epistemic vocabulary:

'Grasp' is in scare quotes above because of its connotations of possession and arrest. These connotations are rarely appropriate when we are talking about the perception or recognition of gestalts, for the mind is then in motion.

> Ernest Klein: **grasp**, tr. and intr. v. — ME. *graspen*, metathesized fr. *grapsen*, 'to grope,' from the stem of OE. *grāpian*, 'to touch, feel, grope.'

What is right about the sense of seizure is its physicality: its Anglo-Saxon refusal of academic refinement. When we experience a gestalt shift, often there is a sense of arrest *in ourselves*: we stand before what we perceive in astonishment. We are struck.

But even to say 'we are struck' is not always accurate — for there is no active form of the verb. It cannot convey the frequent, simultaneous, sense of reaching toward what we need to discern.

'Know' appears to be one of the most etymologically pure words in the English language: it probably means now much what its Indo-European root meant thousands of years ago. But in polite intellectual company, its predicate must always be constructed as a proposition: otherwise it connotes, coyly, a kind of sexual relation. The connotations of erotically intense involvement are appropriate, but the coyness and the Judeo-Christian overtones are not.

20. Max Wertheimer, one of the founders of Gestalt theory, describes thinking in a way that makes transparent both that

and how we think in images. For Wertheimer, all genuine thinking is rooted in gestalts.

> MAX WERTHEIMER: Thinking consists in
> envisaging, realizing structural features and structural require-
> ments; proceeding in accordance with, and determined by,
> these requirements; thereby changing the situation in the
> direction of structural improvements, which involves:
>
>> that gaps, trouble-regions, disturbances, superficialities,
>> etc., be viewed and dealt with structurally;
>> that inner structural relations — fitting or not fitting — be
>> sought among such disturbances and the given situa-
>> tion as a whole and among its various parts;
>> that there be operations of structural grouping and seg-
>> regation, of centering, etc.;
>> that operations be viewed and treated in their structural
>> place, role, [and] dynamic meaning, including realiza-
>> tion of the changes which this involves;
>
> realizing structural transposability, structural hierarchy, and sep-
> arating structurally peripheral from fundamental features — a
> special case of grouping;
> looking for structural rather than piecemeal truth.

21. The idea of inner structural relations is crucial. It is, in fact, the foundation of Gestalt theory.

> MAX WERTHEIMER: The fundamental question can be very
> simply stated: Are the parts of a given whole determined
> by the inner structure of that whole, or are the events such
> that, as independent, piecemeal, fortuitous and blind, the
> total activity is a sum of the part-activities?
> ... For Hume and largely also for Kant the world is like a
> bundle of fragments, and the dogma of meaningless sum-
> mations continues to play its part. As for logic, it supplies:
> *concepts,* which when rigorously viewed are but sums of

properties; *classes,* which upon closer inspection prove to be mere catchalls; *syllogisms,* devised by arbitrarily lumping together any two propositions having the character that ... etc. When one considers what a concept *is* in living thought, what it really means to grasp a conclusion; when one considers what the crucial thing *is* about a mathematical proof and the concrete interrelationships it involves, one sees that the categories of traditional logic have accomplished nothing in this direction.

It is our task to inquire whether a logic is possible which is *not* piecemeal.

22. Wittgenstein, in *Tractatus Logico-Philosophicus,* deploys a virtually identical notion under the rubric "internal relations."

> LUDWIG WITTGENSTEIN: 4.122 ... (Instead of 'structural property' I also say 'internal property'; instead of 'structural relation,' 'internal relation.'
>
> I introduce these expressions in order to indicate the source of the confusion between internal relations and relations proper [external relations], which is very widespread among philosophers.)
>
> It is impossible, however, to assert by means of propositions that such internal properties and relations obtain: rather, this makes itself manifest in the propositions that represent the relevant states of affairs and are concerned with the relevant objects.
>
> 4.123 A property is internal if it is unthinkable that its object should not possess it.

Internal properties and relations are at the root of Wittgenstein's notion of the ineffable, of his idea of logical form, and of his claim that the *Tractatus*'s "fundamental idea is that the 'logical constants' are not representatives; that there are no representatives of the *logic* of facts" [4.0312]. They survive at the core of his later work in the notion of 'forms of life.'

* 23. Wittgenstein and Wertheimer were also deeply interested in music. For both, it was paradigmatically an embodiment of meaning.

> MAX WERTHEIMER: Pictorially: suppose the world were a vast plateau upon which were many musicians. I walk about listening and watching the players. First suppose that the world is a meaningless plurality. Everyone does as he will, each for himself. What happens together when I hear ten players might be the basis for my guessing as to what they all are doing, but this is merely a matter of chance and probability much as in the kinetics of gas molecules. — A second possibility would be that each time one musician played c, another played f so and so many seconds later. I work out a theory of blind couplings but the playing as a whole remains meaningless. This is what many people think physics does, but the real work of physics belies this. — The third possibility is, say, a Beethoven symphony where it would be possible for one to select one part of the whole and work from that towards an idea of the structural principle motivating and determining the whole. Here the fundamental laws are not those of fortuitous pieces, but concern the very character of the event.

24. Inner structural relations, internal properties, 'fitting or not fitting,' are also the foundation of seeing-as: they are the scaffolding, or better, the armature at the centre of any recognition of significant similarity. They are also fundamental to an understanding of lyric comprehension and composition: wholes in which details are at once centres and peripheries, in which there can be no distinction between what is meant and how it is expressed.

Essence and accident belong to the taxonomy of external relations.

> LUDWIG WITTGENSTEIN: It is impossible for me to say one word in my book about all that music has meant in my life; how then can I possibly make myself understood?

25. Focussing on inner structural relations allows us to make sense of our actual phenomenological experience of thinking in images, of seeing-as: it shows us why such experience is an experience of understanding, and why it is paradigmatically an experience of meaning.

26. For meaning lives in gestalt shifts, in the dawning of aspects. The experience of meaning is nothing more, and nothing less, than the recognition of a thing's internal properties or the experience of the *live* interior-structural relationship between two or more things, situations, or contexts.

   I speak of 'internal property' here in the sense of character or attribute: an 'internal property' is the fact that a particular internal relation is thus-and-so. Or: It is an internal property of a thing that its internal structural relations are disposed in certain ways.

27. An experience, perception, or understanding can be more or less meaningful. This is not an observation about a philosophically uninteresting, because 'merely subjective,' phenomenon. It is an observation about the epistemic capacity for experience of ontological truth.

   The experience of meaning comes in degrees.

   The power of an experience of meaning depends on the clarity with which the internal properties of a thing or situation are discerned, or discerned anew.

28. In seeing-as, we move back and forth between one gestalt and another. It is an experience of identity and, yet, difference. Or, difference — and yet identity!

   Understanding is the experience of the *resonance* of inner structural relations that inform two or more contexts.

29. In seeing-as, we perceive analogies — how patterns of meaning intersect and echo one another.

The ability to think analogically is a reflection of sensitivity to ontological form.

Ontological understanding is rooted in the perception of patterned resonance in the world.

30. To understand, then, is to see how things hang together (to use Arne Næss's phrase).

It is not knowing *that* if you follow a series of steps, you will get a certain result, it is seeing *how* the result is contained in that series of steps.

> ARNE NÆSS: It is a maxim of ecology that 'everything hangs together' ... Of course, we know next to nothing about how and why [various interdependencies exist]. But, clearly ... [they do] and [they] form complexes of vast dimensions ... How are things (in the widest sense) related to each other in spontaneous experience? I will argue that they are internally related ...

31. To grasp an analogy is to recognize that if one thing or situation is laid over another, just so, aspects or outlines will spring into focus, a common pattern will be discernible — one that makes a difference to our grasp of the individual things or situations separately.

32. Another way to describe the ontological significance of gestalt thinking: to see as is to see into.

❧

33. Ontological attention is a response to particularity: *this* kingfisher, *this* lagoon, *this* slant-wise smoky West Coast rain. It is impossible to pay such attention and to regard that to which one attends as a 'resource.' In perceiving *this*ness, we respond to having been addressed. (In fact we are addressed all the time, but we don't always notice this.)

LUDWIG WITTGENSTEIN: We want to say: "When we mean something, it's like going up to someone, it's not having a dead picture (of any kind)." We go up to the thing we mean.

34. Or: what-is-meant, meaning, comes up to us.

poetic voices are emptying of self is required to perceive this

35. In the experience of *this*ness we are pierced. The *this* strikes into us like a shaft of light.

Indeed, the power of the experience of the *this* seems equal to everything it isn't — as though all that the *this* is not were experienced in the compression of an instant. It isn't the experience of the rest — by definition, the *this* is the antithesis of the rest — but it has that power.

As though the weight of the universe were balanced on a single point, and that point entered us.

36. *This*ness is the experience of a distinct thing in such a way that the resonant structure of the world sounds through it.

That is: to perceive *this*ness is to perceive a thing's internal relations. It is to perceive it *as* its internal relations.

37. Each *this* is a subset of dispositions within being as a whole. It is unique.

Each *this* focusses the world's resonant structure in a different way.

38. But the structure so focussed — in any given instant — is always the same. There is only one world.

> ARNE NÆSS: The gestalt ontology is a conceptual framework adapted to humans and other conscious living beings. The world we live in spontaneously cannot be degraded by being characterized as being merely subjective. It is the real world we experience. Nothing is more real. Without going into philosophical niceties, I conclude that our life experience is not of 'things in themselves' (Kant's *Dinge an sich*), but this

'experience is not merely 'subjective' either: not 'things for me'
(*Dinge an mich*). Life experience is the experience of gestalts,
[that is, of] a conceptual framework [that] is adapted to the
spontaneous experience of the content of reality.

39. And the resonant structure that the world is now is integral
with the structures that it has been and will become.
The resonant structure that any given thing or situation
is now is integral with the structures that it has been and
will become.

40. Imagination as a way of knowing or perceiving is a sensitivity
to resonance, to inner structural relations.
Imagination perceives the resonance among individual
things; it also perceives the resonance that is the presence
of being *in* those individual things; and it also perceives the
resonance that is being.

41. There is a connection between imagination, in this sense,
and the capacity for abstract thought. Both attend to 'what
is common.'
In the case of imagination, 'what is common' is a set of intrinsic structural features that acts as the axis around which
a gestalt shift occurs. In an engineering case, we go back and
forth between the non-existent ideal and the existing situation, gradually bringing them into agreement. In Yeats's
famous metaphor, we see our heart as a rag and bone shop;
and then we see the rag and bone shop as our heart; and
then we shift back again. *What is common* acts as a hinge
or fulcrum; and the live relation between the two teaches
us something about each. They stand in a resonant relation
that deepens our appreciation of their respective *this*nesses.

42. In some cases in philosophy, too, the perception of structural
commonalities remains the live and flexible basis of insight.

But it is typical of the grasp of shared features in abstract thought that it seizes on those features in a way that eliminates resonance. *What is common* is hypostatized as itself a thing — an isolated particular — rather than serving as the nameless fulcrum around which understanding *of things* turns.

43. Genuine understanding, though, occurs only when the mind is on the move.

The static abstractions of philosophy foreclose on understanding by eliminating movement: *what is common* becomes, itself, the object of our attention rather than the facilitator of attention to distinct-but-connected things. The things themselves fall away as unimportant — for, we think, in abstracting what is common, we have captured their essence. We think we have captured *meaning*.

But when meaning holds still long enough to get its picture taken, it is dead.

> ARNE NÆSS: The atomistic view helps to value the forest in terms of market prices, of extrinsic parts, and tourism. "A tree is a tree. How many do you have to see?"

44. The fullness and the emptiness of things: what is not there because we are embodied, because we are distinct. Because each thing is singular in its resonance.

The emptiness and the fullness of things: what *is* there because to be distinct is not to be separate. Because being is resonance.

III · ETHICS AND INSIGHT

45. Robert Bringhurst has said: "In seeing the moral beauty of a gesture, we see the light in it — the glint of radiance."

46. Rainer Maria Rilke's poem "Archäischer Torso Apollos" suggests what this might mean.

We can't know that fabulous head
where eyes like apples ripened. But
his torso glows still like a candelabra
in which his gazing, though it's shrouded,

rivets us and gleams. Otherwise, the prow
of his breast could not blind you, and no smile
would ripple down the slight twist of the loins,
there, to the core, which held his sex.

Otherwise this stone would stand defaced, cut off
under the shoulders' diaphanous plunge,
and wouldn't shimmer like the pelt of some wild beast;

and wouldn't burst from all its boundaries
like a star: for there is no place
that does not see you. You must change your life.

The poem is a description of seeing-into, and it first enun-
ciates the consequences of *not* seeing-into precisely. "Sonst
stünde dieser Stein enstellt und kurz" — *Otherwise this stone*
would stand defaced, cut off …

But when we see what the archaic torso of Apollo *is*, when
we perceive it as a *this*, we experience its meaning — which is
the radiance of the god's gaze, which is the resonance of light,
and which therefore moves, and moves us. That radiance is
everywhere, and we register the power of this understanding
not only in *being* moved, but in the sense that we *must* move.
A response — a return on this meaning — is required of us.
That everywhere is us, too.

47. A hypothesis: To see the light in a thing, or the beauty in a
gesture, is to experience it in such a way that the resonant
structure of the world sounds through it. To see it, then, with
that faculty most sensitive to resonance, the imagination.

But to see a thing with the imagination is simply to perceive it as a *this,* to become aware of its inner structural relations.

Such perceptions do indeed have the power to set us in motion, to make us change our lives.

48. Other examples of seeing-into:

> - reading character
>   - — the character of persons (which is, for example, the foundation of compelling portraiture, portraiture that, as we say, lives)
>   - — the character of situations
>   - – developing play in sports and games

PETER GZOWSKI: Elite athletes ... like chess masters or artists of the jazz piano, may not so much think differently as perceive differently ... What Gretzky perceives on a hockey rink is ... not so much a set of moving players as a number of situations ... The pattern they [form] [is], to him, one fact ...

> - – perceptive medical diagnosis: the ability to discern what is symptom, what is not, and what the symptoms are symptoms of
> - – military strategy in battle
> - – the conception of causality that underlies the *Yì Jīng*: certain events hang together
> - good editing or teaching: being able to pick up on what someone is driving at
> - being able to sight-read music well
> - appreciating a style of any kind; this includes heightened interpretive abilities which we speak of as a performer's or critic's 'affinity' for certain composers, dramatists, painters, poets, sculptors, thinkers, or artists of other sorts
> - recognizing that the world is populated by an uncount-

able number of beings, most nonhuman, who think and
feel, in varying degrees, as we do

49. The list above is couched, insofar as possible, in the academ-
ically safe vocabulary of positivism. Let me push the boundaries. When we see into something, we say we see its soul
— the glint or gleam of the divine in individual things. What
Hopkins would call inscape. What Herakleitos meant when
he said ἦθος ἀνθρώπῳ δαίμων ("character is spirit"). What
classical Taoism understands by zìrán (自然). And what most
people in sustainable pre-contact North American aboriginal
societies would think a thing simply is.

50. Ontological attention is a form of love.
     Responsibility, responsiveness, better, *responsivity* —
which, were it a word, would share its root with 'spouse' — is
the trace, in us, of the pressure of the world that is focussed
in a *this*. That is *how much* it is possible to attend; that is how
large complete attention would be.

> THE ECONOMIST, 1 March 2008: As [Murlidhar Devidas Amte]
> grubbed in the rain-filled gutter to pick up dog shit, human
> excrement and blackened, rotten vegetables, stowing them in
> the basket he carried on his head, he brushed what seemed to
> be a pile of rags, and it moved a little. The pile was flesh; it was
> a leper, dying. Eyes, nose, fingers and toes had already gone.
> Maggots writhed on him. And ... Amte, shaking with terror and
> nausea, stumbled to his feet and ran away.
>   Most people thought he was crazy to be doing that job any-
> way. Scavenging was a job for *harijans,* for outcastes ... [Mr Amte
> was a successful criminal lawyer in Warora.] But after living with
> Mahatma Gandhi in his ashram in the mid-1940s, something
> had happened to him.
>   At first he let his hair and fingernails grow long, a holy man's
> guise that looked odd in a lawyer. After that, when the scaven-
> gers came to him with grievances one week, he decided to try
> their work, scraping out latrines for nine hours a day ...

It was the encounter with the dying leper, however, that shaped Mr Amte's life ... Where there was fear, he told himself, there was no love ... Deliberately, he went back to the gutter to feed the leper and to *learn his name*, Tulshiram. He then carried him home to care for him until he died, and began — once he had had training in Calcutta — to work in leper clinics all around the town ...

[He subsequently founded his own ashram for the disabled and lepers, which focussed not on charity, but on self-sufficiency through work and creativity. He was] a Gandhian of the pure, old style, who believed that economic development had to be person by person and village by village, by means as small as handwoven threads and fingerfuls of salt ... In his last three decades ... his focus shifted to the preservation of rivers and the well-being of the tribes who lived in the unexploited forest.

51. The hinge swings open in imagination: *our* life could be *that* life.

52. Imagination, as the capacity to see as and into, as sensitivity to ontological resonance, is the most direct route to the good life. It does not *tell* us, it *shows* us, that response is required.

> SIMONE WEIL: To know that this human being who is hungry and thirsty really exists as much as I do — that is enough, the rest follows of itself.

53. But of course it is possible to understand that we must change our lives, and then fail to do so.

The price is, always, a loss of integrity, an absence of interior attunement.

This, then, is why the exercise of moral imagination requires courage: we could, in any instance, be risking everything.

54. To say "imagination shows us" is simply to say "we see into," but to say it in the passive voice.

55. Imagination relieves us of what Simone Weil calls "the ring of Gyges": the refusal to see significant analogies, which is the root of injustice.

> SIMONE WEIL: Gyges: "I have become king, and the other king has been assassinated." No connection whatever between these two things. There we have the ring!
> The owner of a factory: "I enjoy this and that expensive luxury and my workmen are miserably poor." He may be very sincerely sorry for his workmen and yet not form the connection.

56. Imagination reveals the *this* in each thing present to us: the dying leper, the hungry man, the addicted prostitute, the defrauded aboriginal, the broken sculpture, the glittering mountain creek, the ant lurching from the poison we have sprayed, the invisible tree frog singing in the endless winter drizzle, the meat, which is the cooked flesh of a tortured steer, on our plate.

When we see as, see into, the meaning of each situation comes up to us, and we cannot turn away.

57. Hypostatization of 'what is common' is the source of much of philosophy's dryness, its insistence that meaning is not a living relation between things, but an inert abstraction.

Luckily, it is not characteristic of all philosophy in the Western European tradition; nor is it a feature of Taoist thought, nor of philosophical reflection emerging from many sustainable indigenous cultures. To the extent that it dominates a philosophical style or tradition, though, that style or tradition as a whole becomes incapable of meaning. People study the hypostatizations, they engage in refining them and making new ones, but the engagement does not lead to better lives.

58. To be brought to the realization that we must change our lives, we must experience living meaning. We must feel that hinge opening: *our* life could be *this* life.

59. When we encounter an analysis of meaning — an accurate
but lifeless anatomization — we recognize the subject of the
analysis, but the matter does not touch us. Our own soul does
not go out to meet it.

> How accurate can it be if it is also lifeless? — It has all the
external relations correct, but the internal ones are missing.

[handwritten marginalia: Poetry is meeting this space]

60. "The world is a welter of details! We need to establish some
sort of hierarchy or we'll go crazy. Without essence and accident, how do we know what aspects are significant? Which
details *matter*?"

> They all matter. They all are what-is. To see into is, of its
nature, to understand. No excision of detail is required to
make it possible. Only a welter of external relations produces craziness.

61. "But what is Wertheimer's 'separation of structurally peripheral from fundamental features' if not a distinction between
accident and essence?"

> It is a recognition that what needs to be discerned in one
context — in relation to *this* problem that we're trying to
solve — is different from what needs to be discerned in another context, in relation to a different problem. It is not an
insistence that what a thing *is*, in all contexts, is a particular
and unchanging subset of its aspects.

62. Imagination perceives the resonant connections among things
— their ecologies — their internal structural truths.

> Logic damps down resonance — focusses on external re-
lations — grasps things as self-contained essences, the bil-
liard balls that so ably demonstrate the truths of Newtonian
physics.

63. An ethical life can also be achieved through adherence to
principle: an act of will that replaces discernment with faith.
But for this to work, we must have hit on the right principles
to adhere to. And Kant is right: for ethics to be a philosoph-

ical project, we need a way to decide among candidates for the right principles, rather than simply settling for what our culture hands us, no questions asked.

Kant famously believes that pure reason will deliver the grounds for making those decisions, but here I believe he is wrong: reason without imagination is blind.

64. Capacities for seeing-as are as diverse as athletic abilities, or skill at rhetoric or analysis. One can be very good at visual proofs in geometry and hopeless at sensing the developing play in hockey; one can have a talent for getting the best out of one's students and be left cold by the metaphors of Ezra Pound; one can be a superb improviser and a lousy sight-reader; or vice versa.

65. But just as we can get better at logic with practice, so we can improve our capacities for gestalt comprehension.

66. If we do not cultivate the imagination as an organ of onto-logical insight, if we derogate it, we cripple ourselves as ethical beings.

We close the door on our single best chance to espouse the world; to see things for what they are; to testify to that espousal through what we then become.

Alkibiades' Love

Those who think clearly are free.
— ROBERT BRINGHURST

I have always loved the sound of the word *philosophy*. This must be why I first tried to read it as a child. But why did philosophy itself come to matter to me? Why does it matter to me still? Better: *what* is philosophy that it should have held my gaze, since mid-adolescence really, and through its various late twentieth-century and early twenty-first-century North American incarnations?

The spirit of these questions is old, as old as the discipline and its name. In the European literary tradition, philosophy has been wondering about itself since its inception some 2,600 years ago. It has defined, and doubted, and redefined itself with at least as much energy as it has focussed on core questions of ethics, epistemology, and metaphysics. The dictionary tells us it means love of wisdom. But what's that? *Thinking in love with clarity,* I have suggested. *Love of knowing that you do not know,* according to Plato's Sokrates. What, if anything, have these two definitions to do with one another? What would it be to make either a way of life?

Let's start with the Sokratic definition — loving knowing that you do not know — and ask first what it would be to make loving anything a way of life. Love cannot be willed. A 'way of life' connotes a practice, a discipline, something you can get up in the morning and *do*. We cannot get up in the morning and will love.

But we *can* get up in the morning and will attitudes that dispose us to love.

Postures of openness, of attention.

✍

Attentiveness as a way of life, then — a way of *living*.

And what is it that the existence of this participle in so many languages should teach us? — Perhaps that grasp of the synchronic picture, however big, is not the full story. That continuance, ongoingness, practice — *phusis*? — is fundamentally constitutive of the whole.

✍

We can also will honesty.

But I have found that the more important honesty has become to me over the years, the less I have been able to say, or the narrower and more remote the avenues in which I could stand and speak. Stand? More like stumble to my knees, helpless before the loveliness of the world, its violence and terror, the ruin my species — or my species in my culture — has wrought, is wreaking.

✍

No. Have I ever felt I could *say* anything with the hope of getting it right? Always the attempt falls short.

✍

Still: getting up in the morning and assuming a discipline of attentiveness, of alert care, toward knowing that one does not know. What would that look like?

Well, honesty, perhaps: rigorous but not judgemental. Unflinching but not unkind.

A willingness to admit mystery.

Compassion for the self as it wavers in and out of existence in proximity to mystery.

An exercise in courage.

✍

Alkibiades, in Plato's *Symposium*, says to Sokrates: "Let anyone — man, woman, or child — listen to you or even to a poor account of what you say — and we are all transported, completely possessed." And then, turning to the others: "I swear to you, the moment he starts to speak, I am beside myself: my heart starts leaping in my chest, the tears come streaming down my face, even the frenzied Corybantes seem sane compared to me — and, let me tell you, I am not alone. I have heard Pericles and many other great orators, and I have admired their speeches. But nothing like this ever happened to me: they never upset me so deeply that my very own soul started protesting that my life — *my* life! — was no better than the most miserable slave's ... You can't say that isn't true, Sokrates. I know very well that you could make me feel that way this very moment if I gave you half a chance. He always traps me, you see, and he makes me admit that my political career is a waste of time, while all that matters is just what I most neglect: my personal shortcomings, which cry out for the closest attention. So I refuse to listen to him; I stop my ears and tear myself away from him, for, like the Sirens, he could make me stay by his side till I die."

Sokrates makes Alkibiades feel that his life is worthless, and this binds him to him absolutely. What an extraordinary confession.

And Plutarch says of Aristippos, who had heard, second-hand, an account of Sokratic discussion: "... he was so powerfully affected that his body began to deteriorate; he became very pale and thin until such time as he sailed for Athens ... and acquainted himself with the man and his words and his philosophy, whose goal was [for a person] to recognize his own faults and be rid of them."

Plutarch's account may make us think we're dealing with a charismatic and the kind of cult that can grow up around such a figure: someone who Knows the Answers and will provide them at the price of blind obedience. This is not philosophy; philosophy, at its core, is about the rejection of blind obedience. But it is also clearly not what Plato, or indeed Xenophon, thought we were dealing with in the figure of Sokrates. Plato's Alkibiades, a charismatic himself, lets us know we're in the presence of charisma, but there is nothing in his speech, or in the rest of Plato's oeuvre, that suggests we've signed up with a cult. If we haven't, though, this makes Alkibiades' confession, Aristippos' conversion, even more remarkable. Philosophy — *philosophy!* — could do *this* to a person?

❧

Hegel, writing centuries later in a student's album, says: "Not curiosity, not vanity, not the consideration of expediency, not duty and conscientiousness, but an unquenchable, unhappy thirst that brooks no compromise leads us to truth." Hegel was not a charismatic; nor was he particularly susceptible to cults. But we may, I think, imagine that he understood Alkibiades' love. As does the philosophic spirit in each of us when we brush up against any genuinely philosophical gesture: our hearts leap in our chests, the tears come to our eyes, we are prone to think we're crazy and we'd like often enough to set the whole thing down, turn or tear ourselves away. But we're done for, claimed: we belong to what we've scented — unquenchably, uncompromisingly, and indeed sometimes unhappily — until we die.

❧

But what is it that we've brushed up against? — this thing, this discipline, this knowledge or unknowledge, this way of being in the world, that so rivets our attention? What is Alkibiades in love with? *Symposium* offers us several answers, and offers them simultaneously, layering them over one another: Alkibiades is in love with Sokrates; that is, with Eros. He has made the same mistake the sophist, Agathon, and the young untutored Sokrates have made before him: he is in love with love. But this is not quite right. Alkibiades' speech has none of Agathon's rhetorical veneer; in the gesture of telling the truth, Alkibiades embodies it. Look again: Alkibiades *is* in love with what Eros hasn't got: beauty. He is in love with integrity, with ἐγκράτεια or self-mastery, with Sokrates' moral excellence. He is in love with that which opens to reveal divine, golden, utterly beautiful

ἀγάλματα — statues, icons, images honouring the gods. He is
in love with what is hollowed out: nothing in itself; a vessel, an
empty conduit between gods and humans; that is, *erōs*; that is,
awareness of absence; that is, knowing that one does not know.
The phrases crowd on one another as the *agalmata* crowd in
Sokrates' vacant interior. And the intellect's questions: *Is* moral
beauty integrity? Is integrity based on self-control? Could it be
a kind of emptiness? Egolessness? Availability to the divine? Is
any of this knowing that one does not know?

And where in this portrait of Alkibiades' love is philosophy
as dialectic, the grasp of ontological gestalts and their division
according to natural kinds? No one falls in love with the Stranger
from Elea. No one falls in love with the last three-quarters of
Parmenides. (Even though the prospect of its logical exertions
makes Parmenides tremble in fear and anticipation — as when,   * †
he says, in old age one has been compelled to fall in love against
one's will.)

*

After numerous exercises, and abstract characterizations and
applications of dialectic, the Stranger from Elea, in *Statesman*,
says: "… every sort of expert knowledge everywhere throws away
the bad [elements] so far as it can, and takes what is suitable and
good, bringing all of this — both like and unlike — together into
one, and so producing some single kind of thing with a single
capacity."

Whose goal was to recognize his own faults and be rid of them.

*

What is it to be "rid of our faults"? A long tradition of reading Plato understands it as a kind of primness: Prohibition and
non-recreational sex. Put less crudely, should we understand the
excellence with which Alkibiades has fallen in love as an extir-
pation, an emaciation, of the spirit? Indeed, isn't this exactly the
image Plutarch offers us?

Look again: Aristippos becomes pale and thin in his yearning
to *start* the process, not as a result of undergoing it. And look

at Sokrates: drinking everyone under the table, frightening the
enemy in battle with his "swagg'ring gait and roving eye," playing up to the beautiful boys only to turn the tables on them and
become the hotly pursued beloved. He is anything but emaci-
ated. No, this is an excellence whose emptiness is tremendous
interior wealth.

❧

Honesty is not brutality — neither to others nor to oneself. What
is required is to face the demons, not face them down.

Does this mean that compassion is the overriding virtue?
Yes. I think so.

❧

How does one acquire compassion? — One can will oneself to
exercise what one has, but one cannot fill the reservoir by an
act of will.

Imaginative identification: the emptying of the self so that
the shapes of other selves can become real. Others, the world,
becoming real inside one, inside the space where 'one' once was.

And, of course, still is: compassion is useless without a steady
hand and good distance vision.

An attentiveness in which one is, and is not, the other. Identified but distinct. A metaphor.

❧

What is it to be rid of our faults?

My students, when asked to think deeply about this question, respond (hesitantly, with a puzzled tone), "It's as though I
would be more complete" or "I think I would become free." Free
how? "Free to be my self. My real self." And what's that? "I think
that other guy was right. It would be like being free to be my
whole self — what he said about becoming complete." Again,
what extraordinary confessions.

I must, for the sake of honesty, admit that not all students
respond this way. Some say, "Who knows what I'd be like? Who
I am includes my faults. There's no way for the person I am now

to know what it would be like to be different." But this, I think, underlines, makes more astonishing, that some students respond less skeptically. The debater's argument is there, *and it is rejected* in favour of something that is difficult and perhaps even embarrassing to try to articulate.

I think my courageous students are right. To be rid of one's faults is indeed to become the whole — that is, integrated — being that is the precondition of becoming free.

❧

> **integrate**, tr. v., to form a whole. — L. *integrātus,* pp. of *integrāre,* 'to make whole, renew,' fr. *integer.* See **integer** and verbal suff. **-ate.**

> **integrity**, n., wholeness, completeness; uprightness. — F. *intégrité,* fr. L. *integritātem,* acc. of *integritās,* 'completeness, soundness, blamelessness,' fr. *integer.* See **integer** and **-ity**.

❧

If we imagine the mature Sokrates — he of the roving eye and unmatched capacity for booze — to have ascended the ladder of Diotima's higher mysteries, then he has carried each of the rungs up with him. He loves, but instead of seeking to fill his lack, he embraces it. Instead of clogging his interior by stuffing it with the objects of his desire, he remains in the condition of desire. He actively seeks this posture: he loves, but in each instant lets go of what he loves. Better: he loves, but without the desire to possess.   †

At each stage of the ladder, it is achieving this stance that allows us to move to the next. We become more, not less, available to love; we expand our range. By loving without needing to own what we love, we achieve what Hegel might have termed erotic sublation. We offer ontological applause.

❧

Alkibiades tells us that to encounter philosophy is first to discover that we aren't what we thought we were: that what we think most important — the postures and possessions that generate social envy — has little to do with our true nature. It is also to discover that preoccupation with social roles and goods, and neglect of "all that matters ... [our] personal shortcomings," is to be enslaved, to be unfree.

But what then? "Expert knowledge" says that we develop integrity out of a diverse assortment of talents, proclivities, dispositions, and skills by throwing out the bad and collecting the serviceable bits and pieces into "a single kind of thing with a single capacity." And this expert knowledge, according to the Stranger from Elea, just is dialectic: Collection and Division: ontological gestalt and precisation.

*
†

It's as though I would be more complete.

❧

Notoriously, however, Plato never really tells us how dialectic proceeds. Despite the examples and demonstrations in *Sophist* and *Statesman*, despite the agonizing length of the logic-chopping exercises in *Parmenides*, the key questions are never answered. One of them is posed directly at *Statesman* 263a: Young Sokrates asks the Stranger how, in attempts at division, arbitrary 'parts' are to be distinguished from real genera. The Stranger praises Young Sokrates effusively for his discernment, but then declines to answer. The other question — how to tell what species to leave out of the re-collection of fragments — is, to the best of my knowledge, never explicitly framed. *Letter VII*, though enticing, is vague — and, it seems, deliberately so — on all crucial details.

How is it that dialectical expertise produces self-control? What is the relation between *erōs* and integrity? And is it love, or intellectual discipline, that hollows us out — makes us radiant, but empty, vessels for golden ἀγάλματα?

❧

Let us ask again: What is this moral beauty that so overwhelms Alkibiades?

At first it looks like courage — or at least this is how it strikes me when I encounter it in a student, say, or a friend. A breathtaking honesty — someone stepping right out into the open, without a thought for how they might appear, their gaze held by something that has nothing to do with themselves. They are simultaneously vulnerable and untouchable — singular. It might look like stupidity or clumsiness if it weren't for the sense of intelligence behind the gesture, an intellectual firmness. We sense that they are in some way compelled — not helpless, but acting under the pressure of necessity, responding with great attention to something they perceive to be obvious. Moral beauty is always unselfconsciously resolute.

And the lack of self-consciousness is indeed crucial. Heroic postures cannot *be* heroic if they are self-aware. Only from the outside is it possible, with justice, to construe another's actions as heroic. And, if those actions *are* heroic, with this recognition will come the realization that this cannot be communicated to the person in question. The claim will make no sense to her; you will trouble her by demanding precisely the focus that she cannot have if she is to continue to do what she is doing.

And so the impression shifts and deepens: moral beauty looks like courage, looks like intelligence, looks like necessity, looks like humility. It looks simultaneously like integrity, and like defencelessness. Everything is being risked.

The paradox is important here; it is the key. It is in being able to risk everything that we become free. And this freedom allows our useful bits and pieces to settle naturally into place — the result of a kind of chiropractic of the soul. The muscle unclenches, space opens in the joint, and a single, unbroken, continuous motion becomes possible. This is integrity in action.

And what is love if it isn't risking everything?

Earlier, in *Sophist*, before he describes the way of expert dialectical knowing, the Stranger from Elea says: "… the *elenkhos* [cross-questioning, refutation] is the greatest and most efficacious of *katharses* [purifications, cleansings, clarifications]." If we are forced to scrutinize our opinions, and discover that they are inconsistent, then we will "get angry with [ourselves], and become gentle towards others." We will lose our "inflated and rigid beliefs about [ourselves]"; and no loss is more beneficial. Such beliefs clog the soul from the inside just as physical ailments clog the body from the inside and prevent it from benefitting from food. In both cases, health depends on ridding ourselves of these faults or blockages. We must come to know how much we do not know in order to be whole.

⁂

> **whole**, adj. — ME. *hale, hole, hol, hool,* "healthy, whole," fr. OE. *hāl,* "whole, unhurt, healthy, well," rel. to … Goth. *hails,* "complete, alone, whole, healthy, well, sound,"… fr. I.-E. base **qailo-, *quailu-,* "complete, sound, well, happy," whence also OSlav. *cělǔ,* "whole, complete," Lett. *kaîls,* "naked, bare, bald," OPruss. *kailūstikan,* "health," W. *coel,* "omen," and prob. also Gk. κοῖλυ (Hesychius), "beautiful." Cp. **hale**, "healthy," which is a doublet of *whole* …

⁂

Thinking in love with clarity, loving knowing that we do not know: it is the point where these two definitions intersect that each is most potent.

That point is interior silence — not the bunched frustration of failure, nor quietism, but a stillness in which we recognize emptiness, our possibilities for resonance, as home.

⁂

We cannot will love, but love is the goal: an egoless availability, the capacity to touch and be touched by what-is, to become replete with meaning.

What we can will is attempts at attentiveness, the uncluttered vision that both precipitates and is precipitated by love.

⁂

"You can't be serious! Love is madness; it is, as the saying goes, blind. It *distorts* our vision, it doesn't correct it. When we're in love, we see what we want to see, not what's there." Sokrates agrees: love is a species of madness. But he claims it is the most divine division of its genus, and, his sexual abstinence notwithstanding, he is neither stupid nor inexperienced.

I don't wish to deny that love can obscure truth. It produces and depends upon imaginative identification. If we are not skilled and disciplined, the imagination can project rather than discern, and we can identify with those projections. We lack vocabulary here; let us indeed call this blind love. But such love, which projects and then identifies with its own projections, is not Sokratic madness, it is not Herbert's clear-eyed compassion.   *

And, given time, there is no problem *telling* the difference. But how do we learn to live it? How do we become skilled and disciplined in love?

How do we learn to pay attention?

꙳

Seriously to seek moral beauty, Plato argues, is to undergo the *elenkhos*.

To refuse it is to refuse to be released from the greatest of taints (μέγιστα ἀκάθαρτον); it is to acquiesce in deformity (αἰ   *
σχρὸν γεγονέναι). *Eudaimonia*, the well-being of the spirit in us, requires the purity and beauty that results from the refutation of faulty belief.

The Stranger from Elea also suggests that it is failure to be   *
able to collect and divide according to 'forms' (εἴδη) that is at the root of false opinion. We don't see the world as it *is*.

The *elenkhos* rids us of our faults; through it, we embrace humility and are enabled to see what-is. We are cleaned out, unclogged, turned into the emptiness that is *erōs* for the world, and simultaneously made whole.

꙳

To encounter the *elenkhos*, Alkibiades tells us, is to experience oneself as enslaved. Actually to undergo it, my students suggest, is both to become truly oneself, and to become free.

In what sense 'free'? I think perhaps free to trust that one sees the world, and oneself, as they actually are. Free, then, to make a choice, where one perceives that one has a choice; and free to be untroubled by anxiety where one perceives that one does not.

❧

And the connection between freedom and self-control?

What Sokrates has, Plato suggests, is not self-control in some Procrustean sense, but rather the freedom from being shoved around that comes with self-knowledge. It's not that he suppresses his feelings, is cold or removed. Quite the reverse. He becomes free to feel them *all the more intensely* because he need not fear the consequences of such feeling. He will always have a choice about how to act.

❧

Or so the argument goes. Do I believe it? Not entirely. The capacity for intense feeling, even when one knows oneself free to choose, can have devastating consequences. It is, itself, a door to communion: it opens one up, makes one permeable, to both horror and beauty, the dark as well as the light. One needs luck, great luck, to avoid damage if one invites such openness.

❧

Or is it that being *damaged* by the dark, by horror, by ruin is exactly the measure of the extent to which one remains clogged by faults, by false opinions? Is it that pain enters — and leaves — the truly whole, truly empty vessel without trace?

❧

But wait. Why should we think faults are false opinions? Aren't they propensities to act? A tendency to impatience, say, or to self-pity, or to narcissism, to imagining that everything is one's fault. The thought — and it is Freud's and Zhuāng Zi's as much as Sokrates' — is that these propensities will manifest themselves not *just* in actions, but also in beliefs about the world. "Why didn't you speak to Nancy?" "Oh, she snubbed me; she's such a snob." "No, she's not. Where did you get that idea?" "Didn't you see it? Didn't you *see* it? I was standing at the checkout and she walked by without saying a word." "Are you sure she even saw you? What time was it? Was she in a rush to get home?" "You just don't get it: she thinks I'm beneath contempt. Why are you defending her? You think I'm stupid?" *Under* the propensities to act are beliefs that are at least proto-propositional: *the world owes me, I'm worthless, money is the answer, power is the answer, fame is the answer.* We change our behaviour by confronting and rejecting these formational beliefs.

Realizing how *fundamentally* wrong we've been can, if the lesson goes deep enough, open us to compassion: others are as messed up as we are; they, too, act out of pain, out of blindness, out of self-absorption. They, too, fail to see what is right in front of them. They, too, hold profoundly mistaken beliefs about the world. Who are we to judge?

⁂

But now we're talking psychology rather than philosophy, aren't we? Plato didn't distinguish: philosophy — *elenkhos* and *dialectic* — just was psychogogy: lifting the eye of the mind from its bed of slime; leading the enslaved soul out of the cave. But his view is antique, surely: just as physics was distinguished from metaphysics, so, a few centuries later, study of the psyche was distinguished from philosophy proper.

*

*

Note what we have to mean by 'philosophy proper,' though, in order to maintain the contrast: philosophy as 'science,' or at least as an academic discipline from which psychology (as a science) can be distinguished. Is there anything in such a conception of philosophy — let's call it professional academic philosophy — that involves 'a way of life'? Yes: but it looks like the life of Aristophanes' Thinking Shop: at its worst, sophistry; at its best, the cultivation of analytic skill divorced from real engagement with the world.

*

⁂

It's important that Plato himself didn't think such a simple story could be told. You can't tell the truth, he argues, without also acquiring the capacity to lie effectively: both depend on knowing "precisely the respects in which things are similar and dissimilar to one another." The discernment of the *true* rhetorician is thus identical to that of the philosopher. The difference between Sokrates and Kallikles is not to be cashed out in terms of pure and valid argumentation versus mere eristic: Sokrates' elenctic wrestling is full of highly suspect — well, let's be honest, downright bad — arguments. The only reason Sokrates, in Plato's version, isn't a sophist is that he doesn't wish to win for the sake of his own fame, but for the sake of the other's soul.

We cannot tell such a simple story either.

In the first place, many professional philosophers do engage with the world in unsophistical ways: they teach with real passion; they analyze moral and political issues in the media; they serve on the boards of NGOs and advocacy groups. Secondly, many are not analytic philosophers: as so-called continental philosophers, they are much more concerned with literary, existential, cultural, and historical dimensions of Western European thought. There is, increasingly, communication between the two groups; there are, increasingly, young philosophers who are willing and able to read in both traditions.

But there is still, I think many of us would agree, something missing, or perhaps awry — a target that, despite our efforts, we don't hit. Neither our own nor our students' hearts leap from their chests; the tears do not stream down our faces as we contemplate the latest issue of *JPhil*. Professionalism insulates us; we pursue our careers.

And still the story is too simple. Plato was right, I think: the fundamental *skill* is a kind of conceptual διαίρεσις, the capacity for *discrimination* in thought. Call it analysis and synthesis, call it division and collection, it is the same talent that undergirds both legal sophistry and Sokratic self-understanding. In the case of sophistry, the skill is turned on others and the world in an attempt to make money or garner fame. In the case of self-understanding, we turn the instrument on ourselves. The initial attempt, the decision to pursue the *katharsis*, requires a certain amount of courage: often we're forced to it only through catastrophe. But critical self-examination breeds honesty; and honesty brings relief — even in the face of fear. Thus courage grows with exercise.

And so, late in the day, I find myself returning to my early training, what seemed to me at the time to be an exercise in empty eristic. What has held my gaze, without my conscious understanding, is a sensed connection between the capacity for analytic conceptual discrimination and the possibility of leading the good life. It is not, of course, the skill itself that takes our breath away; rather, it is what results when the skill is exercised on the self — a paradoxical combination of vulnerability and integrity, a clarity and directness of vision, a limpid honesty. This is moral beauty. It makes the hair on our forearms rise and our throats go dry. It prompts tears. But although it is indeed such beauty that arrests us, what makes that beauty possible is the same analytic and discriminatory expertise that we cultivate in attempts to define angling or to determine how many angels can dance on the head of a pin. That expertise is at the heart of the *elenkhos*, which we still must practise if we are to find and then to trust ourselves, if we are to see things as they are. If we are to foster genuine attentiveness, make ourselves permeable, skilled in love, able to embrace and sustain the world's darkness without damage.

If we are to learn to think clear of our faults and so become free.

Notes

¶ WHAT IS LYRIC PHILOSOPHY?

A number of entries in this overview are based on or drawn from §§ 2, 7, and 8 of an early version of "Bringhurst's Presocratics: Lyric and Ecology." This essay originally appeared in Lilburn 1995 and appears in a revised version in the present book. Other entries, particularly §§ 35–42, are based on passages in *Wisdom & Metaphor* (Zwicky 2003); and yet others, particularly §§ 43–50, are based on passages in the second edition of *Lyric Philosophy* (Zwicky 2014a).

SOURCES

Notes are keyed to the *section numbers* that immediately precede the quotations.

Preamble   Klee 1964: 77–8, my emphases.

§ 9 Klein 1971.

§ 15 Wertheimer 1938a: 2. The text of this essay, "Über Gestalttheorie," was prepared from shorthand notes taken during a talk that Wertheimer gave in 1924 to the Kantgesellschaft in Berlin. I have chosen to quote from W. Ellis's abridged translation because its English is clearer and more trenchant than N. Nairn-Allison's translation of the full text. The latter, however, more closely approximates the German of Wertheimer's talk. "The fundamental 'formula'" in German runs: "Man könnte das Grundproblem der Gestalttheorie etwa so zu formulieren suchen: Es gibt Zusammenhänge, bei denen nicht, was im Ganzen geschieht, sich daraus herleitet, wie die einzelne Stücke sind und sich zusammensetzen, sondern umgekehrt, wo — im prägnanten Fall — sich *das, was an einem Teil dieses Ganzen geschieht, bestimmt von inneren Strukturgesetzen dieses seines Ganzen.*"

§ 24 Herakleitos, Diels-Kranz Fr 32, trans. T.M. Robinson 1987.

§ 29 Tranströmer 1987, partial line from "Outskirts," trans. Robert Bly.

§ 30 Simic 1990, "Notes on Poetry and Philosophy,": 64.

§ 30 Wittgenstein 1958, § 127, trans. G.E.M. Anscombe.

§ 31 Wittgenstein 1982, § 565, trans. C.G. Luckhardt and M.A.E. Aue.

§ 32 Hardy 1929: 18.

§ 33 Weil 1970: 40, trans. Richard Rees.

§ 34 Wittgenstein 1980: 61e, trans. Peter Winch.

§ 35 Herakleitos, Diels-Kranz Fr 124, trans. Charles H. Kahn 1979, as Fr cxxv.

§ 36 Simic 1990, "Notes on Poetry and Philosophy": 67.

§ 38 Wittgenstein 1980: 7e, trans. Peter Winch.

§ 39 Hass 1984: 274–5.

§ 40 Zagajewski 2000: 116, trans. Clare Cavanagh.

§ 41 Weil 1970: 24, trans. Richard Rees.

§ 51 Necker Cube: The first discussion of this figure occurs in Necker 1832.

§ 57 Simic 1990, "Wonderful Words, Silent Truth": 88.

¶ BRINGHURST'S PRESOCRATICS: LYRIC AND ECOLOGY

Numbers for Herakleitos' fragments are those in Diels-Kranz. I have benefitted from the work of other translators in producing English versions. See Charles Kahn 1979, Kirk & Raven 1963, and T.M. Robinson 1987.

This essay originally appeared in Lilburn 1995. A number of remarks that appeared in that version now appear in "What Is Lyric Philosophy?", the first essay in this volume. See, in that essay, §§ 1–6, 9, 11–13, 17–28, and 56–60.

Notes are organized according to main sections in the text. Under each roman numeral section heading, they are keyed to arabic section numbers.

SECTION I

§ 1 The version of "Herakleitos" printed here appeared in *The Beauty of the Weapons: Selected Poems 1972–82* (McClelland and Stewart, 1982; Copper Canyon, 1985). That book contains the third incarnation of the sequence. The first eight poems, with slight differences, were first published in *Eight Objects* (San Francisco: Kanchenjunga, 1975). These same eight poems with one additional difference, appeared as Section II of *Bergschrund* (Delta, BC: Sono Nis, 1975).

The sequence, including "Herakleitos," was subsequently revised for *The Calling: Selected Poems 1970–1995* (McClelland & Stewart, 1995). In this fourth version, it appears again in a letterpress edition, *The Old in Their Knowing* (Editions Koch, 2005), and in *Selected Poems* (Gaspereau, 2009 and Jonathan Cape, 2010). I have chosen to discuss the third version because its fourth section — the locus of revisions throughout the poem's history — hews most closely to the spirit of Herakleitos' thought as I understand it.

A partial version of the series, chosen by William Arrowsmith, appeared in *Arion*, n.s. 1.4 (1973–74); it was comprised of "Herakleitos," "The Petelia Tablet," "A Short History," and a partial version of "Of the Snaring of Birds" entitled "Strophe from Sophocles." "Herakleitos" and part of "Of the Snaring of Birds" first appeared in *Cadastre* (San Francisco: Kanchenjunga, 1973). Six of the fragments comprising "Empedokles: Seven Fragments" were first published in *Prism international* 13.3 (Spring 1974); § v of the present poem does not appear. Two of the fragments of "Empedokles: Seven Fragments" also appeared as part of an essay, "Postscript to a Translation of Empedocles" in the *Ohio Review* 16.3 (Spring 1975). "Empedokles' Recipes" first appeared in the *University of Windsor Review* 10.2 (Spring–Summer 1975); and "Pherekydes" first appeared in *Prism international* 14.2 (Summer 1975). "Pythagoras" first circulated as a broadside published by Kanchenjunga Press (1974).

§ 3   *... there rustle,*
Heading off one way and another
In the uncertain plain of the sea,
Shadowless roads enough:
But the boatman knows the islands.

§ 5 "The Book of Silences," like "The Old in Their Knowing," exists in many versions. It first appeared in Bringhurst 1986 and most recently in Bringhurst 2009.

§ 6 Burnett 1957: v.

— Hargrove 1989: 17.

— Kirk & Raven 1963: 72–3, 215, 227–8.

SECTION III

Fragment 118   The opening words of this fragment are disputed. I have relied on the judgement of Bollack and Wismann, Diels-Kranz, Kahn, and Robinson, who cite the MS tradition in support of αὐγὴ ξηρὴ ψυχή.

§ 7 Robinson 1987: 158.

§ 9 Rilke 1908. See "Imagination and the Good Life" in this volume for further discussion of this poem.

SECTION IV

§ 3 *Tzuhalem's Mountain*, first published in 1982, is reprinted in all of *The Beauty of the Weapons, The Calling*, and *Selected Poems*.

SECTION VIII

§ 6 Hargrove 1989: 21–2, 26.

§ 7 Letwin 1987: 113.

§ 14 Kirk & Raven 1963: 188.

§ 19 Bringhurst 2009, "Hachadura," § x. "Hachadura" also appears in *The Beauty of the Weapons* and *The Calling*.

§ 20 Aristotle, *Metaphysics* 1010a1–5, trans. John Warrington.

§ 22 Aristotle, *Metaphysics* 1009a27–30, trans. Richard Hope.

§ 23 Aristotle, *Metaphysics* 1009a22–25, trans. John Warrington.

§ 25 Introduction to "The Old in Their Knowing" in *The Beauty of the Weapons* only. The passage Bringhurst is paraphrasing occurs in Aristotle's *Metaphysics* at 1010a, just prior to the passage from the *Metaphysics* with which Bringhurst concludes the prose introduction in *The Beauty of the Weapons, The Calling*, and *Selected Poems*.

✣

Textual bases and relevant commentary for the other poems in "The Old in Their Knowing" include:

▸ "Parmenides": For textual bases, see Diels-Kranz 28B1 and 8 and 28A1–12; or Coxon 1986, Frs 1 & 8 and testimonia; or Kirk & Raven 1963, Frs 339–42, 350–2; especially see Cornford 1935a. For commentary, compare Bringhurst 2004 and 2007; Coxon 1986; Gallop 1984, Introduction; Kirk & Raven 1963, Ch. x; M.R. Wright 1985, xix–xxiii.

▸ "Miletos": For textual background, see Diels-Kranz 11A12, 12A1, 12A9–11, 13A1 (28A3), 13A4–7; or Kirk & Raven 1963, Frs 87, 100, 103, 141–4. For commentary, compare Charles Kahn 1960, and Kirk & Raven 1963, Ch. II–IV.

▸ "A Short History": See citations under "Miletos," especially Diels-Kranz 12A11 (Kirk & Raven 1963, Fr 103). For additional commentary, see John Mansley Robinson 1968, Ch. 3.

▸ "Empedokles: Seven Fragments": For textual bases, see Diels-Kranz 31B24, 57, 61, 62, 105, 115, 127; or Kirk & Raven 1963, Frs 443, 446, 448, 458, 471, 475. For other translations and commentary, compare Inwood 2001; Kirk & Raven 1963, Ch. xiv; and M.R. Wright 1981. The numbering of fragments in both Inwood and Wright is cross-indexed with Diels-Kranz.

▸ "Empedokles' Recipes": For textual bases, see Diels-Kranz 31B6, 96, 98, 31A1 (Diogenes Laertios viii.69–71), 31A78; or Kirk & Raven 1963, Frs 440, 441, and 485. See also, among others, Horace, *Ars poetica* ll. 464–6 and Ovid, *Ibis* ll. 597–8. For other translations and commentary, see previous note.

Of the opening of the third stanza, Bringhurst has said: "There are several references in the fragments to someone or something called Nêstis. E.g., DK 6, where the *téssera pánton hrizómata*, the four roots of everything, are called Zeus, Hera, Aidoneus and Nêstis. There is an old scholiastic tradition (present in Aitios, Stobaios and Diogenes Laertios, and maintained by the likes of Kirk & Raven) that these four gods are personifications of Fire, Air, Earth and Water — in that order. Whatever the virtues of this system of correspondences, I am happy trusting Aeschylus and Homer, to whom *nêstis* means as an adjective, *fasting* or *hungry*, and as a noun, *famine* or *hunger*." (private communication)

› "Pherekydes": For textual bases, see Diels-Kranz 7B1–2 or *Suda Lexicon* s.v. Φερεκύδης. (Kirk & Raven 1963 translate some of the relevant fragments: 44, 51, 54, 56, 57.) For commentary, compare Kirk & Raven 1963, Ch. 1 § 6.

› "Pythagoras": *lemuribus vertebratis, ossibus inter tenebras* ("for the vertebrate ghosts, for the bones among the darknesses"): epigraph by Bringhurst.

For textual background, see Diels-Kranz 14.8*a*, 14.9, 21B7, 36B4, 58B4–8, 58B30–37, 44A23, (58B41), 58C6; or Kirk & Raven 1963, Frs 268, 269, 271–3, 275, 289, 291, 307, 315, 318, 321, 329, 330, 331, 335. For commentary, compare K.S. Guthrie 1987; Kahn 2001; Kirk & Raven 1963, Chs. VII and IX; and John Mansley Robinson 1968, Ch. 4.

› *Gnomon*, a term closely associated with Pythagorean mathematics, has two relevant definitions: (1), a set of units arranged in the form of a carpenter's rule, as shown below, and (2), the index of a sundial.

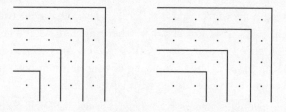

› *Octave*, in addition to signifying a musical interval spanning eight diatonic degrees (sounded when a vibrating string is divided in half), indicates, more loosely, any series of eight. In this connection, it should be noted that the ratio 1:8 is variously cited as the proportion governing the height of Doric order columns. (See, for example, *Encyclopedia Britannica*, 1968, Vol. 16, 1046, or Vitruvius *De architectura* I.1.7–8, where the unit of measure is given as the column's diameter at its base; and compare Kostof 1985, 125, where it is said to be the capital's height.) The word 'style,' in the sense of *gnomon*, is derived from the Greek word for column, στῦλος, from στύειν, 'to make still, erect; to place, set.'

› "Demokritos": For textual bases identified in Bringhurst 2005, see Diels-Kranz 68B156, 171, 277, 67A1, 68A101, of which Kirk & Raven 1963 offer only 554. For background, see Diels-Kranz 68B22,

174, 246; 67A6, 14, 28; 68A37, 40, 47, 119, 135; or Kirk & Raven 1963, Frs 555, 562, 564, 580–3, 585, 591, 594–7. For commentary, compare Kirk & Raven 1963, Ch. xvii, and C.C.W. Taylor 1999.

▸ "Xenophanes": For textual bases identified in Bringhurst 2005 see Diels-Kranz 21B27, 29, 34, 21A33, of which Kirk & Raven 1963 offer 178, 184, 189. For background, see Diels-Kranz 21B11, 14–16, 23, 24, 28, 33; or Kirk & Raven 1963, Frs 169–73, 175, 183, 185, 187. For commentary, compare Kirk & Raven 1963, Ch. v; Lesher 1992, and M.R. Wright 1985: xv–xvi.

▸ "Of the Snaring of Birds": See Sophocles, Antigone, ll. 332–75. In *The Beauty of the Weapons,* an epigraph dedicates Bringhurst's translation of this passage to the memory of Martin Heidegger. In both *Cadastre* and the version published in *Arion,* a parenthesis under the title directs the reader to Heidegger's *Einführung in die Metaphysik* iv.3.

▸ "The Petelia Tablet": See Harrison 1922, Critical Appendix on the Orphic Tablets, § 1: 659–60.

¶ PLATO'S PHAIDROS:
PHILOSOPHY AS DIALOGUE WITH THE DEAD

English translations are often those of R. Hackforth, with minor alterations. I have also relied on H.N. Fowler's translation (Loeb), on C.J. Rowe's, and have benefitted from the work of Alexander Nehamas and Paul Woodruff. Detailed line references are to Burnet's edition of the Greek.

page 59   **commentators**: Commentaries on *Phaidros* are legion, and uncertainties about Plato's intent go back to Hermeias' commentary in the fifth century. As C.J. Rowe puts it, "That the meaning or meanings of the *Phaedrus* are at least partially hidden from view, and have to be searched for, is common to all interpreters" (1988: 224). See the next note for a number of interpretive difficulties mentioned by Hackforth and by Nehamas & Woodruff. Other representative discussions include: Derrida 1972; Burger 1980; Nussbaum 1986, Ch. 7; Griswold 1986; Rowe 1986a; Ferrari 1987; Rosen 1988, Chs. 4 and 5; Heath's exchange with Rowe (Heath 1989); Benardete 1991; Kahn 1996, Ch. 12.1; Kastely 2002; Zuckert 2009, Ch. 5.1.B: 300–32.

Derrida's view is comprehensive, but his reading is not integrative and he has little to say about the fundamental importance of *erōs* to Plato's project.

Burger's approach is perhaps closest to my own, since she argues for a unified vision of the dialogue on the hypothesis that Plato must have been fully aware of the self-reflexive nature of his attack on writing. While I share this hypothesis, I do not go on to draw some of her most significant conclusions: that the dialogue's fundamental modality is ironic, or that perceiving its unity turns on viewing the love-speeches as artful imitations (of allegedly spontaneous speech) that perfectly illustrate the principles of dialectic. As will become apparent though, I think there is much merit to her claim that Plato wished to suggest that "only the written word which points to its illusory appearance as a replacement of memory is able to uncover its own potential as a reminder to the knower" (3).

page 59 **"broken-backed"**: Ferrari 1987: 230.

— **multitude of tensions**: See, for example, Hackforth's introduction to and commentary on his translation of *Phaidros*, or Nehamas & Woodruff's introduction to their own translation. Both address at some length, and with reference to other commentators, the intra-textual problem of ascertaining what the dialogue is about, given its peculiar structure and combination of subjects (Hackforth, 8 *ff.*; Nehamas & Woodruff, xxvii *ff.*). Among inter- and extra-textual difficulties that affect our ability to discern Plato's intentions they note: Sokrates' appearance in the countryside (Hackforth, 14; Nehamas & Woodruff, ix–xi; and compare *Crito* 52b–53a); his uncharacteristic interest in making and listening to speeches (Nehamas & Woodruff, xi; and compare *Protagoras* 334c–335c and *Gorgias* 449b–c, 461d–462a); the fact that "there doesn't seem to have been a time when this meeting between Phaedrus and Sokrates could have occurred" (Nehamas & Woodruff, xiii; compare Hackforth, 8); Phaidros' age (Hackforth, 8; Nehamas & Woodruff, xiv); and the striking tension between this dialogue and *Republic* on the status of poetry (Hackforth, 61). Some additional intra-textual anomalies that may or may not be relevant to the dialogue's philosophical point include: whether or not Lysias' speech is genuinely his or an invention of Plato (Hackforth, 17–18; Nehamas & Woodruff, 7 n. 19); whether

Sokrates' first 'counter-epideictic' speech is to be taken as 'inspired' or not (Nehamas & Woodruff, xix); and the apparent tension between Sokrates' account of the dialectical procedure he claims to have used (265e–266b) and how he has actually proceeded in his speeches (Hackforth, 133 n. 1). The outstanding intra-textual anomaly that definitely, in my view, affects our ability to grasp Plato's intentions concerns the number of Sokrates' speeches. See Hackforth, 125–6 n. 1; Nehamas & Woodruff, 59 n. 142, and the present discussion 60 & 77 ff.

page 60   **Lysias as ... παιδικά**: 236b5; Isokrates as Sokrates' παιδικά (*paidiká*): 279b2. (And Phaidros as Lysias' ἐραστής (*erastés*), the complementary role: 257b4.) Some, for example Hackforth, take these references to be in jest. I agree that the tone of the first two is teasing; but I don't sense that we are to regard their content as *untrue*.

page 61   **myth of the cicadas**: 258e–259d. The cicadas are also mentioned at 230c.

—   **This myth is one of four**: The other three are the myth of Boreas and Oreithuia (229b–d), the myth of the soul (246a–257a, described as a *mythos* at 253c7), and the legend of Theuth and Thamous (274c–275b).

page 62   **as close to death as possible**: *Phaedo* 67e.

—   **Sokrates' suspicion of rhetoric**: In *Gorgias*, the objections are specific: rhetoric's goal is mere persuasion rather than true understanding about matters of right and wrong (454b–455a); rhetoric is a form of flattery, which is bad because it aims at what is merely pleasant, ignoring the good (462b–466a). The objections are also ultimately cumulative: the whole dialogue is aimed at demonstrating the superiority of the life of the philosopher to that of the rhetor-politician.

The objections to rhetoric in *Protagoras* are also cumulative, but more oblique: Protagoras, the sophist and "cleverest of speakers" (310e8), presumes to teach virtue for a fee, but is shown by Sokrates not really to know what virtue is, or at least to hold mutually incompatible opinions about it. Except for a brief skirmish at 334c–335d, however, the subject of rhetoric is not an explicit topic of conversation. Nevertheless I agree with J. and A.M. Adam that "in its formal aspect ... the *Protagoras* may be regarded as an attempt to shew the superiority of Socrates to Protagoras — of dialectic to continuous discourse" (Adam and Adam 1957, xviii–xix).

page 64 **The dialectician selects**: The translation is Hackforth's with minor emendations.

— **In an earlier passage**: 265d–266b.

— **launches into a summary**: 277b–278e.

page 66 **general references to writing and writers**: for example, 235c4, 274b6, 274d2, 275d4, 278c6−7.

— τέχνη ἐν γράμμασι: 275c5; λόγων γραφή 277a10–b1; ἐν πολιτικοῖς λόγοις συγγραφεύς 278c3−4; ποιητής 278e1; λόγων συγγραφεύς 278e1−2; νομογράφος 278e2.

— **Aristotle refers to Sokratic dialogues**: *Poetics* 1447b11. Plato would have known the work of many of the other writers. See Kahn 1996, Ch. 1, for an overview.

— **Not even 'playwright'**: It may be significant that Greek has no such word. The conclusion of *Symposium* provides grounds for thinking that Plato did not wish to be thought of as either a tragic or comic writer.

— **he remembers nothing of it**: 277a8, 277b4, and 277d5.

page 68 **"Oh, but the authorities ..."**: The translation is Hackforth's.

page 69 **Ernest Klein**: Klein 1971.

page 70 **shows us how to do philosophy**: For Sokrates' use of Collection and Division, see especially 243e–245c plus 249d–e, and also 237c–238c and 263b–264e. Sokrates also provides a summary analysis of his use of it at 264e–265c, immediately preceding his explicit definition of the method at 265d–e.

page 72 **Dionysios Halikarnasseus' testimony**: "On Literary Composition," 25, 224–6; and compare Diogenes Laertios, *Lives of Eminent Philosophers*, III. 37.

— **Plato's authorship ... is disputed**: See, for example, Tarrant 1983.

page 73 **has under his cloak**: 228d6–7.

page 75 **Wittgenstein suggests**: *Philosophical Investigations* §§ 455–7.

page 76 **the greatest good**: 256b5–7.

page 79 **Virginia Woolf**: Woolf 1938: 5.

— **other than Plato's**: Examples of philosophers whose work has actively engaged with the thought of non-living philosophers would include Stanley Cavell, Walter Kaufmann, Iris Murdoch, Arne Næss, and Martha Nussbaum, to name but a few.

page 82 **Tranströmer**: In Tranströmer 1987, trans. Samuel Charters.

page 84 **euphoria**: Jameson 1991: 16, 32 *ff*.

⁋ DREAM LOGIC AND THE POLITICS OF INTERPRETATION

page 86 **"The Unconscious"**: Freud [1915] 1957: 166.

— **"the data of consciousness"**: All quotations in this sentence from Freud [1915] 1957: 166–9.

page 87 **"incontrovertible proof"**: Freud [1915] 1957: 167.

— **"legitimate"**: Freud [1915] 1957: 169.

— **"Psychoanalysis demands nothing more …"**: All quotations in this paragraph from Freud [1915] 1957: 169–70. My emphasis in this quotation and the next; Freud's emphasis on "psychical."

page 89 **'preconscious'**: Freud's first published use of the term 'preconscious' appears to have occurred in *The Interpretation of Dreams*, Freud [1900] 1958, Vol. 4: 338. But see, for clarification, Vol. 5: 541, and the discussion in Ch. VII § E. See also Freud [1915] 1957: 173, 189 and § VI: 190–5; and Freud [1923] 1961: 20.

— **jokes and parapraxes**: See, for example, Freud [1905] 1960, especially Part C § VI; and Freud [1901] 1960, especially portions of § V: 68–91 and 102–5.

— **two distinct logoi**: That the two *logoi* are distinct need not entail that there is no overlap, nor that there are not ways of thinking that involve both.

page 90 **"normal mental life"**: Freud [1900] 1958, Vol. 5, Ch. VII § E *passim*.

— **attempt at reductionism failed**: Though it was rejected by Freud as an unsatisfactory attempt to solve the problem of consciousness, the prescience of "The Project" may be measured by the enthusiasm that has greeted the works of George Edelman. Although Edelman does not claim to be a neo-Freudian, there are numerous and significant points of comparison. Freud's suggestion [1895]

that an initial "passage of cathexis" facilitates subsequent passages is echoed in Edelman's central claim that "neurons that fire
together wire together." Freud's notion that thinking is a kind of
"experimental acting" is echoed directly in Edelman's later work.
See also Pribram & Gill 1976.

page 90   **"By the process of displacement"**: Freud [1915] 1957: 186.
Freud's continued use of the word 'cathexis' is one of the strong-
est indicators of the degree to which his later thought remained
indebted to the model sketched in the "The Project." The word
signifies, here, the psychic energy with which an idea, image, or
object is invested; and Freud's understanding of this phenomenon
remained metaphorically, if not literally, quantitative.

Examples may help clarify his notions of displacement and
condensation. According to the theory, we would speak of displacement in the following sort of case: a person, unable to acknowledge childhood abuse at the hands of a parent, displaces
the feelings attendant on the abuse onto a chronic disease from
which the parent suffered, and hence regards the disease with a
degree of terror, anger, and grief that most of us would find puzzling. We would speak of condensation, on the other hand, when
a person anxious about job security, on the outs with a co-worker,
and under siege from a bureaucracy, dreams that a key piece of
equipment keeps malfunctioning. However, it should be noted
that the two do not always function independently. For example,
feelings about a sequence of events — an unexpected visit by a
family member, a quarrel, a disturbing insight about that person's
past relations with someone else — may be focussed in or on a
single apparently minor occurrence, tea staining a napkin, say.
Condensation? Displacement? Arguably both.

Freud himself provides elaborations and examples in Freud
[1900] 1958, Vol. 5, Ch. VI §§ A and B, and also in Ch. VII § E:
595–7.

— **derive their names**: Freud [1900] 1958, Vol. 5: 603.

— **"[exert] on somatic processes"**: Quotation from a letter to Georg
Groddeck dated 5 June 1917, in Freud 1960: 316–18. The characteristics listed prior to the quotation are mentioned in Freud [1915]
1957: 187.

— **Secondary process**: The summary characterization of secondary process in this paragraph must be gleaned from a number of

sources, which in turn must be bolstered by discussions in the "Project" if they are to be fully intelligible. See in particular Freud [1895] 1966: Part I, §§ 1, 14–18, and Part III; Freud [1900] 1958, Vol. 5: Ch. VII §§ E and F, especially 598–611; Freud [1911] 1958: 218–26; Freud [1915] 1957, § VII: 196–204 and 209–15; Freud [1920] 1955: § IV and the opening of § V; Freud [1923] 1961: 19–27.

page 91 **"makes sense"**: Freud [1900] 1958, Vol. 5: 523.

— **Wittgenstein**: Wittgenstein 1958, § 201.

— **"bewildering and ... irrational"**: Freud [1900] 1958, Vol. 5: 597.

— **"the talking cure"**: Breuer and Freud [1893–95] 1955: 30.

page 92 **"a complete divergence"**: Freud [1915] 1957: 194.

page 94 **Freud's answer**: Freud [1930] 1961.

page 95 **jokes ... do not tolerate**: For insightful observations on this and other features of jokes relevant to the present discussion, see Cohen 1983.

— **transparent dreams**: For an example of a 'transparent' dream, see, e.g., Freud [1900] 1958, Vol. 5: 509–10.

— **Rycroft**: Rycroft 1975. Freud himself did not write much about music, priding himself on having a tin ear. Are music and its appreciation products of primary or secondary process thought, on his scheme? An interesting question, whose answer appears to be 'both.' To the extent that primary process is involved, however, it would have to be primary process of which we are aware.

page 96 **'negative capability'**: Letter to George and Thomas Keats, Sunday (21 December, 1817?), address and postmark not recorded.

— **Porter to ... Borges**: See, for example, the excerpt from Katherine Anne Porter, the letter attributed to Mozart, and § 11 of "The Birth of a Poem" by Brewster Ghiselin in Ghiselin 1952. See also "A New Refutation of Time," in Borges 1967: 44–64.

page 97 **"dovetailed in [the] mind"**: John Keats, letter cited above in first note to p. 96.

page 101 **"like a mushroom"**: Freud [1900] 1958, Vol. 5: 525.

— **Emotions**: Freud does not spend as much time on the metapsychological nature of emotions as one might expect. The most explicit clue occurs in Freud [1915] 1957: 178, where Freud writes: "The whole difference [between unconscious ideas and unconscious affects] arises from the fact that ideas are cathexes — basically of memory traces — whilst affects and emotions correspond to *processes of discharge*, the final manifestations of which are perceived as feelings" (my emphasis). Primary processes remain, throughout Freud's work, those which are directed towards discharge, while secondary processes are those responsible for its inhibition. See, for example, the sources cited in the final note to p. 90 (p. 311 above), in particular Freud [1900] 1958, Vol. 5: 601–2, and Freud [1915] 1957: 188.

page 102   **Herakleitos**: Diels-Kranz Fr 32.

— **Plato**: *Phaidros* 278c4–d6, trans. Alexander Nehamas and Paul Woodruff.

page 103   **Wittgenstein**: Malcolm 1984: 27–8.

page 106   **"There is often a passage"**: Freud [1900] 1958, Vol. 5: 525.

¶ ORACULARITY

page 107   **self-designated inception**: The word 'philosophy' occurs sporadically in the written record before Plato, but it is his discussion at *Phaidros* 278d that provides the first notable definition; and it is presented there as a coinage of sorts. It should perhaps be noted, however, that Cicero in *Tusculan Disputations* (v.iii.8–9) recounts a story from Herakleides of Pontos in which Pythagoras is made to describe his own activities in much the same words. Diogenes Laertios (*Lives of Eminent Philosophers* 1.12) reports the same story, citing the same source.

page 109   **Frye**: Frye 1957: 271 (my emphasis).

— **"initiative"**: Frye 1957: 270–81 *passim*.

— **nor systematic**: 'Systematic' denotes thinking characterized by a thorough-going commitment to analytic structure and/or specifiable criteria of justification, which advocates of system maintain is, or are, the proper test[s] of clarity, and/or meaningfulness, and/or truth.

page 110   **insight**: Hartmann 1935: 170. Wolfgang Köhler elaborates: "We can, in our own experience, distinguish sharply between the kind of behaviour which from the very beginning arises out of a consideration of the structure of a situation, and one that does not. Only in the former case do we speak of insight, and only that behaviour of animals definitely appears to us intelligent which takes account from the beginning of the lay of the land, and proceeds to deal with it in a single, continuous course. Hence follows this criterion of insight: *the appearance of a complete solution with reference to the whole lay-out of the field*" (Köhler 1927: 199).

— **'field-as-a-whole'**: Max Wertheimer characterizes the fundamental thesis of Gestalt theory as the view that "there are wholes, the behaviour of which is not determined by that of their individual elements, but where the part-processes are themselves determined by the intrinsic nature of the whole." (Wertheimer 1938a: 2) See note to § 15 in "What Is Lyric Philosophy?", this volume. See also Næss 1989: 58–9.

Hartmann offers the following definition of 'gestalt': "the uncapitalized noun refers to all those organized units of experience and behaviour which have definite properties not traceable to parts, [properties of parts,] and [the mere sum] of their relations. There are many kinds of gestalten in nature, such as physical, physiological, psychological or phenomenal, and logical gestalten. Gestalten always involve formed, patterned or structured processes whether they occur within or without the organism . . . The basic term is the complex organic whole. *All measurable and observable phenomena in nature are differentiations of a pre-existing organic system, whether that be a gravitational field or a human being*" (Hartmann 1935: 311, 72).

— **Herakleitos**: Diels-Kranz Fr 93.

page 114   **a way the world is**: To say 'a way' is not to embrace relativism: Jastrow's duck-rabbit *is* both a duck and a rabbit; the Necker Cube does project both down and up. (See page 266 and pp 17 & 50, this volume.)

page 115   **relations to language**: See Zwicky 2014a, § 124.

— **Herakleitos' book**: Charles Kahn does not use the term 'lyric' in his discussion of Herakleitos' work, but his description coincides with its sense: "At the limit . . . diverse phenomena of resonance, taken together with explicit statements of identity and connection (such as 'war is shared and conflict is justice') will serve to link together *all* the major themes of Heraclitus' discourse into a single network of connected thoughts . . . The stylistic achievement of

Heraclitus is to have contrived a non-linear expression of conceptual structure, a hidden fitting-together . . ." (Kahn 1979: 90)

page 115   **essentially lyric**: If oracular utterance identifies an armature of insight *around which* other observations fall into place, it might seem that it *cannot* occur within the context of lyric composition; for one of the defining features of lyric is the absence of a hierarchy of 'essential' features and 'mere details' (Zwicky 2014a, § 66). But this is to conflate ontological insight and compositional structure. It is the perceptions and assumptions that make up a way of looking at the world that shift and turn around oracular utterance, not the sentences with which it may be keeping company in a lyric composition. The composition does not turn around it, nor require it more than it requires any of its other elements.

page 116   **Herakleitos**: Diels-Kranz Fr 124. No English translation captures the complexity of the original (which inclines me to suspect that Theophrastos' reportage may be more reliable than some have given him credit for). The ambiguity of the term κεχυμένον makes for an utterance that simultaneously claims that refuse-massed-together-at-random *and* a-sweeping-that-has-been-randomly-dissipated constitute the most beautiful universal order. This typical Herakleitean reversal, indicated by the same word, is not available in English.

Kahn's translation may be found in Kahn 1979 as Fr cxxv. See also "What Is Lyric Philosophy?," especially §§ 29–42, this volume.

page 117   **examples**: *Dào Dé Jīng (Tao Te Ching)*, first sentence; Herakleitos: Diels-Kranz Fr 10 (discussed in "Bringhurst's Presocratics," this volume); Wittgenstein 1961, Propositions 1 and 7.

page 118   **engulfed in silence**: For an extended discussion, see Zwicky 2014a, § 249.

— **Frye's 'oracular rhythm'**: Frye's claim that this rhythm is "discontinuous" is, however, puzzling. Even in the example he cites — the lines from Claudio's speech — the basic organization is iambic: the weight of the initial isolated stress is *set in the balance* against the following anapest and three iambs. In many of the examples cited above, the stress-pattern is highly regular. Note, too, the preponderance of trochees.

page 119   **Kahn**: Kahn 1979: 89.

pp 119–20   **Tranströmer, "Track"**: In Tranströmer 1987.

page 121   **logic is ... an intuitive notion**: See for example both Haack 1978: 3 and Quine 1970: xi.

page 123   **semantic coherence**: Some may prefer 'semantic agreement' where I have indicated 'semantic coherence.' I have chosen the latter because it connotes a greater degree of potential interpenetration of the utterance with its context. In the minimal case, however, I take semantic coherence to be satisfied by Tarski's Convention T.

— **Herakleitos**: Diels-Kranz Fr 97, trans. Charles Kahn in Kahn 1979, there Fr LXI.

page 124   **etymology of ... 'analysis'**: Klein 1971.

page 126   **Kahn**: Kahn 1979: 124.

— **'unexceptional' ... speech**: For discussion of the notion of semantically and grammatically unexceptional speech, see "What Is Lyric Philosophy?", this volume, §§ 43–45, "What Is Ineffable?", this volume, §§ IV and V, and Zwicky 2014a §§ 128–29, 133, 230, 269, 271, 276.

pp 127–8   **"most important prospects"**: *Viz*, metaphysics. Immanuel Kant, *Prolegomena to Any Future Metaphysics*: Preface [258], n 2.

¶   MATHEMATICAL ANALOGY AND METAPHORICAL INSIGHT

page 131   **'seeing-as'**: Wittgenstein 1958, Part II.xi.

page 132   **Wertheimer**: Wertheimer 1959. See also the selections from Wertheimer's work in Ellis 1938.

pp 132–3   **"In this square"**: Wertheimer 1938b: 279. For Wertheimer's synopsis of his work with these kinds of examples, see "Dynamics and Logic of Productive Thinking" in Wertheimer 1959: 235–6.

page 133   **"In general we see"**: Wertheimer 1938b: 280.

pp 133–4   **Poincaré**: Poincaré 1929, Ch. III, "Mathematical Creation": 386.

page 134   **Hass**: Hass 1984: 287.

page 134   **Kepler**: Kepler [1604] 1939: 92, trans. E. Knobloch, trans. rev. by G. Shrimpton.

pp 134–5   **Michaels ... Hirshfield [etc]**: Quotations and summaries in this paragraph are drawn from the following sources: Michaels

1995: 179; Hirshfield 1997: 111; Simic 1990, "Notes on Poetry and Philosophy": 67; Knobloch 2000; Polya 1954.

page 135   **Polya [etc]**: Quotations and summaries in this paragraph are drawn from the following sources Polya 1954: v; Butler 1917: 94; Charles Wright 1995: 59; Charles Simic in Charles Wright 1995: 72. See also Simic 1990 "Notes on Poetry and Philosophy": 64, and "Visionaries and Anti-Visionaries": 78.

page 136   **Cohen**: Ted Cohen 1978.

— **Polya**: Polya 1954: 13.

page 137   **Guldin**: Guldin 1641, Book 4, Ch. 4, Proposition 5: 327, trans. G. Shrimpton.

pp 137–8   **Hardy**: Hardy 1929: 18. See also "What Is Lyric Philosophy?" §§ 31–4, this volume.

pp 138–9   **"Red Pepper"**: In Sinclair 2001.

page 139   **Pythagorean theorem**: Brahmagupta and Bhāskara 1973, §§ 146–147.

page 142   **fruitful … and unimportant**: See, for example, Maddy 2000, or Demidov 2000.

— **"most spacious"**: Kepler [1615] 1960: 37.

page 143   **Demidov**: Demidov 2000: 379, 382.

¶   PLATO AS ARTIST

A NOTE ON TRANSLATIONS

Readers will be aware that in places I have played fast and loose with the Englishing of Plato's Greek. (Nowhere, for example, does Plato write a word that requires translation as "Yup.") My intent in such cases has been to render the tone or dramatic sense of the scene as a whole, to try to bring it to life, so that assumptions attendant on reading the dialogue as a 'work of philosophy' will either spring into focus or fall away — or both. Elsewhere, I have relied heavily and with gratitude on the work of many fine translators, often moving silently back and forth among them, occasionally substituting a word or phrase of my own. To make up for this scholarly bricolage, I have tried to give frequent and detailed Stephanus references, keyed to Burnet's edition of the Greek.

Listed below are the translations from which I quote in the main text. Translations of passages that appear alongside the main text are specified in the Notes for Side Quotations which follow.

Kratylos [*Cratylus*], trans. C.D.C. Reeve, in Cooper 1997.

Letter VII, trans. Glenn R. Morrow, in Cooper 1997.

Meno, trans. W.R.M. Lamb, in *Plato*, Loeb Classical Library, Vol. II.

Meno, trans. G.M.A. Grube, in Cooper 1997.

Parmenides, trans. F.M. Cornford, in Hamilton & Cairns 1961.

Parmenides, trans. Mary Louise Gill and Paul Ryan, in Cooper 1997.

Phaedo, trans. G.M.A. Grube, in Cooper 1997.

Phaedo, trans. R. Hackforth, in Hackforth 1972.

Phaedo, trans. Hugh Tredennick, in Hamilton & Cairns 1961.

Phaidros [*Phaedrus*], trans. Alexander Nehamas and Paul Woodruff, in Cooper 1997.

Protagoras, trans. W.R.M. Lamb, in *Plato*, Loeb Vol. II.

Protagoras, trans. Stanley Lombardo and Karen Bell, in Cooper 1997.

Republic, trans. G.M.A. Grube, rev. C.D.C. Reeve, in Cooper 1997.

Sophist, trans. F.M. Cornford in his *Plato's Theory of Knowledge*.

Statesman, trans. C.J. Rowe, in Cooper 1997.

Symposium, trans. Alexander Nehamas and Paul Woodruff, in Cooper 1997.

Theaitetos [*Theatetus*], trans. F.M. Cornford in his *Plato's Theory of Knowledge*.

NOTES FOR SIDE QUOTATIONS

In the following citations, where bibliographical information duplicates that already given in the preceding note, it has been omitted.

page 152   Wittgenstein 1958, § 303, trans. G.E.M. Anscombe.

— *Republic* 596a, trans. after A.D. Woozley, "Universals, A Historical Survey" (1967), *Encyclopedia of Philosophy*: 589.

— *Parmenides* 135b–c, trans. H.N. Fowler, in *Plato*, Loeb Vol. IV.

pp 154–5   Cornford 1960: 266.

pp 155–6   *Phaidros* 249b–c, trans. G.S. Shrimpton, not previously published.

page 156   Carruthers 1990: 29–30.

page 157   *Phaidros* 277b–c, trans. Alexander Nehamas and Paul Woodruff.

page 158   *Statesman* 263a–b, trans. C.J. Rowe.

page 159   *Republic* 510b, trans. G.M.A. Grube, rev. C.D.C. Reeve.

page 160   *Republic* 533d, trans. after G.M.A. Grube, rev. C.D.C. Reeve. (Grube uses 'sciences' and 'science' for ἐπιστήμαι and ἐπιστήμη respectively.)

pp 160–1   *Phaedo* 97b–d, trans. R. Hackforth.

page 162   *Republic* 533d, trans. after G.M.A. Grube, rev. C.D.C. Reeve.

page 164   *Phaidros* 249b, trans. Alexander Nehamas and Paul Woodruff.

page 166   *Republic* 455d–e, trans. G.M.A. Grube, rev. C.D.C. Reeve.

page 169   *Phaidros* 249d–250b, trans. Alexander Nehamas and Paul Woodruff.

page 171   Wittgenstein 1958, § 151, trans. G.E.M. Anscombe.

page 172   *Symposium* 200a, trans. Alexander Nehamas and Paul Woodruff.

page 172   Senechal, in Senechal et al. 2008: xiii.

page 173   Sinclair and Conway 1997: 14–15.

— *Phaedo* 73a, trans. G.S. Shrimpton, not previously published.

page 174   *Kratylos* 390c, trans. G.S. Shrimpton, not previously published.

— *Phaidros* 247b, trans. Alexander Nehamas and Paul Woodruff.

pp 175–6   Aristoxenos, *Elements of Harmony* ii.30–31, trans. J.N. Findlay in Findlay 1974, Appendix 1: 413.

page 176   *Symposium* 215e & 216b, trans. Alexander Nehamas and Paul Woodruff.

page 177   Porphyry, *The Life of Pythagoras*, trans. Kenneth Sylvan Guthrie, in K.S. Guthrie 1987: 135.

page 178   *Protagoras* 358d, trans. Stanley Lombardo and Karen Bell.

— School of Plato: *Definitions* 414b–c, trans. D.S. Hutchinson, in Cooper 1997.

page 179   *Phaidros* 250a, trans. Alexander Nehamas and Paul Woodruff.

page 182   *Republic* 511b, trans. G.M.A. Grube, rev. C.D.C. Reeve.

page 184   *Phaedo* 101d–e, trans. G.M.A. Grube.

— *Republic* 509b, trans. G.M.A. Grube, rev. C.D.C. Reeve.

page 188   *Phaidros* 247b–d, trans. Alexander Nehamas and Paul Woodruff.

page 190   *Phaidros* 252e & 253b, trans. Alexander Nehamas and Paul Woodruff.

pp 197–8   *Symposium* 216d–e, trans. Alexander Nehamas and Paul Woodruff.

page 204   *Phaidros* 249c–d, trans. Alexander Nehamas and Paul Woodruff.

page 205   *Apology* 31d–32a, trans. G.M.A. Grube, in Cooper 1997.

pp 206–7   *Phaedo* 101e, trans. G.M.A. Grube.

¶   WHY IS DIOTIMA A WOMAN?

page 211   **patriarchal character**: This is a commonplace. See, for example, Strayer and Gatzke 1984: 35. For an excellent overview, which draws from a broad range of ancient sources and gives careful attention to the way ideology may inflect reportage, see Blundell 1995, especially Ch. 11, "Women in Athenian Law and Society." See also Schaps 1979.

— **ideology of seclusion**: Xenophon, *Oeconomicus* VII.17–23, 29–30, 35–6; Thucydides, *History of the Peloponnesian War* II.46.

page 212   **mental capacities**: Aristotle's views on the inferior nature of females, and female humans in particular, are well known. See, for example, *Politics* 1254b13–15, 1259b2–4, 1269b13–1270a13 and *Generation of Animals* 728a17–21, 737a27–29, 765b8–766b26, 767a36–767b13, 775a4–22, 784a4–11. For Xenophon's views see *Oeconomicus* VII.23–9, which are belied elsewhere in the same document, for example at VIII.2–3, 10–11, and at IX.18–X.1. Aristophanes, by contrast, appears to have thought women were at least as intelligent as men and that their political situation was unfortunate — see *Lysistrata*. Euripides was also critical of women's political situation, although his attitude toward their intelligence and integrity is less clear — see, for example, *Trojan Women* and *Medea*.

page 212   **mentioning the names**: See Sommerstein 1980. Sommerstein notes that discussions of Xanthippe, Sokrates' wife, appear to defy custom in this matter, and that we have no clear idea why this might have been so: 408–9.

— **Athenian manners**: Sommerstein 1980: 418 n. 56.

— **men's club**: See Lynch 1986: 6–7.

— **taken them in Athens**: Plato *Phaidros* 230c6–e1; *Crito* 52a97–53a4.

— **Plato ... in other dialogues**: See, for example, *Protagoras* 310d–312c.

page 213   **priestess [as] profession**: See Sommerstein 1980: 395–6; also Kosmopolou 2001: 292–99.

— **women in this role**: For an overview, see Burkert 1983: especially 6–11.

— **midwives**: See, for example, Kosmopolou 2001: 299–300 and Brock 1994: 40. The evidence for women working as physicians is not easily traced beyond the Hellenistic period. See Fleming 2007: 258. However, as Parker 1997 points out, Plato himself provides (circumstantial) evidence for the existence of female physicians at *Republic* 454d2 and 455e6–7. Another fourth century source, Demosthenes, rails against Theoris, a Lemnian woman who, he alleges, had a professional practice involving drugs (*Against Aristogeiton* 1 25.79). And there is Phanostrate, a woman whose funerary monument, erected in the middle of the fourth century, describes her as a midwife and physician (*Inscriptiones Graecae* II² 6873). Regarding women practising in the Hippocratic tradition, see Lloyd 1983: 63 and 70. See also Herfst 1922: 55–6.

— **Aiskhines' ... Aspasia**: For an overview of our knowledge of Aiskhines' *Aspasia*, see Kahn 1996: 23–9. Kahn assumes Aspasia is depicted as a teacher of erotics, but notes that this is not established explicitly in the surviving fragments.

— **Xenophon**: Xenophon, *Memorabilia* II.6.36 and *Oeconomicus* III.14.

pp 215–17   **Diotima is a woman because**:

- *male instructor would undermine argument*: That is, Plato's recommendation of 'correct paederastic method' must be *seen to be* disinterested. See Dover 1980: 137 and Zeitlin 1984: 88.

– *male instructor would cloud rationale*: Halperin 1990: 114–6 develops this suggestion following Gould 1963: 193 n. 34.

– *dialogue demands balance*: Corrigan and Glazov-Corrigan 2004: 115–7.

– *Plato gay, therefore unthreatened*: Wender [1973] 1984: 226.

– *Plato gay and subject to pregnancy fantasies*: As Halperin points out, although this response is a popular one, the psychological or psychoanalytical research on which it is based is "less than compelling." See Halperin 1990: 119, especially nn. 28 and 30.

– *Plato sought to dignify relations between sexes*: Halperin 1990: 118. Halperin cites Vlastos 1981: 25 and 40–2 and Saxonhouse 1984: 11–22 as offering "more nuanced understanding[s] ...[but] along roughly similar lines" (Halperin 1990: 193–4, n. 26). The proximity of Saxonhouse's account to the one Halperin sketches is, in my view, clearest in pages 19–25, especially 25. Vlastos, as Halperin notes, does not doubt Plato's homosexual orientation.

– *Plato a proto-feminist*: The idea that Plato was a feminist or a proto-feminist has its roots in his discussion of the 'equality of soul' of female and male guardians in *Republic* v. As Halperin indicates, it is however a highly contested view, given remarks Plato makes elsewhere. In a long note (1990: 192, n. 21) Halperin cites contributions to "the recent controversy," and also Natalie Harris Bluestone's account of the earlier history of the question (Bluestone 1987). For the view that in using Diotima as his mouthpiece, Sokrates "completes the female drama of the second triad of speeches in the *Symposium*," see Ranasinghe 2000: 124, 134–5, 144.

– *dialogue occurred as scripted*: Taylor 1960: 224–5 and Waithe 1987.

– *Diotima a historical figure*: Hug, rev. Schöne, 1909: xlvii, n. 2; Kranz 1926: 438.

– *stand-in for Aspasia*: Halperin 1990: 124, who cites Ehlers 1966: 131–6 in this connection. Ehlers is following Dittmar 1912: 40–1.

– *'Zeus-honouring' mistress*: Nussbaum 1986: 177. Ranasinghe 2000: 161–2 echoes this suggestion. Halperin includes Nussbaum among those who suggest Diotima is a woman in order to make her program in erotics disinterested (1990: 191, n. 8).

– *women knew about sex*: Rosen 1987: 224.

– *spares Agathon humiliation*: Hug, rev. Schöne, 1909: xlvi–xlvii.

– *avoids Aristophanes' charge*: Halperin develops this line himself, but then dismisses it (1990: 127–8).

– Symposium *enacts symbolic matricide*: Cavarero 1995: 93–4.

– *not a woman but a 'woman'*: Halperin 1990: 150.

– *male teacher cannot represent excitement*: Halperin 1990: 129–42. Halperin documents Greek notions of male and female sexual natures, as well as the mores attached thereto, extensively.

page 217   **"Plato's theory"**: Halperin 1990: 138.

page 220   **the thought is ... close**: For additional commentary drawing out connections between the two passages, see Mourelatos 1970: 162 and 178, Sprague 1971, Solmsen 1971, and Kahn 1996: 343–5.

— **its singleness**: See Tarán 1965: 88–93 and Gallop 1984: 64–5 for discussion of textual variants of Fr 8.4. Tarán (1965: 92–3) and Coxon (1986: 195) both note echoes of μουνογενές (if that's what the word is) in Plato's *Timaios* at 31b and 92c. Kahn (1996: 343, n. 17) also notes the earlier of these two parallels.

— **Justice, Fate, and Necessity**: Fragments and lines: 1.14, 8.14, 8.30, 8.37, 10.6.

page 222   **no parallels, except**: *Odyssey* x.501–xi.332 and xii. Cavarero is alert to the feminized contexts in both Plato and Parmenides but reads them as evidence of the cultural ascendency of a patriarchal fear of death, which sublimates the life-renewing spirit of the Great Mother (1995: 36–9 and 98 *ff*). As will become apparent, I believe there is circumstantial evidence that suggests a different scenario. But Cavarero's conjecture has the signal merit of focussing on some of the most striking facts of the matter.

page 223   **real teachers teach**: See, for example, Plato *Protagoras* 325d and *Laws* 808d–e.

page 225   **Santillana**: Santillana 1968: 89.

— **Fr 3**: For various readings of this fragment, see Vlastos 1953, Kingsley 2003, Bringhurst 2007, Gallop 1984. For an extended discussion of other interpretations see Tarán 1965: 41–4. In Coxon 1986 Fr 3 is numbered Fr 4.

— **Cornford and Burnet**: See Cornford 1939, Introduction, Ch. ii: 28–52, and Burnet 1957, §§ 86–95.

page 226   **"Hypsipyle"**: Proklos, *In Platonis Parmenidem* 1.640, ll. 26–8.

— **alert him to a problem**: The correct translation of these lines of Parmenides' text, 8.53–4, is much disputed. See Gallop 1984 for a number of variants including Burnet's, and see Mourelatos 1970: 80–5 for discussion. See also Coxon 1986: 76 and Cornford 1939: 46.

— **Cornford and Santillana**: Cornford 1939: 49–50. Santillana 1968: 88.

— **Don't ask!**: For a very different view of why we should not concern ourselves with the identity of Parmenides' goddess, see Bowra 1937. Bowra believes it is pointless to enquire about her identity because "she is meant to be anonymous. She is a symbol for the poet's personal experience and his own discovery of the truth" (106).

page 227   **Rivaud**: See Rivaud 1905: 73–4.

page 228   **preoccupied with Justice, natural law**: See 1.28 and 8.32 in addition to the references above in the last note to p. 220.

— **Aetius**: Aetius 11.7.1, which appears in Diels-Kranz as 28A37. The passage is also given in Kirk & Raven 1963 as 359.

— **Guthrie**: Guthrie 1965: 63.

page 229   **Rivaud**: Rivaud 1905: 73–4.

— **Walton**: *Oxford Classical Dictionary* 1970.

— **"homologues"**: Santillana 1968: 86. In *Theogony* ll. 411–52, Hekate appears as a powerful divinity, the daughter of Asteria ("the starry one"), herself the daughter of Phoebe ("the bright one"). She is associated with the earth, sea, and sky, but not the underworld. The authenticity of this passage has been disputed. See Albert Heinrich's entry in the *Oxford Classical Dictionary* 1996.

page 230   **"oldest of the Moirai"**: Santillana 1968: 86. Two additional homologues have been suggested: Peitho (Mourelatos 1970: 160–1) and Persephone (Rivaud 1905: 73 and Kingsley 2003: 43).

— **wineless libation**: The scholion appears in what is currently the oldest manuscript of the play, Laurentianus 32.9 (de Marco 1952), which dates from the tenth or eleventh century. The text reads: "WINELESS [ONES]. Wine is not poured in libation to them, but water. Their libations are dubbed 'wineless.' Polemon, in his *Against Timaios*, says that wineless libations are made to certain other gods when he writes, 'The Athenians, being assiduous in these matters and religious in divine things make wineless sacrifices to Mnemosyne, Eos, Helios, Selene, the Nymphs, [and] Aphrodite Ourania.' Philokhoros, moreover, says [the same thing] in the second book of his *Atthides,* concerning other sacrifices performed in the same way, to both Dionysos and the daughters of Erekhtheos, and not only wineless sacrifices but also certain wooden [offerings] on which they used to burn [the other offerings]. Moreover, Krates, the Athenian, says that all of the wooden [offerings] not made from grapevines are called 'wineless.' Philokhoros, however, speaks more correctly when he says it was not vines nor fig branches but those from thyme plants that are called 'wineless,' and that these are the first to be placed on the fire when making such an offering and that the spirit [θύμος, *thúmos*] takes its name from the sound of [the Greek words for] fumigation [*thumíasis*] and burnt offerings [*thúa*]. Certain offerings developed into customs by chance as entirely libation free."

page 230 **drinking party**: Cf. Lynch 1986: 7: "The symposium was an institution lubricated by wine, a wine culture ..."

— **"high speculative terrain"**: Santillana 1968: 117.

page 231 **these two references**: There is a third, oblique reference at 187e, where "heavenly love" of music is described as the province of the "Ouranaic muse."

— **only two other works**: Most of our information about Aphrodite Ourania has been transmitted by later sources: the scholion to *Oidipous at Kolonos,* for example, or Pausanias' *Periegeta* 1.146.

— **astronomical fact**: See Knapp 1934 and discussion in Santillana 1968: 111 *ff.*

page 232 **"time-keeper"**: Santillana 1968: 117.

— **moving image of eternity**: Cf. Plato, *Timaios* 37d5–7. Note that in the passage in *Timaios* that elaborates the image, there is a direct echo of Parmenides Fr 8: regarding being, "we say that it 'is' or 'was' or 'will be,' whereas, in truth ... 'is' alone is the appropriate term" (37e5–38a1). However, that Plato does not identify either being or time with the *planet* Venus is made clear at 38d2–6.

— **"image of the pentagram"**: Santillana 1968: 112. For the definition of *point,* see Aristotle *De anima* 409a6. For the notion that the point or the unit or numbers generates or generate the principle or principles of all things, see the discussion in Kirk & Raven 1963: 245–56. Kirk, Raven and Schofield 1983: 324–42 covers similar material, but with a different focus. See in particular the discussion of Burkert on 324.

page 233   **Diogenes Laertios**: For the stories, see Diogenes Laertios, *Lives of Eminent Philosophers*, VIII: 48 and IX: 21 and 23. For their potential relevance to our understanding of Parmenides' poem, see Fr 8.53–4 and the second note to p. 226 (p. 323 above).

page 235   **feminized ... context ... surprising**: Cavarero 1995 argues that it is precisely the advent of a notion of eternal, atemporal being, presented in and through a feminized context, that signals the breakdown of a culture centred around the Great Mother.

¶   WHAT IS INEFFABLE?

page 237   **cannot be predicated**: See Alston 1956 for a classic statement of this view.

— **language ... involved in all human cognition**: The most recent version of this view — the so-called Language of Thought Hypothesis — was formulated by Jerry A. Fodor. (Fodor 1975. See also Fodor 2008 and 1981.) It is frequently urged that Fodor's notion of epistemic boundedness entails that there are ineffable states of affairs. The reason that this claim is not interesting in the present context is twofold: according to Fodor, these states of affairs are, in virtue of being ineffable, unknowable; and, although they are unknowable, we can know things about them, in particular, that they have linguistic structure.

Donald Davidson's semantic holism also has the consequence that there cannot be ineffable meaning — meanings just are relations among sentences: no sentential relations, no meaning. See Davidson 1974. A clear discussion of the relevant portions of both Davidson and Fodor is contained in Kukla 2005.

— **take serious ineffability claims seriously**: Apart from philosophers who have made serious ineffability claims, such as Herakleitos, Jankélévitch, Nagarjuna, Plotinos, and Wittgenstein, there are a number of recent commentators who have taken ineffability claims seriously. These include most notably William James (1902a), D.T. Suzuki (1957), Ben-Ami Scharfstein (1973 and 1993), André Kukla (2005), and William Franke (2007).

page 238   **then don't fall silent**: This difficulty has been the focus of numerous discussions. In addition to the discussions of Alston 1956, Suzuki 1957, and Scharfstein 1993, see — for example —

Ayer 1952: 118; Hoffman 1960; Stace 1960; Findlay 1970; Pletcher 1973; and Kellenberger 1979. Vladimir Jankélévitch's *La musique et l'ineffable* presents a special case. Arguing that music's meaning is indeed ineffable, he says the ineffable cannot be explained because there is so much to say about it: "such is the unfathomable mystery of God, such the inexhaustible mystery of love" (Jankélévitch 1961: 93).

page 238   **What sorts of things … are ineffable?**: For representative examples, see James 1902b, Ghiselin 1952, Happold 1970, Greeley 1975, and Franke 2007.

page 239   **Langer**: Langer 1951: 197, 206–207; my emphasis on *whole*, Langer's own emphases elsewhere. Langer's quotation from Hans Mersmann is drawn from Mersmann 1935: 40–1. Mersmann's observations are echoed by Jankélévitch 1961: 94.

— **Berenson**: Berenson 1949: 18.

pp 239–40   **Bucke**: Bucke, reported in James [1902b] 1963: 399. James indicates that he is quoting from a privately printed pamphlet, and that a different version of this passage may be found in Bucke 1901: 7–8. *Cosmic Consciousness* has since gone through many editions; the passage in question occurs in § 4 of Part 1.

page 241   **Bringhurst**: Bringhurst 2009, "Sunday Morning."

— **"Two women"**: Weil [1946] 1990: 297–8. There is a striking parallel to Weil's discussion in Polanyi 1958: 57. Polanyi also anticipates a connection between this conception of meaning and Gestalt theory (56–8), and also connects both to a notion of tacit knowledge that, he claims, must remain ineffable (87–95). The latter argument explicitly eschews consideration of so-called mystical experience, however; it depends on a distinction between subsidiary and focal attention, and how these forms of attention function in practical situations.

— **"It is in this way"**: Weil [1946] 1990: 298.

page 242   **hear a melody**: Wertheimer 1959: 242, 252–5, 264–5.

— **Gestalten**: Wertheimer 1938a.

page 244   **not designed to address**: I am not aware of a discussion of ineffability claims as such in Freud's work. The opening chapter of *Civilization and Its Discontents* makes clear that he had little patience with mysticism, which he understood as a form of occultism. He also famously eschewed attempts to offer an epistemology of creativity: "Before the problem of the creative artist analysis must, alas, lay down its arms" ([1928] 1961: 177).

page 245   'Primary process' ... 'secondary process': The idea of primary and secondary processes lies at the centre of Freud's earliest work and influences all his subsequent metapsychological writings. Core texts include Freud 1895, 1900, 1911, 1915, 1920, and 1923.

— "condensation and displacement": Freud [1915] 1957: 186.

— "of a kind ... scorned": Freud [1900] 1958, Vol. 5: 596.

— timelessness: Freud [1915] 1957: 187. See also Freud [1920] 1955, § IV: 28. The detailed editorial footnote attached to the reference to timelessness in Freud [1915] 1957 lists other passages where Freud discusses the subject.

— tolerance of paradox and contradiction: Freud [1915] 1957: 187; and [1900] 1958, Vol. 5: 596. Readers who consult Freud [1915] 1957 will discover that Freud also mentions "replacement of external by psychical reality" as a characteristic of primary process. I will discuss this claim below.

— Secondary process: Freud nowhere lays out the characteristics of secondary process in a list, as he does those of primary process. This characterization is thus the distillate of a number of discussions. See references in fourth note for p. 90 (pp. 310–11 above).

page 246   "reality principle": Freud [1911] 1958: 219. The pleasure principle, whose sway is opposed by the reality principle, is discussed on the preceding page of the same essay.

— "linked with word-presentations": Freud [1915] 1957: 202–3. See also the references given there by the editors in n. 1.

— refusal of reality: See last note to p. 245 and first note to p. 246 above. See also Freud [1911] 1958: 219, n. 3.

— jokes, and ... slips of the tongue: Regarding jokes, see Freud [1915] 1957: 186. Regarding slips of the tongue, see Freud [1900] 1958, Vol. 5: 596, and [1901] 1960: esp. 58–59. Some of Freud's examples in the latter (notably the third and fourth) actually document conscious awareness of the chain of associations underlying a slip of the tongue.

pp 246–7   characteristic of conscious ... artists: For a related view, see Anton Ehrenzweig 1965 and 1967. Ehrenzweig, like Rycroft, argues that primary process is fundamentally important to artistic creativity. However, he views primary process not as Freud and Rycroft do, but as a completely undifferentiated 'scanning'; thus he contends that condensation is not defining of primary process activity but is rather a function of secondary process. In addition, Ehrenzweig equates gestalt comprehension with precision, 'ego rigidity,' and analytic, piecemeal thinking, and so would also be unsympathetic to the view I will be developing below.

page 247   **"impermeable ego boundaries"**: Rycroft 1975: 29.

— **experience of timelessness**: An absence of awareness of time may be the result of an intensity of focus that is not strictly tied to primary process activity. Yet it is repeatedly connected, by both artists and scholars, to creativity. See Mainemelis 2001 and 2002 for an overview. See also the references in the second note to p. 96 (p. 311 above).

— **same ontological 'shape'**: Cf. Næss 1989: 59.

— **Wertheimer**: Wertheimer 1938a: 10.

— **"ratiomorphic"**: Lorenz 1971: 320. Next five quotations also from Lorenz 1971: **"exact" perception**: 281 and 282. **generate statistics**: 320. **"utterly incomprehensible ... illogicality"**: 319–320. **incorrigibility**: 312. **"collect[ing] data"**: 316.

page 248   **Weil**: Weil [1952] 1987: 109.

— **sudden, timeless, and involuntary**: See, for example, Wertheimer 1938b: 279–80; and compare Einstein's words at the end of n. 7 in Wertheimer 1959: 228 with the letter attributed to Mozart in Ghiselin 1952. See also Poincaré [1908] 1932, *passim* but esp. 53–5 and 58; Lorenz 1971, *passim* but esp. 318 and 321; and Wittgenstein 1967, § 151, and Wittgenstein 1982, §§ 564–5.

— **"rationally controlled attention"**: Lorenz 1971: 314. Cf. Næss 1989: 60.

— **Polanyi**: Polanyi 1958: 41.

page 250   **primary process ... a way of knowing the world**: Poincaré — who uses the term *le moi subliminal* to refer to the part of himself that perceives deep, surprising associative connections unsuspected by *le moi conscient* — appears to have come to a similar conclusion. He writes that, concerning his own activity as a mathematician, he came to the following hypothesis: "The subliminal ego is in no way inferior to the conscious ego; it is not purely automatic; it is capable of discernment; it has tact and lightness of touch; it can select, and it can divine. More than that, it can divine better than the conscious ego, since it succeeds where the latter fails" (Poincaré [1908] 1932: 57).

. — **at-oneness with the natural world**: In addition to the excerpt from Berenson quoted earlier, see Auden's superb overview of nature mysticism, "The Vision of Dame Kind," in Auden 1973: 58–62.

page 251   **a word that alliterates**: See Freud [1901] 1960, § 5, for numerous examples. The one I have described may be found on page 63.

— **series of associations**: By a series I intend something less organized than a sequence. A series does elapse in time, but there is no causal or logical shape to it, no constraint on the order of its constituents. So I might notice a purple scarf in a window, think about my friend who is fond of purple, remember that her mother just died, and then be put in mind of the politician who died on the same day. But I might, just as easily, have thought about the dark purplish red of the cloth draped over the politician's coffin, thought of my friend, and have been struck by the coincidence that her mother died on the same day. Or I might have thought about the politician's death, thought about my friend's mother, my friend, and ended up imagining a purple scarf. One cannot as easily perform reversals or juggling tricks in the case of causal or logical sequences without making mistakes: the light coming on does not cause the switch to be flipped; Sokrates' being mortal does not entail that all humans are.

page 255   **et cetera**: It would be useful if everything that might count as an aspect could be fully specified in advance, but it cannot. Douglas Hofstadter and Emmanuel Sander ask a similar question about the degree of resonance among various analogues of a given situation in *Surfaces and Essences: Analogy as the Fuel and Fire of Thinking*. They conclude that "similarity is not only subjective (encodings can vary wildly from one person to the other) but also multidimensional (many aspects of a situation play roles in its encoding)" (163). I agree that the aspects of any given situation are multidimensional, but I am not convinced that they are fundamentally subjective. The alacrity with which we perceive analogies that others draw suggests we all 'get' how someone might have seen something as they did — we pick up on the structural relations immediately. How?

Although Hofstadter and Sander do not document connections between their work and the work of the Gestalt school, what they mean by 'analogy' is 'gestalt shift.' Resonant form, as I am using the term, is an 'analogical structure' of the sort they identify, in which multiple aspects conduce to a final gestalt.

page 256   **the later Wittgenstein**: Also the earlier one. I read the *Tractatus* as an attempt to protect ineffable comprehension from the distorting effects of scientizing thought. If one is precise about what can be made explicit, then one sees clearly the outline of what cannot be made explicit. Wittgenstein's aim was not that of the positivists; he did not wish to reject what cannot be made explicit, but to protect it from misrepresentation.

For "form of life," see Wittgenstein 1967, *passim*; but see especially § 241 and Part II: 226.

— **language becomes meaningless**: Michael Polanyi makes a similar point in the course of an argument with a very different aim. See Polanyi 1970: 92–3. The key notions he employs there are discussed in more detail in Polanyi 1958. See, in particular, the references in the second note to p. 241 (p. 326 above).

page 257   **depress our ability to perceive resonance**: Lorenz 1971: 316, and Polanyi 1970: 93.

— **focus aspects … and form a new gestalt**: When we do this in a methodical way, we are pursuing something close to the method of Collection and Division as Plato understood it: a discipline, he claimed, that was demanded of us if we were to understand rightly the relation of the One and the Many.

— **not … entirely disconfirmed**: In some general respects, Freud's early neuropsychological speculations have indeed been confirmed, and in some particulars, they have been disconfirmed. See Pribram & Gill 1976 and Edelman 1992. Other books by Edelman (1987 and 2006) cover similar ground. For details see second note to p. 90 (p. 309 above).

page 258   **Klein**: Klein 1971. See also "What Is Lyric Philosophy?" §§ 1–10, this volume.

9 IMAGINATION AND THE GOOD LIFE .

§§ 33, 35–8 and 42–3 are based on passages in Zwicky 2014b.

SOURCES

Notes are keyed to the numbers of the sections in which, or following which, the quotations occur.

§ 5 Lorenz 1977: 7.

§ 7 Klein 1971.

§ 14 For this proof, and examples of other visual proofs, see Brown 1999.

§ 19 Klein 1971.

§ 20 Wertheimer 1959, "Dynamics and Logic of Productive Thinking": 235–6.

§ 21 Wertheimer 1938a: 7 and 9–10.

§ 22 Wittgenstein [1921] 1961.

§ 23 Wittgenstein on music: see quotation following § 24.

— Wertheimer on music: see, in addition to quotation following § 23, Wertheimer 1959: 116, 242, 252–5, 264–5.

— Wertheimer 1938a: 11.

§ 24 Ludwig Wittgenstein, reported by M. O'C. Drury in Drury 1973: xiv.

§ 30 Næss 1995: 240–1. A version of the phrase also occurs in Næss 1989: 57, trans. David Rothenberg.

§ 33 Wittgenstein 1958, § 455, trans. G.E.M. Anscombe.

§ 38 Næss 1995: 244.

§ 43 Næss 1995: 245.

§ 45 Robert Bringhurst, private communication.

§ 46 In Rilke 1908.

§ 48 Gzowski 1981: 188 (see also 168).

§ 49 Herakleitos, Diels-Kranz Fr 19.

§ 50 The Economist, 1 March 2008: 93. My emphasis.

§ 52 Weil 1987, § 26, "Attention and Will": 108, trans. Emma Craufurd.

§ 55 Weil 1987, § 30, "The Ring of Gyges": 125, trans. Emma Craufurd.

¶ ALKIBIADES' LOVE

page 283 **thinking in love with clarity**: Zwicky 2014a. The notion of clarity developed there is one that emphasizes the etymological foundations of the word, which link it with resonance rather than analysis.

— **knowing that you do not know**: Plato, *Apology* 21b–e.

page 284 **Alkibiades ... says**: Plato, *Symposium* 215d–216b, trans. Nehamas & Woodruff in Cooper 1997.

page 285 **Plutarch says of Aristippos**: Plutarch, *De curiositate* (Περὶ πολυπραγμοσύνης), *Moralia* 516c, trans. after Kahn 1996: 16, n. 30.

page 286 **Hegel ... says**: Hegel 1960, Vol. 4: 67, trans. Kaufmann 1978: 215.

page 287 **makes Parmenides tremble**: Plato, *Parmenides* 137a. The simile is extraordinarily complex. Parmenides says he feels like the race horse in the poem by the prominent Pythagorean, Ibykos. The speaker in Ibykos' poem, an old man, compares himself to an old race horse who has been entered in a chariot race and knows what's coming — hence the trembling. Ibykos' speaker makes this comparison because he has been compelled to fall in love against his will. The simile appears to involve a gesture towards the myth of the charioteer (see *Phaidros* 246a–257a); if so, the exercises Parmenides is about to undertake may have something to do with the soul's attempt to recall what it saw at the rim of heaven.

— **the Stranger from Elea ... says**: Plato, *Statesman* 308c, trans. C.J. Rowe in Cooper 1997.

page 288 **"swagg'ring gait and roving eye"**: Alkibiades, at 221b in Plato's *Symposium*, appears to be quoting Aristophanes' *The Clouds* 361–2 (... σοὶ δὲ / ὅτι βρενθύει τ'ἐν ταῖσιν ὁδοῖς καὶ τώφθαλμὼ παραβάλλεις). Trans. Nehamas & Woodruff in Cooper 1997.

page 289 **integrate** and **integrity**: Klein 1971.

— **loves, but without the desire to possess**: Compare McKay 2001: 26: "longing ... without the desire to possess."

page 290 **this expert knowledge ... is dialectic**: Plato, *Statesman* 285b, *Sophist* 253d–e and *passim*. Compare Plato, *Phaidros* 265d–e and 273e.

NOTES TO PAGES 290-296

— **gestalt and precisation**: terms first developed in connection with Gestalt psychology, referring to the analgorithmic grasp of wholes and the subsequent discernment of their constituent elements, followed by re-gestalting of the 'precised' whole and subsequent re-precisation, and so on.

page 291   **the Stranger from Elea says**: Plato, *Sophist* 230b–d, trans. Fowler (Loeb).

page 292   **whole**: Klein 1971.

page 293   **Herbert's clear-eyed compassion**: George Herbert, "Love (III)" ("Love bade me welcome ..."). The poem has been collected numerous places. For an authoritative text see Patrides 1974.

— **μέγιστα ἀκάθαρτον ... αἰσχρὸν γεγονέναι**: Plato, *Sophist* 230e.

— **Stranger from Elea also suggests**: Plato, *Statesman* 285a–b.

page 295   **lifting the eye of the mind**: Plato, *Republic* Book VII 533d.

— **leading the enslaved soul out**: Plato, *Republic* Book VII 514a–517c.

— **Aristophanes' Thinking Shop**: Aristophanes, *The Clouds* 94 *ff.*

page 296   **"precisely the respects"**: Plato, *Phaidros* 262a.

— **Sokrates and Kallikles**: See Plato, *Gorgias* 481b *ff.*

References

Adam, J. and A.M. Adam. 1957. *Platonis Protagoras*. New York: Cambridge University Press.

Alston, William P. 1956. "Ineffability." *Philosophical Review* 65: 506–22.

Aristotle. 1952. *Metaphysics*. Trans. Richard Hope. New York: Columbia University Press.

———. 1956. *Metaphysics*. Ed. and trans. John Warrington. London: Dent.

Auden, W.H. 1973. "The Protestant Mystics." In *Forewords and Afterwords*. New York: Random House: 49–78.

Ayer, A.J. [1946] 1952. *Language, Truth and Logic*. New York: Dover.

Benardete, Seth. 1991. *The Rhetoric of Morality and Philosophy: Plato's Gorgias and Phaedrus*. Chicago: University of Chicago Press.

Berenson, Bernard. 1949. *Sketch for a Self-portrait*. New York: Pantheon.

Bluestone, Natalie Harris. 1987. *Women and the Ideal Society: Plato's Republic and Modern Myths of Gender*. Amherst, MA: University of Massachusetts Press.

Blundell, Sue. 1995. *Women in Ancient Greece*. London: British Museum Press.

Bollack, J., and H. Wismann. 1972. *Héraclite ou la séparation*. Paris: Éditions de Minuit.

Borges, Jorge Luis. 1967. *A Personal Anthology*. New York: Grove.

Bowra, C.M. 1937. "The Proem of Parmenides." *Classical Philology* 32.2 (April): 97–112.

Brahmagupta and Bhāskara. [1817] 1973. *Algebra, with Arithmetic and Mensuration, from the Sanscrit of Brahmegupta and Bháscara*. Trans. Henry Thomas Colebrooke. London: John Murray.

Breuer, Joseph, and Sigmund Freud. [1893–95] 1955. *Studies on Hysteria*. In *The Standard Edition of the Complete Psychological Works of Sigmund Freud*, Vol. 2. Ed. and trans. James and Alix Strachey. London: Hogarth.

Bringhurst, Robert. 1982a. *Tzuhalem's Mountain*. Lantzville, BC: Oolichan.

——. 1982b. *The Beauty of the Weapons: Selected Poems 1972–82*. Toronto: McClelland and Stewart.

——. 1986. *Pieces of Map, Pieces of Music*. Toronto: McClelland and Stewart.

——. 1995. *The Calling: Selected Poems 1970–1995*. Toronto: McClelland and Stewart.

——. 2004. *The Fragments of Parmenides*. Berkeley: Peter Rutledge Koch.

——. 2005. *The Old in Their Knowing*. Berkeley: Editions Koch.

——. 2007. "The Fragments of Parmenides: The Poetry of Philosophy and the Fate of the University." *Everywhere Being Is Dancing: Twenty Pieces of Thinking*. Kentville, NS: Gaspereau Press, 129–65. [Berkeley: Counterpoint, 2008.]

——. 2009. *Selected Poems*. Kentville, NS: Gaspereau Press.

——. 2010. *Selected Poems*. London: Jonathan Cape.

Brock, Roger. 1994. "The Labour of Women in Classical Athens." *Classical Quarterly* 44.2: 336–46.

Brown, James Robert. 1999. *Philosophy of Mathematics: An Introduction to the World of Proofs and Pictures*. London: Routledge.

Bucke, R.M. 1901. *Cosmic Consciousness*. Philadelphia: Innes & Sons.

Burger, Ronna. 1980. *Plato's Phaedrus: A Defense of a Philosophic Art of Writing*. University, AL: University of Alabama Press.

Burkert, Walter. 1983. "Craft Versus Sect: The Problem of Orphics and Pythagoreans." B.F. Meyer and E.P. Sanders, eds. *Jewish and Christian Self-Definition*, Vol. III. London: SCM Press.

Burnet, John. [1930] 1957. *Early Greek Philosophy*. New York: Meridian.

Butler, Samuel. 1917. "On the Making of Music, Pictures and Books."
In *The Note-Books of Samuel Butler*. Ed. Henry Festing Jones,
93–109. New York: E.P. Dutton.

Carruthers, Mary. 1990. *The Book of Memory: A Study of Memory
in Medieval Culture*. Cambridge & New York: Cambridge
University Press.

Cavarero, Adriana. 1995. *In Spite of Plato: A Feminist Rewriting of
Ancient Philosophy*. Trans. Serena Anderlini-D'Onofrio and Áine
O'Healy. New York: Routledge.

Cohen, Ted. 1978. "Metaphor and the Cultivation of Intimacy."
Critical Inquiry 5: 1 (1978): 3–12.

———. 1983. "Jokes." In *Pleasure, Preference and Value*. Ed. Eva
Schaper, 120–36. Cambridge: Cambridge University Press.

Cooper, John M., ed. 1997. *Plato: Complete Works*. Indianapolis &
Cambridge: Hackett.

Cornford, F.M. 1935a. "A New Fragment of Parmenides." *Classical
Review* 49.4: 122–3.

———. [1935b] 1960. *Plato's Theory of Knowledge*. London: Routledge
and Kegan Paul.

———. 1939. *Plato and Parmenides*. London: Kegan Paul, Trench,
Trubner & Co.

Corrigan, Kevin and Elena Glazov-Corrigan. 2004. *Plato's Dialectic
at Play: Argument, Structure, and Myth in the Symposium*.
University Park, PA: Pennsylvania State University Press.

Coxon, A.H. 1986. *The Fragments of Parmenides*. Assen/Maastricht
and Wolfeboro, NH: Van Gorcum.

Davidson, Donald. 1974. "On the very idea of a conceptual scheme."
*Proceedings and Addresses of the American Philosophical
Association* 47: 5–20.

Demidov, Sergei. 2000. "On the Progress of Mathematics." In *The
Growth of Mathematical Knowledge*. Ed. E. Grosholtz and H.
Breger, 377–86. Dordrecht: Kluwer.

Derrida, Jacques. 1972. "La Pharmacie de Platon." In *La
dissémination*. Paris: Éditions du Seuil, 69–197. In English as
"Plato's Pharmacy," in *Dissemination*. Trans. Barbara Johnson,
61–171. Chicago: University of Chicago Press, 1981.

Diels, Hermann, rev. Walther Krantz. [1951] 1996. *Die Fragmente des Vorsokratiker*. 6th ed. Zürich: Weidmann.

Diogenes Laertios. [1925] 1931. *Lives of Eminent Philosophers*. Trans. H.D. Hicks. Loeb Classical Library. Cambridge, MA: Harvard University Press.

Dionysios Halikarnasseus. 1985. "On Literary Composition." *The Critical Essays*, Vol. II. Trans. Stephen Usher. Cambridge, MA: Harvard University Press and London: William Heineman.

Dittmar, Heinrich. 1912. *Aischines von Sphettos: Studien zur Literaturgeschichte der Sokratiker*. Berlin: Weidmannsche Buchhandlung.

Dover, Kenneth, ed. 1980. *Symposium*. Cambridge and New York: Cambridge University Press.

Drury, M.O'C. 1973. *The Danger of Words*. New York: Humanities Press.

Edelman, Gerald. 1987. *Neural Darwinism: The Theory of Neuronal Group Selection*. New York: Basic Books.

——. 1992. *Bright Air, Brilliant Fire: On the Matter of Mind*. New York: Basic Books.

——. 2006. *Second Nature: Brain Science and Human Knowledge*. New Haven: Yale University Press.

Ehlers, Barbara. 1966. *Eine vorplatonische Deutung des sokratischen Eros. Der Dialog Aspasia des Sokratikers Aischines*. Zetemata Series 41. Munich: C.H. Beck'sche Verlag.

Ehrenzweig, Anton. 1965. *The Psycho-analysis of Artistic Vision and Hearing*. New York: George Braziller.

——. 1967. *The Hidden Order of Art: A Study in the Psychology of Artistic Imagination*. Berkeley: University of California Press.

Ellis, Willis D., ed. and trans. 1938. *A Source Book of Gestalt Psychology*. London: Routledge & Kegan Paul.

Empedokles. See H. Diels, rev. W. Krantz; Brad Inwood; G.S. Kirk & J.E. Raven; M.R. Wright.

Encyclopedia of Philosophy. 2nd ed. 2006. Donald M. Borchert, Editor in Chief, Farmington Hills, MI: Thomson Gale.

Ferrari, G.R.F. 1987. *Listening to the Cicadas: A Study of Plato's Phaedrus*. New York: Cambridge University Press.

Findlay, J.N. 1970. "The Logic of Mysticism." In *Ascent to the Absolute: Metaphysical Papers and Lectures*, 162–83. London: George Allen & Unwin.

———. 1974. *Plato: The Written and Unwritten Doctrines*. London: Routledge and Kegan Paul.

Fleming, Rebecca. 2007. "Women, Writing and Medicine in the Classical World." *Classical Quarterly* 57.1: 257–79.

Fodor, Jerry A. 1975. *The Language of Thought*. Cambridge, MA: Harvard University Press.

———. 1981. *Representations: Philosophical Essays on the Foundations of Cognitive Science*. Cambridge, MA: MIT Press.

———. 2008. *LOT 2: The Language of Thought Revisited*. Oxford: Oxford University Press.

Franke, William, ed. 2007. *On What Cannot Be Said: Apophatic Discourses in Philosophy, Religion, Literature, and the Arts*. Notre Dame, IN: University of Notre Dame Press.

Freud, Sigmund. *Letters of Sigmund Freud*. 1960. Ed. E.L. Freud. Trans. T. and J. Stern. New York: Basic Books.

Freud, Sigmund. [1893–95] 1955. *Studies on Hysteria*. See Breuer and Freud.

———. [1895] 1966. "Project for a Scientific Psychology." In *The Standard Edition of the Complete Psychological Works of Sigmund Freud*, Vol. 1. Ed. and trans. James Strachey, 281–397. London: Hogarth.

———. [1900] 1958. *The Interpretation of Dreams*. In *The Standard Edition of the Complete Psychological Works of Sigmund Freud*, Vols. 4 & 5. Ed. and trans. James Strachey. London: Hogarth.

———. [1901] 1960. *The Psychopathology of Everyday Life*. In *The Standard Edition of the Complete Psychological Works of Sigmund Freud*, Vol. 6. Ed. and trans. James Strachey, 53–105. London: Hogarth.

———. [1905] 1960. *Jokes and Their Relation to the Unconscious*. In *The Standard Edition of the Complete Psychological Works of Sigmund Freud*, Vol. 8. Ed. and trans. James Strachey. London: Hogarth.

———. [1911] 1958. "Formulations on the Two Principles of Mental Functioning". In *The Standard Edition of the Complete*

Psychological Works of Sigmund Freud, Vol. 12. Ed. and trans. James Strachey, 213–26. London: Hogarth.

———. [1915] 1957. "The Unconscious." In *The Standard Edition of the Complete Psychological Works of Sigmund Freud,* Vol. 14. Ed. and trans. James Strachey, 159–215. London: Hogarth.

———. [1920] 1955. *Beyond the Pleasure Principle.* In *The Standard Edition of the Complete Psychological Works of Sigmund Freud,* Vol. 18. Ed. and trans. James Strachey, 1–64. London: Hogarth.

———. [1923] 1961. *The Ego and the Id.* In *The Standard Edition of the Complete Psychological Works of Sigmund Freud,* Vol. 19. Ed. and trans. James Strachey, 1–66. London: Hogarth.

———. [1928] 1961. "Dostoevsky and Parricide." In *The Standard Edition of the Complete Psychological Works of Sigmund Freud,* Vol. 21. Ed. and trans. James Strachey, 173–96. London: Hogarth.

———. [1930] 1961. *Civilization and Its Discontents.* In *The Standard Edition of the Complete Psychological Works of Sigmund Freud,* Vol. 21. Ed. James Strachey, 57–145. Trans. Joan Riviere. London: Hogarth.

Frye, Northrop. 1957. *Anatomy of Criticism: Four Essays.* Princeton: Princeton University Press.

Gallop, David. 1984. *Parmenides of Elea: Fragments: A Text and Translation with an Introduction.* Toronto: University of Toronto Press.

Ghiselin, Brewster. 1952. *The Creative Process: A Symposium.* New York: Mentor.

Gould, Thomas. 1963. *Platonic Love.* New York: The Free Press of Glencoe.

Greeley, Andrew M. 1975. "Mysticism." In *The Sociology of the Paranormal: A Reconnaisance,* 43–67. Beverly Hills, CA: Sage.

Griswold, Charles L. 1986. *Self-Knowledge in Plato's Phaedrus.* New Haven: Yale University Press.

Guldin, Paul. 1641. *De centro gravitas.* Vienna: Gregor Gelbar.

Guthrie, Kenneth Sylvan, ed. 1987. *The Pythagorean Sourcebook and Library.* Grand Rapids, MI: Phanes Press.

Guthrie, W.K.C. 1965. *A History of Greek Philosophy,* Vol. 11. Cambridge: Cambridge University Press.

Gzowski, Peter. 1981. *The Game of Our Lives*. Toronto: McClelland & Stewart.

Haack, Susan. 1978. *Philosophy of Logics*. Cambridge: Cambridge University Press.

Hackforth, R., trans. 1952. *Plato's Phaedrus*. New York: Cambridge University Press.

——, trans. [1955] 1972. [Plato's] *Phaedo*. Cambridge: Cambridge University Press.

Halperin, David M. 1990. "Why is Diotima a Woman?" In *One Hundred Years of Homosexuality*, 113–51. New York and London: Routledge.

Hamilton, Edith, and Huntington Cairns, eds. 1961. *The Collected Dialogues of Plato*. Princeton: Princeton University Press.

Happold, F.C. 1970. *Mysticism: A Study and an Anthology*. Harmondsworth: Penguin.

Hardy, G.H. 1929. "Mathematical Proof." *Mind* n.s. 38.149: 1–25.

Hargrove, Eugene. 1989. *Foundations of Environmental Ethics*. Englewood Cliffs, NJ: Prentice-Hall.

Harrison, Jane. 1922. *Prolegomena to the Study of Greek Religion*. Cambridge: Cambridge University Press.

Hartmann, George W. 1935. *Gestalt Psychology: A Survey of Facts and Principles*. New York: The Ronald Press.

Hass, Robert. 1984. "Images." In *Twentieth Century Pleasures*. New York: The Ecco Press, 269–308.

Heath, Malcolm. 1989. "The Unity of Plato's *Phaedrus*." *Oxford Studies in Ancient Philosophy* 7: 151–73. Followed by C.J. Rowe, "The Unity of the *Phaedrus*: A Reply to Heath": 175–88. Followed by Malcolm Heath, "The Unity of the *Phaedrus*": 189–91.

Hegel, G.W.F. 1960. *Briefe von und an Hegel*. Ed. Johannes Hoffmeister. Hamburg: Felix Meiner.

Herakleitos. See H. Diels, rev. W. Krantz; Charles Kahn; G.S. Kirk & J.E. Raven; T.M. Robinson.

Herfst, Pieter. 1922. *Le travail de la femme dans la Grèce ancienne*. Utrecht: A. Oosthoek.

Hirshfield, Jane. 1997. *Nine Gates: Entering the Mind of Poetry*. New York: HarperCollins.

Hoffman, R. 1960. "Logic, Meaning, and Mystical Intuition."
    Philosophical Studies 21: 65–70.

Hofstadter, Douglas, and Emmanuel Sander. 2013. *Surfaces and
    Essences: Analogy as the Fuel and Fire of Thinking.* New York:
    Basic Books.

Hölderlin, Friedrich. 1980. *Poems and Fragments.* Trans. Michael
    Hamburger. Cambridge: Cambridge University Press.

Hug, Arnold, rev. Hermann Schöne. 1909. *Symposion,* 3rd ed.
    Christian Cron and Julius Deuschle, eds. *Platons ausgewählte
    Schriften,* Vol. 5. Leipzig and Berlin: B.G. Teubner.

Inwood, Brad. 2001. *The Poem of Empedocles: A Text and Translation
    with an Introduction.* Toronto: University of Toronto Press.

James, William. [1902a] 1963. "A Suggestion about Mysticism." In
    The Varieties of Religious Experience: A Study in Human Nature,
    585–92. New York: University Books.

———. [1902b] 1963. "Mysticism." In *The Varieties of Religious
    Experience: A Study in Human Nature,* 379–429. New York:
    University Books.

Jameson, Fredric. 1991. *Postmodernism, or, The Cultural Logic of Late
    Capitalism.* Durham, NC: Duke University Press.

Jankélévitch, Vladimir. 1961. *La musique et l'ineffable.* Paris: Seuil.

Kahn, Charles. 1960. *Anaximander and the Origins of Greek
    Cosmology.* New York: Columbia University Press.

———. 1979. *The Art and Thought of Heraclitus.* Cambridge:
    Cambridge University Press.

———. 1996. *Plato and the Socratic Dialogue.* Cambridge: Cambridge
    University Press.

———. 2001. *Pythagoras and the Pythagoreans: A Brief History.*
    Indianapolis: Hackett.

Kant, Immanuel. 1977. *Prolegomena to Any Future Metaphysics.*
    Trans. Paul Carus, rev. James W. Ellington. Indianapolis: Hackett.

Kastely, James L. 2002. "Respecting the Rupture: Not Solving the
    Problem of Unity in Plato's *Phaedrus.*" *Philosophy and Rhetoric*
    35.2: 138–52.

Kaufmann, Walter. [1965] 1978. *Hegel: A Reinterpretation.* Notre
    Dame: University of Notre Dame Press.

Keats, John. 1952. *The Letters of John Keats*. Ed. Maurice Buxton Foreman. London: Oxford University Press.

Kellenberger, J. 1979. "The Ineffabilities of Mysticism." *American Philosophical Quarterly* 16: 307–15.

Kepler, Johannes. [1604] 1939. *Ad vitellionem paralipomena, quibus astronomiae pars optica traditur*, etc. In *Johannes Kepler: Gesammelte Werke*. Vol. II. Ed Franz Hammer. Munich: C.H. Beck.

———. [1615] 1960. *Nova stereometria doliorum vinariorum*, etc. In *Johannes Kepler: Gesammelte Werke*. Vol. IX. Ed. Franz Hammer. Munich: C.H. Beck.

Kingsley, Peter. 2003. *Reality*. Inverness, CA: Golden Sufi Center.

Kirk, G.S., and J.E. Raven. [1957] 1963. *The Presocratic Philosophers*. Cambridge: Cambridge University Press.

Kirk, G.S., J.E. Raven, and M. Schofield. 1983. *The Presocratic Philosophers*, 2nd ed. Cambridge: Cambridge University Press.

Klee, Paul. 1964. "On Modern Art." Trans. Paul Findlay. In *Modern Artists on Art*. Ed. Robert L. Herbert, 74–91. Englewood Cliffs, NJ: Prentice-Hall. [First published as *Paul Klee: Über die Moderne Kunst*. Bern-Bümpliz: Verlag Benteli. 1945. First published in this translation as *Paul Klee: On Modern Art*. London: Faber and Faber. 1948.]

Klein, Ernest. 1971. *A Comprehensive Etymological Dictionary of the English Language*. Amsterdam: Elsevier.

Knapp, Manfred. 1934. *Pentagramma veneris*. Basel: Helbig & Lichtenhahn.

Knobloch, Eberhard. 2000. "Analogy and the Growth of Mathematical Knowledge." In *The Growth of Mathematical Knowledge*. Ed. E. Grosholtz and H. Breger, 295–314. Dordrecht: Kluwer.

Köhler, Wolfgang. 1927. *The Mentality of Apes*. Trans. Ella Winter. New York: Harcourt, Brace & Co.; London: Kegan Paul, Trench, Trubner & Co.

Kosmopolou, Angeliki. 2001. "'Working Women': Female Professionals on Classical Attic Gravestones." *The Annual of the British School at Athens* 96: 281–319.

Kostof, Spiro. 1985. *A History of Architecture: Settings and Rituals.*
New York: Oxford University Press.

Kranz, Walther. 1926. "Diotima von Mantineia." *Hermes* 61: 437–47.

Kukla, André. 2005. *Ineffability and Philosophy.* London: Routledge.

Langer, Suzanne. [1942] 1951. *Philosophy in a New Key.* New York:
Mentor.

Lao-Tzu [Lǎo Zi]. 1993. *Tao Te Ching [Dào Dé Jīng].* Trans. Stephen
Addiss and Stanley Lombardo. Indianapolis: Hackett.

Leopold, Aldo. 1949. "The Land Ethic." In *A Sand County Almanac
and Sketches Here and There,* 201–26. New York: Oxford
University Press.

Lesher, J.H. 1992. *Xenophanes of Colophon: Fragments.* Toronto:
University of Toronto Press.

Letwin, Oliver. 1987. *Ethics, Emotion and the Unity of the Self.*
London: Croom Helm.

Lilburn, Tim, ed. 1995. *Poetry and Knowing: Speculative Essays and
Interviews.* Kingston, ON: Quarry Press.

Lloyd, G.E.R. 1983. *Science, Folklore and Ideology.* Cambridge:
Cambridge University Press.

Lorenz, Konrad. 1971. "Gestalt Perception as a Source of Scientific
Knowledge." In *Studies in Animal and Human Behaviour.* Trans.
Robert Martin. Vol. 2: 281–322. London: Methuen.

———. 1977. *Behind the Mirror: A Search for a Natural History of
Human Knowledge.* Trans. Ronald Taylor. London: Methuen.

Lynch, John P. 1986. "The Ancient Symposium as an Institution:
Social Drinking and Educational Issues in Fifth Century Athens."
Laetaberis n.s. 4 (Spring): 1–15.

Maddy, Penelope. 2000. "Mathematical Progress." In *The Growth
of Mathematical Knowledge.* Ed. E. Grosholtz and H. Breger,
341–52. Dordrecht: Kluwer.

Mainemelis, Charalampos. 2001. "When the Muse Takes It All: A
Model for the Experience of Timelessness in Organizations."
Academy of Management Review 26.4 (October 2001): 548–65.

———. 2002. "Time and Timelessness: Creativity in (and out of) the
Temporal Dimension." *Creativity Research Journal* 14.2 (2002):
227–38.

Malcolm, Norman. 1984. *Ludwig Wittgenstein: A Memoir.* 2nd ed. London and New York: Oxford University Press.

de Marco, Vittorio. 1952. *Scholia in Sophoclis Oedipum Coloneum.* Rome: Bretschneider.

McKay, Don. 2001. "Baler Twine." In *Vis à Vis.* Kentville, NS: Gaspereau Press, 11–33.

Mersmann, Hans. 1935. "Versuch einer musikalischen Weraesthetik." *Zeitschrift für Musikwissenschaft* 17: 33–47.

Michaels, Anne. 1995. "Cleopatra's Love." In *Poetry and Knowing: Speculative Essays and Interviews.* Ed. Tim Lilburn, 177–83. Kingston, ON: Quarry Press.

Mourelatos, Alexander. 1970. *The Route of Parmenides.* New Haven and London: Yale University Press.

Næss, Arne. 1989. *Ecology, Community and Lifestyle.* Ed. and trans. David Rothenberg. Cambridge: Cambridge University Press.

——. 1995. "Ecosophy and Gestalt Ontology." In *Deep Ecology for the 21st Century.* Ed. George Sessions, 240–45. Boston: Shambhala.

Necker, L.A. 1832. "Observations on some remarkable Optical Phenomena seen in Switzerland; and on an Optical Phenomenon which occurs on viewing a Figure of a Crystal or a Geometrical Solid." *London and Edinburgh Philosophical Magazine and Journal of Science* 1.5 (November 1832): 329–37.

Nehamas, Alexander, and Paul Woodruff, eds. and trans. 1989. *Plato: Symposium.* Hackett.

——. 1995. *Plato: Phaedrus.* Indianapolis: Hackett.

Nussbaum, Martha. 1986. *The Fragility of Goodness: Luck and Ethics in Greek Tragedy and Philosophy.* Cambridge: Cambridge University Press.

Oxford Classical Dictionary. 1970. 2nd ed. Ed. N.G.L. Hammond and H.H. Scullard. Oxford: Clarendon.

Oxford Classical Dictionary. 1996. 3rd ed. Ed. Simon Hornblower and Antony Spawforth. Oxford and New York: Oxford University Press.

Parker, Holt N. 1997. "Women Doctors in Greece, Rome, and the Byzantine Empire." In *Women Healers and Physicians: Climbing a Long Hill.* Ed. Lilian R. Furst, 131–50. Lexington, KY: University Press of Kentucky.

Parmenides of Elea. See Robert Bringhurst; F.M. Cornford; A.H. Coxon; H. Diels, rev. W. Krantz; David Gallop; Alexander Mourelatos.

Patrides, C.A., ed. 1974. *The English Poems of George Herbert.* London: J.M. Dent & Sons.

Plato. [1924] 1990. Loeb Classical Library. Cambridge, MA, & London: Harvard University Press. For additional English translations of Plato's dialogues, see Adam & Adam; John Cooper; F.M. Cornford; R. Hackforth; Hamilton & Cairns; Nehamas & Woodruff; C.J. Rowe.

Plato. 1961. *Platonis opera.* Ed. John Burnet. Oxford: Clarendon Press.

Pletcher, Galen K. 1973. "Mysticism, Contradiction, and Ineffability." *American Philosophical Quarterly* 10: 201–11.

Poincaré, Henri. [1908] 1932. *Mathematical Discovery.* In *Science and Method.* Translated by Francis Maitland. New York: Dover.

——. 1929. *Science and Method.* In *The Foundations of Science.* Trans. George Bruce Halsted. New York: The Science Press.

Polanyi, Michael. 1958. *Personal Knowledge.* London: Routledge & Kegan Paul.

——. 1970. "Transcendence and Self-Transcendence." *Soundings* 53: 88–94.

Polya, George. 1954. *Induction and Analogy in Mathematics.* Vol. 1 of *Mathematics and Plausible Reasoning.* Princeton: Princeton University Press.

Pribram, K.H., and M.M. Gill. 1976. *Freud's "Project" Re-assessed: Preface to Contemporary Cognitive Theory and Neuropsychology.* New York: Basic Books.

Quine, W.V.O. 1970. *Philosophy of Logic.* Englewood Cliffs: Prentice-Hall.

Ranasinghe, Nalin. 2000. *The Soul of Socrates.* Ithaca and London: Cornell University Press.

Rilke, Rainer Maria. 1908. *Der neuen Gedichte anderer Teil.* Leipzig: Insel-Verlag.

Rivaud, Albert. 1905. *Le problème du devenir et la notion de la matière dans la philosophie grecque depuis les origines jusqà Theophraste.* Paris: F. Alcan.

Robinson, John Mansley. 1968. *An Introduction to Early Greek Philosophy*. Boston: Houghton Mifflin.

Robinson, T.M. 1987. *Heraclitus: Fragments*. Toronto: University of Toronto Press.

Rosen, Stanley. 1968. *Plato's Symposium*. New Haven: Yale University Press.

——. 1988. *The Quarrel between Philosophy and Poetry: Studies in Ancient Thought*. New York: Routledge.

Rowe, C.J. 1986a. "The Argument and Structure of Plato's *Phaedrus*." *Proceedings of the Cambridge Philological Society* n.s. 32: 106–25. See also Malcolm Heath.

——. 1986b. *Plato: Phaedrus*. Warminster: Aris & Phillips.

Rycroft, Charles. 1975. "Freud and the Imagination." *New York Review of Books,* 3 April 1975: 26–30. Reprinted as "Psychoanalysis and the Literary Imagination" in *Psychoanalysis and Beyond*, 261–77. London: Hogarth, 1985.

de Santillana, Giorgio. [1964] 1968. "Prologue to Parmenides." *Reflections on Men and Ideas*. Cambridge, MA and London: MIT Press. Originally published in *Lectures in Memory of Louise Taft Semple*. Princeton: Princeton University Press.

Saxonhouse, Arlene W. 1984. "Eros and the Female in the Political Thought of Plato." *Political Theory* 12.1: 5–27.

Schaps, David M. 1979. *Economic Rights of Women in Ancient Greece*. Edinburgh: Edinburgh University Press.

Scharfstein, Ben-Ami. 1973. *Mystical Experience*. Oxford: Basil Blackwell.

——. 1993. *Ineffability: The Failure of Words in Philosophy and Religion*. Albany: SUNY Press.

Senechal, Marjorie Wikler, Chandler Davis, and Jan Zwicky, eds. 2008. *The Shape of Content*. Wellesley, MA: A.K. Peters.

Simic, Charles. 1990. *Wonderful Words, Silent Truth*. Ann Arbor: University of Michigan Press.

Sinclair, Lister, and John Conway. 1997. "Math and Aftermath." CBC *Ideas* Transcript No. 9723 (13–14 May 1997).

Sinclair, Sue. 2001. *Secrets of Weather & Hope*. London, ON: Brick Books.

Solmsen, Friedrich. 1971. "Parmenides and the Description of Perfect Beauty in Plato's *Symposium.*" *American Journal of Philology* 92: 62–70.

Sommerstein, Alan H. 1980. "The Naming of Women in Greek and Roman Comedy." *Quaderni di storia* 11: 393–418.

Sprague, Rosamund Kent. 1971. "*Symposium* 211a and Parmenides Frag. 8." *Classical Philology* 66: 261.

Stace, W.T. 1960. *Mysticism and Philosophy.* Philadelphia: Lippincott.

Strayer, Joseph R., and Hans W. Gatzke. 1984. *The Mainstream of Civilization,* 4th ed. New York: Harcourt Brace Jovanovich.

Suzuki, D.T. 1957. *Mysticism: Christian and Buddhist.* New York: Macmillan.

Tarán, Leonardo. 1965. *Parmenides.* Princeton: Princeton University Press.

Tarrant, Harold. "Middle Platonism and the Seventh Epistle." *Phronesis* 28 (1983): 75–103.

Taylor, A.E. 1960. *Plato: The Man and His Work.* London: Methuen.

Taylor, C.C.W. 1999. *The Atomists: Leucippus and Democritus: Fragments.* Toronto: University of Toronto Press.

Tranströmer, Tomas. 1987. *Tomas Tranströmer: Selected Poems 1954–1986.* Ed. Robert Hass. New York: Ecco.

Vlastos, Gregory. 1953. "Review of Zafiropoulo, *L'école éléate.*" *Gnomon* 25.3: 166–9.

———. 1981. "The Individual as an Object of Love in Plato." In *Platonic Studies,* 2nd ed., 3–42. Princeton: Princeton University Press.

Waithe, Mary Ellen. 1987. "Diotima of Mantinea." In *A History of Women Philosophers,* Vol. 1. Ed. Mary Ellen Waithe, 83–116. Dordrecht: Kluwer.

Weil, Simone. 1970. *First and Last Notebooks.* Trans. Richard Rees. London: Oxford University Press.

———. [1952] 1987. *Gravity and Grace.* Ed. Gustave Thibon. Trans. Emma Craufurd. London: Routledge.

———. [1946] 1990. "Essay on the Notion of Reading." Trans. Rebecca Fine Rose and Timothy Tessin. *Philosophical Investigations* 13: 297–303.

Wender, Dorothea. [1973] 1984. "Plato: Misogynist, Paedophile, and Feminist." In *Women in the Ancient World: The Arethusa Papers.* Ed. John Peradotto and J.P. Sullivan, 213–28. Albany: SUNY Series in Classical Studies.

Wertheimer, Max. 1920. *Über Sclussprozesse im produktiven Denken.* Berlin: De Gruyter. [Reprinted in *Drei Abhandlungen zur Gestalttheorie.* Erlangen: Philosophische Akademie, 1925, 164–84.]

——. 1925. "Über Gestalttheorie." *Symposion: Philosophische Zeitschrift für Forschung und Aussprache* 1 (1925): 39–60. Also published as a chapbook: Erlangen: Philosophische Akademie, 1925. [Abridged English trans. in Ellis 1938: 1–11.]

——. 1938a. "Gestalt Theory." In Ellis 1938, 1–11. [Abridged English trans. of Wertheimer 1925. Unabridged English trans. by N. Nairn-Allison in *Social Research* 11 (1944): 78–99.]

——. 1938b. "The Syllogism and Productive Thinking." In Ellis 1938, 274–82. [Abridged trans. of Wertheimer 1920.]

——. 1959. *Productive Thinking.* Ed. Michael Wertheimer. New York: Harper & Row.

Wittgenstein, Ludwig. [1921] 1961. *Tractatus Logico-Philosophicus.* Trans. D.F. Pears and B.F. McGuinness. London: Routledge & Kegan Paul.

——. [1953] 1958. *Philosophical Investigations.* Trans. G.E.M. Anscombe. Oxford: Basil Blackwell.

——. 1977. *On Certainty.* Eds. G.E.M. Anscombe and G.H. von Wright. Trans. Denis Paul and G.E.M. Anscombe. Oxford: Basil Blackwell.

——. 1980. *Culture and Value.* Eds. G.H. von Wright and Heikki Nyman. Trans. Peter Winch. Chicago: University of Chicago Press.

——. 1982. *Last Writings on the Philosophy of Psychology,* Vol. 1. Eds. G.H. von Wright and Heikki Nyman. Trans. C.G. Luckhardt and M.A.E. Aue. Chicago: University of Chicago Press.

Woolf, Virginia. [1938] 1986. *Three Guineas.* London: Hogarth.

Wright, Charles. 1995. "Narrative of the Image: A Correspondence with Charles Simic." In *Quarter Notes: Improvisations and Interviews,* 57–74. Ann Arbor: University of Michigan Press.

Wright, M.R. 1981. *Empedocles: The Extant Fragments*. New Haven: Yale University Press.

———. 1985. *The Presocratics*. Bristol: Bristol Classical Press.

Zagajewski, Adam. 2000. *Another Beauty*. Trans. Clare Cavanagh. New York: Farrar, Straus and Giroux.

Zeitlin, Froma I. 1984. "Playing the Other: Theater, Theatricality, and the Feminine in Greek Drama." *Representations* 11: 63–94.

Zuckert, Catherine H. 2009. *Plato's Philosophers: The Coherence of the Dialogues*. Chicago: Chicago University Press.

Zwicky, Jan. [1992] 2014a. *Lyric Philosophy*, rev. 2nd ed. Edmonton: Brush Education.

———. [2003] 2014b. *Wisdom & Metaphor*, 2nd ed. Edmonton: Brush Education.

Acknowledgements

My sincere thanks to the many individuals and audiences who read or listened to earlier versions of these ideas and assisted me in their development. In particular, my thanks to Richard Bosley, Colin Macleod, Roger Shiner, and James Young. To Laurel Bowman, Hélène Cazes, Ian Drummond, Ian Fryer, Tim Green, Mark Griffith, Sue Sinclair, and Dagmar Theison, my thanks for assistance with points of research. To John Barton, my thanks for advice regarding aspects of the index.

Special thanks to Warren Heiti, to Tim Lilburn, and to Gordon Shrimpton for their exceptional generosity and insight.

To Robert Bringhurst for his acute and patient listening as both poet and thinker, my deepest gratitude.

The publisher and author acknowledge, with thanks, permission to reprint the following copyright material: "Herakleitos," § XXI of *Tzuhalem's Mountain* and § X of "Hachadura" by Robert Bringhurst © Robert Bringhurst, reprinted by permission of the author. ¶ "Red Pepper" by Sue Sinclair © Sue Sinclair, reprinted by permission of the author and Brick Books. ¶ The first stanza of Part II of "Baltics" by Tomas Tranströmer, English translation by Samuel Charters © Samuel Charters, reprinted by permission of the translator. ¶ "Track" by Tomas Tranströmer, translated by Robert Bly from *Tomas Tranströmer: Selected Poems*, edited by Robert Haas. Introduction © 1987 by Robert Haas. Reprinted by permission of HarperCollins Publishers.

A version of "What Is Lyric Philosophy?" appeared in *Common Knowledge* 20.1 (Winter 2014): 14–27.

"Bringhurst's Presocratics: Lyric and Ecology" appeared in a significantly different version in *Poetry and Knowing*, edited by Tim Lilburn (Kingston, ON: Quarry Press, 1995), 65–117.

A version of "Plato's *Phaidros*: Philosophy as Dialogue with the Dead" was published in *Apeiron* 30.1 (March 1997): 19–47.

A version of "Dream Logic and the Politics of Interpretation" appeared in *Thinking and Singing: Poetry and the Practice of Philosophy*, edited by Tim Lilburn (Toronto: Cormorant Books, 2002), 121–51. An abridged version of material in the first part of the essay was published under the title "Freud's Metapsychology and the Culture of Philosophy" in *Civilization and Oppression, Canadian Journal of Philosophy* Supplementary Volume 25, edited by Catherine Wilson (1999): 211–26.

A version of "Oracularity" appeared in *Metaphilosophy* 34.4 (July 2003): 488–509.

"Mathematical Analogy and Metaphorical Insight" first appeared in the proceedings of the Eighth Annual Bridges Conference, entitled *Renaissance Banff: Mathematics, Music, Art, Culture* (2005). Subsequently, it was published in *The Mathematical Intelligencer* 28.2 (2006): 4–9 and in *For the Learning of Mathematics* 30.1 (March 2010): 9–14.

"Plato as Artist" was originally published by Gaspereau Press in 2009.

"What Is Ineffable?" appeared in *International Studies in the Philosophy of Science* 26.2 (June 2012): 197–217.

"Imagination and the Good Life" appeared in *Common Knowledge* 20.1 (Winter 2014): 28–45.

A version of "Alkibiades' Love" was first published in *Philosophy as a Way of Life: Ancients and Moderns*, edited by Michael Chase, Stephen R.L. Clark, and Michael McGhee (Chichester, UK: Wiley-Blackwell, 2013), 84–98.

Index

emotion(s), emotional, 6, 8–9, 27,
   58, 101–2, 115, 149, 169, 239,
   242–3, 255, 257–8, 311–12n.
emptiness
  and fullness of things, 14, 275
  as selflessness, 287–8, 292–3
Encyclopedia of Philosophy, 97,
   262–3, 265
Enlightenment, the, 99, 244
  post-Enlightenment, 35
environmental crisis. *See* cultural
  crisis; ecological; *and* evil
epigrams, 113–14
ἐπιστέμη, *epistēmē*, 160, 174, 178,
   185–91, 202–3
epistemology, –ies, 54, 110, 135,
   178, 200, 242, 243, 261, 263
  epistemic anthropocentrism,
   263
  preceded by moral choice, 54,
   263
equilibrium, –ia, 41, 92
Erdős, Paul, 172
eristic, –al, 83, 157, 166, 167, 177,
   296, 297
eros, *erōs*, 27, 59–84 *passim*,
   100, 102, 109, 169, 178, 198,
   211–36 *passim*, 286–90, 293,
   306n. *See also* desire *and* love
  eros of lyric, 5, 16, 109
  eros of philosophy, 5, 6
   philosophy as thinking in love
   with clarity, 6, 99, 283, 292
  erotic sublation, 289
Eryximakhos (in Plato), 214
essence. *See* detail *and* relations,
  external
etymology, –ies, 121, 255
  etymologies of
   analysis, 124
   clarity, 258–9
   clear, 6

διαλέγεσθαι (dialectic),
   69–70
epóptēs, 210
grasp, 267
imagination, 265
integrate, integrity, 289
know, 267
poet, 265
tell, 189
whole, 292
wise, 102
Euclid, 136, 172
eudaimonia, 64, 293
Euler, Leonhard, 131
Euripides, 319n.
Evening Star. *See* Venus
evil, 51
excellence, moral, 51, 144–210
  passim, 213–14, 223, 263,
  286–8, 307n. *See also* beauty,
  moral *and various individual
  virtues*
experience
  of astonishment, 14
  of at-oneness, 239, 243, 250,
   329n.
  of beauty, 12, 217
  of being pierced, 12, 273
  of communicating, 151–2
  of doing philosophy, 217
  of gestalt(s), of gestalt shifts, 11,
   13, 17, 131, 133, 140, 255, 256,
   266, 267, 271, 274
  of 'getting it,' 13, 131–2, 141, 242,
   266
  of ineffability, 238–40, 251, 257,
   260
  of insight. *See most other items
   in this list*
  of language as tool of analysis,
   254
  of mathematical analogy,

information, 171–3, 178–9, 183,
188–90, 256, 258
injustice, root of, 280
insight, 75, 76, 107–29 *passim*, 151,
176, 190, 198, 206, 234, 250,
274, 275–82 *passim*, 312–13n.
lyric insight, 28, 33
metaphorical insight, 130–43
passim
and music, 239
philosophical insight, 14, 108
integrity: etymology, 289
as basis of ability to mean, 98
formal property. *See* is resonant
form *in this list*
of ecologies, 54–5
of gestalts, 110, 242, 251–4
of lyric thought, 4, 6, 8, 16, 54,
109–10, 115–16, 121–3, 126
and also of oracular thought,
109–110, 115–16, 121–3
disintegrative modes of
understanding, 101–2, 121,
124, 127, 258, 260
as 'livingness,' 84
and λόγος (*logos*), 12, 98
as moral virtue, 54, 69, 79, 176,
198, 279, 286–7, 289–91,
297
and ontology, 54, 122, 274
in philosophy, 84, 101–2, 105
precondition of freedom, 289
in Presocratic thought, 52–3, 58
and primary process, 254
is resonant form, 116, 254
in speech, 8, 16
as wholeness, 54, 289
and wisdom, 126
interconnectedness. *See*
connectedness
internal relation(s). *See* relation(s),
internal

interpenetration, 12. *See also*
connectedness *and* integrity
interpretation
dream interpretation, 55, 91–2,
100
literary interpretation, 97

– J –

Jameson, Frederic, 83
Jankélévitch, Vladimir, 325–6nn.
Jastrow, Joseph. *See* duck-rabbit
joke(s), 89, 95, 97, 103–5, 114,
245–6, 250, 259
and metaphor, 136
and philosophy (Wittgenstein),
103
joy: and mystical experience, 240,
243
Jung, Carl Gustav, 199
Justice, Fate, Necessity (in
Parmenides), 220, 226, 228,
230–1, 233

– K –

Kahn, Charles, 43, 57, 116, 119, 126,
313–14n., 320n.
Kallikles (in Plato), 175, 296
Kant, Immanuel, 127–8, 148, 182,
263, 268, 273, 281–2
katharsis, 291–2, 297
Keats, John, 96, 97
Kepler, Johannes, 134–5, 137, 139,
142
Kirk, G.S. & Raven, J.E., 24, 37, 41,
55, 303–5 *passim*, 324n.
Klee, Paul, 3
Klein, Ernest, 6, 70–1, 258–9, 265,
267. *See also* etymologies
Knobloch, Eberhard, 135
Köhler, Wolfgang, 312–13n.
knowledge

wordless, 49, 238, 239, 264. *See also* ineffability
wordlessness, 8, 16
world. *See also* being; ontology; *and* realism
as Beethoven symphony (Wertheimer), 270
as coherent, integrated, nonsystematic, resonant whole, 14, 18, 47–50, 54–6, 111–12, 122–4, 126, 129, 242, 247, 252–3, 258–61, 272–6. *See also* as resonance *in this list*
as collection of discrete entities, 124, 250, 252–4, 259–61, 268, 275
crossword puzzle analogy, 111
espousal of, 282
"fairest order," 12, 50, 116
as geodesic sphere, 255
as gestalt of interlocking gestalts, 247
lyric, moral, ecological order, 49, 51, 54, 261
as machine, 122, 260

meaning of, 13, 47, 128–9
natural. *See* natural world
as resonance, 261
and self, 54
Wright, Charles, 135
writing (in Plato). *See also* literacy
achieves immortality for speech, 223
philosophical status of, 59–84 *passim*
types mentioned in *Phaidros*, 66

– X –

Xenophon, 213, 215, 231, 285, 319nn.
Xenophanes, 237

– Y –

Yeats, W.B., 274
Yì Jīng, 277

– Z –

Zagajewski, Adam, 14
Zen, 96
Zhuāng Zi (Zhuāngzi), 294
zìrán (自然), 278